The Triple Path

by James Kenneth Rogers

Tricruxtide 2020 Edition

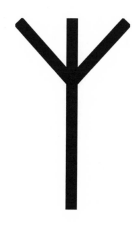

The Triple Path

To get the latest version of this book, visit
TriplePath.org/Download

See TriplePath.org/license for terms governing electronic redistri-
bution. By downloading electronic copies of the book, or by redis-
tributing electronic copies of the book, you agree to those terms.

Inquiries should be addressed to
Inquiries@TriplePath.org.

Tricruxtide 2020 Edition

ISBN-13: 978-1-7923-2827-5
ISBN-10: 1-792-32827-3

*Illustrations on Epigraph and on page 593 from
The Matthew Bible, 1537 (John Rogers, ed.)*

Each who passed through this life, rich or poor,
    Chose a path to walk 'til at death's door.
  You who yet breathe are still choosing yours.

Contents

Preamble

Introduction

The West is increasingly giving up on religion. This is a problem.

The United States remains the most religious of the developed countries[1], and even here the percentage of the adult population claiming no religious affiliation has increased significantly—from 3 percent in 1957, to 8.2 percent in 1990, to 26 percent in 2019. The percentage of Americans self-identifying as Christian declined from 77 to 65 percent between 2009 and 2019. "No affiliation" is now the largest single religious group in America. Only 25 percent of Americans attend church regularly.[2] Even those who claim affiliation with a particular religion are giving up on many of their religion's teachings. A survey of self-identified Catholics found that only 31 percent believed in the core Catholic doctrine of transubstantiation (that the bread and wine at Mass actually become the body and blood of Christ).[3]

The percentage of Americans who report having grown up

---

1   Pew Research Center, "Among Wealthy Nations . . . U.S. Stands Alone In Its Embrace of Religion", December 19, 2002.

2   Pew Research Center, "America's Changing Religious Landscape", May 12, 2015; Pew Research Center, "In U.S., Decline of Christianity Continues at Rapid Pace", October 17, 2019; Barry A. Kosmin and Ariela Keysar, *American Religious Identification Survey (ARIS 2008) Summary Report*, March 2009, p. 5; Mark Chaves, "The Decline of American Religion?", *The Association of Religion Data Archives Guiding Paper Series*, pp. 1-2; Daniel Cox Robert P. Jones, "America's Changing Religious Identity", *Public Religion Research Institute*, September 6, 2017.

with a father who was religiously active decreased from 70 percent for those born before 1900 to 45 percent for those born after 1970. According to one scholar, "every indicator of traditional religiosity is either stable or declining, and there isn't enough new nontraditional religious practice to balance the decline".[4] Secularization is happening even faster in Europe.[5]

Religion is part of human nature—it is found in all cultures worldwide[6], and appears to have been a constant part of human behavior going back at least many tens of thousands of years. There are different explanations for how religion and our tendency for religious behavior developed: it may have directly evolved through natural selection; it may have come about as a cultural byproduct of mental modules (such as agency detection) that developed for other reasons. It most likely developed through a combination of both factors, with religion initially developing as a cultural byproduct of non-religious mental modules, but with innate, biological religious tendencies then developing and strengthening through gene-culture co-evolution. Regardless of how it developed, religiosity is a part of being human, and it is precious.

Over tens of thousands of years, human cultures have accumulated and passed on to future generations much knowledge about morality and right living—about how to create and maintain good relationships and build successful communities, and about what a good life is and how to live it. The principles of morality and traditions that we have developed within the context of religion have enabled us to live in ever more complex and prosper-

---

3 Gregory A. Smith, "Just one-third of U.S. Catholics agree with their church that Eucharist is body, blood of Christ", *Pew Research Center*, August 5, 2019.

4 Mark Chaves (*see* footnote 2), pp. 1, 3.

5 Stephen Bullivant, *Europe's Young Adults and Religion*, Institut Catholique de Paris and The Benedict XVI Centre, Saint Mary's University, Twickenham, London.

6 Donald Brown, *Human Universals*, 1991.

ous societies.[7] Over the last 10,000 years, humans moved from living in simple hunter-gatherer tribes to agricultural societies of increasing complexity and size. The large and complex societies of the last few thousand years could not function without moral principles that were developed, honed, and promoted over the generations by religions—principles such as charity, empathy, honesty, industriousness, sexual restraint, and respect for life and personal property. As more people have more fully lived these moral principles, their lives have significantly improved.

Beyond just giving us moral principles, religion guides us on the path to meaning and illumination, supporting our search for answers to deep life questions and encouraging our individual personal development. It helps us to make parts of our lives sacred and to feel like we are part of something bigger than ourselves in a way that is psychologically nourishing and revitalizing. It helps us draw closer to a higher power and feel serenity, peace, transcendence, elevation, awe, and gratitude.

Religion also gives us outlets for exercising moral goodness towards others, and thus encourages stable, thriving communities. It gives us rites and ceremonies to provide meaning and mark major life events. It provides us with a sense of fellowship and unity with others. It encourages group cohesiveness and provides a social outlet for people to interact, become acquainted, learn from each other, and support one another in their lives and beliefs. And, it provides a public signaling mechanism about our (and others') devotion and trustworthiness.

Most importantly, religion demands that we live better and become greater than we were, calling to us in unique ways that are often more compelling than anything else to lead us to lasting change and improvement.

Almost every adaptive human trait—from altruism to anger—can become unbalanced, turn maladaptive, and lead to negative outcomes. Religion is no different. At least in Western society, how-

---

7   Peter Turchin, *Ultrasociety*, 2016, pp. 208-10.

ever, there is hard evidence that religion is a net benefit. Scholars have found, over and over, that religiosity and belief in God are positively related to better physical and mental health, greater life satisfaction, longer lifespan, and prosocial behavior. The research strongly indicates that religiosity actually causes these effects. The weight of the evidence is astounding. If you have any doubt, please turn right now to the next chapter, on page 29, for a longer discussion (including many references to academic journals).

For psychologically healthy and normal human beings, it is difficult for us to escape religiosity, no matter what church we do or do not go to. Whenever a group of people coalesces around strongly held beliefs or ideas, their religious natures usually emerge, whether it be around Christianity, atheism, environmentalism, or politics.

Even those who formally reject organized religion or belief in God rarely escape their fundamental religious nature—they are still human beings, after all. Like most human traits, each person's innate religious tendencies probably vary along a bell curve. Just as some people are naturally angrier or happier than others, some are more religious than others. The distribution of a natural trait can change in a population over time, but a trend happening as swiftly as secularization in the West is most likely due to principally cultural forces. This is because there have not been enough generations for natural selection to have had much effect (and, if anything, is selecting in the long-term for *greater* innate religiosity, since religiosity is a heritable trait[8] and religious people in the West have higher fertility levels than the nonreligious). Most people who claim no religious affiliation are thus likely doing so because of cultural trends and not because of an innate lack of a religious nature.

One might argue that the growing numbers of people claiming no formal religious affiliation are doing so because they have a

---

8   Laura B. Koenig, et. al., "Genetic and Environmental Influences on Religiousness: Findings for Retrospective and Current Religiousness Ratings", *Journal of Personality*, Feb. 16, 2005.

naturally diminished religious sense and are now giving up on religion because there are fewer cultural constraints against doing so. This is unlikely, however, because most of those who forsake formal religious affiliation continue to manifest an innate religious nature in other ways. Even atheist philosopher John Gray has noted that "secular thought is mostly composed of repressed religion".[9]

Indeed, it is easy to see innate human religious tendencies manifest themselves among the ostensibly non-religious. The new secularists often end up, usually unconsciously, dedicating their natural religiosity to things that scratch their religious itch, but which do not bring as many of the benefits of traditional religion. They are like someone trying to fulfill his body's craving for the wholesome nutrition of fresh, ripe fruit by eating a bag of candy. They devote themselves to things outside the realm of organized religion, but that are still just as strongly religious, albeit distorted and twisted: new kinds of superstitions and strange new modern secular orthodoxies lacking a basis in reality or tradition, and often with unanticipated harmful effects. For example, many modern secularists have transplanted Calvinist notions of original sin and predestination, and superstitious notions of witchcraft and black magic, into their conceptions of race, ethnicity, and gender relations; many have transformed their inclination toward zeal for religious orthodoxy into campaigns to universally impose their ideology by destroying the professional and social life of anyone who does not agree with them.

Even though we have innate behaviors and mental attributes that appear to be hardwired into us, these natural, innate tendencies manifest within the context of the culture around us. For example, language is an innate human characteristic, but the specific language each person speaks is determined by the surrounding culture. When our culture fails to provide a viable option through which we can manifest our natural behaviors, we invent something.

---

9   John Gray, *Seven Types of Atheism*, 2018.

For example, in Nicaragua in the 1980s, deaf children were brought together for the first time to attend a vocational school for the deaf. Teachers did not teach any kind of sign language, instead they tried (unsuccessfully) to teach Spanish and lipreading. The children, though, on their own, created their own sign language so they could communicate with each other. This sign language developed over time into a sophisticated and complete language.

Similarly, when families from different cultures migrate to the same place, the adults usually create a pidgin, which is a simplified language that combines elements of the native languages of the people who created it. Pidgins allow for basic communication, but are not full languages. The children in such communities, though, usually take their parents' pidgin and turn it into a grammatically and lexically complete language. This new language is called a creole, and normally becomes the native language of the children and their descendants.

Left unchecked, the emerging religious orthodoxies and practices of the new secularists would likely develop into a full religion, just like sign language in Nicaragua and creoles developed into new, complete languages. Creoles can develop so quickly because they borrow heavily from the languages of the groups that came together to create it. Similarly, speakers of Nicaraguan Sign Language borrow from outside sources, such as American Sign Language, to fill in gaps.

The secularists, however, seem eager to ignore and forget as much as they can of the rich religious and cultural heritage bequeathed to us by our ancestors. If the new religion they are slowly creating does not collapse, it will survive only at the cost of many years (and likely generations) of painful adjustment as they struggle to come up with new solutions to problems our ancestors already solved long ago.[10]

---

10 For example, it has been nearly three generations since the start of the so-called sexual revolution. Secularists are still struggling to come up with rules and norms to govern the most basic aspects of sexual en-

After the Roman Empire fell, so much knowledge was lost in fields like science, engineering, and art that it literally took centuries to re-develop or re-discover it all. The secularists' rejection of religion and tradition runs the risk of plunging us into an equivalent religious dark age that could take centuries to climb out of.

On the other hand, those who have given up on the old, established religions have a point. The major world religions are pre-modern creations with a lot of baggage that is difficult to accept in light of modern scientific understandings of the world (not to mention the textual, historical, and archeological issues that cast great doubt on the traditional religions' literal truthfulness). This is one of the main reasons why religious affiliation and participation is decreasing so significantly in the West.

This book is addressed to those who have lost their faith in traditional religion. I am one of you. If you are like me, you feel like you have lost something valuable that used to bring value and meaning to your life. But what do we replace it with? The replacement nonbelievers most often seem to turn to is some form of nihilism or social justice grievance fanaticism, or often both. These are a poor substitute for the grandeur and hope and love and meaning and connection we get out of religion.

This book offers a new religion that stays as faithful as possible to the wisdom and traditions of the past while still embracing our modern historical and scientific understanding of the world. It offers a better substitute for the empty nihilism and totalitarian grievance activism that seem to be growing as replacements for traditional religion. If you do not have faith in the old religions: please continue on and see if you do find something worth pursuing.

---

counters, such as consent, whereas centuries of tradition had already come up with a solution that worked very well: sexual restraint outside of marriage, and fidelity within it. And the secularists have done almost nothing to solve the bigger problems caused by the sexual revolution, such as the unstable home environments it forces upon many children (a problem that has so far been getting worse over time).

This book is not an attempt to convince adherents of the old religions about the error of their ways. There are no detailed, polemical attacks on specific religious beliefs—you can find that in plenty of other places. To the faithful of other religions, I invite you also to read on and see if you see something better and more valuable than what you have right now.

So why *can't* we just rely on the religions we have already? The great teachings of the world religions are intertwined with superstitious pre-modern cosmologies (cosmology means our understanding of the universe and humanity's place in it). They are also mixed with legendary retellings of history that we now know are, at best, of dubious veracity, and at worst, outright fabrications. These ancient cosmologies and histories have ever-decreasing relevance as they are contradicted more and more by modern scientific, historical, and archeological discoveries.

For example, when the great religions of the world were founded, many of those religions' adherents believed that the world was flat and that it was at the center of the universe. The most common cosmology found in the Bible presupposes the Earth is a flat disc floating in water or supported by pillars.[11] Other biblical writers say that the Earth is immovable or that the Earth sits at the center of the universe and that everything else, including the Sun, revolves around the Earth.[12] For biblical writers, hell was a literal place below the ground and heaven was a literal place just above the Earth (in different places in the Bible the reason the sky is blue is either because we are seeing a heavenly ocean suspended above the sky, or because the sky is the sapphire floor of heaven).[13]

Many of these types of Bible passages are now interpreted

---

11 Adele Berlin, "Cosmology and creation", in Adele Berlin and Maxine Grossman (eds.), *The Oxford Dictionary of the Jewish Religion*, 2011, pp. 188-89; Othmar Keel, *The Symbolism of the Biblical World*, 1997, pp. 20-21; 1 Samuel 2:8; Job 9:6.

12 Joshua 10:12-13; Psalm 93:1, 96:10; Psalm 104:5.

metaphorically, but there is little reason to believe their writers intended them to be interpreted that way—they almost certainly believed them to be literally true.

It is not hard to notice as you read the Bible that the farther back in time a story was supposed to happen (and thus the more likely the passage was written long after the alleged events happened), the more the stories read like mythology instead of history. It is hard to take literally stories about talking serpents and donkeys or a man emerging unharmed three days after being swallowed by a giant fish; or tales of holy men calling fire from the sky, summoning a bear to kill youths who had mocked his baldness, parting a sea, or stopping the progression of the sun through the sky.[14]

The easier it has become to gather evidence about miracles and supernatural events, the more that claims for their occurrence have decreased. As it has become easier to definitively contradict such claims, they are more rarely made, and even more rarely taken seriously. We have a good grasp of many of the basic laws that seem to govern the operation of the physical universe, and there are no confirmed accounts of any miracles that violate them. There could be a variety of explanations for this, but the most parsimonious is that ancient accounts of such events were not factually correct.

Look at it this way: there are a number of legendary and mythological accounts from dead religions of the ancient world

---

13 J. Edward Wright, *The Early History of Heaven*, 2002, pp. 54-57; The Hebrew word for hell was also used to figuratively refer to death, but was also used in the Old Testament to refer to a physical place, Alan E. Bernstein, *The Formation of Hell: Death and Retribution in the Ancient and Early Christian Worlds*, 1993, pp. 140-42; Exodus 24:9-10 speaks of the sapphire floor of heaven—God's throne was also described as being made of sapphire in Ezekiel 1:26.

14 *See* Genesis 2; Numbers 22; Jonah 1-4; 1 Kings 18; 2 Kings 2; Exodus 14; and Joshua 10.

that, if true, would seem to confirm the veracity of those extinct religions and beliefs. No one today believes these accounts to be true. Doesn't it make sense that the legendary and supernatural accounts in the Bible and the holy books of other surviving religions would be similarly inaccurate?

Because the foundations of the world's great religions are built on legendary and mythological foundations that have become implausibly difficult to accept, these religions are declining as they are forced to confront modernity.

If Western Civilization needs traditional religion to survive, but traditional religion cannot thrive in the modern world and thus cannot fulfill its important historical role, what are we to do? How should we react when we are confronted with modernity-induced religious doubts?

Let us consider four possible responses: 1) the literal approach; 2) the symbolic approach; 3) the rejection approach; and 4) the Triple Path.

The Literal Approach

If history and modern cosmology contradict sacred texts, one approach is to reject history and modern cosmology. This is hard to justify, though, based on a dispassionate weighing of the evidence. Even so, religious believers who take a literal approach sometimes justify this approach by appealing to authority and arguing that their scriptures (or the pronouncements of their religion's holy men) contain the word of God and are thus the ultimate authority, trumping the pronouncements of fallible humans.

There are several problems with this approach to relying on authority.

Believing in the divine authority of teachers or texts merely because they claim divine authority is circular: we have no reason to believe in their claims to divine authority unless we already accept their teachings—merely claiming authority offers no external reason to believe in that authority.

Believing in a leader's or a text's divine authority because of our subjective emotional responses to them is almost equally questionable. Spiritual feelings are subjective. Adherents of wildly different religions—religions with contradictory and mutually exclusive teachings—describe the same sorts of spiritual feelings confirming their belief in these religions. For a much more in-depth discussion of this phenomenon, and a more general discussion on how we can find truth, see the third chapter, on page 45.

Some followers may instead place their trust in stories about a teacher's or a leader's miraculous or supernatural abilities. These stories, if true, possibly could provide some indication of divine authority, but they invariably end up failing objective verification; they are nearly always told second- or third-hand, or the "miraculous" occurrence ends up being explained by charlatanism; they do not stand up to rigorous scrutiny.

Things like feelings, stories of dubious veracity, or a religious text's or leader's own claim to authority are not enough to validate the claims about religious texts' or teachers' authority, especially when some of their claims are directly contradicted by historical or archeological evidence, or by our modern scientific observations of the world.

Furthermore, it is a logical fallacy to believe in a statement's truth merely because it was uttered by an "authority". The statements of authorities should be able to stand up to criticism and independent verification. We discuss this fallacy more on pages 53 to 55.

If an authority's statements are true, they should be consistent with our knowledge of reality. The problem is that questions involving religion and the supernatural are hard to verify. We have no independent means of determining which claims about God are correct, absent a personal direct visitation from God Himself. And even then, without physical evidence or some other corroboration of the visitation, there would be a host of alternative explanations (such as hallucinations or mental illness) for any such visitation that would have to be ruled out first. And as I said, most such claims that can be evaluated fail to stand up to scrutiny.

The Rejection Approach

The rejection approach is to conclude that if verifiable religious claims are often contradicted by scientific discoveries, then perhaps there is not much reason to believe in any religious teaching or ideal—if the verifiable claims are untrue, then the unverifiable claims and teachings probably are not true or worth following either. A rejectionist might conclude that, if the ancients were wrong about their cosmological claims, we should therefore reject (or be skeptical of) *all* traditional religious morals and injunctions, unless we can immediately find a good reason to keep them. The general presumption of rejectionists is "guilty until proven innocent"—all aspects of religion are valueless until proven otherwise.

This is the approach most atheists seem to take.

The problem with this approach is that it ignores our own shortsightedness. Often, it is hard to understand the reason for a traditional rule or taboo until long after the fact. For example, during the sexual revolution of the 1960s and 1970s, it was assumed there was little justification for traditional sexual norms and that they should be abandoned. It turns out, though, that those traditional sexual norms encourage behaviors that are associated with stable family structures, and thus better outcomes for children in our society (and eventually for the future of society itself).

For example, research shows that couples who don't live together before marriage and in which the woman was a virgin on her wedding night have much lower risk of divorce.[15] And divorce

---

15 Anthony Paik, "Adolescent Sexuality and the Risk of Marital Dissolution", *Journal of Marriage and Family*, Vol. 73, No. 2, April 2011, pp. 472-485; Casey E. Copen, *et. al.*, "First Marriages in the United States: Data From the 2006-2010 National Survey of Family Growth", *National Health Statistics Reports*, No. 49, March 22, 2012; Scott M. Stanley and Galena K. Rhoades, "The Timing of Cohabitation and Engagement: Impact on First and Second Marriages", *Journal of Marriage and Family*, Vol. 72, No. 4, August 2010, pp. 906-918; Galena K. Rhoades, *et. al.*, "The pre-engagement cohabitation effect:

is associated with a host of poor outcomes for children.[16] Some comparative anthropological research suggests that widespread cultural acceptance of norms of strict chastity before marriage and absolute monogamy afterwards leads to positive societal outcomes as well.[17]

One lifetime is too short a time to figure everything out. That is why we have culture and tradition. Wisdom about how to live slowly accumulates over huge spans of time, and get passed down as tradition. Rejecting all of it, or large parts of it, is an unwise course. It is far safer only to reject the hard-earned wisdom of the past when it has been clearly and indisputably proved wrong.[18]

Moreover, religion provides important structure and discipline on which to build your life and character. It is difficult to get this structure and discipline in any other way. As Professor Jordan Peterson wrote:

Religion is . . . about proper behaviour. It's about

a replication and extension of previous findings", *Journal of Family Psychology*. Vol. 23, No. 1, February 2009, pp. 107-11; *see also* David Popenoe and Barbara Dafoe Whitehead, "Should We Live Together? What Young Adults Need to Know about Cohabitation before Marriage, A Comprehensive Review of Recent Research", *The National Marriage Project: The Next Generation Series*.

16 Thomas G. O'Connor, et. al., "Are Associations Between Parental Divorce and Children's Adjustment Genetically Mediated? An Adoption Study", *Developmental Psychology*, Vol. 36, No. 4, July 2000, pp. 429-37; Charles Murray, *Coming Apart: The State of White America, 1960-2010*, 2012, Chapters 8 and 15; Brian M. D'Onofrio, et. al., "A children of twins study of parental divorce and offspring psychopathology", *Journal of Child Psychology and Psychiatry*, Vol. 48, No. 7, 2007, pp. 667-675.

17 Joseph Daniel Unwin, *Sex and Culture*, 1936, Oxford University Press.

18 For more about the value and importance of tradition, see pages 59-65, 77-86, and 95-102.

what Plato called "the Good." A genuine religious acolyte isn't trying to formulate accurate ideas about the objective nature of the world (although he may be trying to do that too). He's striving, instead, to be a "good person." It may be the case that to him "good" means nothing but "obedient"—even blindly obedient. Hence the classic liberal Western enlightenment objection to religious belief: obedience is not enough. But it's at least a start (and we have forgotten this): You cannot aim yourself at anything if you are completely undisciplined and untutored. You will not know what to target, and you won't fly straight, even if you somehow get your aim right. And then you will conclude, "There is nothing to aim for." And then you will be lost.

It is therefore necessary and desirable for religions to have a dogmatic element. What good is a value system that does not provide a stable structure? What good is a value system that does not point the way to a higher order? And what good can you possibly be if you cannot or do not internalize that structure, or accept that order—not as a final destination, necessarily, but at least as a starting point? Without that, you're nothing but an adult two-year-old, without the charm or the potential. That is not to say (to say it again) that obedience is sufficient. But a person capable of obedience—let's say, instead, a properly disciplined person—is at least a well-forged tool. At least that (and that is not nothing). Of course, there must be vision, beyond discipline; beyond dogma. A tool still needs a purpose. It is for such reasons that Christ said, in the Gospel of Thomas, "The Kingdom of the Father is spread out upon the earth, but men do not see it."[19]

The Symbolic Approach

The symbolic approach is to look at cosmological reli-

---

19 Jordan B. Peterson, *12 Rules for Life: An Antidote to Chaos*, 2018, pp. 133-35.

gious teachings as being symbolic. It focuses on myth, symbolism, and allegory as powerful tools for teaching and helping us to feel moral truths.

The conservative variety of this approach is to reject only the parts of a religion's teachings that are indefensible, but to retain everything else and hold fast to the old religion. You reinterpret as symbolic teachings about cosmology that have been contradicted by modern science, but you continue believing in the teachings that have not yet been challenged by science. You create space for belief out of the gaps that science has not, or cannot, address. For example, you might discount the idea of a creation in six days, but continue believing that God created the Earth using natural processes over millions of years. If heaven is not directly above the Earth, it is somewhere else, or on another plane of existence.

This conservative approach of discarding the bare minimum is far preferable to the rejection approach. The problem with it, though, is that as scientific and historical knowledge continues to contradict more and more of traditional religion, its foundations continue to weaken, because those foundations were built on an ever-growing corpus of disproved cosmologies and historical claims.

The liberal variety of this approach is to reject or ignore any teaching that seems out-of-date or out-of-harmony with the spirit of the times. You reinterpret as symbolic anything you want. The problem with being this liberal is that religious belief becomes volatile and ever-changing. Groups made up of individuals who apply a liberal approach often lack internal consistency and have little to unite them.

Some people adopt a symbolic approach privately, while maintaining membership in a religion that asserts cosmologically suspect teachings as true. There are cultural and social reasons to do this. For example, if you live in a society or within a group dominated by a certain religion, you may have no practical choice but to remain affiliated and try to make the best of what you have.

This is not a wise or sustainable solution, however. It is morally degrading to live such a double spiritual life, and is difficult to do so without being dishonest. Furthermore, continuing participation in such religions provides institutional strength to them, which helps them perpetuate false beliefs.

The liberal variety of this approach often means joining a liberal religion that endorses the symbolic approach—whether officially or de facto—by rejecting the literal truth of the cosmologically suspect teachings of its foundational spiritual beliefs and texts. In theory, this might sound like a promising way forward, but in practice it has proved to be a dead end. Churches generally adopt this approach while still relying on their previous forms of worship and holy texts. Doing this requires a great deal of organizational dishonesty—maintaining an overt devotion to many aspects of the religion that are based on things the religion has also already partially or completely rejected. Such dishonesty is poison to the moral character of an organization or person.

Applying a "by their fruits you will know them" test shows that the churches that have adopted the liberal symbolic approach are generally failures. Such churches usually do not stop only at rejecting old, false cosmologies, but continue on to also jettison many valuable, foundational moral teachings. They give up not only on the discredited parts of their beliefs, but on tried and true traditions too—often to the point of almost becoming outright rejectionist. This illustrates the greatest problem with the liberal variety of the symbolic approach: it rejects too much. Ever-declining attendance at such churches is a concrete manifestation of the morally bankrupt, dead husk most of them have become.

By itself, a middle-of-the-road symbolic approach is an important tool for getting the most out of religion. The accumulated mythological and legendary stories that have been passed down to us over generations and through the centuries have survived so long for a reason. They are powerful stories illustrating profound moral and psychological truths, and the symbolic approach is the best way to approach them. Psychology professor

Jordan Peterson has been producing a marvelous lecture series discussing the psychological significance and symbolic meaning of major bible stories.[20] These lectures are well worth studying, and are a great example of how the symbolic approach can point us toward wisdom and add rich meaning to our lives.

But the way things are now, applying the symbolic approach to traditional religion is like treating skin cancer with sun block.

Most cosmologically suspect religious teachings were originally put forth as being literally true, even if they also were originally intended to have, or were later re-written to have, multiple, symbolic meanings. (Of course, there are some exceptions: Jesus's parables are profound and full of meaning, but were not taught as being literally true.)

The legendary and mythological stories of the Bible, and the pre-modern assumption that they were true, formed the traditional foundation of religion in the West. Symbolically reinterpreting them—whether in a conservative or liberal way—cannot avoid the irreparable damage the foundations have already suffered from scientific and historical discoveries indicating that most of them are not factually true.

If churches that accept as true the false cosmologies and history inherent in these stories are facing long-term decline, and if the churches that have rejected the false cosmologies and history have fared even worse, then maybe we need another solution.

We need new, strong religious foundations that do not rely on those stories' truthfulness. Then, we can continue to draw meaning and learn important lessons from them (and all the other parts of traditional religion) without them undermining the foundations of our civilization.

The Triple Path Approach

If the previous approaches do not work, then how can we preserve, honor, and practice the valuable traditions, morals, and

---

20   *See* https://jordanbpeterson.com/bible-series/.

stories of our culture? The problem is that the symbolic and archetypal value of our religious traditions and stories are tied too closely to their cosmology. The discredited cosmology pulls down everything else, like concrete shoes dragging someone underwater. Much of what was once in the realm of superstition is now understood. This has caused ever-greater divergences between many traditional religious teachings and our understanding of reality. We need a fresh start to reset these divergences, using the good things from the past to build a new religion unburdened by the discredited ideas. We need something that can integrate our modern understanding of the universe into the traditions and morals of the past—something conservative and traditional, but that is able, when needed, to change in response to new discoveries.

With a new theological foundation not reliant on legendary and mythological stories, we can maintain the useful traditions and morals of the past, and also more successfully apply the symbolic approach to continue cherishing and learning from the legendary and mythological stories of our culture.

There isn't anything out there that does this, so I created it. It is called the Triple Path.

Until now, the only main alternative to traditional religious practice was to integrate into the new, coalescing religion of secularism. The Triple Path offers a different option, rejecting neither traditional nor modernity.

The Triple Path is a new monotheistic religion. At its most basic, its creed is to seek wisdom, practice virtue, and labor with hope.

Seeking wisdom means searching for the truth—not just to learn it, but also to figure out how to learn it. It means having the humility to acknowledge human limitations and to accept truth wherever you find it. It means developing good judgment and character. It means developing a calm and still mind, unmoved by the distractions of life and opinion. And it means doing everything you can to improve your ability to understand God.

Practicing virtue means living morally, doing good, desiring to do good, and doing it for the right reasons.

Laboring with hope is an extension of practicing virtue; it means actively working (even in desperate times) to make things better, starting first with yourself and your family.

A longer creed for the Triple Path is set out starting on page 397. Or, even better, you can take an afternoon to read the rest of this book and get an even better understanding of the Triple Path and the rituals and Church organization it establishes. Its moral and ethical foundations are built on the wisdom of Stoicism and Christianity, seasoned with modern insights from psychology and other schools of Classical thought, and with some added bits from Buddhism, Taoism, and other world philosophical and religious traditions. It is a religion focused less on supernatural beliefs and more on developing moral character and wisdom. Its cosmological foundations are in harmony with modern science, and adaptable to future discoveries. Its theology is theistic rationalism. Its rituals are based on the Anglican Book of Common Prayer and western traditional practices, with influences also from Mormonism. Its ecclesiastical and congregational structure is relatively decentralized and is a combination of elements from the Anglican, Methodist, and Mormon churches. All clergy and leadership are made up of lay-members chosen through sortition and serving temporary terms of service. And it is unapologetically traditional, supporting time-honored morals and gender roles.

Like all religions, the Triple Path has rules for anyone wanting to be a member. A thriving religion must make demands of its adherents. There are several reasons for this: to give adherents a sense of meaning and belonging; to generate a feeling of group identity; to make the religion a valued part of daily life (we do not value things that are easy or free); to learn the importance of sacrifice through lived experience; and to provide a signaling mechanism within the community adherents can use to demonstrate to others their devotion to the religion's principles, and to evaluate others' devotion.

Religions develop their own unique rituals, traditions, and norms that set them apart from other groups. Some of these rituals, traditions, and norms do not have a strong moral component, but instead help ensure conformity with community standards and create a feeling of unity and us-ness. These "norms of cohesion" are rules or expectations that are based less on fundamental principles of morality and more on behavior rules that help members of a community establish their separate identity. These practices serve an important unifying purpose—because these norms of cohesion impose costs in time and foregone benefits, following them provides a way to signal to other group members one's commitment to the group and to its moral principles. They act as powerful, concentrated symbols for the entire set of beliefs and practices of the religion. They serve as outward symbols of adherents' level of commitment to God and their coreligionists. It is important never to confuse the symbol with the thing that it is representing, but even so, the outward symbol and practice are still important in themselves.

Such outward signals of commitment make it easier for group members to spot potential freeriders (who, not being committed to the group or to its moral teachings, will be less willing to follow norms of cohesion that impose costs) and to judge who is worthy of trust and inclusion in the group. The evidence shows that having demanding norms of cohesion strengthen a group, and thus also strengthen cooperation and relationships between members of the group. For example, religious communes that have more demanding norms of cohesion last longer than those that do not.[21]

You are not committed to something unless you are willing to sacrifice for it,[22] and no religion can thrive—or even survive—without committed followers. Who would want to be a member of a religion full of lackadaisical and lukewarm followers?

---

21 Richard Sosis and Candace Alcorta, "Signaling, solidarity, and the sacred: the evolution of religious behavior", *Evolutionary Anthropology*, Vol. 12, No. 6, Nov. 2003, pp. 266-68.

22 *See* Hope 3:17 on page 274 (paraphrased from Jordan Peterson).

Even more importantly, we come into life with an ethical burden to justify our own existence. The purpose of life is not to maximize our ratio of personal happiness or pleasure to suffering, but to take on honorable, worthwhile challenges and to sacrifice to overcome them. Such challenges, voluntarily undertaken, mold and shape us. They bring nobility of soul and allow us to accomplish great things.[23] Practicing self-denial and sacrifice in the context of religious practice helps develop this mature, courageous character. That is why all great religions demand sacrifices.

The purpose of religion is not just to make you feel good or inspired. It is also to demand that you change for the better, and to show you the path to making those changes.

Most of the demands the Triple Path makes of its adherents are standard moral rules you find in most religions, but it also has some unique rules that have the specific intent of setting adherents apart, just as in many other strong, cohesive religions (such as the Jewish prohibition on Pork, the Mormon prohibition on alcohol and coffee, and the Catholic prohibition of meat on Fridays[24]). Because the Triple Path's demands for supernatural beliefs are light (the only requirement is that practitioners believe in God, however they choose to define Him), its demands for lifestyle changes are a bit heavier. Number 10 through 13 of the Creed

---

23 See Hope 3:2 on page 273 (paraphrased from Jordan Peterson).

24 Adherents of each of these religions would probably say they follow these rules because God commanded it, not because of some purpose related to signaling or group identity, but most adherents to these religions would probably also acknowledge that these rules are not universal moral laws binding on people outside their faith. For example, Mormons who own food service businesses often serve coffee and alcohol, including in the City Creek Center mall in downtown Salt Lake City, which is directly owned by the Mormon Church. This is a strong sign that the rules' principle roles are not moral, but have something to do with group identity and membership itself.

(found on page 398), list the practices, Rites, and Feasts that adherents are expected to follow.

Religious rules fall along a spectrum between serving a moral purpose and a cohesion purpose. The most cohesion-targeted rule listed in the Creed is a prohibition on eating gluten. Its purpose is only for signaling and group cohesion. The rule is easy enough that anyone determined to follow it can do so without much disruption, but hard enough that few people will follow it unless they have a real commitment to the religion.

Other major, specific rules are more obviously moral, the best examples being the requirements to love others and follow the Golden Rule, and for celibacy before marriage and fidelity afterwards. Other rules listed in the Creed fall somewhere between the two poles of strictly moral- and strictly cohesion-based rules. Some of these rules are maintaining Sunday as a day of rest, spiritual focus, and family, free from work and spending of money; completely abstaining from tobacco; drinking alcohol only in moderation; eating in a healthy and moderate manner and exercising to keep our bodies fit and strong; avoiding excessive consumption of caffeine and refined sugar; and participating in the religion's Rites and Feasts (which are set out starting on page 401).

The conservative approach inherent in the Triple Path—of creating a new religion that also preserves as much of the West's religious traditions as possible—is because it can be hard to discern right away which parts of a religion are valuable. Often, traditions, rules, practices, and beliefs develop and last, even though no one would have consciously created them, because they confer some benefit that is not readily ascertainable. If a common, traditional, Western religious practice is not demonstrably untrue or harmful, then we should be very slow to discard it, even if it appears to serve no purpose. It may have value or serve a purpose that is not immediately discernible. The Triple Path most assiduously tries to follow this when it comes to morals, practices, Rites, and rules, and less so with cosmological and supernatural claims (for reasons we have talked about earlier in this chapter).

The Triple Path worries less about unanswerable meta-physical questions like the nature of the soul, our fate after death, or future eternal rewards or punishments. In Matthew, Jesus says, "do not worry about tomorrow, for tomorrow will bring worries of its own. Today's trouble is enough for today."[25] Triple Path adherents take Jesus at his word. We care more about the here and now than we do about abstract, indistinct, and indiscernible futures. We begin our approach to morality by seeking to do what is right *because* it is right, not because of some expected reward.

Some people might claim that good behavior is not enough, that you have to be baptized as a Christian or accept Jesus into your heart or adhere to some particular religion's rites and beliefs. That may be true, but how can we prove it? Even if we could, how can we know which religion's practices are right? The potential salvific value of most religions' practices and sacred rites are usually claimed to be exclusive—you have to practice that religion, and only that religion, to be saved. If only the rituals of a certain religion provide salvation, then we are faced with the nearly impossible task of trying to sort through an almost endless number of religions and churches to figure out which one is right. It is far more sensible to focus on moral living and seeking a direct connection to God. If salvific rites, membership in a certain religion, or having the right beliefs were what God really required of us to receive salvation, I cannot help wondering if he would have made it clearer and easier to figure out which were the right ones. It makes far more sense that all of these are inventions of men helping us in our quest to draw closer to God and understand our place in the universe.

The Triple Path teaches that we should be humble about what we know, or what we think we know. We should retain as much as we can of our traditions, but we should also never be afraid to change our beliefs in the face of new evidence, proven discoveries, and better information.

---

25 Matthew 6:34 (NRSV).

At the same time, even in our modern age, we need not limit religion to being just an empirically-based, scientific undertaking. Finding beauty and meaning in life are important too. Some of the most important parts of religion are how it helps us cultivate a sense of wonder and peace; an understanding of our human frailties and imperfections; resilience and meaning in the face of tragedy and suffering; and a respect for the mysteries of the universe.

Human reason and rationality are responsible for the amazing advances in our culture, knowledge, and standards of living. But our brains are finite and surprisingly predisposed to irrationality. What this means is that all of us—even the most intelligent and rational among us—have hidden biases and predispositions that we cannot perceive. This human trait affects the brains of both religious believers and non-believers alike.

Following the Triple Path means trying to clarify your thinking and act more rationally, but also means having humility about your conclusions and beliefs, not losing sight of the importance of feelings and human relationships, and showing ultimate respect and reverence for the divine.

The Codex

In the Creeds, Rites, and Practices section of this book, you will find occasional references to something called the Codex, which is another book that will be a companion volume to this one. The Codex will apply the symbolic approach to continue cherishing and learning from the legendary and mythological stories of our culture (without necessarily believing any of those stories to be literally true) by collecting them into one place—stories from the Bible, Greco-Roman and Germanic myths, and medieval legends. The Codex is still only in very rough draft form. You can find the latest draft at TriplePath.org/Codex.

Theism

If the Triple Path rejects failed ancient cosmologies, then why still believe in God?

Current scientific models give us tremendous insight into

how the universe began and how it works, and into the origins of mankind. These models, however, also have significant gaps and cannot explain the root cause of many scientific observations. Why did the Big Bang happen? How and why do the fundamental forces work? How and why do the elementary particles exist? How did consciousness evolve? What *is* consciousness? We at best have only incomplete answers to these questions.

These gaps and unanswered questions leave room for belief in things that exist beyond the material world we perceive. The unanswered questions of science are "known unknowns"—they are things that we know that we do not know. These known unknowns already leave room open for the possibility of belief.

But it would be wise to have the epistemological humility to also recognize the possibility of "unknown unknowns"—things that we do not even know that we do not know. The inherent limitations of our senses, our scientific instruments, and our brains leave open the possibility that there are realities beyond what we can perceive and measure—things we are incapable of even understanding. Indeed, it is impossible to prove or disprove the existence of God as He is often described in the monotheistic faiths: an invisible, all-powerful, all-knowing being who is present everywhere.

Having this epistemological humility leaves still greater room, even for the most rationally minded person, to believe in the existence of God.

With that room left open for belief, though, the question still remains, why believe? Many people do so after their own personal encounter with the divine. We will talk more about that in a moment, but there are other reasons for believing in God as well. Like William James, you can root it in pragmatic concerns. Just as there is a relationship between well-being and religiosity, there is also a relationship between belief in God and well-being, both physical and mental. People who believe in God are healthier, happier, live longer, and act more morally. As with the research on religiosity, the evidence is compelling. Once again, if you have any doubt, please turn right now to the next chapter on page 29, for a longer discussion (including many references to peer-reviewed academic journals).

Based on what we can measure about belief in God, deciding on theism makes sense. If the question of God's existence is fundamentally unprovable, but belief in Him brings such positive results, then the rational response is to believe in God.

Yet, the world's major religions often teach very different things about God. Looking more granularly, conceptions and definitions of God are almost as varied as the number of individuals holding them. How can we meaningfully discuss the question of God's existence and His characteristics if we do not even have a coherent definition of what He is? Indeed, people with mutually contradictory belief systems claim the same sorts of spiritual, divine feelings as confirmation of the truth of their beliefs about God.

So what does this mean? It might mean that there is one true religion and all the rest are false (and thus that the spiritual experiences of those religions' members are false). Or, it might mean that there is no God. The Triple Path favors a different explanation.

Its explanation is twofold: first, that we human beings are not very good at hearing God and understanding Him. As Paul says in the Bible, "we see through a glass, darkly".[26] Second, we believe that God wants us to figure many things out for ourselves.

We believe that it is impossible to fully define God with words. Each person must experience God for themself—this is each person's right, and solemn responsibility. It is *your* right and responsibility. It is less important to define God with much precision than it is to personally encounter Him and thus come to a greater understanding of Him for yourself.

The Triple Path's conception of God is best described as Theistic Rationalism. We believe that rationalism and religion can be compatible—we can commune and communicate with God,

---

26 1 Corinthians 13:12 (KJV).

but He puts us in control of our actions, and thus also responsible for their consequences.

We pray to God to express our gratitude, goals, and desires. Maybe we even pray for miracles, but we believe that the outcomes of our life are usually the result of our actions, natural laws, random chance, and the choices of others. We thus believe that bad things happen for the same reasons.

Our simple belief in God leaves open many questions about life, existence, and the supernatural. Those questions are important, but no one appears to have found any good, definitive answers to them yet. The lack of those certain answers is not a reason to reject the good that comes from believing in God and practicing religion. A parable from Buddhist scripture helps explains why. This is my adaption of it:

A man was shot with a poisoned arrow. As he lay injured, his family and friends brought a doctor to him to remove the arrow and administer an antidote for the poison.

The man stopped the doctor, saying, "I will not have this arrow removed until I know the surgical technique to be used; until I know whether he who wounded me was wealthy or poor, well-liked or unpopular, sane or crazy, powerful or impotent. I will not have it removed until I know the name of he who wounded me; until I know whether he was tall or short, dark or pale, blond or brunette; until I know whether his eyes were blue, brown, green, or gray; until I know his city, state, and country; until I know the language he speaks; until I know whether the bow firing the arrow that wounded me was a long bow or a crossbow; until I know whether the bowstring was made of natural or artificial fibers; until I know whether the arrow's shaft was wood, bamboo, reed, aluminum, or carbon fiber."

His family begged him to at least receive an injection of the antidote.

He said, "I will not receive an antidote to the poison

27

until I know whether the poison is natural or synthetic; until I know whether it is acid or base; until I know whether it is neurotoxic, carcinogenic, or radioactive; until I know how much poison has entered my bloodstream; until I know the lethal dosage of the poison; until I know the chemical formula of the antidote; and until I know the amount to be administered to me."

The man died and all those things about which he had questioned still remained unknown to him. Indeed, for those around him with the tools to save him—his family, friends, and doctor—the answers to many of his questions were as much mysteries to them as they were to him. And even for the answers they did have, there was not enough time to explain them before the arrow and poison killed him.[27]

Rationalism, empiricism, and pragmatic concerns are important, but so are the subjective and emotional side of things. Religion, God, and tradition add color and meaning to life. They can bring happiness and a feeling of connection to something greater than yourself.

Our time on this earth is limited. Even if we do not understand what they mean or how they work, it makes little sense to reject religion, God, and the traditions of our forefathers if they can help us be better, do better, and find meaning. Do not worry so much about getting the answers to all of life's questions right away—there are more important things to focus on first. Instead, worry about removing the poisoned arrows of selfishness, hypocrisy, ignorance, foolishness, evil, and lazy despair from your life. The evidence shows that religion and God can help you do that. And that is good enough.

So, read on and learn about the Triple Path. Try following it. Test its fruits for yourself. Come back to religion and God.

---

27 *See* Parable 4, The Poisoned Arrow, on page 307, paraphrased from Cula Malunkyovada Sutta, *The Shorter Instructions to Malunkya.*

God and Religion: Practical Evidence

A large body of research shows that believing in God, practicing a religion, praying, and meditating each have a strong relationship with a variety of positive outcomes.

Belief in God

People who perceive having a close connection to God have lower rates of depression and loneliness and greater rates of self-rated health, self-esteem, and psychological adjustment in response to major life stressors. Attachment theorists hypothesize that believers in God can look to him "as a safe haven, a being who offers caring and protection in times of stress" and that this attachment leads believers to "experience greater comfort in stressful situations and greater strength and confidence in everyday life". Indeed, people who "report a closer connection to God experience a number of health-related benefits: less depression and higher self-esteem, less loneliness, greater relational maturity, and greater psychosocial competence". A secure relationship with God is tied to "better self-rated health and better psychological adjustment among people facing a variety of major life stressors". These effects are greater than the effects associated with measures of religiosity or spirituality, and they have not been explained by nonreligious factors.[1]

People who perceive having a close connection to God have lower rates of depression and loneliness and better self-es-

1 Peter C. Hill and Kenneth I. Pargament, "Advances in the Conceptualization and Measurement of Religion and Spirituality: Implications for Physical and Mental Health Research", *American Psychologist*, Vol. 58, No. 1, January 2003, pp. 67-66.

teem, self-rated health, and psychological adjustment in response to major life stressors.[2] People being treated for depression who believed in God had greater reductions in depression and self-harm and greater improvements in psychological well-being than nonbelievers.[3]

This relationship between theism and well-being is not just an American phenomenon. In a 2013 study of ninety-two countries, there was a positive relationship between a person's happiness (as well as life satisfaction) and the self-reported level of importance of God in that person's life, relative to the average level of faith in that person's country.[4]

Religiosity

Similarly, religion is associated with practical, observable benefits to adherents, such as "improved health, survivorship, economic opportunities, sense of community, psychological well-being, assistance during crises, mating opportunities, and fertility".[5] People who are religious are more likely to be honest, law-abiding, give money to charity, volunteer their time to help others, be civically involved, and engage in prosocial behavior. They are also

2   *Same*, p. 67-68.
3   David H. Rosmarin, *et. al.*, "A test of faith in God and treatment: The relationship of belief in God to psychiatric treatment outcomes", *Journal of Affective Disorders*, Vol. 146, No. 3, April 25, 2013, pp. 441-446; *see also* Timothy B. Smith, Michael E. McCullough, and Justin Poll, "Religiousness and Depression: Evidence for a Main Effect and the Moderating Influence of Stressful Life Events", *Psychological Bulletin*, Vol. 129, No. 4, 2003, pp. 614-636.
4   Aleksandr Kogan, *et. al.*, "Uncertainty avoidance moderates the link between faith and subjective well-being around the world", *The Journal of Positive Psychology*, 2013.
5   Richard Sosis and Candace Alcorta, "Signaling, solidarity, and the sacred: the evolution of religious behavior", *Evolutionary Anthropology*, Vol. 12, No. 6, Nov. 2003, pp. 264.

less materialistic, hedonistic, and self-oriented.[6]

Religiosity has a positive relationship with good physical health. "[A]s a predictor of health and longevity, religious involvement rivals nonsmoking and exercise effects."[7] Regular church attendance is associated with a twenty-five percent decrease in risk of mortality, even after accounting for confounding variables; religiosity and spirituality are also associated with decreased risk of cardiovascular disease (but religiosity does not appear to help with cancer or to help recovery from acute illness).[8] Religiosity and spirituality are associated with lower blood pressure and better immune function.[9] A study of elderly patients found a positive relationship between physical and mental health and religiosity, and that non-religious and non-spiritual patients had worse health and higher morbidity.[10] Another study concluded that a 20-year-old who frequently attends church has a life expectancy of 83 years, whereas a 20-year-old who does not attend church has a life expectancy of 75 years. This increased life expectancy appears to be

---

6   David G. Myers, "Religion and human flourishing", in Michael Eid and Randy J. Larsen (eds.), *The Science of Subjective Well-Being*, 2008, pp. 323-46, 330-32; Jesse Preston and Ryan S. Ritter, "Different effects of Religion and God on prosociality with the ingroup and outgroup", *Personality and Social Psychology Bulletin*, Vol. 39, No. 9, September 2013; Arthur C. Brooks, "Religious Faith and Charitable Giving", *Policy Review*, No. 121, October 1, 2003.

7   David G. Myers (*see* footnote 6), pp. 336-38.

8   Lynda H. Powell, *et. al.*, "Religion and spirituality: Linkages to physical health", *American Psychologist*, Vol. 58, No. 1, January 2003, pp. 36-52; David G. Myers (*see* footnote 6), pp. 334-38.

9   Teresa E. Seeman, *et. al.*, "Religiosity/Spirituality and Health: A Critical Review of the Evidence for Biological Pathways", *American Psychologist*, Vol. 58, No. 1, January 2003, pp. 53-63.

10 Harold G. Koenig, *et. al.*, "Religion, spirituality, and health in medically ill hospitalized older patients", *Journal of the American Geriatric Society*, Vol. 52, No. 4, April 2004, pp. 554-62.

caused not only by selection effects (such as unhealthy people being less likely to attend church), but also because religiosity is associated with greater social ties and behavioral factors that decrease the risk of death.[11] A meta-analysis of studies that examined the relationship between religious involvement and mortality found that greater religious involvement is associated with greater odds of survival.[12] It appears that these beneficial effects are not just caused by mundane benefits that religion provides, such as social ties. In studies examining the relationship between religion and health, "salutary effects of religious involvement persist despite an impressive array of statistical controls for social ties, health behaviors, and sociodemographic variables".[13]

Religion also has a positive relationship with mental health. "[S]ystematic reviews of the research literature over the years have consistently reported that aspects of religious involvement are associated with desirable mental health outcomes."[14] Attendance at church is directly related to subjective well-being and is indirectly related to improved physical health through its association with improved mood and also through its relationship with decreased substance abuse.[15] Higher religiosity is associated with lower risk of depression, especially for those under stress; similarly, a meta-analysis of nine studies found a relationship between

---

11 Robert A. Hummer, *et. al.*, "Religious involvement and U.S. adult mortality", *Demography*, Vol. 36, No. 2, 1999, pp. 273-285.

12 Peter C. Hill and Kenneth I. Pargament (*see* footnote 1), pp. 66.

13 Christopher G. Ellison and Jeffrey S. Levin, "The Religion-Health Connection: Evidence, Theory, and Future Directions", *Health Education & Behavior*, Vol. 25, No. 6, December 1998, pp. 700-720, at 702.

14 *Same.*

15 Laura B. Koenig and George E. Vaillant, "A prospective study of church attendance and health over the lifespan", *Health Psychology*, Vol. 28, No. 1, January 2009, pp. 117-24.

religiosity and lower risk of suicide.[16] In another study, higher religiosity and spirituality among elderly patients was associated not only with fewer depressive symptoms, but also with better cognitive function.[17] Among stroke victims, spiritual belief was positively correlated with better mental health (but not with better physical health).[18]

When people were asked what they were striving for in their lives, those with a larger number of spiritual goals had greater purpose in life, life satisfaction, and levels of well-being. Those with a more intrinsic religious orientation have better mental health, self-esteem, meaning in life, family relationships, and a feeling of well-being; they have lower levels of alcohol abuse, drug abuse, and sexual promiscuity.[19] Weekly church attendance has about the same significant positive effect on happiness as being married.[20]

Most of the above studies focused on the United States. Critics might argue that such studies are not generalizable outside the United States because American culture is more religious than other developed nations. Thus, they may argue, the negative comparative effects of irreligion in these studies may come from the stress of being part of a minority group. Studies involving interna-

---

16 David G. Myers (*see* footnote 6), pp. 326, 337; Andrew Wu, *et. al.*, "Religion and Completed Suicide: a Meta-Analysis", *PloS ONE*, Vol. 10, No. 6, June 25, 2015.

17 Harold G. Koenig, *et. al.*, "Religion, spirituality, and health in medically ill hospitalized older patients", *Journal of the American Geriatric Society*, Vol. 52, No. 4, April 2004, pp. 554-62.

18 Brick Johnstone, *et. al.*, "Relationships Among Religiousness, Spirituality, and Health for Individuals with Stroke", *Journal of Clinical Psychology in Medical Settings*, Vol. 15, No. 4, December 2008, pp. 308-313.

19 Peter C. Hill and Kenneth I. Pargament (*see* footnote 1), p. 68.

20 Danny Cohen-Zada and William Sander, "Religious Participation versus Shopping: What Makes People Happier?" *Journal of Law and Economics*, Vol. 54, No. 4, 2011, pp. 889-906.

tional samples, however, contradict this assumption. Data from seventy countries showed that a person's self-definition of being "a religious person" (versus being not religious or atheist) was positively associated with subjective personal life satisfaction. The relationship did not seem to depend on whether a person was a member of the majority or minority religion, but just on whether a person was religious.[21]

This relationship has apparently held across countries for several decades—a 1990 study of sixteen countries found that the relationship between church attendance and a person's happiness and life satisfaction "is not a uniquely American finding, but a general pattern that holds true" across the industrialized world, including in Europe, Canada, and Japan. In the sixteen countries, the people who attended church once a week were satisfied with their lives at a rate eight percentage points higher than those who did not attend, and they were happy at a rate nine percentage points higher than those who did not attend.[22] One study found that religiosity in the United States, Denmark, and Netherlands were all weakly associated with happiness (although the correlations in Europe were not statistically significant).[23] A study of a representative sample of elderly adults in the Netherlands showed that even after adjusting for physical health, social support, alcohol use, and demographic variables, there was a consistent relationship between lower depression and regular church attendance.[24] A

21 Marta Elliott and R. David Hayward, "Religion and Life Satisfaction Worldwide: The Role of Government Regulation", *Sociology of Religion*, Vol. 70, No. 3, 2009, pp. 285-310.

22 Ronald Inglehart, *Culture Shift in Advanced Industrial Society*, 1990, pp. 227-29.

23 Liesbeth Snoep, "Religiousness and happiness in three nations: a research note", *Journal of Happiness Studies*, Vol. 9, 2008, pp. 207-211.

24 Arjan W. Braam, *et. al.*, "Religious involvement and 6-year course of depressive symptoms in older Dutch citizens: results from the Longitudinal Aging Study Amsterdam", *Journal of Aging and Health*,

study of persons in thirty-five European countries found that both traditional religious beliefs and new age religious beliefs were associated with higher levels of subjective well-being, and that atheists had the lowest rates of subjective well-being.[25] A study of 455,104 people from 154 countries found a small positive relationship between religiosity and subjective well-being, after controlling for personal circumstances (but the relationship attenuated in better-off societies).[26] A longitudinal study of 1,500 Germans showed that "individuals who become more religious over time record long term gains in life satisfaction, while those who become less religious record long term losses".[27]

Like all social science research, these results on the effects of religiosity will never be as conclusive as research in hard sciences such as physics and chemistry. People are complicated, and it can be difficult to do the statistics right and create an adequate model to control for all the relevant variables. Moreover, in studies where we look at population-level data, it can be hard to infer causality. It is difficult, and often impossible, to set up double-blind studies, or even studies with control populations, to analyze the effects of religiosity as an independent variable versus a control. The above longitudinal study of Germans, where changes in religiosity over time were related to changes in happiness levels, is highly

Vol. 16, No. 4, 2004, pp. 467-89.

25 Andrej Kirbiš and Sergej Flere, "Conventional religiosity and New age beliefs as predictors of subjective well-being in Europe", *Out of the Box Conference*, May 15-17, 2002.

26 Ed Diener, et. al., "The Religion Paradox: If Religion Makes People Happy, Why Are So Many Dropping Out?" *Journal of Personality and Social Psychology*, Vol. 101, No. 6, December 2011, pp. 1278-90.

27 Bruce Headey, et. al., "Authentic happiness theory supported by impact of religion on life satisfaction: A longitudinal analysis with data for Germany", *The Journal of Positive Psychology*, Vol. 5, No. 1, 2010, pp. 73-82.

suggestive, however, that religiosity was causing the happiness.[28]

One clever study used a natural experiment to test causality, using changes in state laws in the United States in the 1960s and 1970s that led to decreased church attendance. Many U.S. states used to have "blue laws" that prohibited commercial activity, such as retail, entertainment, and sports, on Sunday. Blue laws were repealed throughout the 1960s and 1970s, often in response to court challenges (and thus not, apparently, because people had grown less religious and demanded through democratic processes that the laws be repealed). The repeal of state blue laws led to a decrease in church attendance among white women (but not men). States did not repeal their blue laws at the same time. This allowed researchers to compare demographically and geographically similar states where blue laws were in effect in some and not in others. These conditions allowed researchers to examine the churchgoing behavior and happiness of people before and after the repeal of blue laws. The decrease in church attendance was associated with a significant and substantial negative effect on happiness in white women (but not men). Women's decreased church attendance explained much of the decrease in happiness that they have experienced, relative to men, since 1973.[29] This research is even more suggestive that religiosity causes happiness, and not that happy people merely also tend to be religious.

What is responsible for the relationship between religion and well-being? Religion does not appear to have much of an effect on the "Big Five" major personality traits that psychologists use to describe human personalities (agreeableness, conscientiousness, extroversion, neuroticism, and openness). Religion does, however, seem to have "profound effects on mid-level personality functions such as values, goals, attitudes, and behaviors, as well as on the more self-defining personality functions of life meaning

---

28 *Same.*

29 Danny Cohen-Zada and William Sander (*see* footnote 20).

and personal identity".[30] Religion provides hope, optimism, and purpose, all of which in turn increase a person's well-being.[31] We invest more care and attention into parts of our lives that we view as sacred, and those sacred aspects of our lives give greater life satisfaction and meaning. Not only does religion serve as a general orienting and motivating force, it also provides specific coping mechanisms (such as prayer, meditation, and religious rituals).[32]

Many of religion's benefits may come because it helps "solve significant communication problems inherent in human life".[33] Religions provide social support, companionship, and a sense of community.[34] Indeed, the social aspects of religion have the greatest relationship with increased happiness (both in secular Europe and the more religious United States).[35] Social support from religion often leads to greater self-esteem and a sense of intrinsic self-worth among adherents and also provides a continuous support network in all phases of life. Religious support, however, seems to offer something greater than what comes from other types of non-religious social support—religious support still has a strong relationship with psychological adjustment even after con-

30   Peter C. Hill and Kenneth I. Pargament (see footnote 1), p. 71.
31   Christopher G. Ellison and Jeffrey S. Levin (see footnote 13), p. 708-9; David G. Myers (see footnote 6), pp. 326-28; Sonja Lyubomirsky, et. al., "Pursuing happiness: The architecture of sustainable change", Review of General Psychology, Vol. 9, No. 2, 2005, pp. 111-31.
32   Peter C. Hill and Kenneth I. Pargament (see footnote 1), p. 68; see also Christopher G. Ellison and Jeffrey S. Levin (see footnote 13), p. 707-8.
33   Richard Sosis and Candace Alcorta (see footnote 5), p. 264.
34   Peter C. Hill and Kenneth I. Pargament (see footnote 1), p. 69; Christopher G. Ellison and Jeffrey S. Levin (see footnote 13), p. 705-7; David G. Myers (see footnote 6), pp. 336-38.
35   Liesbeth Snoep (see footnote 23), p. 209-10.

trolling for general social support.[36]

It is also likely some of the health benefits associated with religion come from religion's encouragement of healthy behaviors —people who attend church more often also tend to have other characteristics that are associated with lower risk of dying, such as more physical activity, more social interactions, and being married. These additional healthy behaviors do not explain all the benefit, however. In one study, a twenty-five percent reduction in risk of death still remained among churchgoers even after accounting for these other behaviors that are related to health. Other studies have found that even after controlling for unhealthy behaviors, seventy-five percent of the difference in longevity between the religious and non-religious remains.[37] This added effect of religion has been found outside the United States as well: increased church attendance was found to be associated with lower depression in the elderly in the Netherlands even after accounting for other explanatory variables.[38]

Religious Practices: Prayer and Meditation

Beyond studies of just the general effect of religiosity, prayer and meditation are two specific religious practices that have been shown to have positive effects.

Prayer has a beneficial effect on the person who prays: it increases gratitude and has a strong relationship with hope and adult attachment.[39] Praying for one's partner also decreases infi-

---

36 Peter C. Hill and Kenneth I. Pargament (see footnote 1), p. 69; Christopher G. Ellison and Jeffrey S. Levin (see footnote 13), p. 705-7.

37 Lynda H. Powell, et. al. (see footnote 8), p. 41; see also Christopher G. Ellison and Jeffrey S. Levin (see footnote 13), p. 704 and Laura B. Koenig and George E. Vaillant (see footnote 34); David G. Myers (see footnote 6), pp. 336-38.

38 Arjan W. Braam, et. al. (see footnote 24).

39 Nathaniel Lambert, et. al., "Can Prayer Increase Gratitude?", Psychology of Religion and Spirituality, Vol. 1, No. 3, August 2009, pp. 139-149; Peter Jankowski and Steven Sandage, "Meditative Prayer,

delity in the person who prays (both unfaithful acts and thoughts) by increasing the perception that the relationship is sacred.[40] Praying with and for one's partner or for a friend increases trust and unity with that person. In one study, the participants were instructed to pray together, while control groups were told to engage in daily positive thoughts about their partner, or to engage in a neutral activity. Those in the prayer group were given a sample non-denominational prayer as a starting point in which the person praying addressed God and petitioned for help for the friend. Subsequent self-reported measures and observations by objective observers indicated that the couples in the prayer groups had stronger relationships.[41]

Studies on intercessory prayers (prayers said with the intent to benefit someone else) indicate that such prayers have no effect, or perhaps only a small effect on the other person.[42] Inter-

---

Hope, Adult Attachment, and Forgiveness: A Proposed Model", *Psychology of Religion and Spirituality*, Vol. 3, No. 2, May 2011, pp. 115-131.

40 Frank Fincham, et. al., "Faith and Unfaithfulness: Can Praying for Your Partner Reduce Infidelity?", *Journal of Personality and Social Psychology*, Vol. 99, No. 4, October 2011, pp. 649-659.

41 Nathaniel Lambert, et. al., "Praying Together and Staying Together: Couple Prayer and Trust", *Psychology of Religion and Spirituality*, Vol. 4, No. 1, 2012, pp. 1-9.

42 David R. Hodge, "A Systematic Review of the Empirical Literature on Intercessory Prayer", *Research on Social Work Practice*, Vol. 17, No. 2, March 2007, pp. 174-187; K. Masters, et. al., "Are there demonstrable effects of distant intercessory prayer? A meta-analytic review", *Annals of Behavioral Medicine*, Vol. 32, No. 1, August 2006, pp. 21-26; *but see* Randolph C. Byrd, "Positive therapeutic effects of intercessory prayer in a coronary care unit population", *Southern Medical Journal*, Vol. 81, No. 7, July 1988, pp. 826-9 (Hodge discounts Byrd's results because only 6 of the 26 measured problem conditions had positive results, raising the possibility that Byrd's results were false pos-

GOD AND RELIGION: PRACTICAL EVIDENCE

cessory prayers are "neither significantly beneficial nor harmful for those who are sick. . . . [A]lthough some of the results of individual studies suggest a positive effect of intercessory prayer, the majority do not and the evidence does not support a recommendation either in favour or against the use of intercessory prayer."[43] Praying for another person seems to provide little or no benefit for that person—the collective evidence seems to show that the benefits of prayer come primarily to the person or persons doing the praying.

There is also meditation, which can mean a lot of different things, from following rigid techniques and reciting specific mantras all the way to quietly thinking. My discussion of meditation is focused on the form with which I am most familiar: stilling one's thoughts and emptying one's mind. The National Institutes of Health provides an excellent description:

In meditation, a person learns to focus his attention and suspend the stream of thoughts that normally occupy the mind. This practice is believed to result in a state of greater physical relaxation, mental calmness, and psychological balance. Practicing meditation can change how a person relates to the flow of emotions and thoughts in the mind.[44]

This type of stillness meditation has tremendous benefits. Randomized controlled trials into meditation techniques that fo-

---

itives) and William S. Harris, et. al., "A Randomized, Controlled Trial of the Effects of Remote, Intercessory Prayer on Outcomes in Patients Admitted to the Coronary Care Unit", *Archives of Internal Medicine*, Vol. 159, No. 19, October 25, 1999, pp. 2273-2279.

43 L. Roberts, et. al., "Intercessory Prayer for the alleviation of ill health", *Cochrane Database of Systematic Reviews*, November 9, 2011.

44 National Institutes of Health, National Center for Complimentary and Alternative Medicine, "Terms Related to Complementary and Alternative Medicine", http://nccam.nih.gov/health/providers/camterms.htm (accessed May 12, 2013).

cus on stilling one's thoughts and achieving mental silence show significant effects (greater than other common stress management techniques) on work-related stress and depressive feelings.[45] Beyond effects on stress and mental health, meditation actually causes physiological changes in practitioners' brains and bodies.[46] Meditation improves physical and mental well-being for people suffering from a variety of physical and mental ailments.[47] Meditation is associated with lower blood pressure, lower cholesterol, lower stress hormone levels, and better health outcomes.[48] Other related practices are also beneficial: praying the rosary and saying mantras both have a positive effect on cardiovascular health, and transcendental meditation (which also involves saying mantras) modestly reduces blood pressure.[49] Even just cultivating sacred moments has positive effects on subjective well-being, psychologi-

45 Ramesh Manocha, "Meditation, mindfulness and mind-emptiness", *Acta Neuropsychiatrica*, Vol. 23, No. 1, Feb. 2011, pp. 46-47; *see also* Ramesh Manocha, *et. al.*, "A Randomized, Controlled Trial of Meditation for Work Stress, Anxiety and Depressed Mood in Full-Time Workers", *Evidence-Based Complementary and Alternative Medicine,* June 2011.

46 B. Rael Cahn and John Polich, "Meditation states and traits: EEG, ERP, and neuroimaging studies", *Psychological Bulletin*, Vol. 132, No. 2, March 2006, pp. 180-211.

47 Paul Grossman, *et. al.*, "Mindfulness-based stress reduction and health benefits: A meta-analysis", *Journal of Psychosomatic Research*, Vol. 57, No. 1, July 2004, pp. 35-43.

48 Teresa E. Seeman, *et. al.* (*see* footnote 9).

49 Luciano Bernardi, *et. al.*, "Effect of rosary prayer and yoga mantras on autonomic cardiovascular rhythms: comparative study", *British Medical Journal*, Vol. 323, No. 7327, December 22, 2001, pp. 1446-1449; Robert D. Brook, *et. al.*, "Beyond Medications and Diet: Alternative Approaches to Lowering Blood Pressure: A Scientific Statement From the American Heart Association", *Hypertension*, vol. 61, No. 6, June 2013, p. 1360-1383.

cal well-being, and on stress reduction.[50]

The research strongly suggests that prayer and meditation have real beneficial effects on mental, physical, and relationship health. Why? How? We do not know exactly. It may be only because it helps us reduce stress and break out of harmful thought processes. I think it may also be because it helps us connect to God and the divine, but regardless of the exact mechanism of action for prayer and meditation, and regardless of whether the mechanism of action is natural or supernatural, the fact is that the research shows they work.

Given how easy and simple it is, it makes sense to learn how to effectively pray and meditate and regularly practice them. The studies I cite above generally allowed participants to define the meaning of prayer for themselves, or encouraged them to use generic non-denominational prayers addressed to God. I address my prayers to God, then express gratitude, express my hopes for the current situation and the future, and then end by saying "Amen". I use formal language and archaic pronouns for God, because that helps it feel more sacred.

My limited expertise in meditation is based on a free class on meditation I took at Harvard when I was there as a law student. But what I learned has worked well for me. I find a quiet place where I can sit comfortably. I close my eyes, take deep breaths, and clear my mind of thoughts. To help me clear my thoughts, I sometimes use visualizations I learned at a meditation class. The most effective one for me (and that I still often use) is to imagine (while continuing to breathe deeply) that my mind is a stormy sea and that my thoughts are violent stormy waves undulating across my mind. Then, I imagine the sun rising over the sea of my mind, gradually burning off the storm clouds and slowing and stilling the winds. I think about the waves of thoughts in my mind slowly

---

50   Elisha David Goldstein, "Sacred Moments: Implications on Well-Being and Stress", *Journal of Clinical Psychology*, Vol. 63, No. 10, 2007, pp. 1001-1019.

weakening and subsiding. I continue to breathe deeply and imagine my mind becoming the glassy smooth surface of a perfectly calm sea. Other times, instead of the sea visualization, or together with it, I recite in my mind a simple mantra as I breathe in and out —usually I will think the word "stillness" as I breathe in and then think the word "peace" as I breathe out. Whatever method I use, once my thoughts have been stilled, I continue to breathe deeply and enjoy the serenity of a still mind, I imagine a window in my heart opening and drawing in heat and love, which induces feelings of elevation to add to the serenity. When I have been more regularly practicing meditation, I find I need to use the visualizations less frequently—I can more easily just sit and start to breathe deeply and gradually switch my mind over into "meditation mode". Another technique we used in the class that I liked was to begin our meditations by breathing deeply while staring at a candle's flame.

I recommend taking a class on meditation to get more ideas and to find something that works for you.

Conclusion

Just because a lot of people engage in a religious practice, does not by itself mean the practice is optimal or worth following. Path dependency can mean that useless or harmful religious practices become widespread because they are part of a "religious package" that a lot of people have come to accept, often because other aspects of a religion do bring real benefits, or because the religion has become widespread because of macro socio-political forces or even because of random chance.

But it is likely that many, if not most, religious practices become widespread because they bring real benefit. It is worth learning about and examining the religious practices of others to evaluate whether those practices are worth following, especially when different, unrelated religions have ended up adopting similar practices. For prayer and meditation, the evidence that they are worth adopting is strong, as is the evidence for religion and belief in God in general.

Some Thoughts on Truth

Our desire for truth is one of the most fundamental human yearnings. What is truth, though? And how we can come to know it? Thinking about these questions, and their answers, is an important step to shedding our foolishness.

Our Senses and Objective Reality

The most fundamental question in a quest for truth is if some sort of truth in the universe even exists. If the answer is yes, the next question is whether we can discover that truth. Based on our experience with our senses, most of us readily assume without thinking that there is some sort of objective reality. Our perception of reality, however, is limited and imperfect. We only perceive a small part of what we normally think of as being real.

Even someone with 20/20 eyesight has imperfect vision. The level of detail that we can see is limited by the number of rod and cone receptor cells in our eye. Moreover, there are holes and imperfections in the picture our eyes pick up because the distribution of receptor cells in our retina is uneven and because there are not receptors where the optic nerve connects to the retina. Our perception of seeing a complete picture with no holes in it is merely an illusion created by our brains filling in the gaps. Worse still, our eyes can see only a small part of the available light—visible light (the only part we can see) is only two percent of the electromagnetic spectrum.[1] This means that we are blind to potentially ninety-eight percent of what there is to "see". These limitations of perception do not apply only to sight—all of our senses are similarly constrained.

---

1   Lisa Yount, *Modern Astronomy: Expanding the Universe*, 2005, p. 36.

Moreover, our brains have to further filter and interpret all the information our senses receive. Seeing a good magic show is easy proof at how quickly our senses can be fooled.

Beyond just the fallibility of our senses, the very physical properties of the universe make it impossible to be certain about some things. Quantum physics indicates that it is impossible to have complete certainty about certain aspects of subatomic particles: as certainty about a particle's momentum goes up, certainty about its position goes down, and vice versa. Gaining knowledge about one aspect of the particle makes it impossible to gain knowledge about another. A few scientists have even hypothesized that the physical laws of the universe may not be constant—they may have changed over time, or may be different in other parts of the universe.[2]

In spite of all these uncertainties and limitations, most of us intuitively believe that some sort of objective truth exists. We perceive an apparently unchanging and constant exterior environment, and we experience the consistency of cause and effect. While our perception of physical reality may be imperfect and flawed, the consistency of those perceptions leads us to assume that our perceptions of reality have a high probability of being generally accurate. Indeed, our continued survival as living beings requires that we act as if objective physical reality exists—for example, without thinking about it, we presuppose that the food we see is real, and we eat it when we are hungry; anyone who does otherwise would soon die.

Our experience indicates that there are physical laws governing the operation of the universe and that, on the scale of human lifetimes, these laws are unchanging. This consistency in our daily experience leads us to assume that truth exists and that we can discover and understand it. Just as we learn through repeated ex-

---

2   John Webb, "Are the laws of nature changing with time?" *Physics World*, April 2003, pp. 33-38; Michael R. Wilczynska1, *et. al.*, "Four direct measurements of the fine-structure constant 13 billion years ago", *Science Advances*, Vol. 6, No. 17, April 24, 2020.

perience from a young age that the sun always rises, we come to expect consistency in other areas, so long as we can discover some sort of pattern.

Our experiences with the consistency of reality contrast with a common unreal experience: when dreaming, we often look at something, look away, then look at it again only to discover that the object has changed in some fundamental way. We perceive "real life" as being qualitatively different from our dreams because we presume that our dreams are generated by our own minds and are thus changeable, whereas our waking perceptions of the universe and the physical world are consistent and appear to be governed by unchanging laws. We feel time flowing on, cause and effect seemingly unchanging and unalterable.

The business of living requires that we assume there is a reality to our existence and that we can come to an understanding of it. We should be bold in moving forward on the best truth we have, and in seeking more of it. It would be wise in this boldness, however, to still have the humility to recognize we will never have perfect understanding. As we confidently seek, we should also humbly understand that the best we can hope is only that our imperfect knowledge and understanding become slightly better approximations of reality. Because of our human limitations, we can never have complete certainty about any of our perceptions.[3]

---

3   While dreaming, most people do not notice the inconsistencies in their perceptions and usually do not even notice they are dreaming—within the context of the dream, the inconsistencies appear perfectly natural. This raises the question: is anything like this happening while we are awake? If so, how could we tell? Psychology research in recent decades into the phenomena of change blindness and inattention blindness suggest that, even when we are awake, we do not perceive such changes very well. *See, e.g.*, Daniel J. Simons and Daniel T. Levin, "Failure to detect changes to people during a real-world interaction", *Psychonomic Bulletin & Review*, Vol. 5, No. 4, 1998, 644-649; Christopher Chabris and Daniel Simons, *The Invisible Gorilla*, 2010.

When I write in this book about facts or truths or reality, it is because I am communicating with the normal words of everyday language. I write based on my limited perceptions and experiences of an outside world that seems to exist. Of course, there is uncertainty about everything I represent as being true or real, but just as it is wise to have the humility to recognize the uncertainties of life, it is also foolish to be crippled by that uncertainty.

Different Notions of Truth

Enlightenment and scientific notions of objective truth are often the only way we are taught to conceive of truth in school and university. This can cloud our understanding and keep us from considering other ways of conceiving of truth.

Truth from a scientific perspective could perhaps be defined as "a set of facts that are derivable from materialistic reductionism".[4] Some ideas, however, are outside the realm of facts capable of verification in this manner, yet appear in practice to be no less true. In many ways, they seem to be *more* true. The American Pragmatist school of philosophy offers a way of evaluating the veracity of such ideas. It teaches that we should determine the truth of an idea by examining its practical consequences. For example, on the question of God, William James said "[o]n pragmatic principles, if the hypothesis of God works satisfactorily in the widest sense of the word, then it is 'true'."[5]

Following the Pragmatist line, Professor Jordan Peterson defines truth in Darwinian terms, arguing that fundamental truth is that which guides you to action and allows you to survive and reproduce, or more broadly, that which ensures viability across the broadest domain of time.[6] He argues that truth in the Darwinian sense is

---

4   Jordan Peterson, July 5, 2018, https://twitter.com/jordanbpeterson/status/1014983453173878784.

5   William James, *Pragmatism: A New Name for Some Old Ways of Thinking*, "Lecture 8: Pragmatism and Religion", 1907.

6   Jordan Peterson, Podcast 4: Religion, Myth, Science, Truth, 32:00, 1:12:00, and 1:13:50.

that which is uniquely useful and valuable, as opposed to the New-tonian notion that only what is objectively observable is real.[7] Finding truth can thus mean not only seeking greater understanding about the "world as a place of things", but also about the "world as a forum for action".[8] Whereas Newtonian or scientific truths teach us facts about the material world, lessons about the world as a forum for action teach us moral truths: truths about values and how we should act in the world—human truths about being and meaning.

These moral truths have usually been passed down to us in stories. Our problem now is that many, if not most, of our traditional narratives have been proved historically and cosmologically inaccurate. Just because the stories are not factually true, however, does not necessarily mean that the moral claims embedded in them are also untrue. As the Fourth Century Roman writer Sallust said of the Romans' pagan myths: "Now these things never happened, but always are."[9] When he wrote that, paganism was already on the decline and would soon collapse, in spite of his efforts (and those of the final pagan Roman Emperor, Julian).[10] His justification for the myths was not enough to salvage belief in stories in which ever-growing numbers of people had lost confidence.

But as we discussed in the last chapter, it is getting harder and harder to rely just on our faith in the stories passed down to us. What is the answer, then, as we seek truths about the world as a forum for action—truths about acting, being, and meaning? Perhaps we need new stories, or a new way of using our old ones. The Triple Path's main purpose is to move to a solution to this problem. We have already discussed how it takes as many as possible of the ingredients available from traditional religion and bakes them

---

7   *Id.* at 1:37:00.

8   Jordan Peterson, *Maps of Meaning: The Architecture of Belief*, 1999, pp. 15 (page numbers from 2002 PDF version).

9   Sallust, *On the Gods and the Cosmos*, ca. 360.

10 *See* Edward J. Watts, *The Final Pagan Generation*, 2015.

into something new and nourishing and more resilient, but it does something else too. It calls for each individual to get better at learning how to find truth, especially moral truths, and then having more faith in the moral truths themselves, and in their Source.

There are many such truths to be discovered, or re-discovered. In the next chapter, we will discuss these questions of morality and ethics in more detail. Here, we focus on the methods we can use to discover truth.

How Can We Discover Truth?

If we assume there is some kind of real truth, and that we can gain knowledge about it (both of which are reasonable assumptions, based on our perceptions of existence), the next step is to figure out how we may gain knowledge of it.

Some ways of gaining knowledge are more effective than others. Many complement each other. Some are better for discovering Newtonian truths and some are better for discovering moral truths. I have separated them into seven categories: sensory observation, experience and common sense, trial and error, authorities, empirical rationalism, emotions, and religion and tradition. These categories are artificial. In real life, there is no clear separation between them, and we often use multiple methods at the same time. But separating them is a useful way to think about the different ways we gain knowledge of the truth. Each category has an important place in our quest for truth. Let us discuss each of them in turn.

1) Sensory Observation

The most fundamental way to gain knowledge is through passive observation using our senses. Imperfect though they are, our senses seem to be the only way our internal selves receive information about the outside material world.

There are three problems with observation. First, as I discussed above, our senses are imperfect, limited, and not always reliable. Second, mere observation does not tell us anything about the root causes of things. Determining causes requires interpretation and reasoning, rather than just observation. Third, observation is backward-looking and limited: it only tells us about what has already happened in the past, and it limits us to only learning about what we can directly perceive.

2) Experience and Common Sense

Gaining knowledge through observation involves accumulating memories of previous sensory experiences. Using experience and common sense means interpreting the information we have gained to make conclusions and predictions. We notice cause and effect, and gain experience to make conclusions about future events. A child remembers the time he burned himself by touching the hot stove, and he thereafter avoids touching that stove until he has first checked whether it is hot.

We apply our innate and learned cognitive abilities to reason and extrapolate from previous experience to make inferences about things we have not yet observed or experienced, and to make predictions. We notice patterns and learn to generalize from them. The child extrapolates from his experience with a particular stove to conclude he should be careful about touching all other stoves and even things that are not stoves that he knows might be hot.

The problem with common sense is that our brains did not develop to be truth-seeking machines, but to be survival machines. At the most basic level, our brains' purpose is to help us survive into adulthood and pass on our genes by having and raising children. We have all sorts of cognitive shortcuts and biases hardwired into us that increase our probability of survival but that may sometimes decrease our ability to find truth. We tend to be much more biased toward false positives than false negatives—we are much more likely to assume that something is there when it is not (a false positive) than to assume that something is not there when it really is (a false negative). The frequently used stylized example of this tendency is that the person who assumed that the rustling in the grass was caused by a predator and fled tended to survive. Even if most of the time the rustling was only caused by the wind, it would only take an occasional hidden lion to cull from the gene pool those not prone to the false positive bias.

Thus, while it confers survival advantages on the savanna, neolithic farms, and even in urban jungles, our innate basic intuitive reasoning can be wrong. We naturally commit all sorts of fallacies:

- we falsely attribute causation to unrelated events that happen close together (like the Aztecs believing their blood sacrifices caused the sun to rise or our tendency to feel aversion to a food we ate just before we felt sick to our stomach, even if the illness had nothing to do with the food);
- we misunderstand the true causes of events (such as the belief up until the 19th century that bloodletting helped cure disease or that bad air caused malaria);
- we trust too much in our senses without understanding their limitations—we believe that our senses give us a completely accurate understanding of world, but then make false conclusions based on them (like the belief in the ancient world that the world was flat);
- we falsely attribute personality and intentionality to inanimate objects (like people talking to their car).

Beyond our cognitive and sensory limitations, we are also temporally and spatially limited—we cannot be everywhere and everywhen at once. There is only so much one person can figure out using personal experience and common sense on his own. Relying on observation, experience, and common sense is enough to get us into adulthood and pass on our genes to the next generation, but there are other ways to get to more knowledge of the truth.

3) Trial and Error

Trial and error is a rudimentary form of experimentation. It involves observation and experience, but instead of just passively observing, we take action to test our ideas. Trial and error means testing different options until we come to one that works. Think of Thomas Edison inventing the light bulb by testing new materials over and over until he found something that would work as the filament.

Discovery through trial and error is often time-consuming. Relying on trial and error to discover new truth means that each of us is limited in what we can discover during our lifetime. Imagine if each of us had to invent the light bulb again on our own. We can only personally do so much. Moreover, trial and error will not always lead to the complete truth. If we discover something that seems to work, it does not necessarily mean it is optimal in all situations (for example, fluorescent and LED bulbs last longer and are more energy efficient than Edison's light bulb).

Even if it leads us to the optimal solution, the bigger problem with trial and error is that, just like with observation, it does not usually lead to an understanding of the root causes of things. Just because we find a solution that works does not mean that we will understand why it works. The inventors of the light bulb, or fire or the wheel, did not understand why or how their inventions worked.

4) Authorities

Our time and our ability to observe, experience, and experiment are limited. Language is a powerful tool that allowed us to pass knowledge to others, first through oral traditions, and now through the written and recorded word. We do not have to start from scratch in our quest for knowledge. We are thus not limited to our own personal experience. The accumulated store of human-generated information is now so amazingly vast that it would be impossible for even the greatest genius to rediscover and recreate it all through observation, trial and error, and common sense. Because of this, we all rely on a body of gradually developed knowledge and wisdom that we often call "culture" or "tradition" (more on these in a few pages). We also rely on experts: people who have gained knowledge in a particular subject area and who then share that knowledge with others.

As we briefly discussed in the first chapter, in spite of the importance of experts, it is a logical fallacy to rely on the truthfulness of a statement just because an expert said it. There is nothing wrong, however, with relying on a statement made by an expert because of the inherent merit of the statement itself. It is thus not a fallacy to argue that something said by an authority is true. The fallacy comes from believing that something is true *because* an authority said it. The status of the person making a statement does not magically make the statement true.

Every statement made by an authority should be subject to criticism. It is always a big warning sign when authority figures (whether as individuals, groups, corporations, associations, or governments) claim their statements to be above reproach and beyond criticism, and especially when they try to silence the speech of those whom they oppose. Whatever the justification given, anytime people try to stop you from subjecting their statements to critical examination, the real reason will almost always be because they are afraid you will discover their statements are false, or because they themselves are afraid their claims might be false, and they do not want to expose themselves to the cognitive dissonance of considering they might be wrong. If they had good evidence and justifications to back up their claims, why would they not want you to critically examine their pronouncements?

Another similar tactic to be wary of is when anyone tries to shout down, shame, harass, or publicly humiliate dissenting voices (often by using some pretextual excuse about the dissenter violating orthodoxies or being "offensive"). It would be wise to automatically discount any statements, and to disregard any claims to authority, made by such people. If an authority's claims are true, why would he or she need to resort to such oppressive tactics to defend those claims? Legitimate authorities do not shrink from challenges to their ideas, because they know they have nothing to fear. It is the charlatans who try to suppress others' voices, because they are scared of being disproved.

Almost as bad are those who create, spread, or promote propaganda, which are messages intended to convince or change opinions by misrepresenting facts, as if their feeble words have the power to change truth. Soviet propaganda trying to justify the superiority of communism did not change its inherent defects. The supermarket shelves were still always bare. Its 100 million victims were still dead. And it still collapsed.

This is why free speech is one of the foundational values of the West. We have progressed so far and so fast since we enshrined free speech during the Enlightenment because free speech is such a powerful tool for cutting down the lies and mistakes of the powerful and the charlatans among us, and thus bringing us closer to the truth.

The pronouncements of an authority are worthless unless they are backed up by good justifications, but, it is important to apply the proper methodology for the kind of claim being made, and across the right timescale.

5) Empirical Rationalism (the Scientific Method)

Empirical rationalism means applying reason and logic to our perceptions and experiences to come to conclusions. It means employing a systematic approach to gaining knowledge and finding answers to questions; it means following the evidence where it leads, even if it proves your previous ideas wrong. The scientific method is an application of empirical rationalism where scientists openly share their results and ideas. Others critique those results and ideas and build on them. This becomes an iterative process that builds more and more knowledge, leading to improved conclusions and ideas. It requires freedom of speech to work.

The scientific method involves observation and experimentation. Sometimes, scientists start with an unanswered question. The question might be more implicit than explicit and be as simple as "what more can we learn about this species living in this habitat?" Other times, scientists create and then test a hypothesis using the knowledge they have gained from observation, experience, trial and error, authorities, and previous applications of the scientific method.

Whether it be a formal hypothesis or question, or just an implicit question focused on gaining more knowledge, scientists design experiments or tests to disprove their hypothesis or to provide data to help answer the question. They then share those results with other people who examine and critique the methodology and results, and perhaps try out the experiments or tests themselves to see if they can replicate the results. If the results stand up to scrutiny, and can be replicated by others, then our level of confidence in the validity of the hypothesis or the answer to the question is increased. The hypothesis, however, will always be subject to further testing and attempts to disprove it. If further experiments disprove it, then it is rejected (Newtonian physics stood for hundreds of years until Relativity came along). If it stands up to further experimentation, then our level of confidence in it increases even more.

My description of the scientific method is simplified. There are as many ways of doing science as there are scientists. No matter the exact approach, the distinguishing characteristics of science are 1) subjecting one's results to others' review and criticism; 2) an analytic and systematic approach to solving problems and answering questions; 3) rejecting conclusions that are not supported by evidence; and 4) making a sincere, good faith effort to be unbiased and to base one's views and opinions on the evidence, as opposed to trying to force evidence to fit one's preconceived notions.

More than just being simplified, my description of the scientific method is also idealized. In real life, things do not happen so cleanly or clearly. Results are often ambiguous or misinterpreted. Even worse, just like everyone else, scientists can be dogmatic and set in their ways, refusing to change their opinions in the face of new evidence. For example, geologists regarded theories about plate tectonics and continental drift as ridiculous fringe ideas for decades before the ideas were accepted.

There are even problems with the process of what gets presented as science in the first place. A new theory usually will not be disseminated and get widespread acceptance unless it is published in a peer-reviewed journal. Scientists rightfully expect new claims to stand up to criticism and review. Publishing in peer reviewed journals helps provide a system that ensures experts in the field vet new scientific claims, but the people who decide what gets published in a scientific journal also have the power to suppress papers presenting theories with which they disagree, such as when a new concept contradicts their own pet theories. More and more often, reviewers reject papers because they contradict the reviewers' political and ideological beliefs. Some so-called "academic" disciplines have become so infected with such practices that they are not worthy of any consideration or respect.[11]

Relying on the scientific method also means accepting that we are capable of correctly perceiving and understanding reality and causality, which (as I discussed above) is not necessarily something we can be sure of.

Most scientists are aware of the problems I have described above. Many of them really do care about maintaining the integrity of the scientific process, and they work to overcome or minimize its potential flaws and problems. Mistakes usually get corrected, eventually. If we adopt a "by their fruits ye shall know them" standard, the scientific method has proven itself over and over. No other approach to discovering factual truth has yielded better results. Do you use smartphones, the Internet, or modern medicine? Then you have already experienced some obvious fruits of the achievements of science. If you had a serious illness and your options were to get treatment from a modern doctor (who was trained based on our modern scientific understandings of biology, anatomy, and physiology) or a tribal witch doctor from a hunter-gatherer tribe (whose "expertise" is based solely on observation, experience, trial and error, and authorities), who would you choose?

6) Feelings

Feelings are also important parts of knowing truth and in the decision-making process. When certain areas of the brain associated with emotions are damaged, a person's decision-making abilities are often significantly impaired.[12] In spite of the benefits of

---

11 These fields are increasingly called "grievance disciplines."

12 Antoine Bechara, "The role of emotion in decision-making: Evidence from neurological patients with orbitofrontal damage", *Brain and Cog-*

empirical rationalism, our brains are not, and likely can never become, passionless rationality machines (much to the chagrin of many economists, New Atheists, and rationality enthusiasts). Letting emotions influence your decisions means you are a normal human being. Rather than being an impediment to rationality, emotions are often a great help. Your feelings can help you subconsciously integrate what you learn using the previous five methods and come to the right conclusion.

In his 1971 essay "The Eureka Phenomenon", Isaac Asimov explains that many discoveries are made when someone has a sudden flash of inspiration about the solution to a problem the person had been mulling over.[13] Such "eureka" moments do not come from a rational, conscious process, but probably from subconscious processing by the brain. Even after we have stopped consciously thinking about a problem, our brain seems to continue to work on it subconsciously. Einstein and many other scientists have described experiencing sudden flashes of insight when making some of their most important discoveries.[14] Indeed, the very term "eureka" originates from a (possibly apocryphal) story about the great ancient Greek mathematician Archimedes, who had a sudden flash of insight while visiting the public baths; when the insight came to him, he reportedly leaped out of the bath, shouted "eureka!" (Greek for "I've got it") and ran home right away because he was so eager to test his discovery.[15]

There is much we do not understand about how the brain works and how we form opinions and make decisions. We would like to think we understand why we do what we do—that we are

---

nition, Vol. 55, January 2004, pp. 30-40; see also Antonio Damasio, *Descartes' Error: Emotion, Reason, and the Human Brain*, 2004.

13 Isaac Asimov, "The Eureka Phenomenon", *The Left Hand of the Electron*, 1972.

14 For example, see Albert Einstein, "How I created the theory of relativity", *Physics Today*, August 1982, pp. 45-47.

15 Isaac Asimov (see footnote 13).

good at introspection and self-understanding. Research indicates, however, that we do not understand our own decision-making processes as well as we think we do.

More often than we realize, we rely on emotion to shape our beliefs. Rather than using our powers of rationality to come to a conclusion based on the available information, we usually work the other way round: we use our powers of reason to justify our already-held, emotion-based beliefs. We decide what to believe based on what "feels" right, rather than a conscious application of any of the five ways for discovering truth we have already discussed above. We start with a conclusion and then reason backwards, after the fact, to come up with a justification for that conclusion, even though we do not fully consciously understand the real reasons why our brains arrived at that decision or belief.[16]

Cognitive shortcuts such as our feelings and subconscious make us into the amazing thinking beings that we are. At the same time, though, they create mental blind spots and biases that are impossible to see ourselves. Because we lack conscious awareness of this, it is easy to fool ourselves into making bad choices. The scientific method has proven itself to be so powerful because peer review requires that other people critique, evaluate, and test a scientist's work. On a more personal level, it would thus seem that peer reviewing ourselves—a continuous, iterative process of exposing our decisions and conclusions to others' critiques—would help us find more personal truth and guidance for how to live.

But how can we do this over the span of a human life about every idea and decision? Turning to friends for advice is a good idea, but friends can only take us so far, since they are usually about the same age as us and share the same general life experience and thus many of the same blind spots and biases. Parents, grandparents, and wise older mentors can offer advice based on a lot more life experience, but each of them has only lived one life.

16 Jonathan Haidt, *The Happiness Hypothesis: Finding Modern Truth in Ancient Wisdom*, 2006.

SOME THOUGHTS ON TRUTH

There is only so much wisdom in any one person. And turning to family and friends for advice is not really peer review, not in the same way that science uses it. It is not a step up from older methods of finding truth because it *is* one of the oldest ways of finding truth. Humans undoubtedly have been turning to family and friends for advice as long as there have been humans. Peer review implies a systematic, rational, repeatable, and replicable process.

Can science and technology offer a solution? Maybe if we had big datasets with details about huge numbers of people's decisions and lives; and maybe if there was some computer monitoring everything about you; then maybe there could be a way to compute meaningful information that would be generalizable from other people's lives to provide good advice to you about your life. But how would we get huge number of people to consent to such intrusive monitoring to create such datasets? And who would want something so cold and intrusive controlling his or her life?

And even if such a thing were possible or desirable, for it to offer good advice for your life, you would have to tell it what kinds of outcome you want. As we have already discussed, our minds are not transparent to ourselves. So how can you even know what kind of life you really want to live? And how can you know what kind of life you *should* want to live? And how can you predict how that will all change as you grow older and (hopefully) wiser? And how can you avoid making decisions now that will lock your future self into a life you will end up detesting?

How do you peer review what is right and wrong? How do you peer review existence?

When it comes to knowing facts, empirical rationalism has proved itself, but when it comes to finding moral truth—to living the good life, as the ancient philosophers called it—empirical rationalism's track record is lacking. We must turn elsewhere.

7) Tradition and Religion

Because we understand ourselves so poorly, it is all too easy to fail to understand the real motivations for our desires and

60

decisions, let alone the likely long-term consequences of our decisions on ourselves, our families, and our community. By middle
age, almost everyone can look back on their life and remember
times when they were certain about some fact that later turned out
to be wrong, or when they were sure about a decision that later
proved to be a big mistake.

While every situation and person is unique in some ways,
there are also remarkable similarities too, more than most of us
would like to admit.[17] Tradition and religion are two tools humanity has developed to "peer review" ourselves across large swaths of
territory and people, and even across huge timescales. And they
have worked remarkably well. It appears that the emergence and
development of the great universal religions of the Axial Age were
the necessary precursors to the rest of modernity that followed.[18]

Religion and tradition provide generalized guidance that
would be difficult to figure out for yourself, especially at the beginning of life, without the experiential wisdom that comes with old
age and a life well-lived. They represent the collective body of wisdom passed down to us from multitudes of our forebears, developed slowly over time, based on the lessons they learned the hard
way.

Many elements of religion and tradition can seem arbitrary
and nonsensical in the moment, only for their purpose to become
clear much later, when we are older and wiser. We would all do
well to respect the traditions of our ancestors, as voices echoing
hard-earned wisdom out of the past to us.[19]

"What about slavery?", you might ask (or about any other
evil thing in the world that religion at some point encouraged, allowed, or even just failed to eliminate)—after all, every major religion at least tolerated slavery (and some still do). Well, I would first
point out that slavery's end in the West, and then in most of the

---

17 *See* Parable 12, The Sand in the Hourglass, p. 317.
18 *See, e.g.,* Peter Turchin (*see* footnote 7, page 3).
19 Hope 9:3; Parables 63.

rest of the world, came about mostly through the long, tireless efforts of fervent Protestant Christians acting *because* of their religious convictions. Nevertheless, it is true that slavery persisted as a practice for a long time before it was abolished, and that most religions at least tolerated its practice. We must, of course, acknowledge that tradition and religion are not perfect guides. We already discussed in the first chapter how religion has failed us in its cosmology.

Could we not use reason and the scientific method and all of our modern knowledge to create something better, then? Well, two of the major 20th Century attempts at this—communism and fascism—were terrifying, terrible, murderous disasters. And secular humanism is not some new system. It is really just secular Christianity. Moreover, it has failed until now to prove itself as a viable replacement for religion and tradition, likely because it not only removes just the false cosmology, but God too, and most of the rituals, and the community, and the sense of tradition and rootedness, and the awe and transcendence. What makes it so attractive, though, is that it also removes most of the parts that require any sacrifice or difficulty.

Moreover, secular humanism has not proved itself a stable replacement. It appears to be rejecting more and more of its Christian roots and evolving into an incoherent medley of secular nihilism and social justice grievance activism. This is a path leading in the direction of collapse, just like fascism and communism before. If so, let us hope it neither gains as strong a foothold as its communist and fascist intellectual forebears, nor as cataclysmic a collapse.

This question of using science and reason to replace religion goes to the is-ought problem articulated by David Hume: there is a difference between knowing what *is* and what *ought* to be, and it is not clear how we get from knowing what *is* to deducing what *ought* to be. As Hume said, "let us see, that the distinction of vice and virtue is not founded merely on the relations of objects, nor is perceived by reason".[20]

As we have discussed, science is the best method we have found for discovering what *is*, but it has failed miserably at helping us understand the *ought*. For guiding us toward right living—toward the good life—religion and tradition have a millennia-long proven track record. They are the best we have. As Professor Jordan Peterson has pointed out:

How is it that complex and admirable ancient civilizations could have developed and flourished, initially, if they were predicated upon nonsense? (If a culture survives, and grows, does that not indicate in some profound way that the ideas it is based upon are valid? If myths are mere superstitious proto-theories, why did they work? Why were they remembered? Our great rationalist ideologies, after all—fascist, say, or communist—demonstrated their essential uselessness within the space of mere generations, despite their intellectually compelling nature. Traditional societies, predicated on religious notions, have survived—essentially unchanged, in some cases, for tens of thousands of years. How can this longevity be understood?) Is it actually sensible to argue that persistently successful traditions are based on ideas that are simply wrong, regardless of their utility?

Is it not more likely that we just do not know how it could be that traditional notions are right, given their appearance of extreme irrationality?

Is it not likely that this indicates modern philosophical ignorance, rather than ancestral philosophical error? . . .

There appears to exist some "natural" or even—dare it be said—some "absolute" constraints on the manner in which human beings may act as individuals and in society. Some moral presuppositions and theories are wrong; hu-

---

20 David Hume, *A Treatise of Human Nature*, 1739, book III, part I, section I.

man nature is not infinitely malleable.

It has become more or less evident that pure, abstract rationality, for example, ungrounded in tradition—the rationality which defined Soviet-style communism from inception to dissolution—appears absolutely unable to determine and make explicit just what it is that should guide individual and social behavior. Some systems do not work, even though they make abstract sense (even more sense than alternative, currently operative, incomprehensible, haphazardly evolved systems). Some patterns of interpersonal interaction—which constitute the state, insofar as it exists as a model for social behavior—do not produce the ends they are supposed to produce, can not sustain themselves over time, or even produce contrary ends, devouring those who enact them and profess their value. Perhaps this is because planned, logical and intelligible systems fail to make allowance for the irrational, transcendent, incomprehensible and often ridiculous aspect of human character . . . .[21]

I will repeat: religion and tradition are not perfect guides. However, "incomprehensible, haphazardly evolved" though they are, they are the best we have got.

And religions and traditions *do* develop and update themselves in response to changing circumstances and current situations. Christianity today is radically different from the practice and beliefs of Jesus's followers in 40 AD. Sometimes, though, circumstances change enough that a religion or tradition cannot keep up, and it collapses. This can happen quickly. The paganism of the classical world was strong and widely practiced for centuries, likely millennia. Romans at the beginning of the fourth century AD were born into a pagan world they assumed would continue long after they were dead. But within their lifetimes, Christianity replaced it as the dominant religion of the Empire, and paganism swiftly col-

---

21 Jordan Peterson (*see* footnote 8), pp. 19, 22.

lapsed.[22]

I believe we are seeing the same thing happen with Christianity right now.

Even as paganism collapsed, though, there was still much of value in it. The Christians saw this too. Significant elements of pagan belief and practice were thus incorporated into the Christianity that replaced it. Pontiff, Easter, Yule—these words are all pagan in origin, as are many of the practices underlying them, along with many other elements of Christianity.

So too should we use as much as we can of Christianity in what replaces it. This is one of the main purposes of the Triple Path: not to create some new system from scratch, but to provide a replacement religion that keeps as much of our Western Christian practice and heritage as possible. This is what sets it apart from systems like fascism and communism that were "rationally" constructed from scratch, as well as from secular humanism and its offshoots, which increasingly reject as much as possible of Western tradition and Christianity.

Spiritual Feelings, Religion, and Morality

So now let us discuss where emotion intersects with religion. One of the areas where feelings affect our beliefs most profoundly are in matters of religion and morality. People frequently form religious convictions about a religion's truthfulness based on personal emotional experiences with the religion. Many Christian churches call this religious emotional experience feeling the spirit, or accepting Jesus in your heart. This feeling is often described as a feeling of warmth, peace, and light flowing into your mind and a burning in your heart that makes you want to do good.

The Book of Galatians in the New Testament says that "the fruit of the Spirit is love, joy, peace, patience, kindness, generosity, faithfulness, gentleness, and self-control".[23] In the Gospel of John, Jesus says that "[w]hen the Advocate [or Helper] comes,

---

22 *See* Edward J. Watts (*see* footnote 10).

23 Galatians 5:22-23 (NRSV).

whom I will send to you from the Father, the Spirit of truth who comes from the Father, he will testify on my behalf".[24] From these and other passages, many Christians have come to believe that spiritual feelings are an indicator of truth that "testifies" on behalf of God. But what kind of truth is it testifying about?

Psychologists who study this spiritual feeling have named it "elevation". They describe it as involving a desire to act morally and being characterized by a feeling of warmth in the chest.[25] (Elevation is a big part of spiritual feelings, but not the only part; other emotions such as awe and transcendence and tranquility are also important.) As we will see in the next section, elevation is a common human experience across cultures and religions. This makes it difficult to believe that feelings of elevation communicate knowledge about the material, factual truth of a religion's cosmological and historical claims.

The Purpose of Elevation

So what is the purpose of elevation?

It appears that one of its functions is to help encourage altruism and community in the appropriate circumstances. Laboratory studies have shown that participants who were induced to feel elevation were more likely to act altruistically afterward.[26]

There is much research that shows that almost every human behavioral and cognitive trait has a significant heritable component.[27] Assuming that it is heritable like most other traits, why would our ability to feel elevation have evolved? Why would natu-

---

24 John 15:26 (NRSV).

25 Jonathan Haidt, "Elevation and the positive psychology of morality", in Corey Keyes and Jonathan Haidt (eds.), *Flourishing: Positive psychology and the life well-lived*, 2003.

26 Simone Schnall, *et. al.*, "Elevation leads to altruistic behavior", *Psychological Science*, Vol. 21, No. 3, March 2010, pp. 315-320.

27 Thomas J. Bouchard, Jr., "Genetic Influence on Human Psychological Traits: A Survey", *Current Directions in Psychological Science*, Vol. 13, No. 4, August 2004, pp. 148-51.

ral selection have favored it?

We are social and communal. We band together with others to cooperate, share resources, and provide mutual protection. Altruism and sociality help communities survive and thrive. But too much altruism can also lead to their downfall, as freeriders and sociopaths take advantage of the community's foolish over-generosity. Perhaps elevation evolved as a way of encouraging us to engage in altruism and sociality at the right times, to guide us toward appropriate moral action within our human environment.

On a less rational note, I believe that there is an element of divine communication or influence involved in it that helps us better understand moral truths.

Whatever the explanation for how and why we developed the ability to feel elevation, it seems to be a valuable way to guide us to moral action. It does not, however, seem to work well as a guide to finding objective facts about the material world.

A Short Experiment—Comparing Different Religions

When I was a youth, I was taught that feeling elevation was a sign I had encountered truth and that feeling it within the context of our religion meant that God was telling me that all the truth claims of our religion were true. When I later encountered convincing evidence that contradicted things I had previously "felt" to be true, I began to question this. What did these spiritual feelings mean? I decided to investigate by comparing what people from other religions had to say about their spiritual experiences.

I searched the Internet for narratives about religious or spiritual experiences that used words describing elevation; I specifically sought writings from people of different faiths. It was not hard to quickly find examples from every religion I checked. Everywhere I looked, people described the same feelings leading them to faith in their religion. Whether it was Christianity, other monotheistic faiths, polytheistic religions, non-theistic religions, or even new age beliefs—adherents always gave a similar story about their emotional conversion to the religion.

If you do believe that spiritual feelings can only be found

within one, "true" religion, then try the exercise on the following pages. It contains a representative selection from the descriptions I found[28] and lets you test yourself to see whether you can recognize which description comes from which religion.

The following fourteen quotes are from practicing Buddhists, Catholics, Hindus, Mormons, New Agers, Protestants, and Unitarians in which they describe how they felt during their conversion to the religion or during important, defining spiritual experiences. Try to guess which quote comes from which of the seven religions (some religions are used more than once). I have standardized the language, with changes indicated by brackets, so that differences in terminology between religions will not tip you off (for example, the Bible and all other religious texts become a [text] or [sacred text]). At the very end of this chapter, for each quote you can find citations and further explanatory notes about the context of each statement. Following each quote is the list of seven religions so you can circle the religion that you think the person in each quote is writing about. Answers are at the end of each page:

1. "As I read [the sacred text] . . . I felt a burning in my heart that I should come and investigate."

Buddhist Catholic Hindu Mormon New Age Protestant Unitarian

2. "I was praying . . . when I felt a burning shaft of [God's] love come through my head and into my heart."

Buddhist Catholic Hindu Mormon New Age Protestant Unitarian

Answers: 1. Catholic; 2. Catholic.

---

28 The omitted descriptions are all similar in tone and language to the ones included here. I omitted some for the sake of space and others to avoid mentioning religious traditions with members having more delicate sensibilities about the mention of their faith.

3. "I . . . wanted to know [the truth]. After a few weeks, I stumbled onto [a sacred text] which . . . answered my questions in a way that I had not heard of before. I read everything . . .and I even tried the experiment of asking [God] . . . . After about 6 weeks, I felt a burning in my chest and a sensation that was unlike anything I had ever felt. It was pure happiness and peace."

Buddhist Catholic Hindu Mormon New Age Protestant Unitarian

4. "Every time I was with the [church members], I felt this warm feeling, a feeling of peace and for the first time in my life since my church-going days, I wanted to follow [God] . . . ."

Buddhist Catholic Hindu Mormon New Age Protestant Unitarian

5. "About 10 years ago, when Jenny and I decided to start a family, we began looking for a [church] for our kids. During my first service here at [the church],. . . . I was hooked. I recall the feeling of peace that I felt when I was attending . . . ."

Buddhist Catholic Hindu Mormon New Age Protestant Unitarian

6. "The sense I had of divine things would often of a sudden kindle up, as it were, a sweet burning in my heart; an ardor of soul, that I know not how to express."

Buddhist Catholic Hindu Mormon New Age Protestant Unitarian

7. "I felt a burning in my heart, and a great burden seemed to have left me."

Buddhist Catholic Hindu Mormon New Age Protestant Unitarian

Answers: 3. New Age; 4. Mormon; 5. Unitarian; 6. Protestant; 7. Protestant.

8. "[Even as a child], [w]ithout understanding much about the complex [doctrine] . . . he was attracted to [church]. There he often felt a strong feeling of peace flowing through his body."

Buddhist Catholic Hindu Mormon New Age Protestant Unitarian

9. "The power of [God] came into me then. I had this warm and overwhelming feeling of peace and security. It's hard to explain."

Buddhist Catholic Hindu Mormon New Age Protestant Unitarian

10. "[After praying,] [i]mmediately I was flooded with a deep feeling of peace, comfort, and hope. . . . It was real, it was utterly convincing, it was entirely unexpected."

Buddhist Catholic Hindu Mormon New Age Protestant Unitarian

11. "[The religious leader] looked into my eyes deeply for a moment, and I experienced a feeling of peace and love unlike anything I had ever experienced before."

Buddhist Catholic Hindu Mormon New Age Protestant Unitarian

12. "For the first time I not only felt accountable for my past [sins,] but I had to fight back tears. I knew that I had let down [God and] my family. . . . However, I also knew I was forgiven! . . . [It] gave me a feeling of peace that I have never felt . . . in my whole life. I felt like I had a huge weight lifted off of me and that I was finally home and free . . . . I felt like a new person."

Buddhist Catholic Hindu Mormon New Age Protestant Unitarian

Answers: 8. Hindu; 9. Catholic; 10. Protestant; 11. Hindu; 12. Catholic.

13. "A feeling of peace seemed to flow into me . . . . I felt very peaceful from inside and also felt [warmth]."

Buddhist Catholic Hindu Mormon New Age Protestant Unitarian

14. "Every time I am there [at church], a feeling of peace overcomes me."

Buddhist Catholic Hindu Mormon New Age Protestant Unitarian

Answers: 13. Hindu; 14. Buddhist.

The point of this exercise is not to question anyone's spiritual or religious beliefs, but to help us understand the role of spiritual feelings in finding truth. Since the cosmological and historical claims of the above religions are largely contradictory and mutually exclusive, if one of the religions were true in the material factual sense, many or most of the others would be false. Many or most of the above people's religious experiences, therefore, could not have been reliable indicators of factual truth about the material world.

But what about moral truth? Might spiritual feelings be leading us to truths about the world as a forum for action? It would be difficult to follow up with the individuals quoted above to find out how their experiences affected them in the short- or long-term, but from the way they wrote about them, they seem to highly value their spiritual experiences and consider them milestone events in their lives. I know I consider my important spiritual experiences as not only milestone events, but as life-changing events.

I mentioned above that elevation induces a desire to act altruistically, and we discussed in the last chapter the research that shows religious people are more likely to engage in a variety of pro-social behaviors.[29] I cannot help but believe there is a connection.

---

29 *See* text accompanying footnote 6 on page 31.

Conclusion

Recent history has led to radical changes in how we discover and pass on truth. The Enlightenment and Scientific Revolution have transformed how we understand the material world. The invention of the printing press, and the increased literacy it brought, has encouraged increased reliance on authority and has transformed how tradition and religion and knowledge spread to new people and get passed down to future generations.

Jesus said "you will know them by their fruits".[30] On the question of *is*, the scientific method and the rest of the great intellectual heritage of our modern Western tradition and culture have done more than anything in history to guide humanity to greater factual knowledge about the material world and also to previously unfathomable increases in standards of living.

Scientific discoveries about the material world are often proven wrong, but virtually always by someone else applying the scientific method. While the scientific method is not always right, it has proven far more accurate at discovering truth about the material world than anything else we have been able to come up with.[31] But rationalism and the scientific method have been inadequate tools at helping us find truth about the world as a forum for action. Science does well at helping us discover new facts, but does poorly at helping us find meaning.

When it comes to *ought*—figuring out what is right and wrong, how to live a good life, and how to live with meaning, then tradition and religion have shown themselves to be our best guides. Their proven track record to help us be healthier, happier,

---

30 Matthew 7:20 (NRSV).

31 A philosopher might point to the problem of induction to argue against science's utility in discovering truth. The counterargument, though, is that science has produced the best results so far. We should, of course, never stop looking for better ways of coming to the truth, but for coming to factual conclusions about the material world, the scientific method is the best thing we have.

and behave better suggest that we should adopt as much of their practices and moral teachings as possible, rejecting only the factual and historical claims that are clearly mistaken.

No one has all the answers. We are all fallible and imperfect. Each of us believes things that are wrong. We cannot change and improve our thoughts and ideas and actions to more closely match reality if we cannot recognize when we are wrong. May we all seek for more of the right kind of humility. But may we also have the right kind of courage also, to boldly seek truth and then act confidently based on the best knowledge and wisdom we have found.

Most of the time, we seek truth only haphazardly. How much more could each one of us find by being more thoughtful and wise in our quest for truth? How much more could humanity find if we all collectively were more wise and thoughtful?

Notes About Spiritual Descriptions Exercise:

The following references give the source and an explanatory note for each quote in the spiritual descriptions exercise on pages 68 to 71. If any source becomes unavailable on the Internet, copies of all quotes are in the possession of the author and available upon request:
1. Mark Miravalle, Interview dated January 12, 2008, htt p://wap.medjugorje.ws/en/articles/mark-miravalle/; talking about his experience reading about a famous apparition of the Virgin Mary in the former Yugoslavia.
2. Maria Christi Cavanaugh, "Meet our Novitiate", http:// web.archive.org/web/20120924142308/http://olivben.org/Novitiate /Our_Newest_Novitiate/; describing when she felt called to become a nun.
3. Reverend1111, "Re: How can you be sure of what happens after death if.... (beliefs, belief)", City-Data Forum, General Forums, Religion and Spirituality, September 23, 2010, http://ww w.city-data.com/forum/religion-philosophy/1057532-how-can-you-sure-what-happens-7.html; a forum post describes finding information on a website that stated it contained information from divine beings describing the afterlife.
4. Emily Mockus, "A Longing For The Spirit", http://www .mormonconverts.com/catholic/a-longing-for-the-spirit.htm; a former Catholic describing her conversion to Mormonism.
5. Dave Flynn, "My journey to Universal Unitarianism at First Parish Church", Mindful Parenting Blog, October 25, 2009, http://mindfulparenting.blogspot.com/2009/10/my-journey-to-univ ersal-unitarianism-at.html; describing his experiences with Unitarian Universalism.
6. Jonathan Edwards (colonial American preacher and theologian, 1703-1758), "Personal Narrative", ca. 1740, in William P. Trent and Benjamin W. Wells (eds.), *Colonial Prose and Poetry, Third Series*, 1903, https://archive.org/stream/colonial prosean01wellgoog/colonialprosean01wellgoog_djvu.txt.

7. Alonzo Johnson and Paul T. Jersild, *Ain't Gonna Lay My 'ligion Down: African American Religion in the South*, 1996, p. 29 (quoting Clifton Johnson, *et. al.*, God Struck Me Dead: Voices of Ex-Slaves, 1969, p. 126), http://books.google.com/books ?id=FKbHRp_z3uoC&pg=PA29. This is from an oral history of a black woman from the American South after the American Civil War.

8. Jean-Philippe Soule, "The Way of the Sadhu", January 2003, http://www.nativeplanet.org/health/yoga/swami/swami2.htm; a description of a Hindu guru's spiritual experiences as a boy.

9. Dan, "Conversion Story from Dan", December 7, 2009, http://conversionstories.org/2009/12/07/conversion-story-from-dan; describing a visit to Medjugorje, Bosnia and getting a blessing from a Catholic priest.

10. asteroid, "Re: Evangelical 'born again' experience: real, exaggeration, or hoax?", Catholic Answers Forum, http://forums.c atholic.com/showthread.php?t=22192; a description of a born again experience of a Protestant (who later converted to Catholicism) after saying the sinner's prayer.

11. Bob Bishop, "WHO IS 'HAN' (aka Bob Bishop)? And What Does He Know that Might be Worth Learning?", All Awaken, http://www.allawaken.net/html/who_am_i_.html; describing an encounter with Maharishi Mahesh Yogi.

12. Carmel Brizzi, "My Journey Back to the Catholic Church", http://www.ancient-future.net/cbstory.html; a lapsed Catholic describing her return to Catholicism and experiencing the sacrament of reconciliation.

13. Siddhaloka (Siddha Yoga Dham, Bangalore), "Newsletter 2010", http://www.siddha-loka.org/newsletter2010.html; descriptions from two people about encountering a Hindu guru.

14. Debasish, Review of Dhauli Peace Pagoda, http://www .localyte.com/attraction/11416-Dhauli-Peace-Pagoda—India-Orissa —Bhubaneswar; describing feelings experienced at the Buddhist stupa on Dhauligiri in India.

Some Thoughts on Morality

What is morality?

Most broadly, it is recognizing that there is a difference between right and wrong, and then doing what is right. More than that, though, it provides a framework for how to live and *be*. It shows how to live with meaning—how to live the good life, as the ancient philosophers called it.

It is also about resolving conflict. Within you, different parts of yourself may disagree about what is best in the moment; more broadly, the you in the moment may conflict with your potential self as it beckons to you out of the future.[1] Your personal interests, or those of your family, may conflict with other families' or the community's; your community's interests may conflict with those of other communities or with the nation; and the nation's may conflict with other nations and peoples. It is easy to inflate the fault of others and rationalize away your own mistakes, or those of your group. A lot of morality is about resolving these conflicts correctly, helping you, or your group, see where you are in error, so you can correct your mistakes and resolve your conflicts.

Morality is also part of our quest for truth. Moral questions are so inherently interesting to most people because of our yearning to find truth about the world as a forum for action. Our aspirations for what ought to be also motivate our quest for morality, with morality providing principles, guidelines, and rules to tell us how we should behave and how we should treat each other so that we can turn our aspirations into reality.

When it comes to rules, though, we each have a natural

---

1   *See* Hope 8:5.

tendency to make exceptions for ourselves and rationalize our bad behavior. The higher someone rises in a hierarchy, the more he can enforce exceptions for himself; the more he can bend rules and make new ones to excuse his immorality. One check on this problem, however imperfect, is always having someone higher up in the hierarchy to prevent abuses of those under him. At the very top always used to be God, from whom all morality flowed. The Bible and traditions of the church could provide absolute standards that even the king and the church leaders, at least in theory, could not controvert.

But now that religion is in retreat—now that so many of us doubt the material, factual truth of much of the Bible or Christianity, what are we left with? Even if you believe in God, to where do you turn to know His will?

In the early drafts of this book, in this chapter I argued that it was possible to use reason to create a universally applicable rational moral system, and then I tried to elucidate that system. I failed in my attempt. I ended up just using logic and reason to justify the basic moral precepts of Western culture and Christianity that we already have. In the few places where my reasoning went beyond those traditional precepts, I now have strong doubts about whether I was right.

Plenty of philosophers and ethicists have tried to do the same thing as me and have also failed. Many have advanced our understanding of ethics and morality, but none has created a self-evidently superior, universal system of morality based only on reason and logic. This all goes back to the is-ought problem we have already discussed. Every moral system must start from some basic axiomatic premises that define the system's objectives or the system's highest ideals.

But how do you rationally and scientifically justify the system's axiomatic premises?

Neuroscientist and New Atheist Sam Harris recently tried to do it by arguing that an ethical system should maximize the "well-being of conscious creatures" and that "science can tell us

78

what values lead to human flourishing".[2] But how do you define "conscious," "well-being," and "human flourishing"? How do you measure them? And across what time span? How do you account for differing, contradictory preferences within the same individual, or between different individuals? When there are disagreements—and there will be disagreements—who gets to be the final arbiter of what constitutes "well-being" and "human flourishing"? The very fact that there will be those inevitable disagreements casts strong doubt on whether we can ever bring morality into the same realm as material facts and science.[3]

In the context of morality, this is how Professor Jordan Peterson defined the is-ought problem:

The painstaking empirical process of identification, communication and comparison has proved to be a strikingly effective means for accurately specifying the nature of the relatively invariant features of the collectively apprehensible world. Unfortunately, this useful methodology cannot be applied to determination of value—to consideration of what should be, to specification of the direction that things should take (which means, to description of the future we should construct, as a consequence of our actions). Such acts of valuation necessarily constitute moral decisions. We can use information generated in consequence of the application of science to guide those decisions, but not to tell us if they are correct. We lack a process of verification, in the moral domain, that is as powerful or as universally acceptable as the experimental (empirical) method, in the realm of description. This absence does not allow us to sidestep the problem. No functioning society or individual can avoid rendering moral

---

2   Sam Harris, *The Moral Landscape: How Science Can Determine Human Values*, 2010.

3   This is the "open-question argument". *See* G.E. Moore, *Principia Ethica*, 1903, § 13.

judgment, regardless of what might be said or imagined about the necessity of such judgment. Action presupposes valuation, or its implicit or "unconscious" equivalent. To act is literally to manifest preference about one set of possibilities, contrasted to an infinite set of alternatives. If we will live, we must act. Acting, we value. Lacking omniscience, painfully, we must make decisions, in the absence of sufficient information. It is, traditionally speaking, our knowledge of good and evil, our moral sensibility, that allows us this ability. It is our mythological conventions, operating implicitly or explicitly, that guide our choices. But what are these conventions? How are we to understand the fact of their existence? How are we to understand them?

This "problem of morality"—is there anything moral, in any realistic general sense, and if so, how might it be comprehended?—is a question that has now attained paramount importance. We have the technological power to do anything we want (certainly, anything destructive; potentially, anything creative); commingled with that power, however, is an equally profound existential uncertainty, shallowness and confusion. Our constant cross-cultural interchanges and our capacity for critical reasoning has undermined our faith in the traditions of our forebears—perhaps for good reason. However, the individual cannot live without belief—without action and valuation—and science cannot provide that belief. We must nonetheless put our faith into something. Are the myths we have turned to since the rise of science more sophisticated, less dangerous, and more complete than those we rejected? The ideological structures that dominated social relations in the twentieth century appear no less absurd, on the face of it, than the older belief systems they supplanted; they lacked, in addition, any of the incomprehensible mystery that necessarily remains part of genuinely artistic and creative production. The fundamental propositions of fascism and communism were rational, logical, statable, comprehensible—and terribly wrong. No great ideological struggle presently tears at the soul of the world, but it is difficult to believe that we have outgrown our gullibility. The rise of the New Age movement in the West, for example—as compensation for the decline of traditional spirituality—provides sufficient evidence for our continued ability to swallow a camel, while straining at a gnat.

Could we do better? Is it possible to understand what might reasonably, even admirably, be believed, after understanding that we must believe? Our vast power makes self-control (and, perhaps, self-comprehension) a necessity—so we have the motivation, at least in principle. Furthermore, the time is auspicious. The third Christian millennium is dawning—at the end of an era when we have demonstrated, to the apparent satisfaction of everyone, that certain forms of social regulation just do not work—even when judged by their own criteria for success. We live in the aftermath of the great statist experiments of the twentieth century, after all. . . . [4]

Schools of Thought on Morality

Several schools of thought have developed different approaches about how to think about ethics and morality. Ostensibly, each explains what ethics is and provides a framework for how we can evaluate whether a given action is moral or not. Each's proponents might claim that their school is authoritative and prescriptive. Really, though, each is more descriptive than anything else, mostly only telling us what people already generally agree to be moral and immoral (or, in a few cases, perhaps what the school's proponents *wish* were moral and immoral), but then also offering that school's own justification for why.

Even though most adherents of the different schools agree

---

4   Jordan B. Peterson (*see* footnote 8, page 49), p. 21-22.

on most moral questions (such as murder, adultery, and stealing being wrong), their descriptions and justifications are useful ways for better understanding our general Western system of morals and some potential justifications for its principles and rules.

There are some differences between the schools, and they do occasionally come out on different sides of some questions. It is on those edge cases that we can best see the differences between the schools and argue their relative merits. We will shortly discuss one of those cases, the "lying to the murderer" scenario. Thinking about these edge cases can help us think more carefully about moral questions. Free tree to do so.

Overall, in spite of the intellectual merits of each school of thought, and in spite of the best efforts of their proponents, the justifications and explanations offered by the different schools cannot replace the effectiveness of the old order of traditional morality, which was justified because it came from God. The harsh reality is that if there is no higher, sacred standard of morality, then each individual feels somewhat free to determine his own standards. And if each person determines his own morality, he will all too easily make exceptions for himself when right conduct is hard or undesirable in the moment. Even within the framework of a given school of thought of ethics, if a dispassionate application of its tenets would yield an answer you do no like, it is not too hard to create reasonable-sounding rationalizations for whatever you want to do. The sexual revolution has shown us that.

If there is no easy way to derive a universal system of ethics, then to what do we look for our source of ethics and morals in our modern, post-Enlightenment world? Where can we find a source of morality and ethics beyond ourselves—something that we cannot rationalize away? And especially, how do we do this in the Triple Path—a religion that readily acknowledges "we see through a glass, darkly"[5] and do not always understand very well the will of God?

The old order functioned as well as it did for two reasons:

---

5   1 Corinthians 13:12 (KJV).

first, because its moral principles worked, and second, because people believed those principles came from God.

But even in those days, when everyone in the Christian West accepted as authoritative and divine the traditions of the church and the Bible, humans still were really the ones who made the traditions, and the church, and the Bible.

But how did they make it? Christianity is a fusion of first century apocalyptic messianic Judaism with significant elements of Greek and Roman culture and philosophy. The initial, recognizable beginnings of the system date back at least 30 centuries, when the ancient Hebrews, Greeks, and Romans each began to emerge as peoples. There were hundreds of thousands of people (and very likely millions) who had significant impact on how it all developed —authors and scribes and compilers who made the texts; religious leaders who established and enforced traditions, rules, and practices; and many laypeople who followed those traditions, rules, and practices and, in following them, molded and adopted them to their lives, passing their modifications to their children. Many of these people tried to do their best to represent God's will. Some did not. The whole system, though, grew up gradually, over a long stretch of time. What we have now was distilled out of thousands of years of experience and practice. No one person made it.

Now that so many people recognize that the system is man-made, can it still survive? Well, the moral principles have not changed—they still work when people follow them. The problem is the growing lack of belief that God is at the head of the system. This makes people less likely to follow it.

So then with what do we replace God at the head of our moral system? The Triple Path's solution is to put God back at the head, but without the grand unsupportable claims of the past. We can do this by seeing the slow development of our traditional moral system as a gradual manifestation of God's will to us.

Traditional morals were put to the test over many years by many individuals. The parts that brought people closer to the divine and to living the good life were more likely to win continued acceptance over the years. Similarly, the parts that did not lead people closer to the divine and to living the good life were more likely to fade away as they proved ineffectual. Just as the process of natural selection and evolution can be understood as the way God created modern humans, the process of the natural selection and evolution of tradition and religious practices can be understood as the way God revealed his will to us about morality and how to live.

On a spiritual note, I believe that God can speak to us through divine impressions, and maybe even visions to some, but considering the experiment in the last chapter that compared people's descriptions of their spiritual experiences, it appears those manifestations from God often do not come with the clarity and precision of mathematics, or even spoken language. They can thus be easy to ignore or misinterpret without paying careful, humble, attention. Even so, I believe those divine impressions—foggy and faint, but always pointing the same general direction—have been nudging us to move the right way as well.

Let us thus acknowledge that the system we have inherited is imperfect and not necessarily a perfect representation of God's will, but it is also the best we have got. And let us recognize that breaking a complicated, well-functioning system is a lot easier than fixing it—this means change must be careful and very, very slow.

When slight modifications to the traditions of the past are needed, we should rely on the collective wisdom of elders who have proven themselves over a lifetime of moral conduct to decide to make those changes. And these changes should be small and happen gradually and incrementally, after much time for deliberation and examination. As stated later in this book:

Truth lies open for all; it has not yet been monopolized. There is plenty of it left for us and our posterity to discover. The teachers of the past are not our masters, but our guides. We usually follow in their footsteps on the old road they have trod before. If we find a way along the path that appears shorter and smoother to travel, let us scout out miles far ahead to verify the soundness of the proposed change. And let us always beware that we do not shortsightedly fool ourselves into following what ends up being a dangerous or faulty path, when the safety of the old road was there all along.[6] The chapter on Church organization and Practice in this book outlines a general system of Church governance that follows these principles—respect for tradition, and modifications made only gradually and slowly by elders with a proven track record of moral conduct.

I acknowledge that, just like the other schools of thought on ethics, what I set forth above is only a descriptive justification for traditional morality. The difference, though, is that whereas post-Enlightenment culture (and most particularly post-modern culture) has weakened our moral system by removing God from its head without offering a compelling replacement to submit to, the Triple Path puts God back at the head, but in a way that is compatible with modern cosmology and science.

In spite of my criticism of Sam Harris above, there must be a role for science and reason in morality. We should use reason to help us understand and evaluate rules and competing interests. We should use the scientific method to assess the outcomes of different choices and life courses. We should never, however, be so arrogant to think that our own reasoning can be the primary source of our morality. In matters of morality, it is too easy to use reason to justify things we want in the moment, but which are ultimately bad for us. We should be on guard to not let reason mislead us and always remember to let all reasoning be silent when experience gainsays its conclusions.[7]

As we have already seen, and will see again below, research supports many aspects of traditional morality, showing that people who live according to the old, traditional standards live happier, more fulfilling lives.

To get a better picture of the current state of moral think-

6   Hope 9:11.
7   Wisdom 1:24.

ing, let us discuss briefly some of the various schools of thought on morality, and then let us discuss some foundational principles of Western morality.

In many ways, as far as practically applicable morality, humanity still has not advanced much beyond the Golden Rule, so let us start there.

The Golden Rule

The Golden Rule has been around for thousands of years, with forms of it being taught in Ancient Egypt,[8] Greece,[9] and China.[10] The negative form frames the rule in terms of what you should *not* do:

What you do not want done to yourself, do not do to others.[11]

Jesus taught the most famous version of the positive version, telling us what we *should* do:

Do to others as you would have them do to you.[12]

The negative form of the rule, though, is contained within the positive. Doing to others also includes not doing to others.

George Bernard Shaw criticized the Golden Rule because

---

8 Richard Jasnow, *A Late Period Hieratic Wisdom Text: P. Brooklyn 47.218.135*, 1992, p. 95. "That which you hate to be done to you, do not do it to another."

9 Isocrates (436-338 BC), 1:14 (Democritus), "Conduct yourself toward your parents as you would have your children conduct themselves toward you."; Isocrates, 2:24 (Nicocles), "Deal with weaker states as you would expect stronger states to deal with you."; Isocrates, 3:61 (Nicocles or the Ciprians), "Do not do to others that which angers you when they do it to you."

10 Confucius, Analects, 15:24; Confucius, Analects, 5:12, "What I do not wish men to do to me, I also wish not to do to men"; Confucius, Analects. 12:2, "[Virtue is] not to do to others as you would not wish done to yourself."

11 Confucius, Analects, 15:24.

12 Matthew 7:12 (NRSV).

it does not take into account that our preferences might be different from others'.[13] This is a valid criticism, but most people really following the Golden Rule will already take into account others' preferences because they will want others to take their preferences into account.[14] This is not always obvious just from hearing the Golden Rule, though, and philosopher Karl Popper offered an interesting reformulation of it to make this point clearer:

[Do] unto others, wherever possible, as *they* want to be done by.[15]

The Golden Rule is a major part of how we think about ethics and morality, and has been for more than 2,000 years. But Popper's inclusion of "wherever possible" hints at a flaw: what if you (or the other person) desire evil or immoral things? In a vacuum, the Golden Rule would appear to require immoral acts toward others, so long as the other person desired it. What if Alice *wants* Bill to kill her? And what if Bill wants to kill Alice too? Does this magically make it moral for Bill to kill Alice? Can the Golden Rule transform murder into a moral act?

Thus, Immanuel Kant criticized the Golden Rule because "on this principle the criminal might argue against the judge who punishes him".[16] In other words, the convicted criminal being sentenced could argue to the judge that the Golden Rule requires his release, since the judge himself would not want to be sentenced to prison. Even if the judge were a deeply moral person who would want to be sentenced for a crime he had committed, Shaw's and Popper's reformulation would appear to require respect for the

---

13 George Bernard Shaw, *Maxims for Revolutionists*, 1903.

14 Walter T. Stace, *The Concept of Morals*, 1937, p. 136. "'[D]oing as you would be done by' includes taking into account your neighbour's tastes as you would that he should take yours into account."

15 Karl Popper, *The Open Society and Its Enemies, Vol. II*, 5th ed., 1966, p. 501 (2011 printing).

16 Immanuel Kant, *Fundamental Principles of the Metaphysic of Morals*, 1785, Second Section.

criminal's preferences and thus compel his release.

Another problem with the Golden Rule is that it does not mention the need for reciprocity in our altruism. We briefly discussed in the last chapter the problem of freeriders and sociopaths taking advantage of the altruism of others. In the face of repeated attempts at exploitation from freeriders, how can altruistic behavior persist in human populations? The answer is reciprocal altruism. We start out with a default of guarded benevolence—our initial inclination is generally to respond to someone kindly, but if that person mistreats us or takes advantage of us, we reciprocate. We cease our altruistic behaviors, and we respond to that person's mistreatment in kind with our own defensive negative and selfish behavior. If, however, the other person responds positively to us, we also respond in kind again, and we enter a cycle of increasing, and then eventually stable, altruism towards each other. In this way, we can punish freeriders, prevent them from taking advantage of our generosity, and ensure that only those people who are also willing to act with altruism will get the benefit of our own continued altruism.

In simulations and games designed to test human interactions, people who engage in reciprocal altruism do better than those who play entirely selfishly or those who play entirely selflessly. Reciprocal altruism is usually the best strategy in most human interactions. Yet, the Golden Rule fails to explicitly take into account the need for reciprocal altruism.

The requirements of the Golden Rule thus must be limited by other moral considerations. It cannot stand on its own as the only foundation of all morality. It is most definitely *one* of the foundations of morality, but not the only one. In day-to-day life, reasonable people implicitly understand that there are limits to the Golden Rule such that judges can still sentence criminals to prison; that murder is still wrong, even if the murderer and the victim consent to it; and that there are limits to our moral obligations to others.

Any reasonable person practicing the positive formulation of the Golden Rule takes into account all of these criticisms. The

Golden Rule is really a shorthand for something like this:
> Do to others as you would have them do to you, including doing to others, where possible and moral, what they would want done to them. Cease so doing to others who fail to reciprocate. Do not do to others that which is harmful to them, that which wrongfully interferes with their autonomy or accountability, that which would harm third parties or the community, or that which would cause you to act immorally.

The Categorical Imperative and Deontological Ethics

The problems with the Golden Rule bring us to our first modern school of ethics. Kant's solution to the Golden Rule's shortcomings was his Categorical Imperative: "Act only according to that maxim whereby you can at the same time will that it should become a universal law".[17]

In some ways, the Categorical Imperative improves on the Golden Rule, solving its problem with how to deal with the immoral idiosyncratic preferences of individuals. Kant's rule has its own problems, though, such as the "lying to the murderer" scenario French philosopher Benjamin Constant proposed: the Categorical Imperative would appear to demand that you always tell the truth, no matter what. This would make it immoral to lie to a murderer about the whereabouts of his intended victim, even if doing so would protect the victim.

Or what about sheltering an innocent family condemned to the gulag? When the secret police come knocking, the Categorical Imperative would seem to require that you tell the truth about the family's presence in your house.

Constant's solution to the "lying to the murderer" scenario is that we only owe a duty to tell the truth to someone who has a right to the truth. In the scenario, the murderer has no right to the truth about the whereabouts of his intended victim, and

---

17 Immanuel Kant, *Grounding for the Metaphysics of Morals*, 1785, 3rd edition.

thus you would not have any duty to disclose it to him.

Kant wrote an essay responding to Constant's criticism in which Kant maintained that if remaining silent was not possible for some reason, then the Categorical Imperative require telling the murderer where to find his victim.[18]

Similar to the Golden Rule, the Categorical Imperative has a problem in not accounting for the need for reciprocity. If everyone followed the Categorical Imperative, then maybe you could blindly follow it too, but when others do not and you still do, they can take advantage of you. An ethical system with real-world applicability needs to take into account that some people cheat when they can get away with it, or even ignore the rules altogether. It is foolish to pollyannishly proclaim the importance of having universal duties or rules that would expose those who respect them to exploitation or even ruin. Thus, reciprocal altruism must be a clear and explicit part of the foundation of human morality.

Kant's theory of ethics (and Constant's response) was deontological, which is an approach to ethics that considers the morality of an action based on duties and rules and on whether the act itself is right or wrong, regardless of the outcome. He opposed consequentialism.

Consequentialism

Consequentialist theories of ethics hold that the results of an act are what matter. They thus judge an act's morality based on its consequences, not on whether it conforms to the law, or some set of moral rules, or even based on the actor's intent. The consequentialist resolution to the "lying to the murder" scenario is that lying to the murderer is the most moral act to take, because it would achieve the result of protecting the victim.

The most well-known branch of consequentialism is utilitarianism. Eighteenth Century English philosopher Jeremy Bentham founded utilitarianism, with its "fundamental axiom" that "it

---

18 Immanuel Kant, *On a Supposed Right to Tell Lies From Benevolent Motives*, 1798.

is the greatest happiness of the greatest number that is the measure of right and wrong".[19] Bentham called the principle of maximizing happiness and pleasure "the principle of utility",[20] hence the name utilitarianism. Proponents of later versions of utilitarian theories have argued for maximizing other things as well, such as well-being, personal interests, and even beauty and love.

All things being equal, it would make sense that we want more well-being than less and that more happiness, beauty, and love are better than less of them. But like each moral theory, utilitarianism has its faults (many of these same criticisms can be leveled against other kinds of consequentialist theories).

One problem with pure utilitarianism is that it can be cold and impersonal, which is alienating to our innate, emotional moral sense. It just feels wrong to be so calculating in our moral judgments. A practical moral system has to take into account natural human emotion.

Another problem is that it is often hard to predict the consequences of one's acts. The fruits of some bad decisions do not become apparent for years, or even decades—long after it is too late to do anything about the bad choice. It is also difficult to sort out competing interests, such as when an act has bad consequences for some and good consequences for others; or when it brings huge positive consequences for a few people, but small negative consequences for a lot of others; or when it brings small, diffuse positive consequences for a lot of people, but huge negative consequences for a few. It would be easy to make compelling arguments for either side in many of these kinds of situations.

Bentham came up with equations to show how to compare and evaluate different kinds of pain and pleasure to determine their relative worth. Even with equations, though, how precise can you be when measuring and comparing subjective human

---

19 Jeremy Bentham, *A Fragment on Government*, 1776.
20 Jeremy Bentham, *An Introduction to the Principles of Morals and Legislation*, 1789.

experiences? And how practical is it to work out equations when trying to make a decision in the heat of the moment?

If you noticed that some of these critiques of utilitarianism sound similar to the criticisms above about Sam Harris's conception of ethics, that is because Harris's system is a kind of utilitarianism.

Because it has to account for so many competing interests, and because of the problems in accurately measuring utility, Utilitarianism makes it too easy to rationalize what would be good for you and costly for someone else. No one is omniscient, and no one is purely selfless; it is easy to convince yourself that what you want is also moral. This is especially true with Utilitarianism, which tends to eliminate any kind of transcendent authority that is over the system. Relying exclusively on utilitarianism means that the human rule-makers at the top can too easily justify moral rules they have created for their own benefit.

The communists who starved millions to death, sent millions more to their deaths at gulags and reeducation camps, and who committed genocide against their own people rationalized the bloody horror of their acts with utilitarian excuses.

Utilitarianism is not the only type of consequentialist ethics.

Ethical egoism teaches that each individual should maximize his own self-interest. Economists and libertarians love this one. The tremendous success of modern capitalism shows how well this principle can work to create a thriving, prosperous society. When taken to extremes, however, or when held up as the highest value, ethical egoism can go very wrong: just look at the general economic stagnation experienced by most people in the West since the 1970s, as the wealthy have captured for themselves almost all the extra income productivity gains; or at the causes (and effects) of the financial collapse of 2008; or at the moral malaise of modern times, as people are increasingly seen, and treated as, nothing more than economic production units.

Ethical altruism takes the opposite stance, saying that the morality of your acts depend on how they impact other people, regardless of the consequences to yourself. There are many examples of self-sacrifice that we all recognize as noble and commendable. The main problem, though, is that too strong a focus on selfless altruism makes it too easy for freeriders to take advantage. Furthermore, many people claiming (even to themselves) to be altruists are not necessarily acting out of pure motives. As philosopher Max Scheler said, altruism is not noble when "love for the small, the poor, the weak, and the oppressed is really disguised hatred, repressed envy, and impulse to detract. . . directed against the opposite phenomena: wealth, strength, power, largess".[21]

Deontology defines morality in terms of ensuring your actions conform to the rules and fulfill your duties, while consequentialism defines it in terms of the results of your acts. The last of the major three schools of ethics focuses on neither.

Virtue Ethics

In virtue ethics, having a virtuous character is seen as its own end, not as a means toward some other greater end. In virtue ethics, you cannot reduce virtue to some other more important *ought*, such as maximizing utility or fulfilling your duty. Beyond just having a virtuous character, though, virtue ethics also requires having what is usually translated from Ancient Greek as "practical wisdom", which means being able to figure out what is right in a given situation. These ancient ideas obviously have had a strong influence on the Triple Path.[22]

In contrast to virtue ethics, many modern theories explain why people conform to laws and norms in terms of maximizing their personal self-interest. For example, the "control theory of deviant behavior" holds that:

[p]eople conform when they believe they have more to lose by being detected in deviance than they stand to gain from

---

21 Max Scheler, *Ressentiment*, 1913.

22 "Virtue" in the context of virtue ethics does not mean quite the same thing as virtue in the context of the Triple Path. Virtue ethics is an important part of morality in the Triple Path, but not the only part.

the deviant act. Some people deviate while others conform because people differ in their stakes in conformity. That is, some people simply have far less to lose than do others. A major stake in conformity lies in our attachments to other people. Most of us conform in order to maintain the good opinion of our friends and family. But some people lack attachments. Their rates of deviance are much higher than are those of people with an abundance of attachments.[23]

These types of theory describe only a part of human nature. They fail to adequately account for why people who have a lot to lose sometimes go against the majority and stand up for what they believe in, even at tremendous cost to themselves. Most people in Nazi Germany or Stalinist Russia or Maoist China kept their heads down and went along with the rest of their society, but not all of them.

Most people want to do the right thing and have an inherent sense of morality. I suspect that many or most of the people who went along with the Nazi, Stalinist, or Maoist regimes privately disagreed with them, but lacked the moral courage to stand up and say so.

This is where virtue ethics has tremendous power. It helps explain why people act morally even when there is little personal upside, but still much personal risk: because they have an inherent sense of morality and enough moral courage to act on it. Beyond just its explanatory power, virtue ethics has transformatory power to help us develop the necessary moral courage to stand up for what is right. Virtue ethics helps us become the kind of people who *would* stand up to a Hitler, Stalin, or Mao in power over us.

Critics of virtue ethics question its potential universality, given cultural differences in what is considered virtuous. Furthermore, they charge that its focus on personal character attributes, as opposed to right action, means that it cannot provide clear rules to follow.

---

23 Rodney Stark, *The Rise of Christianity*, 1996, p. 17.

Furthermore, critics argue that while you cannot get from *is* to *ought*, the *ought* cannot ignore the *is*. There are limits on what is possible and what can be expected of people. The virtues and behaviors expected of people must take into account our human limitations and the limitations of existence.

These criticisms are worth considering. On the other hand, virtue ethics has survived since the times of Ancient Greece until now, and is still taken seriously as a way of approaching morality. It most definitely should play a big part in how we conceive of morality.

Now let us move from the oldest school of ethics to the newest: moral relativism.

Moral Relativism

In its most mild form, moral relativism is merely the recognition that people disagree about what is moral. At its most pernicious, it takes Hume's is-ought problem to an absurd extreme and holds that because people disagree about what is right and wrong, and because there is no way to use science and reason to resolve the question, this means that there *is* no right and wrong, and we should therefore tolerate others' behavior even if we personally think it to be immoral.

The general influence of post-modernism on society has also brought with it—to our collective shame and detriment—a strong undercurrent of moral relativism to much current public discourse and opinion. Moral relativism is worthless as a moral philosophy, as it does not even attempt to help us make judgments about what is moral and what is not. It is an anti-morality, tearing down what came before without even pretending to offer anything useful as a replacement. It represents the worst of post-Christian nihilism in the West.

Moral relativism is a dead end and not worth further discussion. So, let us move on to one of the most compelling modern schools of ethical thought: pragmatic ethics.

Pragmatic Ethics

Pragmatic ethics grew out of the general American philosophical tradition of pragmatism. It holds that societies can progress morally just as they do scientifically, through a process of inquiry and social innovation. It calls itself pragmatic because one of its core tenets is that we should keep what works and discard what does not. It recognizes that we can never fully understand the truth and must seek ever-closer approximations by testing ideas through human experience, evaluating them based on their practical uses and effects.

So far, this is not much different from the approach of the Triple Path. There are differences, though. The first is that most proponents of the pragmatic ethics approach are wholly materialist, not making much allowance for the divine or the spiritual. The next big difference is that its main focus is on society, whereas the Triple Path's focus is on first taking ethical responsibility as individuals and families.[24]

The biggest difference is that for ethical pragmatism, everything is subject to revision—nothing is sacred. It holds that all moral principles should always be subject to inquiry and reexamination with no regard to established tradition. Because of this orientation, pragmatic ethics too quickly rejects the wisdom of tradition in areas where quick experimentation and analysis can yield misleading results that only become clearly wrong much later. This is where pragmatic ethics goes most wrong. The wisdom of tradition is not always apparent at first glance. Change is more likely to get things wrong than right. It is highly likely that our descendants will consider to have been grave mistakes many of the social "innovations" of the last 60 years that were breathlessly praised at the time by their proponents as great progress.

Even the very willingness to so quickly reject the sacred weakens a moral system. All human societies sacralize things. Every culture has taboos. Our natural psychology appears to create a mental hierarchy in which the values and beliefs at the top are considered so sacred and important that they are inviolable, and

---

24 See Virtue 11:1-11 and Hope 1:2-.

the things at the bottom are so reprehensible that they are always worthy of contempt and should be shunned.

In his book, *The Happiness Hypothesis*, psychologist Jonathan Haidt discusses research that indicates that one of the major groups into which our moral concepts cluster is "the ethic of divinity".[25] When people apply the ethic of divinity, "their goal is to protect from degradation the divinity that exists in each person, and they value living in a pure and holy way, free from moral pollutants such as lust, greed, and hatred".[26] "The core idea of the ethic of divinity is that each person has divinity inside, so the ideal society helps people live in a way consistent with that divinity."[27]

Even if we never end up tearing down any of our most sacred values, and even if we never accept that which we now reject, a moral system that encourages a ready openness to tearing down the previously sacred and uplifting what had been considered reprehensible is inherently weak. The very willingness to tear sacred parts of it down makes none of it feel sacred in the way that we psychologically need. And being willing to uplift that which was once considered evil makes nothing proscribed feel very bad anymore. With the moral system being thus weakened in our minds, it is easy to ignore important, valuable moral rules when they are hard to follow. Even worse, beyond just making it easier to ignore moral rules, a mindset open and willing to tear down what is sacred and to uplift what is evil creates a general predisposition to tear down sacred things and accept what was once thought evil, even when the sacred parts are true and valuable and divine and the proscribed things really are evil.

When someone's prior hierarchy of sacred values has been torn down in his mind, it is not a dispassionate, rational process to replace them. It is often psychologically shattering. It usually takes a long time to find something with which to replace it and then re-

---

25 Jonathan Haidt (*see* footnote 16, page 59), pp. 187-211.

26 *Same*, p. 188.

27 *Same*, p. 209.

build a new internal hierarchy. Tearing down the sacred hierarchy also usually removes the stigma (at least temporarily) of the taboos as well. While someone is seeking and rebuilding a replacement set of values, it thus becomes all too easy to justify dysfunctional and evil behavior, to the point where, to avoid cognitive dissonance, someone can come to permanently accept evil and start to think of it as unobjectionable, or even good. In this way someone who starts out applying pragmatic ethics can become a moral relativist.

Even worse, the most common available alternatives compatible with science and rational cosmology are, on the whole, terrible replacements. Like candy that over-satisfies our natural taste for sweetness without providing any of the nutrition of real fruit, the common secular replacements for religion only momentarily gratify the natural moral and religious longings of the soul by providing empty spiritual calories that leave it still hungering. The most insidious influence of pragmatic ethics and of moral relativism is that they have created a greater willingness to tear down the old order without offering a viable replacement.

This helps explain why it is such a big problem that religions are stuck with pre-modern cosmologies and historical claims that are clearly false. Once you recognize the parts of a religion that are incorrect, the next emotionally natural step is to reject all of it, since none of it feels as sacred as it used to. As Professor Jordan Peterson wrote:

Our inability to understand our religious traditions—and our consequent conscious denigration of their perspectives —dramatically and unfortunately decrease the utility of what they have to offer. We are conscious enough to destabilize our beliefs, and our traditional patterns of action, but not conscious enough to understand them. If the reasons for the existence of our traditions were rendered more explicit, however, perhaps we could develop greater intrapsychic and social integrity. The capacity to develop such understanding might help us use our capacity for reason to support, rather than destroy, the moral systems that discipline and protect us.[28]

Part of the Triple Path's purpose is to help solve this problem by making it harder to "denigrate" what religion has to offer. The Triple Path is compatible with current knowledge and better able to accommodate our growing understandings. It is thus more resilient and less likely to bring on a shattering moral experience.

But this aspect of pragmatic ethics does raise a valid point: what should we do when something held sacred *is* wrong? No moral system is absolutely perfect, and a resilient moral system has to make allowance for that. The problem with pragmatic ethics and moral relativism is they are too ready to change. I daresay that many of those sympathetic to their views *relish* such change. In contrast, the Triple Path's approach is that change should be infrequent, slow, and considered, and that we should entrust decisions about such change to elders who have proved themselves through a lifetime of upright living. With great respect for tradition, such elders can reconcile and apply the relevant aspects of the different schools of thought to make small changes when they are needed.

While the Triple Path is a new creation, it was created out of the hard-earned wisdom and longstanding, proven traditions handed down to us by our forbears. And one of the most important sources for the Triple Path is the wisdom of the philosophers of Ancient Greece and Rome, who taught an important concept that can help us reconcile the conflicts between the different schools of thought on ethics.

The Golden Mean and Tradition

One of the maxims inscribed outside the Ancient Greek temple at Delphi was "nothing to excess". Aristotle expanded on this with his concept of the Golden Mean:

> Moral virtue is a mean . . . between two vices, the one
> involving excess, the other deficiency . . . it is such because
> its character is to aim at what is intermediate in passions

---

28 Jordan B. Peterson (*see* footnote 8, page 49), p. 189.

and actions. . . . [29]

It is the nature of . . . things to be destroyed by defect and excess, as we see in the case of strength and of health. . . . ; both excessive and defective exercise destroys the strength, and similarly drink or food which is above or below a certain amount destroys the health, while that which is proportionate both produces and increases and preserves it. So too is it, then, in the case of temperance and courage and the other virtues. For the man who flies from and fears everything and does not stand his ground against anything becomes a coward, and the man who fears nothing at all but goes to meet every danger becomes rash; and similarly the man who indulges in every pleasure and abstains from none becomes self-indulgent, while the man who shuns every pleasure, as boors do, becomes in a way insensible; temperance and courage, then, are destroyed by excess and defect, and preserved by the mean. [30]

Thus, for Aristotle, most virtues fall in the middle between two vices, one caused by excess and the other by deficiency. [31]

As with virtues, so too with schools of ethics. The four schools of ethics we have discussed (I exclude moral relativism as not being a legitimate school of ethics) all have their strengths and weaknesses. Deontology, consequentialism, virtue ethics, and pragmatic ethics each has a different focus: on rules and duties, on consequences, on virtues, and on moral progress and change. If you take any of the four schools to its extreme, it yields perverse results, such as deontology teaching that you should help a murderer find his victim. Conversely, each school shines when you apply it at its Golden Mean between the excess and deficiency of its guiding

---

29 *Aristotle, Nicomachean Ethics*, Book 2, part 9.

30 *Same* at Book 2, part 2.

31 Aristotle admitted that this principle did not hold in all cases. For example, it did not hold for things universally recognized as bad, such as adultery, theft, and murder. *Same* at Book 2, part 6.

principles.

And not just for each school by itself. Holding up each school as something separate in competition with each of the others is the wrong approach. When a situation forces one school into deficiency or excess, then another one can step in to offer better guidance. When you take all four schools together, each at its Golden Mean, then you really have something.

I am not the first to have pointed out that, in practice, each of the four major schools incorporates elements of the other three. Most forms of deontology and consequentialism incorporate notions of virtue. Real-world application of deontology and virtue take into account the results of actions (Constant's solution of the "lying to murderer" problem was an appeal to duty, but it seems to me that he specifically created his solution to avoid a bad result). Virtue ethics and consequentialism acknowledge the role of moral rules and the importance of fulfilling duty. And pragmatic ethics incorporates the elements of each of the other three that have proven useful.

Each school complements the others. Together, the four of them can best be compared to the four legs of a table holding up modern Western morality. But that table (to continue the metaphor) rests on the solid, firm ground of tradition. The four moral schools of thought only work because they were built up on the tradition of the past, relying on the moral rules and practices slowly developed through hard experience and then proved true over generations of practice. The four moral schools have advanced morality because they examined what already worked and then offered explanations for why they worked, thus helping us understand better our moral system to be able to advance it a little. None of the four schools got the explanation exactly right, which is why they work better in concert, complementing each other's deficiencies. This is also why we will likely always need the guiding hand of tradition, since it has provided us more of what is true and right than any of the four schools by themselves have ever been able to.

Looking at moral systems that try to divorce themselves

from tradition shows us that. Some moral systems make a lot of logical sense, but do not actually work. I briefly mentioned communism, which purports to be set forth on rational, logical, and scientific principles. Communism preaches the *necessity* of revolution to overturn the old order. In practice, every time a regime tried to implement communism, it sought to break the "shackles" of the past to bring about a promised communist utopia. The utopia never came. Instead, the communists perpetrated some of the worst horrors of the 20th Century: the Holodomor, the gulags, the cultural revolution, and the killing fields of the Khmer Rouge, to name a few.

Nazism, the ideology responsible for the most of the rest of the terrible horrors of the 20th Century, also rejected the accumulated wisdom of the past, as manifested in Christianity. Nazism was antagonistic toward Christianity—had they been victorious in World War Two, the Nazis planned to eradicate Christianity in Germany.[32]

The moral rules provided by religion and tradition do not always make sense. Someone trying to create a rational system of morality and practice would probably not have created the traditional system we have inherited. But what we have inherited *actually works*. The "reason-based" alternatives cannot claim that.

Now that we have discussed the different schools of thought on morality, let us turn to some other foundational principles of morality.

_____

32 U.S. Office of Strategic Services, *The Nazi Master Plan, Annex 4: The Persecution of the Christian Churches, July 6, 1945,* published in Rutgers Journal of Law and Religion, Winter 2001 ("[T]he destruction of Christianity was explicitly recognized as a purpose of the National Socialist movement."); George Lachmann Mosse, *Nazi Culture: Intellectual, Cultural, and Social Life in the Third Reich,* 2003, p. 240 ("Had the Nazis won the war their ecclesiastical policies would have gone . . . to the utter destruction of both the Protestant and Catholic Church."). It is well-documented that Hitler was an atheist.

Autonomy, Accountability, and Free Will

Each person is a separate, autonomous individual. For each action a person chooses to take, there is natural consequence. Choosing something also means choosing its consequences. Because of this, most of us also assume that each of us should be held accountable for the consequences of our actions.

But what if our choices are not really freely made? Does free will exist, or are our actions determined by preexisting circumstances?

The distinction implicit in these questions, between determinism and free will, is a false dichotomy. Debates about free will are mostly just debates about semantics and definitions. Determinists, who do not believe in free will, argue that our actions are entirely governed by the conditions that pre-existed our actions. They thus argue there is no free will, because if you had perfect information about a person's physical state and all the preceding events of his life, you could perfectly predict his future actions. The problem is that no one has been able to experimentally prove if this is possible, and perhaps uncertainty at the quantum level means that it will never be possible. Even the most devoted determinist would have to admit that no one has ever conclusively proved you can predict a person's actions and choices based on the antecedents.

The idea of determinism is often set against a definition of free will that holds that we are free to make choices independent of constraints (with different free will defenders offering different explanations or definitions of those constraints). Even the most ardent free will advocate would have to admit, however, that the physical desires and sensations of our body exercise a powerful influence on our choices and that physical laws and principles govern the function of our brains and bodies. Even if it were true that we could choose to act independently of the physical realities of our bodies, there would still be other constraints on our decisions, such as social and psychological constraints. Thus, no one who talks about free will can really claim that we are free of all constraints on our actions except for our own will.

The debates about free will versus determinism are fruit-less—neither position is strong, and the arguments end up being more of a pointless debate about definitions of words than something that will yield useful ideas about morality and how we should act and be. The purported dichotomy between determinism and free will is false. There is validity to both concepts, and only considering both of them together can we really understand human nature and behavior. The idea that free will and determinism can both be right is called compatibilism.

Holding each of us accountable for our choices does not require that there be free will in some metaphysical sense. Outside constraints and pre-existing conditions *do* influence our decisions. It is equally true, though, that individuals are capable of independent action and of learning from their choices—we change our future behavior in response to the results of our past actions. As autonomous individuals, we accumulate experience and knowledge and adjust our behavior in response to our environment and to incentives.

Furthermore, in spite of the constraints on us, there is pragmatic evidence that we possess some sort of free will: the history of human experience clearly shows that we flourish when freedom is maximized.[33] We thrive when others treat us as if we have free will. Even just reducing a person's belief in free will makes that person less helpful and more aggressive.[34]

Being accountable for our actions, though, is as important as our freedom to act. Because our actions affect everyone around us, we must be held accountable not only for the natural personal consequences of our actions, but also for the effect our actions have on others. Laws and moral rules do this.

---

33 *See, e.g.*, Fraser Institute, *Economic Freedom of the World: 2004 Annual Report*, pp. 22-25.

34 Roy F. Baumeister, *et. al.*, "Prosocial benefits of feeling free: disbelief in free will increases aggression and reduces helpfulness", *Personality and Social Psychology Bulletin*, Vol. 35, No. 2, February 2009.

Whether or not we are free in some metaphysical sense, the physical reality is that both individuals and societies progress and flourish when individuals are free to determine their actions and then held accountable for the results.

We think of our "self" as one continuous being, existing from birth until death. It can sometimes be helpful, however, to consider the "you" of the present moment as a finite entity, one which will soon no longer exist, and of the different "yous" at future times as separate independent selves. The condition of each of your future selves, though, is largely determined by your actions in the present. Taking a moment from time to time to look at your future selves as separate, independent beings for whom you have complete responsibility helps you remember your obligation to work in the present to ensure the welfare and personal development of your future selves.

We often make mistakes, though, in predicting what will happen in the future. Over time, almost every mutual fund underperforms when compared with the market average. Pundits and so-called experts generally avoid making specific predictions that can be easily measured and evaluated, and when they do, they are usually wrong (of course, they love to trumpet the rare occasions when they are right, but conveniently fail to mention the times they were wrong). On a more personal note, we are bad at predicting how we will feel in the future, and how potential life events will affect our future levels of happiness.[35] Traditional moral precepts, proven through hard experience, are the best tool we have for figuring out how best to exercise our free will.

Pathological Altruism

The research of psychologist Jonathan Haidt and his colleagues has discovered six foundations of human morality: care/harm, fairness/cheating, loyalty/betrayal, sanctity/degradation, authority/subversion, and liberty/oppression.[36] Many of these foun-

---

35 *See*, Daniel Gilbert, *Stumbling on Happiness*, 2006.

36 Jonathan Haidt (*see* footnote 16, page 59), pp. 9-11.

dations have been hollowed out by post-modernism and moral relativism to the point that only love, altruism, and freedom of action
(but with no consequences for one's bad choices) have come to be
enshrined as almost the only virtues, to perverse results. These
modern watered-down principles of morality focus on just one
and a half of the moral dimensions. There are many other virtues,
however, covering the full scope of the moral dimensions: honesty,
loyalty, courage, honor, chastity, faithfulness, patience, industriousness, perseverance, discipline, and fatherliness/motherliness, just
to name a few. All of them are important and have their place. A
whole, virtuous person must integrate every virtue.

A singular focus only on altruism and universal love can
quickly become pathological. Virtue does not require unlimited selflessness. None of us is obligated to sacrifice everything to help a
stranger. You, like every other person, have a right and an obligation to work for the welfare of yourself and your family and to protect yourself and your family from harm. These obligations take
precedence over your obligation to help strangers. This is so obvious I almost hesitate to write it, but given modern discourse, it
needs to be explicitly articulated.

A useful way to conceptualize our moral obligations to
others is to think of our relationships with others as forming concentric circles of obligation. Imagine a chart showing a person at
the center of a set of concentric circles. The circles map out the
person's relationships. The people with whom the person has the
strongest and most important relationships fall inside the closest
circles—such as children, spouse, and other similarly close family
and friends. Moving out from the innermost circles, the next expanded circles would contain relationships of decreasing strength
and importance. We have greater moral obligations to those in the
innermost circles, with waning obligations to those farther out. Our
greatest obligations are to our children, spouse, and other close
family and friends, then to other friends, then to acquaintances,
then to other members of our communities, then to nation, and

then to others more broadly.[37]

Wise altruism requires that you carefully consider the welfare of yourself and those closest to you. It is good to be softhearted, but only if you are hardheaded too. There is no virtue in showing altruism for strangers at the expense of your family, friends, community, and nation. Most people implicitly recognize this. It appears we tend to judge those who show preference in helping a stranger over kin, "as less morally good and trustworthy than those who did the opposite." Similarly, someone who neglects a stranger is usually considered "less morally bad and untrustworthy" than someone who neglects kin.[38]

You have decreasing obligations to those who are not as close to you. Wise altruism means not putting others' needs above those to whom you owe your greatest obligations. It means acting with prudence to ensure that your and your family's own welfare is not disproportionately or wrongly, unnecessarily compromised.

Especially since each person's resources are limited, it is often unwise to show a great deal of altruism in the following circumstances: to those who are in need of help because of their own poor choices and are unlikely to change; when altruism will create a cycle of dependence such that the recipient of help will likely never become self-sufficient; and to those who will never reciprocate.

There should be a balance, of course. Your obligations to

---

37 Virtue 16:3; Alistair Sutcliffe, Robin Dunbar, et. al., "Relationships and the social brain: Integrating psychological and evolutionary perspectives", *British Journal of Psychology*, Vol. 103, 2012, pp. 149-168.

38 Ryan M. McManus, et. al., "What We Owe to Family: The Impact of Special Obligations on Moral Judgment", *Psychological Science*, January 28, 2020. Interestingly, study subjects also recognized when showing a preference for kin became immoral nepotism: "When occupying roles requiring impartiality, agents who helped a stranger instead of kin were judged as more morally good and trustworthy than agents who did the opposite."

those who are close to you are not an excuse to mistreat or completely ignore others in need. And it is never moral to harm other people to gain an advantage for yourself or for those who are close to you.

A great benefit of religion is that it helps us strike the right balance between self-preservation and altruism, between the extremes of narcissistic selfishness and pathological altruism. It gives us a community that facilitates the practice of selflessness and altruism, where we have easy access to others in need of our selflessness but who are less likely to take advantage of it—our coreligionists' willingness to participate and practice their religion provides a signal they take seriously their obligation also to practice altruism and not take advantage of our kindness.

Hypocrisy

Hypocrisy is claiming to have beliefs, qualities, or motivations that you do not really possess. It is making criticisms of others or having expectations of others that you do not apply to yourself. It is living in moral self-contradiction. Hypocrites are parasites who willingly reap the benefits of others' moral acts, but who are unwilling to reciprocate.

We all condemn hypocrisy, but no one is free from at least a little of its taint on his or her personal character.

When we practice hypocrisy, we get the external social benefits of gaining others' trust and of earning a respected place in the community, but without sacrificing anything to truly earn that trust and respect.

Such hidden immorality usually imposes greater costs on society than the short-term personal benefits the hypocrite gains for himself. Because of this, hypocrisy makes a perverse sort of short-term sense to selfish individuals unconcerned about the greater good, but the hypocrite does not come out ahead either: his hypocrisy is always bad for himself too, in the long-run. If he is discovered, it will destroy his reputation. And even if he is not, he will have cankered and polluted his soul.

Furthermore, there are many ways in which your wrongdoing can cause you to suffer its bad consequences, even if you manage to keep your misconduct concealed from others. Professor Jordan Peterson has said that, after thousands of hours of clinical practice as a psychologist, he has observed that no one ever really gets away with anything—the consequences for your immoral acts always come, somehow.

Every culture's norms call for strictly punishing hypocrisy when it is discovered. Indeed, dealing with the problem of hypocrisy is likely one of the reasons moral rules, and punishments for violations, developed. Professor Peter Turchin explained:

> For example, one way to suppress within-group variation in cooperativeness is "moralistic punishment." Cooperators are of course vulnerable to exploitation by selfish free riders. But what if they become angry and impose sanctions on those who refuse to contribute to the common good? This is where moralistic punishment comes in. If punishment is severe enough (and in the presence of lethal weapons it can grade all the way up to execution), even rational free riders calculate that contributing pays better, because the alternative is worse.

> Groups still need enough moralistic cooperators who will force non-cooperators to pull their weight. If there are not enough moralists, cooperation unravels (and the moralists themselves stop contributing, because they don't want to be taken advantage of). But in groups that have achieved cooperation, moralistic punishment enforces the social norm that everybody contributes equally (some voluntarily, others because the alternative is worse). In other words, cooperators are no longer at a disadvantage compared with free riders. Moralistic punishment is basically a "leveling mechanism" that makes everybody equal within the group and, thus, shuts down within-group competition.[39]

Such enforcement helps discourage hypocrisy, but no en-

---

39   Peter Turchin (see footnote 7, page 3), p. 111.

forcement system is perfect. External incentives are never enough
to force hypocrites to always follow the rules—there are just too
many opportunities to cheat. This is when virtue ethics shows its
strength. People who believe in doing good for its own sake are
less likely to change their actions when they think no one else is
watching.

Wisdom also leads you to try to stamp out hypocrisy within
yourself. The aggregate of all of our actions creates the human
world in which we live. If you really want to live in a good, moral,
just, fair, and prosperous society, then you have an obligation to
work to make it a reality by being good, moral, honest, just, fair,
and hardworking, even when no one is watching. If you avoid doing these things when you can get away with it, then you are demonstrating through your actions that you do not really want to live in a
good, moral, just, fair, and prosperous society.

Certain situations make hypocrisy more likely. For example, an experiment with college students showed that those occupying positions of power were prone to act with greater hypocrisy
by judging others more harshly for moral failings while judging
themselves leniently, even though they were less likely to actually
follow those same moral requirements. Conversely, those who felt
that their power was illegitimate were more honest than the average person, judging themselves more harshly than they judged others.[40] Other laboratory experiments have shown that people who
move into a position of power get better at deceiving others.[41]

This means that in your personal life, the more power you
get, the more you should be aware of the potential for you to act
with hypocrisy. On a broader scale, it also means we should set up
our societal hierarchies—in government, business, private institu-

---

40 Joris Lammers, et. al., "Power Increases Hypocrisy: Moralizing in
    Reasoning, Immorality in Behavior", *Psychological Science*, Vol. 21,
    No. 5, May 2010, pp. 737-744.
41 Dana R. Carney, et. al., "The Powerful Are Better Liars but the Pow-
    erless Are Better Lie-Detectors", Unpublished Manuscript, 2019.

tions, church, and everywhere else—in ways that force extreme transparency on those in power, to make it more difficult for them to get away with the hypocrisy to which their position may naturally predispose them. There should also be accountability. Everyone, no matter how powerful, should always be accountable to others who have real power to oversee and supervise them (and those people overseeing should also be accountable to others, in a circle of overlapping accountabilities that is wide enough to prevent cronyism).

Moreover, since people who feel that their power is illegitimate act with less hypocrisy, perhaps we should reevaluate the ways in which we select people to fill positions of power in the first place. The Ancient Athenians used a system of sortition to select many of their leaders. In this system, they had a lottery among those qualified to fill a position. The winner of the lottery took up the position.

There are almost always at least several qualified candidates who can capably fill any vacant leadership job. The "winner take all" nature of top positions means that there are often very small differences (if any) in the competency of different potential candidates. Starting from a candidate pool of similarly-qualified people, leaders often rise to the top through some combination of luck, uninhibited ambition, and cheating. These three things are hardly a sound basis for putting someone in charge. Our current systems for choosing people to fill positions of power tend to favor the selection of traits associated with sociopathy. By introducing some randomness into leadership selection, the person in charge hopefully will feel less deserving of the position (especially if the list he was chosen from was not too short) and more likely act with integrity. It will also make it harder for people with sociopathic tendencies to manipulate their way to the top. We should also strengthen the ways we make those in authority accountable and impose higher penalties for leaders who violate laws and moral rules, to provide incentives to counteract the potential for hypocrisy.[42]

And personally, we should focus less on criticizing hypocrisy in others and more on rooting it out within ourselves. Almost since the invention of writing, we have records of people thinking and debating about morality and ethics. Some people devote their entire career to it. Many of the rest of us think it interesting to ponder and discuss moral questions. No matter how long and how much we think and write about morality, the human condition is too complicated and nuanced for someone to be able to write down a set of moral rules that are always applicable at all times.

The incompleteness of any moral system may lead to the temptation to use that incompleteness to justify unethical behavior. When clear, established moral rules and norms do not directly address a particular situation, it would be easy to use that moral ambiguity to justify misconduct. We are good at rationalizing and justifying our bad behavior because we all have some natural tendencies toward hypocrisy.

But the inherent flaws and gaps of any moral system do not give license to act unethically. We must all be on guard, and we must encourage transparency in all facets of life to combat our natural hypocritical tendencies—we are less likely to act hypocritically when we know others are watching or if we know we will be held accountable.

Rules of Cohesion and Purity

One of the ways religions and communities create unity is through rules of cohesion, which we discussed earlier on pages 20 to 22. Closely related to rules of cohesion (and often overlapping with them) are rules of purity centered on helping us grow closer to the divine. Our desire for purity is related to the natural emotion of disgust, which is centered on the sanctity/degradation dimension of morality. We normally feel disgust in relation to sev-

---

42 For this reason, the Triple Path establishes a church structure that uses sortition to fill positions of authority, imposes limited terms on those positions, and requires oversight.

eral areas: "food, body products, animals, sex, death, body enve-lope violations, and hygiene",[43] and rules of purity usually focus on these areas. Examples of these types of rules range from the di-etary rules of many cultures and religions (such as pork for Jews and coffee for Mormons) to rules about hygiene (such as taking off shoes before entering the home in many Asian cultures) to rules about sexual morality and courtship (which are found in every cul-ture and religion).

Many rules of purity serve practical real-world purposes. As we have seen, rules about sexual purity encourage productive, prosocial behavior that makes people happier and feel more mean-ing, and that encourages the creation of more resilient, well-ad-justed, flourishing families. Or some purity rules have health ben-efits, such as prohibitions on tobacco. Some rules are focused only on the external (such as our prohibition on gluten, or the Jewish prohibition on pork). All of these rules, even the purely external ones, serve as rules of cohesion as well.

Beyond this cohesion function, following rules of purity serves another function. We seem to feel a natural emotional, psy-chological connection between physical purity and internal feel-ings of moral advancement and spiritual transcendence. Moral pu-rity rules help us separate aspects of the outside world that appear to be profane and dirty from an inner world of purity and divinity. Following these rules thus helps encourage feelings of the divine within us, which invigorates our desire to seek inward purity in our thoughts and intentions, which positively affects our outward actions towards others. These rules of purity are thus also rules of divinity that help us live more elevated, virtuous lives.

Family

There are two places where you should most focus efforts to live morally: on yourself, and then on your family. There are two reasons for this: 1) this is where your personal accountability is greatest and 2) this is where you will have the most impact. Each

---

43 Jonathan Haidt (*see* footnote 16, page 59), p. 188.

of us was given life by our parents. If we were fortunate to have good parents, we owe it to them to do just as well or better with our own children. If we experienced the misfortune of having bad parents, then we owe it to society and to ourselves to do a better job than our parents did to make things better for the next generation.

The most lasting contribution most of us can make to humanity's future, and the greatest long-term influence we can have. is through the children we leave behind. In all that we do apart from our family life, few of us will make lasting contributions of great magnitude to the future of humanity. After you die, more than likely only a few people will remember your contributions or life's story. After a few generations, almost no one will remember. Virtually none of us will be remembered in history books or encyclopedias. The vast majority of even the famous people of today will be barely remembered in 100 years, relegated to footnotes in books that nobody reads. Many will be completely forgotten in 1,000 years. If we live well and make an impact for good in our descendants' lives, however, there is a good chance we will be well-remembered for some time at least by them. And even when our descendants have forgotten us, part of us will very literally continue to live on in them through the DNA we have left behind in them, and hopefully also through the wisdom and traditions we taught to our children and grandchildren that got passed down through the generations.

Because our greatest impact on the future is through our children, we should put a proportionate amount of time and effort into them, but not in the way that most people would think. Things like dance lessons or piano practice, private school tuition and tutors, extra homework, or sports practices are not the most important places to direct our efforts. In the balance between nature and nurture, many of us vastly overestimate the power of nurture to shape children.

There are three main factors that determine how a child will turn out: heredity, the home environment, and non-home environment (which just means all other environmental factors not common to all the children in the family). A large and growing body of research examining a variety of life outcomes shows that the home environment is the least important factor.[44]

The home environment is also referred to as the shared environment, and includes all environmental factors that siblings reared in the same household share in common. Researchers can assess the relative influence of heredity and environment by examining the differences in how identical twins, fraternal twins, biological siblings, and adopted children turn out.

We know that biological siblings and fraternal twins share about fifty percent of their DNA, identical twins share essentially one hundred percent, and adopted siblings share no more DNA than would two complete strangers. Researchers can look at how these different kinds of siblings turn out on a variety of different measures, compared with how much DNA they share, to figure out how much of their life outcomes and personal characteristics can be attributed to heredity, how much can be attributed to their shared environment of being raised in the same household, and how much is attributable to other factors (such as random chance and differing environments outside the home). Over and over, the studies have conclusively shown that the least important variable is the home environment. Newer studies have examined this ques-

---

44 *See* Steven Pinker, *The Blank Slate: The Modern Denial of Human Nature*, 2011 (particularly chapter 19); Judith Rich Harris, *The Nurture Assumption*, 2009; *see also* Kenneth S. Kendler and Jessica H. Baker. "Genetic influences on measures of the environment: a systematic review", *Psychological Medicine*, Vol. 37 No. 5, May 2007, p. 617; Thomas J. Bouchard Jr., "Genetic and environmental influences on adult intelligence and special mental abilities", *Human Biology*, Vol. 70, No. 2, April 1998, pp. 257-79; Alexander Weiss, *et. al.*, "Happiness is a personal(ity) thing: the genetics of personality and well-being in a representative sample", *Psychological Science*, Vol. 19 No. 3, March 2008, pp. 205-10.

tion in a completely different way by looking directly at the genotypes of unrelated people, and they also confirm that important human traits are highly heritable.[45] In other words, parents' influence is the weakest determinant of how their children turn out. Genetics is by far the biggest determinant of how kids will turn out. Adopted siblings who are raised together in the same home, but who have different biological parents, are almost as different from each other when they grow up as complete strangers, while twins and biological siblings reared apart are almost as similar to each other in adulthood as twins and biological siblings who were reared together by their parents. As one study explained, "[o]n multiple measures of personality and temperament, occupational and leisure-time interests, and social attitudes, [identical] twins reared apart are about as similar as are [identical] twins reared together".[46]

Heredity is strongly related to a variety of outcomes: personality, intelligence, and mental illness; antisocial behavior (including criminality, delinquency, aggression, and diagnoses of antisocial personality and conduct disorders); psychopathology such as conduct, oppositional defiant, and attention-deficit/hyperactivity problems; depression and anxiety; risk aversion and altruism; lifetime income, educational attainment, and psychological aptitude; job stability, levels of independence/self-reliance, and levels of conscientiousness/reliability; body mass index levels, weight, obesity, and consumption levels of healthy and unhealthy foods; political and social attitudes (including about issues such as gay rights and immigration); and even moral traits, such as levels of honesty. The non-home environment also affects each of these to a lesser ex-

---

45 G. Davies et. al., "Genome-wide association studies establish that human intelligence is highly heritable and polygenic", *Molecular Psychiatry*, Vol. 16, No. 10, October 2011, pp. 996-1005.

46 Thomas J. Bouchard, Jr, et. al., "Sources of human psychological differences: the Minnesota Study of Twins Reared Apart", *Science*, Vol. 250, No. 4978, pp. 223-8.

tent, and the home environment has the least influence.

Judith Harris, a research psychologist who specialized in the study of these nature/nurture issues summarized what the research shows:

> two people reared in the same home by the same parents were not noticeably more alike [in personality] than two people picked at random from the population, once you deducted the similarities due to shared genes . . . . Siblings are alike in personality only to the extent that they share genes; if they do not share genes (if they are adoptive siblings or stepsiblings) they aren't alike at all. Growing up together—going on the same trips to the museum or the ballpark, coming home to the same city apartment or house in the suburbs, living for 18 years with the same parent or parents—does not make them more alike. . . . In stark contrast to the here-today-gone-tomorrow results so common in psychological research, [these] behavioral genetic results have been resoundingly consistent. Despite differences in the ways personality is measured (standard personality tests, judgments by parents or teachers, direct observations of behavior, etc.), and differences in the kinds of subject pairs who participate (adoptive siblings, biological siblings or half-siblings, identical and fraternal twins, reared together or apart), the conclusions are almost invariably the same. Siblings are alike only to the extent that they share genes. Genes make biological siblings more alike in personality; growing up together does not. . . . Regardless of what is measured and how it is measured, the results are almost invariably the same: genetic factors account for 40 to 60 percent of the variance; shared home environment accounts for little or none."[47]

---

47 Judith Rich Harris, "Why Can't Birth Order Account for the Differences Between Siblings?", 2001, http://judithrichharris.info/tna/birth-order/sibdiff.htm.

What this means is that when you look at outside influences, genetics and biology, and how you parent your child, the least important force to shape who your child will become is your parenting.

This does not mean that parenting is unimportant. The studies on heritability and environment look at normal families in the developed world. This means that children in these studies had a certain minimum level of care—their basic physical needs were met (they had food, clothing, shelter, etc.) and they did not have abusive parents.

Parenting is thus very important, but not in the way that most people think. Good parenting is obviously better than bad parenting. Mostly, though, this is because bad parenting can have such disastrous effects. Abuse can have significant lifelong negative impacts on children. Your parenting can thus have major beneficial effects on your children, but those major effects come from not being a bad parent. You might also be able to have an effect on some aspects of your children's non-home environment and their friends based on where you choose to live and the school you send your child, but the effect is likely minor—if parents could exert much influence in this way, it would most likely show up in the research as being part of the effect of the home environment, since circumstances of children that can be influenced by parents generally show up as being an effect of the home environment.

While the effect of the home environment is small, it is not nonexistent. Good parenting can have effects at the margins. If your child is on the edge of taking one path or another, the home environment's small effect could be enough to put your child on the right path. Parents thus need to love their children and show them affection, take care of them, teach them spiritual and moral truths, teach them basic manners and social norms, and give them access to an education.

Furthermore, parenting does have a significant effect on important, foundational issues we have already discussed—on issues of religion, culture, and tradition.

Children's political party[48] and religious denomination[49] are largely determined by environment and are likely to match their parents'. Parenting also has a significant effect on children's level of religiosity.[50] Parents can also have a significant effect on their children's use of tobacco, alcohol and drugs, on juvenile delinquency, and on when daughters start having sex.[51] Parents also have a significant effect on children's occupational interests, but genetic influences are greater.[52]

There is plenty to stress about when you are a parent, but it is important to remember that many of the things we think are important for a child's future success will not actually make much of a difference. On many big issues (income, IQ, level of happiness, personality traits) your parenting will not make much of a difference. You can make a difference, though, by working to pass on your values, religion, culture, and traditions.

You can also have an effect on many other smaller aspects of your children's lives that can add value and make for a richer life—for example, most adults who play a musical instrument learned because their parents made them learn as children. When approaching parenting decisions, such as deciding activities for your children, remember that much of what you do (so long as you are not abusive) will only affect the smaller aspects of your children's lives. You should make those decisions based on what will likely

---

48 Peter K. Hatemi and Rose McDermott, "The genetics of politics: discovery, challenges, and progress", *Trends in Genetics*, Vol. 28, No. 10, October 2012, pp. 525-533. Political orientation (conservative or liberal), however, has a strong heritable component and is less likely to be affected by parenting. *See also* Thomas J. Bouchard, Jr. (*see* footnote 27, page 66).

49 Thomas J. Bouchard, Jr. (*see* footnote 27, page 66).

50 *Same* (though genetic influences have a slightly larger effect).

51 Bryan Caplan, "The Breeders' Cup", *The Wall Street Journal*, June 19, 2010,

52 Thomas J. Bouchard, Jr. (*see* footnote 27, page 66).

add the most value to your child's future life, for the lowest cost (not just in money, but also in time and aggravation). When making such decisions, you could try asking yourself the following four questions to help decide what would be worthwhile:

1. Does my child enjoy it?
2. Do I enjoy it?
3. What are the potential long-run benefits?[53]
4. What are the potential long-run harms?

Parenting will not do much to change your child's intellectual achievements, salary, or personality as an adult. Most of the benefits of good parenting (both for children and parents) come from the personal relationships you build with your children, the kind of family you create, and the values, religion, culture, and traditions you pass down. Beyond this, there is little you can do to give your children some kind of great extra advantage later in life. (other than also giving them good genes).

The other thing you can create through your parenting is a greater sense of meaning in your life and that of your children. There is probably no better way for most of us to learn about self-sacrifice, love, and empathy than by becoming a parent. Most of us are born with a tendency toward thinking that the world revolves around ourself. There is no quicker way to start on the road toward abandoning this poisonous attitude and to start learning about sacrifice and selflessness than by becoming completely responsible for the life and well-being of a helpless baby, a baby who has no understanding of your needs or desires or schedule, who needs almost constant attention, and whose care and well-being require that you rearrange your own life to fit his or her needs. It can be exhausting, but there is almost nothing more rewarding.

The strongest evidence for the positive impact of becoming a parent is that almost all parents would still become parents if they had to choose all over again, and most of those who never

---

53 The first three questions are from Brian Caplan, *Selfish Reasons to Have More Kids*, 2011.

end up becoming parents regret it. When asked if they would still have children if they had to do it over again, ninety one-percent of parents they would. Another poll found that seventy-one percent of childless adults over age forty said that if they could do things over again, they would have had children.[54] A study of parents in several European countries found that parents generally agreed that watching children grow up is one of life's greatest joys. Eighty-seven percent of parents in the United States rate parenting as providing a great deal or a lot of fulfillment. Mothers with children living at home as well as those with grown children who have moved away both report higher life satisfaction than childless women. Parents feel greater meaning in their lives than non-parents, and they report feeling greater meaning when taking care of their children than when doing other daily tasks.[55] Parents experience more daily positive emotions than non-parents, and they experience more positive emotions when they are with their children than when they are not. Men living with their children have higher rates of happiness than childless men and than fathers living apart from their children.[56] A study from Poland showed that women's happiness levels go up following the birth of their first child, and that there are also happiness gains for second, third, and subsequent children. There were similar patterns for men, but the happiness levels did not increase as much.[57] A study of the brains of middle-aged women found a

---

54 Brian Caplan (see footnote 51).

55 Kostadin Kushlev, *Exploring Parental Well-being: Is Childcare Associated with Parental Well-Being and What Factors Can Enhance It, Masters Thesis*, Reed College, 2008, pp. 7-8, 10-12, 26.

56 S. Katherine Nelson and Kostadin Kushlev, "The Pains and Pleasures of Parenting: When, Why, and How Is Parenthood Associated With More or Less Well-Being?", *Psychological Bulletin*, Vol. 140, No. 3, May 2014, pp. 846-895, pp. 876, 880.

57 Anna Baranowska and Anna Matysiak, "Does parenthood increase happiness? Evidence for Poland", in *Vienna Yearbook of Population Research, Vol. 9, Reproductive decision-making*, pp. 307-325, 2011.

positive relationship between the number of times a woman had given birth and having a "younger-looking" brain.[58]

Like anything, there are of course also downsides to having children. Having children is related to a slight decrease in marital satisfaction and to increases in personal and marital stress.[59] Parents feel significant worry about their children's welfare. They report feeling more negative feelings associated with anxiety than do non-parents and also more feelings of anger. Being a parent is also associated with sleep deprivation and greater fatigue. Having children in the home is associated with higher levels of financial stress. Parents of higher socioeconomic status report feeling less meaning when taking care of children than those of lower status, and having more education is associated with more negative views toward motherhood among women and with finding less value and fulfillment in parenthood among men and women. Working mothers with children have higher levels of worry than those without children.[60]

Contradicting the Polish study mentioned above, a survey in the United States showed that having a first child decreased happiness levels a small amount (each subsequent child also decreased happiness, but not by much).[61] These negative effects were most pronounced when children were young and weakened as children got older. Indeed, another study has shown that having older children is associated with greater feelings of closeness and connectedness.[62] Furthermore, the idea that having children, by itself, causes lower happiness is questionable, because the studies showing lower

---

58 Ann-Marie G. de Lange, *et. al.*, "Population-based neuroimaging reveals traces of childbirth in the maternal brain", *PNAS*, October 29, 2019.

59 Kostadin Kushlev (*see* footnote 55) at 2-3; S. Katherine Nelson and Kostadin Kushlev (*see* footnote 56) at 852 and 877.

60 S. Katherine Nelson and Kostadin Kushlev (*see* footnote 56) at 877-78 and 882-83.

61 Brian Caplan (*see* footnote 51).

62 S. Katherine Nelson and Kostadin Kushlev (*see* footnote 56) at 880.

happiness levels have also failed to control for the marital status of the parents. It appears that what causes unhappiness is not having children per se, but having children outside of wedlock. Unmarried people who become parents, especially fathers, end up with higher rates of depression. In fact, one study showed that married women who became mothers actually had lower rates of depression than their childless counterparts, whereas unmarried mothers had higher rates of depression than their childless counterparts.[63] Another study showed that never-married parents had more depression and lower happiness and self-esteem than married parents. Similarly, married parents had higher or similar levels of well-being as married non-parents, but single parents had lower well-being than single non-parents. Some studies have also shown that biological parents have lower levels of depression and unhappiness as compared to adoptive parents, step-parents, and non-parents.[64]

Beyond just the negative effects of singe-parenthood on the parents, it has big negatives effects on children too. Other than abuse, one of the worst things that parents can do to negatively influence their children is to divorce or get pregnant outside of marriage. Some of the negative outcomes observed in children of divorced or single parents are behavioral problems, emotional problems, substance abuse, aggression, criminality, higher rates of injury and illness in childhood, early mortality, school problems, lower levels of achievement, and lower levels of social adjustment. Whether a divorced parent stays single or remarries makes little difference to these outcomes, and the children of never-married women fare even worse than those of divorced parents (children of widowed parents do just fine).[65]

Just like most other behaviors and life events, propensity

---

63 Kei M. Nomaguchi and Melissa A. Milkie, "Costs and Rewards of Children: The Effects of Becoming a Parent on Adults' Lives", *Journal of Marriage and Family*, Vol. 65, No. 2, May 2003, pp. 356-374.

64 S. Katherine Nelson and Kostadin Kushlev (*see* footnote 56) at 881, 883.

for divorce appears to have a genetic component—the heritability of getting divorced is between twenty-nine and fifty-three percent.[66] This means that between twenty-nine and fifty-three percent of the variation in someone's likelihood of getting divorced can be attributed to heredity, and not to any environmental facts in that person's life. Some of the bad outcomes observed in children of divorced parents are likely also genetic: the personality traits that make someone more likely to get divorced (such as disagreeableness, for example) are heritable. Children of divorced couples would thus be likely to inherit those same negative traits, but some of the negative outcomes experienced by children of divorced parents, such as behavioral problems and substance abuse (and very possibly others), appear to be caused largely by the divorce itself, and not by genetic factors.[67] This means that one aspect of good parenting is being committed to waiting until marriage to have children and to lifelong monogamy thereafter.

The behaviors associated with traditional sexual morality are among the factors that increase the probability of a stable, enduring marriage. Among women who get married, those who delay their first sexual encounter until at least age 18 have much lower divorce rates after ten years of marriage: twenty-seven percent, versus forty-seven percent for those who have sex before age 18.

---

65 Thomas G. O'Connor, *et. al.*, "Are Associations Between Parental Divorce and Children's Adjustment Genetically Mediated? An Adoption Study", *Developmental Psychology*, Vol. 36, No. 4, July 2000, pp. 429-37; Charles Murray, *Coming Apart: The State of White America, 1960-2010*, 2012, Chapter 15.

66 Kenneth S. Kendler and Jessica H. Baker. "Genetic influences on measures of the environment: a systematic review", *Psychological Medicine*, Vol. 37, No. 5, 2007, p. 617.

67 Thomas G. O'Connor, *et. al.* (*see* footnote 65); Brian M. D'Onofrio, *et. al.*, "A children of twins study of parental divorce and offspring psychopathology", *Journal of Child Psychology and Psychiatry*, Vol. 48, No. 7, 2007, pp. 667-675.

Women who have sex before marriage, even if it is only with their future husband, have higher divorce rates than women who wait until marriage. Women who have multiple sexual partners before age 18 have higher divorce rates than women who do not have multiple partners before 18.[68] Similarly, people who live together before marriage (and especially if before getting engaged) are more likely to have lower quality relationships and are more likely to divorce. As with the research about the effect of divorce on children, it is possible that some other factor makes a woman both more likely to have sex as an adolescent and also to get divorced later in life. Researchers, however, have applied statistical techniques to attempt to infer causality, and the results indicate that having sex at an early age itself makes women more likely to get divorced.[69]

Beyond just the positive effect of marriages on children, strong lasting marriages are also good for married individuals and for society. Being married has a strong positive relationship with

68 Anthony Paik, "Adolescent Sexuality and the Risk of Marital Dissolution", *Journal of Marriage and Family*, Vol. 73, No. 2, April 2011, pp. 472-485.
69 Casey E. Copen, et. al., "First Marriages in the United States: Data From the 2006-2010 National Survey of Family Growth", *National Health Statistics Reports*, No. 49, March 22, 2012; Scott M. Stanley and Galena K. Rhoades, "The Timing of Cohabitation and Engagement: Impact on First and Second Marriages", *Journal of Marriage and Family*, Vol. 72, No. 4, August 2010, pp. 906-918; Galena K. Rhoades, et. al., "The pre-engagement cohabitation effect: a replication and extension of previous findings", *Journal of Family Psychology*, Vol. 23, No. 1, February 2009, pp. 107-11; David Popenoe and Barbara Dafoe Whitehead, "Should We Live Together? What Young Adults Need to Know about Cohabitation before Marriage, A Comprehensive Review of Recent Research", *The National Marriage Project: The Next Generation Series*, 1999.

happiness.[70] Young men are much more prone to violent and criminal behavior than women, and getting married and having children decreases these criminal tendencies.[71] Traditional norms of sexual morality encourage men to marry and have children, thus decreasing their criminality and encouraging them to become contributing members of society.

A wide range of parenting styles fits within the kind of nonabusive parenting that will avoid harm to children and let them develop as they otherwise would to their full potential. There is thus a lot of room to choose the parenting style that works best for you and your children. In our family, what we have found works best for us is attachment parenting, which focuses on building strong bonds between parent and child. If you are interested, a more complete defense and introduction to attachment parenting (and also a generally all-around good parenting advice book for new parents) is *The Baby Book: Everything You Need to Know About Your Baby from Birth to Age Two* by Dr. William Sears, Martha Sears, Dr. Robert Sears, and Dr. James Sears.

To bring this discussion back to where we started, if our parenting does not have much effect on the big outcomes for our children, like intelligence and income, I hope you now understand why I still claim that our parenting can leave a mark on the world for the better.

First, if you are a good, decent person who is contributing to society, your biological children will likely turn out that way too. So, you can contribute to future society by focusing on having more

---

70 Charles Murray (*see* footnote 65), Chapter 15.

71 John Wright, *Handbook of Crime Correlates*, 2009; Robert J. Sampson, *et. al.*, "Does Marriage Reduce Crime? A Counterfactual Approach To Within-Individual Causal Effects", *Criminology*, Vol. 44, No. 3, pp. 465-508; Kathryn Edin, *et. al.*. "Fatherhood and Incarceration As Potential Turning Points in the Criminal Careers of Unskilled Men", pp. 46-75, in Mary Patillo, *et. al.*, (eds.), *Imprisoning America: The Social Effects of Mass Incarceration*, 2004.

biological children (what you can reasonably provide for, both physically and emotionally) and less on micromanaging the minutiae of your children's upbringing (unless you and your children like minutiae, so long you do not let it tire you out and sour you on having more children!).

Second, your parenting will leave a big mark on the world because parents have a huge influence on passing on our values, religion, culture, and traditions.

The research shows that parenting is hard work. It is associated with more stress, but for married couples, it is also associated with fulfillment, meaning in life, and happiness, especially for biological parents. So, when weighing the number of children to have, consider all of these factors, and the potential costs and benefits. More importantly, consider that greatest of personal benefits that will come to the new person whom you will be creating—the gift of existence. Also consider the benefits your future child might bring to society and to your community.

When deciding whether to have another child, remember that your parenting style (within the bounds of normal, non-abusive first-world parenting styles) will have little effect on many of the ways your child will turn out, so you can relax a little from the normal worries about your child's future and whether you are doing enough, or doing it right. Then, finally, consider whether you have the financial and emotional resources to support another child, and decide whether having another is right for your situation. For middle class, intelligent, productive parents who are married and contributing to society (and thus likely to have a positive experience raising children and to produce children who will contribute to society), my opinion is that the optimal number will usually be somewhere between three and six children.

Conversely, if you are not a decent person and not contributing to society, your children will most likely be like you, so you should not have children (or have very few), to minimize your negative impact on future generations. Also, if you are not married, you should not have children—it will lead to negative outcomes in your own life and also in your children's.

Unity, Diversity, and Identity

The history of religious and moral thought over the last three millennia has led toward expanding notions of whom we include in our conceptions of "us", but even with this expansion, we still maintain different categories of "us". We probably always will. Imagine you see two people standing in the road in the path of an oncoming truck. One of them is a stranger and the other is a close friend or a family member. You only have enough time to push one person out of the way. Who do you save first? Almost everyone would, without hesitation, save their close friend or family member.

We are primates, and just like other primates, we are social animals with an innate need to maintain social contact with others. We are adapted to flourish and thrive as members of a mutually supportive group, and there appear to be physical cognitive limits to the number of people we can emotionally and intuitively include in our group. British anthropologist Robin Dunbar first proposed the existence of such a cognitive limit.

Dunbar found that among primate species, the best predictor of the average size of a social group in a species was the size of that species' neocortex region in the brain. When a primate group grew beyond the average limit for the species, the group would become unstable and break apart. He hypothesized that the amount of neurons in a primate's neocortex limited how many relationships the primate could keep track of at the same time.[72]

Applying his results from other primates to humans, Dunbar found that, based on humans' average neocortex ratio, the expected natural human group size would be about 150.[73] This 150-person limit is now known as Dunbar's number. Dunbar found

---

72 Robert I. M. Dunbar, "Neocortex size as a constraint on group size in primates", *Journal of Human Evolution*, Vol. 22, No. 6, June 1992, pp. 469-493.

73 At a 95 percent confidence level the range was between 100 and 230.

real-world evidence from a variety of fields supporting his hypothesis. Modern hunter-gatherer tribes commonly live in groups averaging 148 members (with a range of 90 to 222). Archaeologists' population estimates for ancient stone-age villages in Mesopotamia showed a range of 150 to 200 people. Hutterite[74] farming communities limit their size to 150 people; army units from Roman times until the present have remained between 100 and 200 men; and businesses (or sub-organizations within larger businesses) do not function well when they have more than 150 individuals.[75]

Two anthropologists, H. Russell Bernard and Peter Killworth, used surveys to study the size of personal networks in the United States and found a similar, but larger, limit to the number of meaningful social ties in modern society: a mean of 290 (and a median of 231).[76] Why is there a difference between Dunbar's number of 150 and the Bernard-Killworth number of 290? Perhaps it is because of differences in methodology or what was being measured. Or maybe our move to agriculture and living in larger groups has selected for better cognitive adaptations beyond just neocortex size that make us a little better at handling the larger, more complex societies of modern life.

Whether the number is 150 or 290, the takeaway is that there appears to be a maximum number of people with whom we are mentally capable of maintaining meaningful social ties, and that number is, at most, only a few hundred. We may intellectually believe that all people—even those outside our core social network—

<hr />

74 The Hutterites are an Anabaptist group similar to the Amish.

75 Robert I. M. Dunbar, "Coevolution of neocortex size, group size and language in humans", *Behavioral and Brain Sciences*, Vol. 16 No. 4, 1993, pp. 681-735.

76 Peter D. Killworth, H. R. Bernard, *et. al.*, "Comparing Two Methods for Estimating Network Size", *Human Organization*, Vol. 60, No. 1, Spring 2001, pp. 28-39; *see also*, H. R. Bernard, Peter Killworth, *et. al.*, "How Much of a Network does the GSS and RSW Dredge Up?" *Social Networks*, Vol. 9, No. 1, 1987, pp. 49-63.

are worthy of equal moral consideration, but in the real world, when a truck is barreling toward two people, we push our friend out of the way first.

We are well-adapted to maintaining social cohesion in small groups, so it is relatively easy. In larger groups, however, we lack the cognitive and emotional capacity to intuitively self-organize the way we can in smaller groups. The large institutions of modern life are foreign to our natural mental disposition.

In light of Dunbar's number, it thus becomes clear why the universalistic tendencies of the major world religions were necessary for the flowering of human culture and development that has happened over the last few thousand years. Such moral rules give us cognitive and emotional tools to step beyond our normal mental limits to reach out of our social circles and act morally to "others", but universally applicable moral rules do not come naturally to us. Thus, while our intellectual conception of whom we include in "us" has expanded, in practical terms, our innate biological tendency is to morally and emotionally commit ourselves to relatively small social groups.

As we discussed, a useful way to conceptualize our moral obligations is to imagine our relationships with others as forming concentric circles. Later research by Dunbar and his colleagues supports this conceptualization of our ties to others forming concentric circles.[77]

Color gradients provide another way to visualize this. Imagine again a chart showing your social relationships, with you at the center, your closest relationships near the middle, and ever-weakening relationships as you move farther from the center. This time, though, there are no concentric circles—just color. At the center is a deep, warm, vibrant red. The color gradually fades the farther from the center you go, getting paler, weaker, and colder. As you look at the people marked on such a chart, there is no one particular step as you move outward where you can definitively say your

---

77 Alistair Sutcliffe, Robin Dunbar, et. al. (see footnote 37).

social obligations have materially changed, because the color weakens gradually. There is a clear difference, however, when you compare the very center of the chart to its outermost periphery. Similarly, we usually do not perceive a stark either/or dichotomy between a homogeneous "us" in our core social network versus an undifferentiated "them" in the outside world. Rather, we feel the strongest connection with those closest to the center of our relationship circle (usually our immediate family and close friends); they are the people we most closely identify as "us". The ties weaken gradually as we move farther from the center until we reach our core social network of 150 to 300 people for whom we have devoted our brains' limited capacity for building strong social ties.

Most of us have contact with more than just 150 to 300 people in a given month. The farther those people are from our social core, the more we start to emotionally consider them as being "other". As our social distance from others grows, the emotional ties we feel toward them weaken; we start to apply learned rules of morality to our interactions rather than our brains' natural social capacity. Someone will be more or less of an "us" and more or less of a "them" based on that person's social distance from us. The more different a person is from us—such as having a different regional accent, geographical origin, native language, religion, ethnicity, or nation—the greater our tendency to consider that person as being an "other". We naturally see the world in terms of a small group of "us" to whom we owe strong moral duties, a weakening "us" made up of members of our community, ethnicity, and nation, and then a larger group of "them" to whom we owe fewer moral obligations.

Our great human abilities for learning, rational thinking, and adapting to novel situations make universally applicable moral rules possible; the good fruits of these moral developments have become obvious over the last few thousand years as violence in human societies has gradually decreased and stability has increased (along with accompanying increases in material welfare).[78] But no practical moral system can ignore the realities of human biology. The "ought" of our moral system must take into account the "is". Living in the society of people you regard as "us" is important. We naturally organize ourselves into groups and communities, and much of the meaning and fulfillment of life comes from our membership and participation in them. More than that, a lot of the material and emotional support we need during times of difficulty comes from the people in our social networks who are closer to us. Community members care for each other, and are willing to make sacrifices for each other that perfect strangers would be unwilling to make.

In recent decades, there has been a growing move toward claiming that increasing the diversity and the differences between individuals in society is of supreme importance. In the Untied States, proponents of this idea are prone to frequently repeating the mantra that "diversity is our strength". Sometimes they quote as support our national motto, "*e pluribus unum*", which is Latin for "out of many, one". They seem to ignore the final word "one". Historically, America's great national strength was creating unity, not cultivating diversity.

Harvard political scientist Robert Putnam has found that, in the United States, greater ethnic diversity in a community decreases the trust residents have for those of other ethnicities. More surprisingly, greater diversity decreases trust that residents have for people of their *own* ethnicity.

Putnam found other detrimental effects of ethnic diversity. The more diverse the community, the less likely it was that residents would work together on community projects, give to charity, or volunteer. Residents of more diverse communities had fewer close friends, lower happiness, and lower perceived quality of life.

---

78 For a detailed description of the evidence that violence has been decreasing, and a discussion of causes, see Steven Pinker, *The Better Angels of Our Nature: Why Violence Has Declined*, 2011.

Even when controlling for a variety of variables (such as age, ethnicity, socioeconomic class, and poverty and crime levels), the relationship still held between ethnic diversity and these negative effects. Putnam found that "the difference between living in an area as homogeneous as Bismarck, North Dakota, and one as diverse as Los Angeles is roughly as great as the difference between an area with a poverty rate of 7 percent and one with a poverty rate of 23 percent, or between an area with 36 percent college graduates and one with none".[79]

Putnam, a liberal progressive, was so shocked and dismayed by his results that he waited over six years to publish them while he searched for other potential explanations. He never found any.[80]

A robust body of research from a variety of fields such as psychology, sociology, political science, and international relations confirms Putnam's results.[81] A recent meta-analysis of 87 studies found "a statistically significant negative relationship between ethnic diversity and social trust across all studies".[82] A sociologist and a psychologist who together ran millions of computer models of different hypothetical neighborhoods concluded that it appeared impossible to have diverse neighborhoods that were also socially co-

79 Robert D. Putnam, "E Pluribus Unum: Diversity and Community in the Twenty-first Century The 2006 Johan Skytte Prize Lecture", *Scandinavian Political Studies*, Vol. 30, No. 2, June 2007, pp. 137-174.

80 *Same* at 153; John Leo, "Bowling With Our Own: Robert Putnam's sobering new diversity research scares its author", *City Journal*, June 25, 2007.

81 Oguzhan C. Dincer, "Ethnic Diversity and Trust", *Contemporary Economic Policy*, Vol. 29, No. 2, April 6, 2011 (this study found a negative correlation between ethnic polarization and trust, but a U-shaped relationship between ethnic fractionalization and trust).

82 Peter Thisted Dinesen, et. al., "Ethnic Diversity and Social Trust: A Narrative and Meta-Analytical Review", Preprint, September 2019, DOI: 10.13140/RG.2.2.20314.70081.

hesive; the sociologist commented that "these trends are so strong, it's unlikely policy can change it".[83]

Researchers find that ethnic diversity has negative effects not just in the United States, but around the world. Studies have found that higher levels of diversity are associated with decreasing levels of social trust or cohesion in: a sample of 60 countries[84] (this study also found that Protestant traditions also had a positive effect on social trust); in Europe[85]; in Denmark[86]; in Germany[87]; and in Australia.[88]

An 18-year longitudinal study of British households found that increased diversity caused decreased emotional attachment to, and feeling of belonging in, one's community.[89] Higher diversity in Dutch schools increased the likelihood of schoolchildren choosing

83 Zachary Neal and Jennifer Neal, "The (in)compatability of diversity and sense of community", *American Journal of Community Psychology*, Vol 53, Nos. 1-2, pp. 1-12, March 2014; Michigan State University, *MSU Today*, November 18, 2013.

84 Jan Delhey, "Predicting Cross-National Levels of Social Trust: Global Pattern or Nordic Exceptionalism?", *European Sociological Review*, Vol. 21, No. 4, 2005, pp. 311-327.

85 Conrad Ziller, "Ethnic Diversity, Economic and Cultural Contexts, and Social Trust: Cross-Sectional and Longitudinal Evidence from European Regions, 2002-2010", *Social Forces*, Vol. 93, No. 3, March 2015, pp. 1211-1240.

86 Peter Thisted Dinesen and Kim Mannemar Sonderskov, "Trust in a Time of Increasing Diversity: On the Relationship between Ethnic Heterogeneity and Social Trust in Denmark from 1979 until Today", *Scandinavian Political Studies*, Vol. 35, No. 4, May 31, 2012.

87 Ruud Koopmans and Susanne Veit, "Ethnic diversity, trust, and the mediating role of positive and negative interethnic contact: A priming experiment", *Social Science Research*, Vol 47, 2014, pp. 91-107.

88 Rebecca Wickes, et. al., "Ethnic Diversity and its Impact on Community Social Cohesion and Neighborly Exchange", *Journal of Urban Affairs*, Vol. 36, No. 1, April 2013.

same-ethnic friends.[90] A study comparing Puerto Rican youths raised in New York versus Puerto Rico found that growing up as a minority increased rates of depression, anxiety, and psychological distress.[91]

Ethnic diversity is also associated with higher levels of societal conflict and instability. Heterogeneity decreases cooperation between different groups.[92] Higher levels of ethnic and linguistic diversity in a country are correlated with higher levels of political instability and lower levels of democracy.[93] An analysis of 187 countries found that the level of ethnic heterogeneity explained 55 per-

---

89 James Laurence and Lee Bentley, "Does Ethnic Diversity Have a Negative Effect on Attitudes towards the Community? A Longitudinal Analysis of the Causal Claims within the Ethnic Diversity and Social Cohesion Debate", *European Sociological Review*, Vol. 32, No. 1, Feb. 2016, pp. 54-67.

90 Anke Munniksma, et. al., "The Impact of Adolescents' Classroom and Neighborhood Ethnic on Same- and Cross-Ethnic Friendships Within Classrooms", *Journal of Research on Adolescence*, Vol. 27, No. 1, Jan. 2016.

91 Margarita Alegria, et. al., "The effect of minority status and social context on the development of depression and anxiety: a longitudinal study of Puerto Rican descent youth", *World Psychiatry*, Vol. 18, No. 3, October 2019, pp. 298-307.

92 Ozan Aksoy, "Effects of Heterogeneity and Homophily on Cooperation", *Journal of Mathematical Sociology*, Vol. 33, pp. 303-22, 2009.

93 Christopher Clague, et. al.. "Determinants of Lasting Democracy in Poor Countries: Culture, Development, and Institutions", *Annals of the American Academy of Political and Social Sciences*, Vol. 573, No. 1, pp. 17-41, January 2001; Curtis Thompson, "Political Stability and Minority Groups in Burma", *Geographical Review*, Vol. 85, No. 3, July 1995, pp. 269-285; James Rogers, *Honors Thesis: The Importance of the Middle Class in Political Stability and the Strength of Democracies*, Brigham Young University, 2005.

cent of the variation in ethnic conflicts between countries.[94] A study of diversity and conflict found that "population diversity, and its impact on the degree of diversity within ethnic groups, has contributed significantly to the risk and intensity of historical and contemporary civil conflicts".[95] Ethnic diversity even has a negative effect on a country's level of innovation.[96]

Switzerland is one of the few counterexamples of a multiethnic society that has enjoyed long-term stability and lack of conflict. An analysis found, however, that Switzerland's stability was not based on "integrated coexistence, but rather on well-defined topographical and political boundaries separating linguistic and religious groups", as opposed to India and the former Yugoslavia, where the lack of such boundaries was associated with increased conflict.[97]

We flourish when we live in a community of people we see as being "us" and not "them". Since strong communities and strong social ties are so beneficial, the best future outcomes for humanity will come from building strong and cohesive communities of ethical, relatively homogeneous individuals who try to integrate themselves into a unified group. We should thus seek to become part of communities where we fit in and where we can easily perceive other members as being part of an "us". Communities should re-

94   Tatu Vanhanen, "Ethnic Nepotism as Cross-Cultural Background Factor of Ethnic Conflicts", *Open Journal of Political Science*, Vol. 4, No. 3, 2014.

95   Cemal Eren Arbath, *et. al.*, "Diversity and Conflict", NBER Working Paper No. 21079, September 2019.

96   Bala Ramasamy and Matthew C. H. Yeung, "Diversity and innovation", *Applied Economics Letters*, Vol. 23, No. 14, 2016, pp. 1037-41.

97   Alex Rutherford, *et. al.*, "The Geography of Ethnic Violence", in P. Fellman, *et. al.* (eds), *Conflict and Complexity, Understanding Complex Systems*, 2015; Alex Rutherford, *et. al.*, "Good Fences: The Importance of Setting Boundaries for Peaceful Coexistence", *PloS ONE*, Vol. 9, No. 5, May 21, 2014.

strict admittance of new members to those who will easily assimilate into the group. Research shows that when a minority group reaches a certain critical mass, its members do not assimilate and continue to maintain a distinct identity from the surrounding culture.[98] Communities should thus also limit the number of people they admit to manageable levels that can be assimilated. Most importantly, we should seek to assimilate ourselves to the norms, idiom, and culture of the communities of which we are a part. It is impossible to create an "us" unless each person is willing to change themself to become a part of the group.

And of course, none of this creates a right for an "us" to unjustifiably mistreat a "them". We have universal obligations to all human beings. Even though we owe our strongest moral duties to those closest to us, we still have moral duties to everyone else and are never justified in treating outsiders immorally. It is never right to mistreat, be dishonest with, or take advantage of an outsider in an attempt to get some benefit for yourself or those close to you. On the other hand, it is morally justifiable—indeed, morally required—that you protect those who are close to you from threatened harm, even to the point of using violence in self-defense when threatened. For example, it is not moral to beat up your neighbor and steal his possessions. It is moral, however, to use force against a neighbor who is trying to steal your possessions or harm you or your family.

Maybe it would be better if we could conceive of humanity as one unified whole, but our brains are likely just too limited to emotionally conceive of a single community of 7 billion us-es. Universal moral rules help us understand our obligations to other people, even if those people are very different. These rules are important, but for a moral system to be robust, long-lasting, and effective, it also must take into account our biological and cognitive

---

98 Arun Advani and Bryony Reich, "Melting Pot or Salad Bowl: The Formation of Heterogeneous Communities", *Institute for Fiscal Studies*, IFS Working Paper W15/30, October 2015.

limits. Thus, it is not only morally justifiable, but also desirable, for us to focus on building strong, unified smaller communities.

Ethnicity and identity are malleable, but not infinitely so. A person of Western European descent would probably never completely fit into a Pygmy tribe, even if raised from birth among them. But ethnicity and identity can change to some extent. There is thus some element of choice to our identity.

Passive identities tend not to last. Every identity needs to have an element of setting itself in opposition to and in conflict with other identities—otherwise it will not survive as other forms of identity that *are* more oppositional and confrontational take it over or wear it down until it no longer exists. How many Roman pagans are there nowadays?

But a productive, meaningful identity needs to be more than just oppositional in nature, nor should confrontation or opposition be its main focus. Too often today, especially as religion declines in importance in most people's lives, too many people increasingly define their identities in terms of confrontation against, or opposition to, the identities of others.

It is far more constructive to focus on defining your identity in terms of what you *are*. And it is even better to build identity in terms of being and becoming, to choose an identity that calls you to do good courageously, that demands you rise higher and be more. This is what following the Triple Path offers.

Do you feel something lacking in your life? Do you feel destined for something greater? When you honestly appraise yourself and your life, could you be aiming higher? Perhaps existence is calling to you to do more, to be more. Perhaps the Triple Path is calling to you.

Meditations and Parables

This section begins the part of this book considered canonized scripture for followers of the Triple Path. The next four chapters are mostly written in the second person, following the style of Marcus Aurelius's *Meditations*. It adapts the words of many of the world's great religious and philosophical thinkers, arranged in each part by subject matter. Next, there is a chapter of parables. A set of references at the end of each chapter lists the sources that inspired each statement's ideas and words (sometimes with significant changes from the original words). The following are the main works relied on, along with some explanatory notes about abbreviations:

- Marcus Aurelius, *Meditations* (abbreviated "Meditations")
- Seneca, *Moral Letters to Lucilius* (abbreviated "Lucilius")
- Aristotle, *Nicomachean Ethics* (abbreviated "Nicomachean")
- Epictetus, *Enchiridion* (abbreviated as "Enchiridion") (the Final Charge on page 593 was inspired by Enchiridion 51)
- The Delphic maxims
- The Bible (the reader's knowledge of the names of its books is assumed; references refer only to specific books)
- Jesus, *Gospel of Thomas* (abbreviated as "Thomas")
- Jordan B. Peterson, assorted talks and writings, including *Maps of Meaning: The Architecture of Belief* (abbreviated as "Maps") and *12 Rules for Life* (abbreviated as "12 Rules")
- Joseph Smith, *The Book of Mormon* (abbreviated as "BoM")
- Joseph Smith, *Doctrine and Covenants* (abbreviated as "D&C")
- Buddha, *Dhammapada*
- Chuang Tzu, *Chuang Tzu*
- Tao Te Ching

Foundations

Contents

1. The Triple Path

1   Follow the Triple Path: seek wisdom, practice virtue, and labor with hope—nothing is more important than these.

2   The Triple Path molds and constructs the soul. It orders your life, guides your conduct, and shows what you should do and what you should leave undone. It shows you the course to follow when you waver amid uncertainties.

3   If you would be strong enough to bear suffering; able to stand tall and unashamed; and, most important, free, then: boldly and courageously seek wisdom, practice virtue, and labor with hope. There is no other way to this end.

4   If you would have all things under your control, put yourself under the control of wisdom, virtue, and hope.

5   How great is the help we receive from the Triple Path in everything, everywhere; it not only succors us in the greatest matters, but also descends to the smallest.

6   Understanding wisdom, virtue, and hope is like looking at

three parallel lines stretching to infinity. In the distance, the lines converge into one point. The Triple Path is the single path. Wisdom, virtue, and hope all join together.

7 When you understand the Triple Path, you follow it for its own sake, not for external reward or benefit.

8 Better than wealth or power is taking your first step on the Triple Path.

9 Following the Triple Path, you will start to see that you are limited in an infinite number of ways, but that the different manners in which you might seek wisdom, practice virtue, and labor with hope are still limitless.

10 From the Triple Path, you will see the world in a new light, as if everything is new again.

11 The most helpful remedies for your soul are those not interrupted. Thus, never stop seeking wisdom, practicing virtue, and laboring with hope.

12 Once on the Triple Path, press forward until the end with steadiness, having a perfect brightness of hope, continuing to seek wisdom, practice virtue, labor with hope, and trust in God.

13 Walk your journey through life on the Triple Path always with your eyes open and your speech true, facing and balancing equally the chaos of the unknown on your left and the tyranny of the known on your right.

14 Chaos is the capacity of the infinite world to disrupt your finite considerations. Order is always susceptible to such disruption. We are each called—*you* are called—to contend with this chaos. And while contending, never succumb to the nihilism of those whom chaos has defeated, nor to the tyranny of those who have grown too terrified of order's defeat.

15 Wake up and follow the Triple Path. The day seems short when you sleep through it; life seems meaningless when you are not seeking wisdom, practicing virtue, and laboring with hope.

16 Now is the time to wake up, for the day is at hand, and an eternal night is coming upon you. Why would you sleep through the daylight of your life? Cast off your works of darkness and put on

the armor of light. Walk in the daylight, with wisdom, virtue, and hope; walk not in the shadows, in revelry and drunkenness, in licentiousness and debauchery, in discord and jealousy.

17 Let your resolve to live the Triple Path and your practice of it be like a fortified city built on a mountain, strong and not hidden.

18 Wisdom, virtue, and hope are free to you, if you seek them. These three will save you if you have them to bring forth from within yourself. They will destroy you if you do not receive them within you to bring forth.

19 Grazing animals do not worry about a change of pasture; fish do not worry about a change of stream. They accept the minor shift so long as the all-important constant remains. Let your constants be wisdom, virtue, and hope.

20 It is hard to concentrate on the best things if you spend your time on what is less important. Never let your practice of the Triple Path be merely a distraction or afterthought. So doing, you leave the Path anyway, losing the wisdom, virtue, and hope you could have found.

21 Become an experienced traveler on the Triple Path. Then, even when you are tempted by foolishness, you still will seek wisdom; when you feel like doing evil, you still will practice virtue; and in the most desperate of times, you still will labor with hope.

22 To heal your soul, you must first know what is making it sick. Wisdom, virtue, and hope will transform you into someone who sees more of your own faults, things of which you used to be ignorant. And recognizing them, you will start, by the grace of God, to conquer them and reform yourself.

23 Be patient and tireless in seeking to fill your mind with wisdom and your actions with virtue and hopeful labor, even if they only happen little by little. A bucket can be filled drop by drop, but not if there are no drops! Many small good acts can still fill a lifetime with wisdom, virtue, and hope.

Do not think lightly of foolishness, evil, and lazy despair, flippantly excusing your mistakes and follies, even if they are small and only impede your practice of the Triple Path little by little. A bucket can also be emptied drop by drop. Many small bad acts can still empty a life, leaving foolishness, evil, and lazy despair instead.

24 Even on top of a garbage heap, a flower can grow, full of sweet perfume and delight. Your wisdom, virtue, and hope can also grow, no matter your circumstance.

25 There are many who follow the Triple Path, but call it something else, or call it nothing at all. To the degree any others seek wisdom, practice virtue, and labor with hope, they follow the Triple Path partway. Seek them out and show them its fullness.

26 How can you recognize when you are following the Triple Path? By the fruits of your acts. The Triple Path brings good fruits. Do not despair if you do not see them right away. They will come.

Do not be a fool who either loves the vine and hates the fruit, or who loves the fruit and hates the vine. Such inconsistency only leads to sorrow, for you cannot have the fruit without its vine, nor the vine without its fruit. Some bad fruit may appear to be sweet at first, but they show their true nature, sooner or later.

You will never harvest grapes from thorn bushes. A thorn bush can never change the fruit it produces, but you can change where you seek fruits.

27 When wisdom, virtue, and hope rule in a family, more happiness and success will be found. When a community practices them, its condition improves. When a country's leaders and representatives follow them, it will have more peace and prosperity. But do not confuse cause for effect, and do not look for the wrong fruits. The Triple Path's fruits are principally spiritual, not material. Because of the randomness of life and the limits of perception, individuals, communities, and countries may temporarily appear to enjoy good fruits, especially material prosperity, even when they practice foolishness, evil, and lazy despair. Thus, never take good fortune as a sign of your wisdom, virtue, or hope. Instead, humbly try to ensure you ever-more faithfully follow the Triple Path. Do not be blind to your own failings; never interpret success,

especially material success, as a sign of your wisdom, virtue, or righteous labors.

28 As leaves cannot flourish by their own efforts, but need a branch to which they may cling and from which they may draw sap, so your soul withers on its own and must be grafted upon a religion to be sustained by its teachings, precepts, community, and rites; graft yourself onto that which offers the most sustenance: the Triple Path, with its roots in wisdom, virtue, and hope.

29 Wisdom, virtue, and hope will not—cannot—adapt themselves to your desires. Rather, you must adapt yourself to their demands.

30 Praise the good.

31 Walk not in evil paths of darkness, but come into the light of the Triple Path. For, the fruit of the Triple Path is all that is good and right and true. Have nothing to do with vain works of darkness. Instead, expose them—the light makes visible all things upon which it shines.

32 Your earthly journey on the Triple Path ends with your death, just as a fire's light ends when its last embers are extinguished. The Triple Path's principles, though, can never die so long as there is someone who thinks on them and lives them. Spread them, therefore, and help fan them into many flames of wisdom, virtue, and hope burning bright in the hearts of your posterity and fellow man.

33 Stop vacillating off and on the Path. Move ever more directly forward toward seeking more wisdom, practicing more virtue, and laboring more with hope.

34 Strive not to seem happy to others, but instead to live well, with wisdom, virtue, and hope, in possession of yourself, so that at the end of your life, come when it may, you may cry out with courage and with greatness of soul, "I have fought the good fight, I have finished the race, I have stayed on the Path".

2. This Book

1 The study of the Triple Path is not the study of words, but the study of being and meaning, and the development of your soul.

2   How easily these words, as all words, become a prison of paper and ink, or sound—the fruits of a crooked, broken, scattered, and imperfect language from which only God may deliver us.

3   Just knowing the words of this book will not make you great, only practicing them will; then, these words will burn in your soul like a furnace.

4   Better than a thousand senseless words is one word of wisdom that brings stillness and peace when you understand it; or one word of virtue that touches your soul with meaning when you practice it; or one word of hope that moves you to work for a better future when you believe it.

5   Read this book, think on it, and seek greater understanding. However, be not just a reader of these words, but a doer of them also. This book is not the Triple Path. The Triple Path is a way of life, not words on a page.

6   Do not confuse the sun with the finger pointing at it.

7   Even if you could recite every word of this book from memory, it would mean nothing if you did not follow them. You would be like an investor who carefully tracks someone else's money while neglecting his own finances. It does not matter if you learn any of these words if, having forsaken foolishness, evil, and lazy despair, you always seek greater wisdom, practice more virtue, and ever labor hope.

8   Internalize these principles and follow them until seeking wisdom, practicing virtue, and laboring with hope become an inseparable part of your character. Just as a pure diamond is always clear and solid no matter where it is, so too should wisdom, virtue, and hope always be a part of your nature, no matter your circumstance.

9   If you read these words and act on them, then you are like a wise man who builds his house on a foundation of rock. When rain falls, floods come, and winds blow, that house will not fall down. If you do not follow these words, then you are like a foolish man who builds his house on a foundation of sand. When rain falls, floods come, and winds blow, that house will fall down.

10 Following the Triple Path is a call to action, not to just considering words. Make these words become your words, then live in harmony with them, even in thought, so that your inner life is not out of harmony with your doings.

11 A journey does not begin when you see your route on a map. It starts when you take your first step. This book is just a map marking the way of the Triple Path. It will direct you onto the Triple Path and orient you, but you can only follow it by living its principles in your thoughts and actions.

12 A map is useful because it simplifies reality. A map, therefore, cannot perfectly and completely represent the real world—it could only do this by being as big as the thing it was representing; so doing, it would lose most of its utility.

13 You will never learn to play a musical instrument just by reading about how to do it; you must also practice it as much as you can. You will never learn to follow the Triple Path just by reading about it; you must also follow it, practicing it as much as you can.

14 Remember the parables of the testing sower and the three treasure seekers.

3. Improvement and Imperfection

1 Improving your life means taking on much responsibility. And effort. And care. And living less in arrogance, deceit, and resentment, breaking the bonds of the slavery of opinion.

2 While working to improve yourself, it can be helpful to look to the good examples of others to emulate. But when evaluating your progress, compare yourself to where you were yesterday, not to where someone else is today.

3 It is when things are at their worst that you most often need improvement. In such situations, cling to whatever improvement you can manage. On a sinking ship, making it on a cramped lifeboat is cause for celebration.

4 How vain and foolish is it to plan only for future repentance and reformation. You have need to do so now! If you are waiting for some future time to begin, how much are you missing

out on, and will continue to lose! Do not deceive yourself. The same rationalizations you make now, and new ones, will tempt you ever more as you persist in your foolish, lazy evil. What makes you think you will be any better-placed in the future to repent and re-form, after you have further corrupted your soul, than you are right now? And what if you die tomorrow, still wallowing in your foolishness, evil, and lazy despair? If you discovered you had been given deadly poison, would you delay in seeking out and taking the antidote? Then seek out the antidote to that which is poison-ing your soul.

5   When you are doing something you know, however dim-ly, to be wrong, start to stop doing it—now, today. Do not waste time questioning how you know it is wrong, or why it is wrong. Such questioning will confuse without enlightening, and stop you from acting. You can know something is wrong without knowing why.

6   Remember the parable of the two young men.

7   Sometimes it is not enough to only change what you are doing—you must also change how you think.

8   How do you get better? Study, meditate, and watch your-self to gain greater understanding; use this understanding to find things you need to improve; set attainable, measurable, and dis-crete goals; record your progress and reward yourself in achieving them; follow up to evaluate your progress; and then set new goals. Make this an ever-repeating cycle of improvement and progression.

9   When something goes wrong, or when you need to im-prove or change, seek to understand what happened to you and why; where you are and where you are going; what is keeping you from moving forward; and how to expose yourself voluntarily and gradually to what it is you are afraid of doing to move forward.

10   Even if you do not always manage to keep up the same pace, if you ever travel the same path, you can still make much progress.

11   Improvement in individuals and communities rarely hap-pens through abrupt shifts, but rather through slow, gradual change.

12   The more radical a necessary change is, the more painful

it will be. How much better, then, it is to make the needed adjustments through small corrections along the way.

13 When progress stalls, consider whether it is because not that you have lacked opportunity, but that you have been too arrogant to take full advantage of what is already in front of you.

14 Too often, you only learn how to improve when forced, through pain and anxiety. Often those lessons are difficult lessons. When you avoid necessary lessons, you just make the lesson you must learn even harder when it comes again in the future. Seek to learn without needing to be forced. Thus, be humble. Humility does not mean debasing yourself. It means understanding that you do not know enough to avoid the potential misery and tragedy and malevolence waiting for you in life and thus taking every chance you have to learn to improve.

15 Do not be discouraged when you make mistakes. Every person does. When you falter, return again to the Triple Path. Be satisfied if most of what you do is consistent with the Path; be satisfied if you are improving and more faithfully following it. If you are not improving, then you must change something in your life.

16 Watch yourself to recognize when you are starting to wander off the Path. You are more likely to wander off of the Path when you are walking at its edge. If you wander off of the Path, the probability you will wander still further increases. But as you progress forward along the center of the Path, the probability you will progress further still also increases.

17 When you wander off of the Path and lose yourself, you must first figure out how you erred, not only so you can find your way back onto the Path but also so you can figure out how to avoid the same mistake again.

18 You are weak and imperfect. Seek to overcome your weaknesses and turn them into strengths. Recognize your mistakes. You should feel regret and shame for them, but do not let these feelings consume or paralyze you. Instead, use them to lead yourself to improvement. Change your mind and character to overcome whatever weakness led you to your mistakes.

19 The consequence of evil acts is often suffering—either to yourself or others. Sometimes the suffering will humble you enough to repent. How much better, though, would it have been to avoid the suffering to begin with? Be humble. Seek wisdom, practice virtue, and labor with hope, and you will avoid much unnecessary suffering.

20 Follow these three steps to repent of your sins and mistakes: First, stop doing whatever caused the need to repent. Second, make amends, as much as possible, for any harm you caused. Third, work to change and channel your desires away from evil and toward wisdom, virtue, and hope. Your actions shape your desires, and your desires shape your actions. As you work to change both, each will reinforce the improvements you seek to make in the other.

21 Seek to end each day a better person than when you started.

22 You cannot see everything. You naturally focus your attention on what you seek and on the obstacles to it, ignoring most everything else. When you are in crisis, it may be because of what you have been ignoring, because you were seeking the wrong things. If life is not going well, it may be that your knowledge, not life, is lacking. If you cling too tightly to the wrong desires, you may be blinding yourself to what you really need. Sacrifice your prior, wrong goals. Change what you seek, and you will change what you see. Seeking after wisdom, virtue, and hope, you will start to perceive what was previously hidden—great things calling to you.

23 It is impossible for you to relive your life so that you would have followed the Triple Path at all times until now. However, you may still profit from your past. Use your past mistakes to understand how much better it is to follow the Triple Path. You must choose how to live the rest of your life. Show more wisdom, practice more virtue, and labor more with hope than you have in the past. Live the Triple Path!

24 Wisdom will not fall upon you by chance. You must seek it. Virtue will not fill your character by luck. You must practice it.

You will not fulfill your life's work through inaction. You must labor to complete it.

25 Strive for greatness of soul. Strive to seek all wisdom, to practice all virtues, to labor ceaselessly with hope.

4. Light

1 If you walk in the day, you do not stumble, because you see by the light of this world. But if you walk in the night, you stumble, because there is no light to guide you.

2 Receiving wisdom is like turning on a light in a dark room —it lets you better perceive everything around you. The brighter light of greater wisdom brings truer understanding.

3 Just as the brightness of the sun dims all lesser lights in comparison, so virtue, by its own greatness, can shatter and overwhelm evil, pain, wrongs, and annoyances. Wherever its radiance reaches, all lights that shine without its help appear extinguished.

4 Laboring with hope is not naively seeing light where there is none, but fighting the darkness with what you reflect from God's Divine light.

5 Remember the parable of the light.

5. Meaning

1 The purpose of your life is not to find pleasure, or satisfaction, or comfort, or peace, or even joy. Your purpose is to live with meaning.

2 There is no guarantee that seeking to live with meaning will bring lasting satisfaction or happiness or peace, but pursuing meaning above all else is more likely to bring these other three than seeking any of them out as ends in themselves.

3 Do not ask, "what is the meaning of life?", making demands on existence. Instead, recognize what existence demands of *you*—that your life have meaning. You answer this ultimate demand through the life you live. *You* determine whether to live with meaning. No matter your circumstances, you choose your reaction to them. To the demand of existence, the only proper response is to take responsibility.

4 Figure out what you should do and become to justify your

life. Then, go: do and become.

5   He who has a why can bear almost any how.

6   When you are aiming at something profound enough, then it becomes worth passing through much anguish to participate in bringing it about.

7   Meaning does not come from having rights and freedom, but from having responsibilities.

8   Live with meaning, so that you might keep at bay the corrupting influences of foolishness, evil, and lazy despair.

9   Do not sacrifice meaning for immature expedience. Expedience is the cowardly avoidance of responsibility. It blindly seeks to satisfy the urges of the moment, narrowly and selfishly seeking short-term gain. Expedience is dumping the consequences of your mistakes onto someone else, or onto your future self. It casts hell into the future—into your future.

10   Stop uttering falsehoods. Live according to the dictates of virtue and your conscience. Courageously stay faithful and true to the highest of ideals, even in the face of the ultimate threat. This is the path to profound meaning.

11   Living with meaning is better than having what you think you want or need. Do you know what you want? Do you know what you really need?

12   You cannot force meaning. It comes upon you of its own accord when you are doing the right things, when you are following God and seeking wisdom, practicing virtue, and laboring with hope while striving to achieve worthy goals.

6. God

1   Prostrate before God, and none else.

2   It is impossible to fully define God with words. It is your right—and your responsibility—to come to a personal understanding of Him for yourself.

3   You do not come to know God through reason or analysis; you come to know God by experiencing Him.

4   Behold the incredible and grand mystery of existence, feel the awe of contemplating the universe, and recognize that behind it

all lies an ineffable power and mystery beyond your reckoning or imagination.

5   Follow and respect God, and falter not. Even when your will is weak and wicked, still follow on.

6   When your soul is weary and heavy-laden, come to God for rest, righteousness, and salvation.

7   Rather than merely saying you believe in God, act as if He exists.

8   Your mind and heart are before God, always. He knows when you allow to dwell in them arrogance; spite; deceit; cruelty; resentment; malevolence; love of destruction; and hatred of God, man, and being. When your heart and mind are full of such evil, then are you ripe for destruction.

9   Whatever you treat as your highest value becomes your god. There are no atheists, only those who fail to recognize the god they serve. Let yours always be *the* one and true God.

10   You are a weak, watery being standing in the midst of un-realities; therefore turn your mind to the things that are everlasting and real—God, truth, and wisdom, virtue, and hope.

11   Lift up your soul to God; put your trust in Him and the Triple Path, and you will not be ashamed.

12   Faith in God is not believing in that which you know to be false. It is not the childish belief in magic. It is not reveling in ignorance and willful blindness.

13   God exists. He is above all things. You will only ever have an imperfect knowledge of His nature. To attain even this imperfect knowledge, you must reverence the spark of God's divinity that is within you, and keep it pure.

14   No one can be good without the help of God. If you seek Him, you can feel God near you, with you, within you. You can feel His influence dwelling in you, marking your good and bad deeds. Or maybe rather, it is your good and bad deeds that mark your soul, drawing it closer to, or farther from, God. So, draw yourself closer to Him. Whatever you do or say that makes you feel ashamed or weak, do not do or say. Whatever you do or say that

is true and makes you feel confident, strong, and holy, and which conforms to the standards of wisdom, virtue, and hope, then that should you do and say.

15 It has been said that man and woman were created in the image of God. Would that not mean that *you* also were so created? And if you can feel the spark of His divinity within you, might that mean you are a fragment of God, having within yourself a part of Him? Are you, then, ignorant of your noble birth? Why do you not consider the source from which you have sprung? Why do you not remember, when you are eating, who you are that eat, and whom you feed? When you are in the company of the opposite sex, when you are conversing, when you are exercising, when you are disputing, is it the divine you make speak, the divine you feed, the divine you exercise? Are you bearing God about with you, poor wretch, and know nothing of it? If so, then it is within yourself that you carry Him, and profane Him, by impure thoughts and unclean actions. In the presence of even an image of God, you would not dare to act as you do. And with God Himself present within you, seeing and hearing everything, are you not ashamed to think and act thus, insensible of your own nature and at enmity with God?

16 God is worshiped by those who truly know Him and those who want to know Him. Would you worship God? Then imitate Him. If God is goodness and wisdom, virtue, and hope, then you will approach Him and understand Him—and thus purify and refine your soul—by being a good man or woman, by seeking wisdom, practicing virtue, and laboring with hope.

17 An essential part of piety towards God is to have the right ideas about Him: that He exists and encompasses pure wisdom, virtue, and hope. Resolve yourself to obey Him, and yield to Him, and always willingly follow Him. For thus you will never find fault with Him, nor accuse Him of neglecting you. And always remember that in whatever situation God has placed you, it is your duty to labor to improve it.

18 Do not just obey God, but train yourself to agree with

Him. Obey Him not because you must, but because your soul wills it.

19 You are a weakling and a degenerate if you struggle and malign the order of the universe and would rather reform God than reform yourself. Winter brings on cold weather, and we must shiver. Summer returns, with its heat, and we must sweat. Misfortune and evil bring their pain, and we must suffer. In bad circumstances, always strive to overcome. But that which you cannot reform, it is best to endure, and to attend uncomplainingly upon the God under whose notice everything progresses. When you cannot change the order of things, what you can do is acquire a stout heart worthy of the virtuous, thus courageously enduring chance and placing yourself in harmony with God and the Triple Path.

20 At peace are those who take refuge in God.

21 Commend your soul to God. In Him let your hope and trust rest. Let Him be your rock and fortress of shelter, His faithfulness and truth your defense. Follow Him with clean hands and a pure heart, not lifted up unto vanity, nor working deception upon your neighbors. Let Him guide and lead you, and you shall dwell under His illumination. Stand firm in your resolve, not shaken even in the face of terror by night and war by day, pestilence and sickness, death and plague.

22 Be wary of anyone you hear of who has said, "I have seen God" or "I speak for God" or "Thus sayeth the Lord". Of such, many have been misquoted or proved to be liars, crazy, or self-deluded.

23 To know God, do not obsess yourself with the tales of others or with labored reason and analysis. Go to the source and experience God for yourself, for that is how you will come to know Him.

24 If you discovered a seashell hundreds of miles inland, you might put it to your ear, listen, and think you knew what the ocean is like.

Or, if someone came to you and told you what it is like to be at the coast, you might think you then understood the sea.

But a wise man wanting to know whether the seashell or the tales of others were right would go to the seashore, get in a boat, and go out on the water himself. Once he had listened and looked and touched and smelled and felt and experienced, he would have no need for the weak imitations from a seashell or someone else's explanations to understand.

Even the most precious of memories fade. To retain his knowledge, he would need to go back again and again to the ocean to refresh his knowledge and experience it anew.

25 Good and true religion speaks to man about drawing closer to God. Should religions, which are of man, claim to speak for God?

26 Do not be so prideful as to assume that God is on your side. Rather, concern yourself about whether you are on His side.

27 Follow the Triple Path and rise and mold yourself to kinship with God. Your money will not place you on a level with Him, for God has no bank account, no investments, and no titles to land; your degrees and earthly honors will not do this either, for God has no degrees, no medals, no trophies; your reputation does nothing either, for God continues on the same whether He is known by everyone or by no one.

28 The path of God is the path of truth and wisdom, virtue, and hope.

References

1. The Triple Path
1- Meditations 3:6. 2- Lucilius 16:3. 3- Lucilius 37:3. 4- Lucilius 37:4. 5- Lucilius 17:2 (quoting Cicero). 7- Chuang Tzu, Sec. 1 (Free and Easy Wandering), Watson translation, p. 26. 9- Dhammapada 178. 10- 2 Corinthians 5:17. 11- Lucilius 69:2. 12- BoM, 2 Nephi 31:20. 13- Jordan Peterson, Podcast 38: Cathy Newman and Analysis, 1:08:30. 14- Jordan Peterson, 12 Rules for Life Tour: Iceland Lecture 1, 36:00. 15- Dhammapada 60. 16- Romans 13: 11-13. 17- Thomas 32; Matthew 5:14. 18- Thomas 70. 19- Chuang Tzu, Sec. 21, (T'ien Tzu-Fang), Watson translation. 20- Meditations 3:6. 21- Tao Te Ching 27. 22- Lucilius 6. 23- Dhammapada 121-122. 24- Dhammapada 58-59. 26- Thomas 43 and 45; BoM, 3 Nephi 14:16-20; Matthew 7:16-20. 27-Tao Te Ching 54. 28- Lucilius 95:47, 50. 29- Dorothy Sayers. 30- Delphic maxim 24. 31- Ephesians 5:8-14. 32- Meditations 7:2. 33- 12 Rules, p. 259. 34- Lucilius 12:9 and 110:20; Timothy 4:7.

2. This Book
1- Lucilius 108:23. 2- Joseph Smith, November 27, 1832, to William W. Phelps. 3- Lucilius 75:7; Ecclesiasticus 48:1. 4- Dhammapada 100. 5- James 1:22; BoM, 3 Nephi 17:3. 6- Maps, p. 25 (quoting Northrop Frye). 7- Dhammapada 19-20. 8- Meditations 7:15. 9- Matthew 6:24-27. 10- Lucilius 20:2. 12- Jordan Peterson. 13- Rod Dreher, "What Pope Francis Unveils", *The American Conservative*, September 7, 2019.

3. Improvement and Imperfection
1- 12 Rules, p. 131. 2- 12 Rules, p. 142. 3- 12 Rules, pp. 141-42. 4- John Rogers, *The Nature and Necessity of Repentance*, 1728, pp. 66, 68, 71. 5- 12 Rules, pp. 188-90. 7- Maps, p. 25. 9- Jordan Peterson Podcast 2.06, 58:00. 10- Lucilius 20:2. 12- Jordan Peterson, Podcast 44, 2:45. 13- 12 Rules, pp. 393-97. 14- Jordan Peterson, Podcast 44, 2:45. 15- Meditations 5:9; Ecclesiastes 7:20. 16- Jordan Peterson, 12 Rules for Life Tour: Iceland Lecture 2, 1:31: 00. 17- Jordan Peterson Podcast 2.08, 1:53. 18- BoM, Ether 12:

26-27. **19**- BoM, Alma 32:13. **20**- D&C 58:43. **21**- Lucilius 108:4. **22**- 12 Rules, pp. 129-31. **23**- Meditations 8:1. **24**- Lucilius 76:6. **25**- Nicomachean, Book 4, part 3.

4. Light
1-John 11:9-10. **2**- D&C 50:23-25. **3**- Lucilius 66:20.

5. Meaning
1-2-Jordan Peterson, Podcast 57, 2:27:00. **3**- Viktor Frankl, Man's Search for Meaning, 1946. **4**- 12 Rules, 119-21. **5**- Friedrich Nietzsche, *Twilight of the Idols, or, How to Philosophize with a Hammer*, 1889 (Maxims and Arrows, no. 12). **6**-Jordan Peterson Podcast 5, 38:00. **7**-Jordan Peterson, Podcast 62, 56:00. **8**- 12 Rules, p. 60. **9**- 12 Rules, pp. 230-34. **10**- 12 Rules, pp. 198-203. **11-12**- 12 Rules, pp 230-34.

6. God
1- Delphic maxim 57 (alternate numbering, *see* Al. N. Oikonomides, "Records of 'The Commandments of the Seven Wise Men' in the 3rd c. B.C.", 63 Classical Bulletin 67, 76 (1987). **3**- Razib Khan, "Variation in general intelligence and our evolutionary history", *GNXP Blog*, December 29, 2018. **4**- Wency. **5**- Delphic maxims 1 and 3; Enchiridion 53 (quoting Cleanthes). **6**-John Rogers, *The Nature and Necessity of Repentance*, 1728, p. 9. **7**-Jordan Peterson, Debate with Sam Harris, Part One, 1:24:00. **8**- Peter Turchin, Ultrasociety, 2016. pp. 208-10; 12 Rules, p. 212. **9**- 12 Rules, pp. 255-58. **10**- Lucilius 59:27. **11**- Psalm 25:1-2. **12**- 12 Rules, p. 139. **13**- George Long (Translator), *The Thoughts of the Emperor Marcus Aurelius Antoninus*, 1862, Introduction by the Translator. **14**- Lucilius 41:1. **15**- Epictetus, *Discourses*, Book 2, Chapter 8. **16**- Meditations 5:21; Malachi 3:2-3; Lucilius 94:47, 50. **17**- Enchiridion 31. **18**- Lucilius 96:2. **19**- Lucilius 107:7, 12. **20**- Psalm 2:12. **21**- Psalm 24:3-4, 31:1-6, and 91:1-10. **22**- Matthew 24:23-26. **26**- Clyde Lewis. **27**- Lucilius 31:10-11 (quoting *Aeneid* 8:364). **28**- Psalm 25:10.

Wisdom

Contents

1. Wisdom

1   Wisdom is still and formless, standing alone and unchanging, reaching everywhere and in no danger of being exhausted; yet within you it causes action and change and gives form and under-

standing to what you perceive. Wisdom is the mother of all things; it is the center of the universe; it is a good man's treasure, and a bad man's refuge. Wisdom does not compete, yet wins. It does not speak, yet always responds. It cannot be summoned, but comes of its own volition. It does not command, yet is obeyed.

2 Prepare yourself to receive wisdom, and it will flow in—not when you want it, but when you have earned it.

3 You contain wisdom that you cannot comprehend.

4 Wisdom is simple. Yet, even if you spent your whole life seeking, you would never receive a fullness of it. But spend your life seeking all the same. The more you seek, the more you will receive, and the closer you will come to a fullness.

5 Wisdom comes bit by bit. Be patient in seeking it. The large redwood grows from the tiniest seed; the construction of the tallest building begins with a single shovelful of dirt; the journey of a thousand miles starts with a single step.

6 So long as you are ignorant, keep learning, even to the end of your life. And never forget, you are always ignorant about something. Your knowledge is ever incomplete. Spend your time liberally seeking more of it. And live always seeking greater wisdom, like a swift river always flowing toward the great expanse of the sea.

7 Wisdom is broad and unhurried; foolishness is cramped and busy.

8 Wisdom is not passive. It fearlessly cuts down foolishness.

9 When you contemplate raw wisdom, often you will gaze upon her with bewilderment and awe, like being in a far-off remote area at night and looking upwards at the star-filled heavens, staring in wonder, as if seeing them again for the first time.

10 The infinite mysteries of wisdom sometimes unexpectedly cut through your limited understanding; be ready so that when they do, you recognize, integrate, and act on them.

11 The wise recognize small things without considering them paltry and large things without considering them unwieldy.

12 The wise do not delight if they acquire something, nor do they worry when they lack something or lose it.

13 The wise recognize how much of their merit comes from what they have learned from others. They realize they have many weaknesses—both known and unknown to themselves.

14 The wise rest where rest is to be had and do not try to find rest where there is none. The foolish try to rest where there is none and do not rest where it is to be found.

15 The wise learn what others do not learn. They thus desire what others do not desire, and do not prize what others prize. They often value what the multitude has passed by and cast aside as worthless.

16 As a solid rock is not shaken by the wind, the wise falter not amidst blame or praise.

17 When a knife edge is blunt, you need much effort to cut with it. Wisdom is like a sharp blade, helping you more easily cut through the obstacles of life.

18 Know what you have learned.

19 Long for wisdom.

20 Observe and perceive, then discern rightly.

21 Make a habit of careful inquiry. Be persistent; do not stop investigating and seeking, even though you feel satisfied with initial appearances and with what you think you have discovered. Consider things carefully, in an orderly way, and vigorously and consistently.

22 Learn to recognize rightly. You will never find wisdom if you imagine truth in untruth and see untruth in truth, or if you believe that which is unimportant to be essential and that which is essential to be unimportant.

23 Not all irrefutable arguments are actually true.

24 Do not let reason mislead you. Let all reasoning be silent when experience gainsays its conclusions.

25 Seek wisdom everywhere—hold onto every bit you find, no matter its source.

26 Do not be surprised to find wisdom in the unlikeliest of places, even in the minds of your opponents—especially in the minds of your opponents. On the other hand, if someone has many

clearly wrong ideas, there is a good chance his other ideas are wrong too.

27 Others can point you to the never-ending path of wisdom, but you must travel it yourself to find what lies along the way.

28 Wisdom is a mystery that few seek and even fewer find. Heed the quiet voice of wisdom rather than the shouts of the foolish crowd.

29 Praise wisdom.

30 What good is it if you say you have wisdom, but you do not have virtue and hope? Is wisdom enough? No! You need all three. You cannot really seek wisdom without also practicing virtue and laboring with hope.

2. Foolishness and Ignorance

1 How blind and impenetrable are our understandings, for we will not seek wisdom, neither do we desire that she should rule over us!

2 Getting rid of your foolishness is the beginning of wisdom.

3 Fools stare at their hazy reflection in troubled, muddy water and think they have a clear understanding of themselves and the world. They hear, yet do not understand, see and do not perceive.

4 Foolishness is low, abject, mean, slavish, and exposed to many of the cruelest passions. These can be banished from you by wisdom, virtue, and hope, which are the only real freedoms.

5 There are none so blind as those who will not see.

6 Many willfully blind themselves by accepting the foolishness of those around them. Others blind themselves by refusing to recognize what would be plain if they were looking, or obvious if they were watching.

7 That of which you are ignorant is often less a danger to you than that of which you are certain, yet wrong.

8 Do not tell yourself lies that seem like truth. The fool who knows he is foolish has at least some measure of wisdom. The fool who thinks himself wise is hopeless. He perceives the reality and truth around him as well as a spoon perceives the taste of soup.

9 Your mind often tries not to notice even that which lies

before your eyes; force, therefore, upon it the knowledge of things that should be perfectly seen and understood.

10 A fool's greatest enemy is his own shortsightedness. While his foolishness does not yet bear fruit, he anticipates sweetness, but when it ripens he reaps only bitterness.

11 Fools are puzzled, surprised, or even angry when they encounter wisdom.

12 Speak wisdom to a fool and he will call you foolish.

13 No one is born wise. Many never find wisdom because they let the inertia of their youthful foolishness carry them through life. They are too lazy or too careless to pull themselves off of the path of foolishness and onto the Triple Path.

14 When a bird stops briefly to rest near your home, you do not invite it in and share with it your dinner. If this happened, your food would make it sick, and you would have wasted your time.

15 Some fools understand and accept wisdom when they encounter it. Many never do. Often, they are incapable of doing so. You cannot recognize fools just by looking at them. Thus, share wisdom widely and freely, but do not waste your time on those who prove themselves unable to receive it.

16 The rebuke of the wise is better than the song of fools.

17 The wise have eyes to see; fools grope around in darkness.

18 Fools, lacking understanding, laugh at wisdom.

19 One heedless fool can destroy much good.

20 Fools return again and again seeking water from a bucket dipped into a dry well.

21 Remember the parable of the travelers and the dry well.

22 Fools wear themselves out in vain pursuits. The wise satisfy themselves accomplishing worthy ends.

3. Truth

1 Seek the truth. And when you find the truth, it will set you free.

2 Your pursuit of truth is a process, not an end.

3 Never tire of learning.

4   We all live in error. Strive for truth that you may discover where you are in error.

5   Take every truth you find—no matter from where or whom it may have come—and make it your own.

6   There are different kinds of truth. Our myths never happened, yet always are.

7   The world is not just a place of things, but also a forum for action and being. Seek not only the truth about things in the objective world, but also the truth about how you should act and be. There are three aspects to the world as a forum for action: the unexplored territory of nature and chaos; the explored territory of culture and ancestral wisdom; and the process by which you mediate between the two.

8   Seek to understand what is; what to do about what is; and the difference between understanding what is and what to do about it. And also realize that skill in doing any one of these three does not equate to skill in the others.

9   When you encounter truth, it will make other things you had previously known fit together, giving an ampler understanding than you had before, like puzzle pieces connecting into a more complete picture.

10   Truth reigns supreme. It exists independently of all else.

11   Any opinion at variance with truth is wrong. You must change your opinion to match the truth, for truth will not change itself to match your opinion.

12   You can contend with reality and shape a few of its contours, but reality is boundless, and you are not.

13   Fools live on in blissful ignorance of the truth until it blindsides them and destroys their understanding of the world.

14   Truth cares not about what you want or makes you happy or brings good feelings. Seek it all the same, for ignoring the truth will not change it, and one day you must have a reckoning with it. Thus, seek to understand as much as you can, as soon as you can, so that you are prepared to face reality.

15   If you seek truth, you may find comfort. But if you seek

comfort above truth, you will find neither comfort nor truth—only wishful thinking to begin with and, in the end, despair.

16 When you encounter an unwanted truth, pretending you do not know it is a sin against truth. Be not as an infant who thinks that whatever he refuses to look at does not exist.

17 Diverting your attention from something you do not want to know about will not make it go away.

18 Even if you do not believe in brick walls, you will still be hurt when you smash into one.

19 Reality that you ignore tends to degenerate into ever more monstrous chaos.

20 Good and wise ideas do not need many lies to be told about them to gain acceptance.

21 How cynical, how hopeless, how evil it is to believe that lies and falsehoods will improve reality! Shun this poison that accuses the truth as insufficient and honest men as fools, and cast out those trying to dispense it to others.

22 Lies deform the structure of being. Individual lies corrupt individual souls. Group lies corrupt whole communities and nations.

23 Do not be surprised if some of the things you most fiercely deny are those things you also most fear to be true.

24 Never value anything more than the truth. Those who hate truth do so because of that which they value most. They usually even start out valuing truth greatly, but by not valuing it above all else, whenever the truth runs counter to those things they value most, they reject whatever measure of truth they need so they may hold on to those other things. And so they slowly descend until they end up hating the truth for the sake of propping up their foolish dead faith in false idols.

25 You can judge a person's character by the amount of truth he can tolerate.

26 If you wish to know what you really consider to be truth, look at what you do, not what you say you believe. Beware of those hypocrites who betray what they claim to believe through their ac-

tions.

27   The most important aspects of things are often hidden because of their simplicity and familiarity, because they are always before your eyes. And thus you are not struck by what, once perceived, is the most striking and powerful.

28   Remember the parable of the truck driver.

4. The Unknowable

1   We look at wisdom, yet do not see it; we hear it, yet do not listen to it; we try to grasp it, yet cannot get hold of it; we write about it, yet cannot describe it.

2   A frog in a well cannot imagine the ocean, nor can an insect in summer conceive of ice. How then can someone who thinks he has nothing left to learn understand wisdom? He is restricted by his own learning. Your mind is limited. Much is unknowable.

3   The unknown surrounds you, like an ocean enveloping a small island. No matter how much land you reclaim from the sea, the waters still encircle you.

4   You see only a mirror's reflection, darkly.

5   Recognize what is already around you, and the hidden will start to be made manifest.

6   It is not until you come to the limits of the shore that you can begin to understand the vastness of the ocean. Start to understand the limits of your knowledge, and you will begin to understand the limitlessness of wisdom. Recognize the magnitude of the unknowable, and your mind will start to reach into illumination.

7   Your mind is like a small gem sitting on Mount Everest. See the smallness of yourself; cease your self-pride in the luster of your little stone. Look around you and see the great, beautiful mountain of wisdom surrounding you.

8   A blind person cannot understand a fine painting, nor can a deaf person comprehend beautiful music. The blind know they cannot see; the deaf know they cannot hear. They hone their other senses and learn to compensate.

9   Tally up everything that you know, and it cannot compare to all the things that you do not. Calculate the time you have been

alive, and it cannot compare to the time before you were born or the time that will pass after you die.

10 Do not treat the unknown as known.

11 Know that your knowledge is incomplete and may be wrong. It is a disease of the soul to think you know when you do not. Recognizing this as a disease is the first step to curing it.

12 When you stand, even though your feet rest on a small space, they also depend on the support from the surrounding ground. Your paltry knowledge and understanding also depend on the support that comes from all the things you do not know. Recognize this and find comfort and repose in the support of the unknown and the unknowable.

13 Beware of too adamantly claiming certainty and rightness. False certainty impedes further progress, putting you at risk of rejecting new and more correct truths when you encounter them. The wisest do not claim to have a monopoly on truth or wisdom; they do not claim exclusive knowledge; they seek to learn new things; they freely change their opinion when confronted with more truth. Their continual uncertainty drives them to endless seeking and thus to greater wisdom.

5. Humility

1 Be humble. The root of humility is to recognize that there is much you do not know, and that there is much you will never know.

2 Do not be arrogant about what you think you know.

3 Those who think they know everything have no way of finding out they do not.

4 Beware of pride, lest you do evil or great foolishness.

5 In this age of reason, the necessity for humility calls out. Reason flies high and sees far, but it is also prone to pride. Pride falls in love with itself, worshiping its productions as absolutes and glorifying itself until it sees nothing else.

6 Do not mix your practice of the Triple Path with pride. Let the Triple Path strip off your faults, rather than assist you in condemning the faults of others.

7   When you are humble you do not mind reproof or criticism, no matter your station in life or that of whomever is criticizing. You honestly consider the reproof and actively seek to correct your mistakes and failings, acting with discernment and with wisdom, virtue, and hope.

8   How often you fail to recognize your faults, blind to your own sins! The blind of sight ask for a guide, yet you wander without one, oblivious to your own evil. You thus find wisdom and virtue with so much difficulty, because you do not even know you are diseased.

9   Too often, you try to excuse your faults and claim you do not deserve to suffer the consequences of your actions. Too rarely, you accept your mistakes and faults without trying to excuse them and without trying to avoid their consequences. Be humble, and make the rare become frequent and the frequent become rare.

10   It is easy to succumb to the temptation to ignore your own mistakes. When things go poorly, or when they fall apart completely, accept responsibility. Do not pridefully rationalize away the outcome, blaming the world or other's faults. Ask yourself: "How did I contribute to this? What mistakes did I make? What could I have done differently?". Ask with real intent and a heart open to knowing the truth. You probably will not like the answer, and that is why you must ask the questions; for, the answer will show where you have erred and how you must change.

11   There never was, and never will be, someone who is always blameworthy or always praiseworthy. Strive to be indifferent to praise, so you do not become vain or blind to your weaknesses. Search criticisms to learn ways to improve yourself, but do not become so immersed in them that they sap your will to improve.

12   When Themistius, a Roman Senator and philosopher, heaped praise upon the Emperor Julian, this was the nature of Julian's response: "I am fully conscious that by nature there is nothing remarkable about me. I have neither sufficient training nor natural talents above the ordinary. Any success that I achieve should not be attributed to any personal attributes of my own, but to God."

Let this be your attitude as well when others heap praises on you.

13 Do not claim to be wiser than you are. Remember too, that it is nearly impossible for you to know how much wisdom you really have. Also remember that you are more likely to think you have more wisdom than you actually do, than you are to think that you have less.

14 Like every person, you are full of weaknesses and short-comings. Work to turn your weaknesses into strengths: seek to discover them, frankly acknowledge them, and work to overcome them; but, do not let your failures to overcome weaknesses discourage you—instead let them remind you always to be humble. Even if you only use your weaknesses to teach yourself humility, they have started to become strengths to you.

6. Prayer

1 When you pray and meditate, with whom are you communing? With yourself? Be careful, then, for you are likely communing with a bad person! Pray instead to God and commune with that Source of wisdom and virtue that is never exhausted.

2 Pray for things possible.

3 Pray always, that by God's grace: in your seeking, you find wisdom; in your desires and actions, you practice virtue, with a grateful heart and love for others; in your labors, you cultivate hope and the fortitude to continue laboring; and you keep yourself from entering into temptation or falling prey to evil desires.

4 Use prayer to focus yourself on that which is most important, and thus draw yourself closer to God. When you pray, give thanks for all that is good in your life. Express your virtuous desires. Do not expect that expressing your desire for blessings for yourself or others carries magic to make them happen with no effort on your part. Work to make them a reality.

5 Is it reasonable to pray to God that He upend the eternal laws of the universe, just to ameliorate your troubles? Should you expect that your problems be solved by magic? Pray to know what you should be doing to fortify your resolve and character; pray to know how you have erred; and pray that you might more clearly

see the truth so that you can conceive of the right path to struggle your way out of your predicament.

6 Develop good judgment about that which you pray for. Take care that you not pray with good intentions for bad things. And do not confuse your good intentions with the goodness of the thing you pray for. Can your intentions transform bad into good?

7 Lift up your heart to God in singing, for the song of the virtuous is a prayer unto God. Listen to and sing music that will illuminate and uplift you.

7. Meditation and Mindfulness

1 How long will you blaspheme and love vanity and seek after lies? When you are tempted or disturbed, sin not; stand in awe and stillness, ponder and be silent.

2 Still your mind and find tranquility and insight. Still your mind so you may perceive when God comes to commune with you.

3 Your mind is limited and finite; wisdom is not; peace is not. Still your mind, empty it, and let infinite wisdom and peace flow through it.

4 Seek for heat as well as light in your meditations, that they be intense, effectual, and affecting, that your heart burn within you, your soul alight with a divine flame.

5 The coldness of confusion, worry, and judgment freeze your mind into foolishness, like a glacier in winter. Let the warmth of peace shine through your frozen mind and melt it, making it run like spring runoff flowing toward the deepest and most profound wisdom, to an infinite ocean.

6 Let churning, cloudy, muddy water be still, and it will become clear on its own. Let your mind be still, and you will empty it of what clouds it; then, you will find clear wisdom left behind.

7 You cannot see a reflection of yourself by looking into turbulent water. Only staring into still water can you see yourself. Stare into the stillness of your mind and begin to understand.

8 Do not fill your mind with your worries, fears, and distress. Empty your mind and find the wisdom that comes when you are not full of yourself.

9   Remember the parable of muddy water.

10   The empty space in the middle of a wheel makes the axle move. A container is useful because it is empty. A home is inviting because of the empty living space within. These physical objects are much valued, but it is the emptiness within them that actually makes them useful. If your mind is always full, how can it be useful? Empty your mind, still your thoughts, and be present, and you will find wisdom, peace, and purpose.

11   What benefit is a quiet neighborhood, if your emotions and thoughts are in an uproar? And what detriment is a neighborhood in commotion if you are at peace? If it is contentment you seek, know that it is your mind that creates it.

12   People seek retreats for themselves—in the country, mountains, and seashore. It is in your power, though, at any time to rest from your worries and petty thoughts. Constantly then, give to yourself this greatest of retreats and renew yourself.

13   Control your mind, shaken by wandering thoughts, so that it may at last come to rest and be steadfast and content with itself.

14   Do not let your thoughts mindlessly flit to and fro like a leaf blown in the wind. Instead, root yourself in the serenity of a peaceful, controlled mind.

15   Just like a fish taken out of the water and thrown on dry ground, your thoughts tremble and jump aimlessly. In its natural state, your mind is difficult to grasp, flighty, rushing wherever it wants, following every fleeting whim. You daze yourself with quivering, mean, little worries and overwhelm yourself with great fears. Still your thoughts, and tame your mind.

16   Remember the parable of the traveler.

17   If you work without resting, your body will wear down, and your work will remain unfinished. If you live without stilling and emptying your mind, your mind and spirit will wear down, and your life's work will remain unfinished.

8. Action and Engagement

1   Act when you know.

2   Wisdom is not mere passive learning and contemplation.

171

It is also action. How do you know you have found wisdom? It drives you to action.

3   Too often, the best lack all conviction, while the worst are full of passionate intensity. Realizing the limits of your knowledge is not an excuse for inaction. Humility does not mean passivity. Fools let their doubts paralyze them. Go forward, acting on the best knowledge and wisdom you have. Stand firm in the wisdom you have found, yet seeking even more. Be unrelenting and diligent in practicing virtue and laboring with hope as best you can, while still striving for improvement.

4   Be brave and not afraid to deal with heavy difficulties. Solve them and do great things that others fear to do. Be prudent too and anticipate challenges before they arise, when their solution is easy. Then, act to prevent the problem so that your small acts also accomplish greatness.

5   Make time to still your mind and remove yourself from the distractions of the outside world, but do not cut yourself off from the world, with an always-empty mind. Also use your mind for careful thoughts. Also fill your life with deliberate and diligent action. You must, if you are to practice virtue and labor with hope. Make time for stillness, but also fill your life with engagement.

6   It would be easy to find constant serenity and peace by cloistering yourself from the world and outside obligations. But, this is the way of the selfish fool. There is no wisdom in shirking your obligations. If everyone acted thus, it would be the end of humanity. Real wisdom comes when you learn how to find stillness and peace and live in the present moment even while busily engaged in doing good and laboring with hope.

7   When water is at rest, nothing is more still and soft, but when it moves, it reshapes the landscape and overcomes the hardest obstacles it encounters. Even a small trickle of water can carve a deep canyon. So let your periods of stillness and action be.

9. Gratitude

1   Be grateful.

2   Give thanks to God. The wise do this instinctively. Fools

lack this sense as much as a blind man lacks sight.

3   Cultivate gratitude within yourself. You have much for which you should be thankful. Make time every day to consider those things. Pray to God in gratitude for them.

4   It is too easy to let yourself become so accustomed to the good things in your life that you lose your appreciation for them. Do not think of yourself as entitled to them. Consider them unconditional gifts from God, received unsolicited and undeserved, and then cultivate a level of gratitude in proportion to your having received such generous gifts.

5   Think not about what you do not have, but about what you *do* have. Of these, think on the best ones. Reflect how eagerly you would seek them if you did not have them and then be grateful that you do have them. At the same time, however, take care that you do not let your gratitude for them lead you to overvalue them, so that you would be disturbed, angry, or disappointed if you should ever not have them.

6   Never forget the good there is in your life. Set aside time each day to dwell on everything for which you should be grateful. List them. Contemplate them. Pray in thanks for them. Be grateful.

7   The fool's life is empty of gratitude and full of fears.

10. Cosmology

1   Remember the parables of the poisoned arrow and the cure for the blind.

2   Do you have a soul? Is it eternal? Will it continue after death? Is there a heaven or hell? Will you be reborn again?

Do not let these questions, or the answers you believe about them, be a net trapping you in dogma and speculation.

Even so, find wisdom and peace in your contemplation of God and the universe; about the beginnings of all things; how the universe was molded by the Great Architect of the Universe; and the Mystery of death and what awaits beyond it.

3   Does chance drive and toss our affairs without method, leaving us to fend for ourselves, without God's intervention? Or, is

existence unity, order, and purpose ordained by God? It matters little. If it is all confused disorder, then you can create wise and virtuous order out of the chaos by following the Triple Path. If it is divinely ordered purpose, then unity and providence lead to the principles underlying the Triple Path. The Triple Path leads us to obey God cheerfully, but to submit to chance only defiantly, after remaking our destiny.

4   Do not overly concern yourself with how to gain rewards after this life, but instead concern yourself with living well right now. Seek wisdom, practice virtue, and labor with hope, and then leave the rest in God's hands.

5   We are all born as foreigners entering a strange land; or, as empty vessels waiting to be filled. We start without knowledge or wisdom, observing and copying those around us, or relying on what others give to fill us of what they have. Just as those who came before taught you, you must do the same for the next generation. Pass on to them what you have learned from others and what little you have been able to add to and improve of that learning. So doing, with each generation, we slowly grow in wisdom and knowledge, with a better understanding of who and what we are, and our place in the universe.

11. Duality and Free Will

1   Observe good opposed to evil, highness set against lowness, existence versus non-existence, beauty contrasted with ugliness. Each exists because of the other. Wisdom exists because there is foolishness. Virtue exists because there is evil. Hope exists because there is despair. This does not mean you should tolerate or seek out foolishness, evil, and lazy despair to know wisdom, virtue, and hope. You will experience foolishness, evil, and lazy despair as a natural part of life without ever seeking them out. And even if everyone were full of wisdom, virtue, and hope, their opposites would yet exist because each person would still be free to choose them.

2   The forces of opposition are not equally strong. Wisdom, virtue, and hope, if sought after and practiced with persistence,

will conquer foolishness, evil, and lazy despair. In the midst of foolishness, seek wisdom. Surrounded by evil, practice virtue. Encircled by lazy despair, labor with hope.

3   Chaos is the abhorrent lack of order, and tyranny is the obscene excess of it: both are evil extremes to be banished. The virtuous Golden Mean between them is responsible freedom.

4   Evil and good are real. They are black and white. But there are many shades of grey between them. Encircled by greys as you try to move forward on the Triple Path, it can be hard to judge whether you are moving toward the white or the black. Maintain a searching, far-reaching perspective to help you see forward far enough to understand whether the shade of grey you are heading toward is lighter or darker than the shade behind you. Brighter light also helps you see better to detect the difference between the greys around you. Thus, as you move along the Triple Path, also let the Source of all light and goodness shine on you. Only doing these two things can you tell whether you are moving forward or backward on the Triple Path.

5   You are free to choose. No matter the external influences, you are accountable for your acts. The conflict of evil in opposition to virtue is universal, from the history and development of the great civilizations all the way down to your life and that of each individual. Stand firm in your freedom to choose, and use that freedom to choose the Triple Path. Help others to do likewise, to bring a day when all people choose to seek wisdom, practice virtue, and labor with hope.

12. Transience

1   Everything flows. No one steps in the same river twice.

2   Time is like a river of passing events; strong is its sweeping current. As soon as something comes into view, it is swept away and another takes its place, then this too is swept away.

3   All things perish, everything passes; even the universe, immortal and enduring as it is, changes and never remains the same. Only God stands firm, perfectly unchanging.

4   All the good of mortals is mortal. But wisdom, virtue, and

hope do not perish; they are among the few immortal things that fall to us mortals.

5 The rising sun is the setting sun. The thing born is the thing dying.

6 The years pass, time goes on. Decay, growth, fullness, and emptiness end and then begin again.

7 The universe is transformation; your interpretation of reality is opinion; life is fleeting.

8 All that which the crowd gapes after ebbs and flows. Fortune gives us nothing that we can really own.

9 The paths of glory still lead to the grave.

10 Think not about anything, "I have lost it", but only, "I have given it back", for it all comes from the Giver of all things. Thus, what concern is it of yours by what instrumentality the Giver called for its return? So long as He may allow it to you, take care of it as something that is not yours but that has been entrusted to you.

11 Things naturally tend to break down, but hastened by the blindness and evil of men.

12 More than two thousand years ago, a list of the seven wonders of the world was made to catalog the grandest and most beautiful things built by man. Six have been completely destroyed; the seventh lies in ruins, its riches looted.

13 Look back over the past, with its changing empires that rose and fell, and you see the future too.

14 What is free from the risk of change? Neither earth, nor sky, nor the whole fabric of our universe, though it be controlled by the hand of God. Existence will not always preserve its present order; it will be thrown from its course in days to come.

15 Nothing takes place without change. Change is what created you. You cannot even be nourished unless the food you eat goes through a change. What you see today is already changing and will never exist again exactly as you see it. Amid the changes, though, some patterns repeat over and over again. Learn to recognize them. And never forget that there is still wisdom, virtue, and hope, always firm amid change's rhythms.

16 The past is rolled up into the present, and the present is always unrolling itself out into the future.

17 Your life is either past (and unchangeable) or future (and uncertain). Your present self exists for but a moment, transient and changing. Live in the present, but also be ever-mindful of the past and future. The past made you who you are now. Living for the future carries your existence forward. Learn from your past selves' mistakes and think on the well-being of your future selves to avoid present errors.

18 Who knows what the future brings? The race does not always go to the swift, neither the battle always to the strong. Time and chance happen to all men. You do not know when misfortune will come, just like the fishes that are caught in a net or the birds in a trap. Even following the Triple Path is not a guarantee of a favorable destiny. Unpredictable misfortune comes to all: to wise and foolish, virtuous and evil, laborer and lazy. The wise understand this and still follow the Triple Path.

19 You have no sure promise of anything during life, not even of life itself. Fate makes no guarantee of leading you into old age, but will let go of you whenever she sees fit. While you yet have time, then, follow the Triple Path.

20 Remember the parables of the sand in the hourglass and the ring of truth.

13. Death and Oblivion

1 He who is privileged to be born is destined to die.

2 What is death? Some say it is the end; others say it is merely a change. Why should you fear either possibility? If it is ceasing to exist, then it is the same as not having ever begun. And why would you shrink from changing into another state, if that which is you continues on?

3 In the universe, the whole earth is just a small point; how small a place in the world is your home and how few the number who live in it.

4 Contemplate the vast spread of time's abyss; consider the universe; and then contrast your short, small life with infinity.

5   You are dying every moment. With each day that passes, you lose a little more of your life. Counting even yesterday, all past time is lost time; the very day in which you read this is shared between yourself and death. Your final hour does not of itself bring the end, it merely completes the process. You reach death at that moment, but you have been a long time on the way.

6   Most people awoke on the day of their death with no inkling or expectation that that day would be their last. You do not know where death awaits you, so always be ready to face it.

7   When you lie down to sleep, say to yourself, "I may not wake again"; when you wake, "I may not go to sleep again"; when you leave your house, "I may not return"; and when you return, "I may never go out again".

8   Death hangs over you. Your days are but a breath. Your life is a vapor that appears for a little time and then vanishes away. Soon you shall lie down in the dust, and, if others seek you in the morning, you shall be gone. On that very day all your plans will perish. Do not distract yourself by the pursuit of wealth, power, pleasure, or praise. While you are alive and it is in your power, seek wisdom, practice virtue, and labor with hope. Let your faults die before you do, and leave behind instead a living legacy of the good you have built.

9   Life seems short to those who measure its length by pleasures, which are empty and can never deeply or permanently satisfy.

10   Are you offended by someone? Do you idolize another? Remember: shortly all of you will be dead and soon not even your names will be left behind. All things pass away and become a mere tale; complete oblivion soon buries them. With what then, should you occupy your time and effort? Focus your thoughts and actions on following the Triple Path rather than on finding offense, or on gossip, or on adulation, or on trivialities.

11   The deep flood of time rolls over all. Neither the infamy of the fool, nor the renown of the wise, will endure forever. The wise die just like fools. Eventually all will be forgotten and every-

one will depart into the same realm of silence. Yet, the wise still follow God and the Triple Path; to them, the need to do so is self-evident.

12 After you die, all who knew you will also die soon after, as will the next generation; then again also they who succeed them, until no one remembers even your name. But suppose your fame *was* immortal, what is that to you? What are fame and praise to the dead? Nothing. What are fame and praise to the living? Less than nothing, a distraction from the Triple Path.

13 See how soon everything is forgotten. Look at the chaos of infinite time on each side of the present and then understand the emptiness of applause, and the changeableness and lack of judgment in those who pretend to give praise. Finally, quiet your vanities at last. Think on the serenity and peace of following God and the Triple Path, and content yourself with this.

14 The universal law of death—which is part of the universal law of life—is that the man who works, the man who does great deeds, in the end dies as surely as the idler who encumbers the earth's surface; but he leaves behind him the great fact that he has done well. And the effect of his life may last long after he is gone, indeed long after even the very memory of him is no more.

15 That you will one day be forgotten in the far future is no argument for nihilism; it does not mean you are irrelevant. It means you are choosing the wrong frame of time to look at. What you do in the moment matters for the moment; so, do it well and wisely.

16 Remember the parable of the empty tomb.

14. Seeking and Becoming

1 Your life is not perfect; *you* are not perfect. Your current knowledge and wisdom, therefore, are not enough. Thus, always seek greater knowledge, greater truth, and greater wisdom.

2 Most of the great things now commonly known were at one time unfathomable, until someone courageously explored the unknown.

3 Seek what should be sought and avoid what should be avoided.

4   Seek that which is good for your soul, not what you want in the moment.

5   Keep seeking wisdom until you find it. When you find it, you may first become troubled, then you may be astonished. But, it will always transform you. And finally, you will realize you have found that which is most precious.

6   Let wisdom free you from a life chained down by the burdens of ignorance and foolishness.

7   Be as a strong tree, firmly rooted in the solid ground of wisdom, virtue, and hope, yet flexible enough to sway when the storm winds come, so that you do not break, and changing your direction of growth to always point toward the light.

8   You must defeat your personal foolishness twice. First, replace the ignorance with which you were born. Then, shed the folly you have learned.

9   Be less concerned about having the right answers than with asking the right questions.

10   Improve yourself by maintaining an attitude of honest self-appraisal: seek out different perspectives; relish discovering new ideas and new ways of looking at things; listen to the words of those with whom you disagree; consider criticisms and contrary arguments; and incorporate whatever you find that is of worth into your thoughts and actions.

11   Do not heed the false, selfish, contorted words of those seeking to justify foolishness, evil, and lazy despair.

12   The foolish look to so-called "teachers" who parrot back to them only what they already wanted to hear, who never challenge them to do more, to improve, or to carry a heavier load than they had been; the foolish elevate those whose words assuage their guilt and tell them there is nothing wrong with their foolishness. And thus they blind themselves to the abundant wisdom so easily available around them.

13   Be vigilant that you seek for the truth and not for self-serving lies. It is easy to confuse the two. No one is always right. Truth will sometimes highlight your failures and errors and show that

you had been doing wrong. If your quest for truth only ever confirms the righteousness of your current path or the correctness of your current beliefs, beware whether you have really been seeking truth. Following the truth often demands that you change. The most valuable truths you can discover are the ones that lead you to stretch and sacrifice to improve, or ones that force you to change your way of thinking or acting or being, for these are the truths that lead to wisdom.

14 You will become what you seek. Thus, seek out what you wish to become. Intelligence holds fast to intelligence; wisdom receives wisdom; truth embraces truth; virtue loves virtue; light clings to light; mercy has compassion on mercy and claims her own; justice continues its path and claims its own.

15 Masons chisel stone; carpenters work timber; blacksmiths forge iron; farmers till the soil and direct irrigation water; the wise transform themselves.

15. Self Knowledge and Self-Mastery

1 Know thyself.

2 Consider your ways. Examine and reflect, with your spirit searching diligently, asking yourself: "What am I? What have I done? What am I doing? What have I thought? What am I thinking? What have I desired? What do I now desire? Where am I going?"

3 To chart your course on the Triple Path, you must first know where you are. Where you start is less important than where you are heading. Once you know where you are, proceed forward on the Path with purpose. Otherwise, you could waste your entire life in random wanderings.

4 Not understanding what is in the mind of another person is seldom cause for unhappiness; real unhappiness comes from not understanding what is in your own mind.

5 When you know other people, you are clever; when you know yourself, you are illuminated. When you overcome others, you are strong; when you no longer need to overcome yourself, you are mighty.

6   Understand well your own peculiar traits of personality and regulate them properly. You do not need to try to make some other person's personality your own, for the more peculiarly your own that your personality is, the more likely it will fit you well.

7   Do not be too confident in your ability to rationally consider alternatives and come to a decision—it may be that you have already emotionally and subconsciously made a choice and are just using reason to justify it.

8   Know yourself, but do not dwell on yourself; love yourself, but also love others. Adopt the concerns of wisdom, virtue, and hope as your own.

9   No matter your external environment, no one may stop you from seeking wisdom, practicing virtue, and laboring with hope in whatever circumstance you find yourself. No one else is your master; your reaction to external influences comes from yourself.

10   If you have lost control and acted unwisely, quickly come back to yourself; do not continue out of step. It is always better to return as quickly as you can to the Triple Path than it is to continue reveling in your state of lost control on dark, hidden paths.

11   Never fool yourself into believing that finding pleasure is your ultimate goal or purpose in life. Thieves, tyrants, and murderers have all felt much pleasure.

12   Unless you keep pleasure within bounds, it will tend to carry you headlong into the abyss of sorrow.

13   Be neither someone who eats too much nor too little; neither someone who sleeps excessively nor insufficiently. Be moderate in your eating, recreation, working, sleeping, and waking.

14   Your habitual thoughts color the character of your being. Dye it then with such thoughts as these: "I will seek wisdom, practice virtue, and labor with hope".

16. Travel

1   If you try to find respite and rejuvenation only in vacations and retreats from home and work, you will still find something to distract your mind in every place. What a blessing it would be for you to wander instead away from your old self! No matter the

character of whatever place you go as a retreat, you will still bring to it your own. If you would escape your troubles, you do not need a new place, but a new character.

2   Your journey on the Triple Path is a voyage of your character, not a trip to some new physical place. Thus, focus not on much travel, but on much self-improvement.

3   What benefit has travel of itself given you? It cannot give you judgment or shake off your errors; it merely holds your attention for a moment by a certain novelty, as children pause to wonder at something unfamiliar. What travel will give is familiarity with other nations: the shape of new mountains, the emptiness of strange deserts, the powerful cascade of great waterfalls, the smells of foreign foods. It will not bring the stillness and expanse of wisdom, the strength of virtue, or the improvement that comes from laboring with hope.

4   Rather than mindless travel, you ought instead to focus on study and self-improvement. Cultivate not your knowledge of new places, but of those who are masters of wisdom and virtue. Indeed, so long as you are ignorant of what you should avoid or seek, or of what is necessary or superfluous, or of what is right or wrong, you will not be traveling, but merely wandering.

5   What is the benefit to you in hurrying to and fro in foreign travel? If you are traveling with your uncontrolled passions and desires, then you are also always followed by your afflictions. It is of no use to run to some other place to get away from them. That from which you are running is within you. Accordingly, reform your own self, get the burden off your own shoulders, and keep within safe limits the cravings which ought to be limited. Wipe out from your soul all trace of sin. It is medicine, not scenery, for which the sick man must go searching.

6   Where lies the truth, then? Can wisdom or virtue be picked up by wandering? No! Travel as far as you like, you can never establish yourself beyond the reach of desire, beyond the reach of bad temper, or beyond the reach of fear; had it been so, the human race would long ago have banded together and made a

pilgrimage to the spot.

7   When you spend too much time in traveling, you become a stranger to your own native country.

8   Spend all your time in foreign travel, and you will end by having many acquaintances, but no friends.

17. The Riches of Wisdom

1   He who is wealthy yet still foolish, unvirtuous, or in lazy despair is poor in the midst of his riches. Being poor and wise is better than being rich and foolish. Seek first for the riches of wisdom.

2   What shall it profit you if you gain the whole world and forfeit your own soul?

3   There is no end to the wealth of wisdom. When you have found some, share that abundance.

4   Be frugal with your money and material possessions but liberal in gathering and sharing the true wealth of wisdom.

5   Be modest in your apparel and possessions and instead carry the priceless treasures of wisdom in your soul. If you have material wealth, use it without arrogance, and live modestly—do not selfishly use it to satisfy your vanity, but instead to bless the future of your posterity and of humanity.

6   The foolish are idle, having eyes full of meaningless greediness, never coveting the riches that would truly satisfy them.

7   Remember the parable of the two young men.

18. Argumentation

1   Do not waste time in unprofitable discussions filled with sophistry and quibbling about words and insignificant things, tying knots and binding up words in double meanings, and then trying to untie them. Rather, proceed with your whole soul, cutting with wisdom, virtue, and hope through such knots that others make, lest things, as well as words, deceive you.

2   Seek out the truth, in a direct and simple manner. Do not bicker with others over petty details or insignificant distinctions, futilely trying to sharpen your wits on useless objects. How much better it is to follow the open and direct road, rather than to map out

for yourself a circuitous route which you must retrace with infinite trouble.

3   Sophistry and quibbling waste effort on that which is useless. Rush past all that is clever nonsense, and hurry on to that which will bring you real progression.

4   The hairsplitters and the nitpickers, with their illusory, misleading, and unfounded arguments are like jugglers, throwing the same things in circles over and over, never accomplishing anything of lasting import.

5   Leave off all the word-play of the philosophers and teachers of religion who reduce the most glorious subject to a matter of syllables, and lower and wear out the soul by teaching fragments; who by their teaching do their best to make philosophy and religion seem difficult, rather than great.

6   Instead of these absurd discussions, why not rather discuss something that is useful and wholesome to yourself, questing after the path that will take you toward seeking wisdom, practicing virtue, and laboring with hope?

7   Let your thoughts and conversations dwell on those things that exercise and sharpen the mind, occupying it honorably, that it will accomplish some sort of good.

8   Do not use false words to manipulate.

9   Consider that the person speaking may know something you do not. When someone opposes you, do not succumb to the temptation to distort, oversimplify, or parody his position into a straw man. If you truly understand his perspective, you will be able to find whatever value it might have. And if you still find it lacking in value, you can sharpen and strengthen your arguments against it.

10   When you find yourself headed down the path of fruitless argumentation, follow this practice: each person may speak for himself only after faithfully restating the other's ideas and feelings to that person's satisfaction. Thus, each person must enter the other's frame of reference, being in his mind and heart sufficiently to understand his thoughts and feelings. So doing, you may find

yourself revising your own thoughts—the argument's emotion dissipated, your differences reduced, and the remaining differences more rational and understandable. You also run the risk of being changed yourself, but equally face the great prospect of bringing yourself more into alignment with the truth.

19. Sages

1   Be not a follower of any person. Instead, be a follower of God and the Triple Path.

2   Place your ultimate trust in God, not in sages, leaders, or any other person.

3   Do not trust in some sage or leader to show you perfect wisdom. Emulate the good you see in others, but never be foolish enough to believe you will ever find someone worthy of perfect emulation. If you place blind and complete trust in others, then when you come to know their foolishness, you will either trick yourself into believing that their foolishness is wisdom, or you will become disillusioned and reject the good things you had learned from them.

4   Consult the wise.

5   In your seeking of wisdom, read the great works and spend your time in the company of all the best; no matter in what lands they may have lived or in what age. Consider the words of anyone you might consider a sage as if he was not aware of the full truth but was seeking it obstinately.

6   There is no hidden path. Truth and wisdom should not be hidden, indeed cannot. The Triple Path is there for all to see.

7   Share the wisdom you have with others and learn from their wisdom in turn. Help them overcome their personal foolishness and accept their help in overcoming your own.

References

1. Wisdom

1- Tao Te Ching 25:1, 32:1, and 62:1 (Steve Mitchell Translation), Tao Te Ching 73:3 (Byrn and Walker Translations). **2-** Tao Te Ching 29:1. **3-** 12 Rules, p. 188. **4-** Tao Te Ching 32:2. **5-** Tao Te Ching 64:2; D&C 93:12-13. **6-** Meditations 1:4; Lucilius 76:3; BoM, 1 Nephi 2:9; Dhammapada 258. **7-** Chuang Tzu, Sec. 2 (Discussion on Making All Things Equal), Watson translation, p. 32. **9-** Lucilius 64:6. **10-** Maps, pp. 26-7. **11-12-** Chuang Tzu, Sec. 17 (Autumn Floods), Watson translation, p. 98. **13-** Tao Te Ching 77:3-4. **14-** Chuang Tzu, Sec. 17 (Autumn Floods), Watson translation, p. 98. **15-** Tao Te Ching 64:4. **16-** Dhammapada 81. **17-** Ecclesiastes 10:10. **18-** Delphic maxim 6. **19-** Delphic maxim 23. **20-** Delphic maxim 7, 78. **21-** Meditations 1:16. **22-** Dhammapada 11-12. **23-** Maps, p. 11. **24-** William Harvey, *On Animal Generation*, 1651; John Dickinson, U.S. Constitutional Convention, 1787. **25-** BoM, Moroni 7:20. **26-** Jonathan Haidt, *The Happiness Hypothesis: Finding Modern Truth in Ancient Wisdom*, 2006, p. 242. **27-** Marcel Proust, *In Search of Lost Time: Volume 2, Within a Budding Grove*, 1919, Chapter 3. **28-** Ecclesiastes 9:17. **29-** Delphic maxims 26 and 62. **30-** James 2:14-18, 3:13.

2. Foolishness and Ignorance

1- BoM, Mosiah 8:20. **2-** Horace, *Epistles*, I:1, line 41. **3-** Chuang Tzu, Sec. 20 (The Mountain Tree), Watson translation; BoM, 2 Nephi 16:9; Isaiah 6:9. **4** Lucilius 37:4. **5-** English Proverb. **7-** Attributed to Mark Twain. **8-** Hesiod, *Theogony*, line 27 (Norton Anthology, Third Edition, Vol. A, p. 40). **9-** Lucilius 94:25. **10-** Dhammapada 66, 69. **12-** Euripides, *The Bacchae*, 405 BC, 478-9. **13-** Bhagavad Gita 14:8. **14-** Chuang Tzu, Sec. 19 (Mastering Life), Watson translation, pp. 192-30. **16-** Ecclesiastes 7:5. **17-** Ecclesiastes 2:14. **18-** Tao Te Ching 41:1. **19-** Ecclesiastes 9:18. **20-** Thomas 74. **22-** Ecclesiastes 10:15.

3. Truth

1- John 8:32. **2-** Jordan Peterson, "Freedom of Speech: Not Just

WISDOM

Another Value", talk on May 13, 2017. **3-** Delphic maxim 121. **4-** Jordan Peterson, "Freedom of Speech: Not Just Another Value", talk on May 13, 2017. **5-** Lucilius 12:9. **6-** Sallust, *On the Gods and the Cosmos*, ca. 360. **7-** Maps, pp. 13-14. **8-** Maps, p. 15. **9-** Jordan Peterson. **11-** Lucilius 76:22. **12-** Jordan Peterson, Podcast Season 2, 47, 47:00. **15-** C.S. Lewis, *Mere Christianity*, 1952. **16-** Leo Tolstoy, "The First Step" in *Essays and Letters*, 1909, pp. 82-91; Mary Eberstadt, "A Time of Reckoning", *The Weekly Standard*, June 15, 2018. **17-** 12 Rules, p. 307. **18-** 12 Rules, p. 263. **19-** 12 Rules, p. 313. **20-** Dan Davies, 108573518762776451: The D-Squared Digest One Minute MBA, *D-Squared Digest*, May 27, 2004. **21-** 12 Rules pp. 244-45. **22-** 12 Rules, p. 248. **25-** Jordan Peterson, quoting Nietzsche, http://www.c2cjournal.ca/2016/12/we reteaching-university-students-lies-an-interview-with-dr-jordan-peter son. **26-** Jordan Peterson, "Freedom of Speech: Not Just Another Value", talk on May 13, 2017. **27-** Ludwig Wittgenstein, *Philosophical Investigations*, 1968, p. 50.

4. The Unknowable

1- Tao Te Ching 14:1, 21 (Mitchell Translation). **2-** Chuang Tzu, Sec. 17 (Autumn Floods), Watson translation, p. 97; D&C 12:8, comments from BK. **3-** Maps, p. 49. **4-** 1 Corinthians 13:12. **5-** Thomas 5. **6-** Chuang Tzu, Sec. 17 (Autumn Floods), Watson translation, p. 97, comments from BK. **7-** Chuang Tzu, Sec. 17 (Autumn Floods), Watson translation, p. 97. **8-** Chuang Tzu, Sec. 1 (Free and Easy Wandering), Watson translation, p. 27; Thomas 34. **9-** Chuang Tzu, Sec. 17 (Autumn Floods), Watson translation, p. 99. **10-** Cicero, *De Officiis*, 1:18. **11-** Tao Te Ching 71:1-2 (Legge, Beck, and LeFargue translations). **12-** Chuang Tzu, Sec. 24 (Hsu Wu-Kuei), Watson translation.

5. Humility

2- 12 Rules, p. 230. **3-** Attributed to Leo Buscaglia. **4-** D&C 23:1. **5-** 12 Rules, pp. 241-42, 251-52. **6-** Lucilius 103:5. **7-** Dhammapada 143-144. **8-** Lucilius 50:3-4. **9-** Chuang Tzu, Sec. 5 (The Sign of Virtue Complete), Watson translation, p. 66. **10-** 12 Rules, pp. 244-47, 388-90. **11-** Bhagavad Gita 12:18; Dhammapada 228. **12-**

188

Edward J. Watts, *The Final Pagan Generation*, 2015, p. 117. **13-** Romans 12:16. **14-** BoM, Ether 12:27.

6. Prayer

1- Lucilius 10:1. **2-** Delphic maxim 52. **3-** D&C 19:38, 31:12. **5-** 12 Rules, p. 380, 388-90. **6-** Lucilius 31:2. **7-** D&C 25:12-13.

7. Meditation and Mindfulness

1- Psalm 4:2-4. **2-** Anguttara Nikaya 4:94. **3-** Dhammapada 88; Chuang Tzu, Sec. 3 (Secret of Caring for Life), Watson translation, p. 46. **4-** John Rogers, *The Nature and Necessity of Repentance*, 1728, pp. 52-53. **5-** Tao Te Ching 15:2, 26:1, 43:1. **6-** Tao Te Ching 8:2, 15:3, 22 (Mitchell Translation). **7-** Chuang Tzu, Sec. 5 (The Sign of Virtue Complete), Watson translation, p. 65. **8-** Tao Te Ching 15:4; Dhammapada 82, 205. **10-** Tao Te Ching 11:1. **11-** Lucilius 55:8, 56:5. **12-** Meditations 4:3. **13-** Lucilius 32:5. **14-** Dhammapada 82, 205. **15-** Dhammapada 34-35. **16-** Chuang Tzu, Sec. 31 (The Old Fisherman), Watson translation. **17-** Chuang Tzu, Sec. 15 (Constrained in Will), Watson translation.

8. Action and Engagement

1- Delphic Maxim 88. **2-** 1 Peter 1:13. **3-** William Butler Yeats, "The Second Coming", 1919; Bertrand Russell, Mortals and Others, ("The fundamental cause of the trouble is that in the modern world the stupid are cocksure while the intelligent are full of doubt."). **4-** Pittacus (as quoted in Diogenes Laertius, Lives of the Great Philosophers, 77-78); Tao Te Ching 63:2. **7-** Tao Te Ching 43:1.

9. Gratitude

1- Delphic Maxim 106. **2-** Psalm 92:1, 6. **3-** Sonja Lyubomirsky, *et. al.*, "Pursuing happiness: The architecture of sustainable change", *Review of General Psychology*, Vol. 9, No. 2, 2005, pp. 111-31; Robert A. Emmons and Michael E. McCullough, "Counting blessings versus burdens: An experimental investigation of gratitude and subjective well-being in daily life", *Journal of Personality and Social Psychology*, Vol. 84, No. 2, February 2003, pp 377-89; Jeffrey J. Froh, *et. al.*, "Counting blessings in early adolescents: An experimental study of gratitude and subjective well-being",

Journal of School Psychology, Vol, 46, 2008, pp. 213-233. **5**- Meditations 7:27. **7**- Lucilius 15:9 (quoting Epicurus).

10. Cosmology

1- Cula Malunkyovada Sutta, The Shorter Instructions to Malunkya. **2**- Lucilius 65:19-20; Brahmajala Sutta 72; Majjhima Nikaya 63, 72. **3**- Meditations 6:10; Lucilius 16:5. **4**- Dhammapada 15-18.

11. Duality and Free Will

1- BoM, 2 Nephi 2:11; Tao Te Ching 2:1-2. **3**- Inspired by Jordan Peterson. **5**- D&C 29:35-42; BoM, Mosiah 23:13.

12. Transience

1- Heraclitus, as quoted in Plato, Cratylus, 402a. **2**- Meditations 4:43. **3**- Denis Diderot, *Salon of 1767*; Lucilius 58:24. **4**- Lucilius 98:9 (quoting Metrodorus). **5**- Chuang Tzu, Sec. 33 (The World), Watson translation (this is one of Hui Shui's ten theses). **6**- Chuang Tzu, Sec. 17 (Autumn Floods), Watson translation, p. 103. **7**- Meditations 4:3. **8**- Lucilius 72:7. **9**- Thomas Gray, *Elegy Written in a Country Churchyard*, line 36. **10**- Enchiridion 11. **11**- Jordan Peterson, Podcast Season 2, 30, 29:30. **13**- Meditations 7: 49. **14**- Lucilius 71:12. **15**- Meditations 7:18. **16**- Jordan Peterson, Podcast 33: Jacob's Ladder Biblical Lecture, 36:30:00. **17**- Meditations 3:10. **18**- Ecclesiastes 9:11-12, 10:14. **19**- Lucilius 99:22.

13. Death and Oblivion

1- Lucilius 99:8. **2**- Lucilius 65:24. **3**- Meditations 4:3. **4**- Lucilius 99:10. **5**- Lucilius 24:19-20. **6**- Lucilius 26:7; "As Overdose Deaths Pile Up, A Medical Examiner Quits the Morgue", *New York Times*, October 7, 2017. **7**- Lucilius 49:10; John Rogers, *The Nature and Necessity of Repentance*, 1728, pp. 49. **8**- Meditations 4: 17; John Rogers, *The Nature and Necessity of Repentance*, 1728, pp. 69; Lucilius 27:2; Job 7:16-17, 21; Psalm 146:4; Dhammapada 287. **9**- Lucilius 78:27. **10**- Meditations 4:6, 4:33. **11**- Lucilius 21: 5; Ecclesiastes 2:16. **12**- Meditations 4:19. **13**- Meditations 4:3. **14**- Theodore Roosevelt, National Duties—Address at Minnesota State Fair, September 2, 1901, p. 9. **15**- 12 Rules, p. 116.

14. Seeking and Becoming

1- 12 Rules, pp. 287-88. **2**- Maps, p. 49. **3**- Lucilius 66:6. **4**- 12

Rules, p. 106. **5-** Thomas 2. **7-** 12 Rules, pp. 287-89. **10-** BoM, Helaman 13:26-28. **12-** BoM, Helaman 13:26-28. **13-** Joseph Smith, Lectures on Faith 6:7. **14-** D&C 88:40. **15-** Dhammapada 80.

15. Self Knowledge and Self-Mastery
1- Delphic maxim 8. **2-** John Rogers, *The Nature and Necessity of Repentance*, 1728, pp. 23-24, 50, 52, 53. **3-** 12 Rules, pp. 95-96, 123, 315. **4-** Meditations 2:8. **5-** Tao Te Ching 33:1. **6-** Cicero, *De Officiis*, 1:113. **8-**Tao Te Ching 72:3 (Walker). **9-** Meditations 2:9. **10-** Meditations 6:11. **11-** Meditations 6:34. **12-** Lucilius 23:6. **13-** Bhagavad Gita 6:16-17. **14-** Meditations 5:16.

16. Travel
1- Lucilius 104:7-8. **2-6-** Lucilius 103:13-21. **7-** Rene Descartes, *Discourse on the Method*, 1637, Part I. **8-** Lucilius 2:2.

17. The Riches of Wisdom
1- D&C 11:7; Ecclesiastes 4:13; Lucilius 74:4. **2-** Mark 8:36. **3-** Tao Te Ching 77:3-4. **4-** Tao Te Ching 67:2-3. **5-** Meditations 1:16; Tao Te Ching 70:3 (World translation). **6-** D&C 68:31. **7-** Thomas 63.

18. Argumentation
1- Lucilius 45:4-5, 113:1. **2-** Lucilius 102:20, 113:1, 26. **3-** Lucilius 117:26, 30. **4-** Lucilius 102:20, 113:1, 26. **5-** Lucilius 71:6. **6-** Lucilius 102:20, 113:1, 26. **7-** Lucilius 124:21. **8-** 12 Rules, 241-42. **9-** 12 Rules, 279-80, 289. **10-** Carl Rogers, "Communication: Its Blocking and Its Facilitation, *Northwestern University Information*, 1952, 20:25. pp. 9-15.

19. Sages
2- Psalm 118:8-9. **4-** Delphic maxim 53. **5-** Lucilius 45:4, 62:2. **6-** Greg Cochran, "The Advent of Cholera", *West Hunter Blog*, October 17, 2014.

Virtue

Contents

1. Virtue

1 Seek not just to live, but to live well, practicing virtue.

2 Let your commitment to practicing virtue be like a tall mountain: firm, steadfast, and immovable.

3 Never let yourself tire of acting with virtue.

4 What is virtue? It is doing good and desiring good—doing the right thing for the right reasons. It is avoiding evil acts and intentions. It is honoring and fulfilling your duties, especially to those closest to you. It is following the Golden Rule.

5 Universal moral absolutes exist. Individuals and societies that reject them condemn themselves to misery and breakdown.

6 Just because there is some disagreement about what is right does not mean there are no moral absolutes. Consider the parable of the fair jar: no one in the crowd knew how many candies were in the jar, and each had guessed a different number. Yet even so, the same, unchanging number of candies was always still in the jar. And the collective wisdom of all the individuals, who were diligently

and in good faith trying to find the correct answer, came close to getting things exactly right.

7   How may you practice virtue and avoid evil? There are too many ways to do good, and evil, for anyone to list them all. Develop good judgment. Cultivate a powerful and consistent character so that it becomes easy to do good deeds and hard to do bad ones. Learn from your mistakes. So doing, you will understand what is right, and freely choose good actions without being told what to do by others.

8   Many virtues are to be found in a Golden Mean that lies between excess and deficiency, with either extreme destroying the virtue. Take, for example, the virtue of courage: cowardice is its deficiency, and recklessness its excess.

9   Remember the parable of Icarus.

10   You practice virtue most fully when you engage in virtuous actions knowingly, chosen for their own sakes, and chosen not on a whim, but according to a stable disposition.

11   The wisdom of the past and of tradition give us general rules about what ought to be done or left undone. But as to what you are to do in the moment, you must take counsel in the presence of the actual situation. Thus, be present and vigilant, and wise, that you not choose wrongly. And watch carefully that you not rationalize away the wisdom of the past and of tradition to fool yourself into thinking your situation to be some special case exempting you from traditional standards. It is far more likely you are trying to rationalize and justify what ought not to be done than that an exception truly exists.

12   Rules are necessary to give you structure and discipline, but rules conflict, and they do not always apply. There must be an ethic underlying the rules you follow, and you should have more respect for the ethic: seek wisdom, practice virtue, labor with hope, tell the truth, and orient yourself toward the good—an alliance with God.

13   You are free to choose good or evil. Let yourself always delight in doing good. Be anxiously engaged in a good cause, and

do much good of your own free will.

14 Just speaking about good deeds is not enough. Pretending to act with virtue is useless. You cannot fool your soul.

15 You will not find virtue written in ink on a page, but by showing it in your actions, thoughts, speech, and character. Thus, act with self-control in body, mind, and spirit.

16 Stay devoted to the ideals of your best moments, even when those moments have passed and you feel uninspired. Doing good, or seeing others do good, can inspire and elevate anyone—virtuous or not—with a desire to do good. But no one keeps such feelings forever. The real measure of your virtue is how you act when you do not feel inspired to do good, or when you desire to do evil. Virtue does not mean having perfect desires, but having the strength of character to continue doing good even when your desires are imperfect.

17 Since you know that your desires are imperfect, put yourself in situations that stimulate you to do good. You will avoid evil and do good most easily not by resisting temptation, but by avoiding situations where you are most likely to be tempted.

18 Feel the charming beauty of virtue, and shun the foulness and deformity of evil.

19 Seek most of all to understand and practice the four cardinal virtues, which subsume almost all other virtues: prudence, justice, temperance, and fortitude.

20 Smooth and easy is the road that leads down to wickedness, in all its variety and abundance. Long and steep is the path to virtue, and rough at first; but when you reach the top, the road becomes easy, the air smells sweet, and the vistas are glorious to behold.

21 These things lead away from virtue and toward evil: wealth without work; pleasure without conscience; knowledge without character; commerce without ethics; science without humanity; religion without sacrifice; morality without faith; politics without principle; rights without responsibilities; actions without consequences; freedom without tradition; and confidence without God.

22 Praise virtue.

23 What good is it if you say you have virtue, but you do not have wisdom and hope? Is virtue enough? No! You need all three. You cannot really practice virtue without also seeking wisdom and laboring with hope.

2. Evil

1 Despise evil. Shun evil.

2 Evil is arrogance, spite, deceit, cruelty, conscious malevolence, love of destruction, and hatred of God, man, and being itself.

3 Evil tries to infiltrate that which is most good. Be vigilant, therefore, against evil, lest the best things end up becoming tools for evil.

4 It is rare for those doing evil to recognize their evil. They justify themselves in their own eyes, trying to make their evil seem good.

5 A desire for revenge against God is the root motivation for many evil deeds, even among those who claim not to believe in Him.

6 There are many who do terrible evil by fooling themselves into believing that God approved or commanded it. No one's words—not even those of the highest prophet or king—has magic to turn evil into good. And you are accountable for all the evil you commit, even if someone claiming authority commanded it or preached that it was good.

7 The evil are ashamed of what they should not be and are not ashamed of what they should be. They fear when they ought not to fear, and do not fear when they ought to. They forbid when there is nothing to be forbidden, and do not forbid when there is something that should be.

8 It is the motto of the decadent, and also of the evil, to enjoy what is unusual, and not only to depart from that which is right, but to leave it as far behind as possible, and finally even to take a stand in opposition to it.

9 When others do evil to you, do not let it lead you to ni-

hilism and to doing evil yourself. Instead, learn the wrongness of that evil and let it motivate you to fight it, still practicing virtue.

10   Resentment, arrogance, and deceit lie at the heart of much evil.

11   Many become evil by pursuing and avoiding pleasures and pains they ought not, or when they ought not, or as they ought not. If you deal with pleasure and pain as you ought, you will be able to practice much virtue and avoid doing much evil.

12   If you continue to choose evil, it will consume you from the inside out, like termites destroying a beautiful house.

13   Do not let evil overcome you; instead, overcome evil with good. Do not let lies overcome you; instead, overcome lies with truth.

14   It may be impossible to prove whether heaven exists, but there is no doubt that hell on Earth is possible. If you do not want hell to manifest itself in the world, you must understand your role in producing it and then act with courage and virtue to stop it.

15   The line between good and evil cuts through the heart of every human being.

16   If you gaze for long into an abyss, the abyss gazes also into you.

17   Guard against complacency. You are human; therefore, be not so foolish as to haughtily think that anything human could be alien to you.

18   Beware of pridefully criticizing the evil of others, putting yourself above doing such things. All those horrible things were done by human beings. You, too, are a human being. You cannot conquer the evil in your heart, and thus cannot practice a fullness of virtue, until you understand how you could succumb to the terrible evils of the world—until you understand that there is evil in your heart and that you are capable of committing it.

19   Consider the terrible evils done in the world. Then, remember that people like you played a roll in them and that people like you were thus responsible for those evils. Look in yourself for the motivations that drove people like Hitler, Mao, Stalin, and

their followers, because those motivations are there inside you too. View how you could become the perpetrator of archetypal evil, then conquer the evils in yourself that beckon you onto that path.

20 Be not blinded by the evil of those around you.

21 Evil people fight against virtue when they encounter it.

22 When you give evil an entrance into your soul, soon, you begin to think or speak thus, "Wisdom, virtue, hope, and God? Focusing on these is not living. They are but jargon and empty words. The only way to be happy is to do what thou wilt. To eat, drink, be merry, and spend your money is the only real life, the only way to remind yourself you are mortal. Our days flow on, and life—which we cannot restore—hastens away from us. Why hesitate? This life of ours will not always admit pleasures; enjoy it while you can. What profit lies in practicing virtue? Get ahead of death, and let anything that death will filch from you be squandered now upon yourself." Shun these voices just as Ulysses shunned the Sirens. He would not sail past them until he was lashed to the mast. And these words are no less potent; they lure people from country, parents, friends, spouse, children, and virtuous ways. They wreck whoever heeds them upon a life of baseness. How much better it is to follow a straight course and attain a goal far more glorious and honorable.

23 The follower of evil is proud and cares not for God. He tells himself, "There is no God. I will never suffer the consequences of my evil." His mouth is full of cursing, deceit, vanity, and fraud. He secretly lies in wait, like a predator, to seize and destroy the virtuous. He thinks, "God has forgotten, he hides his face and will never see what I have done. I will never be held to account".

24 Remember the parable of the ring of Gyges.

3. The Adversary

1 Renounce the adversary and all his works.

2 Resist the adversary, who is the enemy of mankind, that he flee from you.

3 Be disciplined and vigilant, resisting evil with steadfastness, for your adversary goes about as a roaring lion seeking whom he

may devour.

4　Foolish and accursed is he who plays with the adversary. You cannot drink from God's cup and the cup of the adversary too.

5　The adversary always tries to assume a pleasing shape, yet all the while he is devising as many ways as he can to deface and obscure God's glory.

6　The adversary, too, can cite scripture for his purpose.

7　O how you have fallen from heaven, Lucifer, son of the morning! You dared to scowl against your Maker. You tried to exalt yourself because of your beauty; you corrupted your wisdom because of your brightness; you profaned the sanctuaries; and you did lay low the nations. And so, you will be cut down.

You said in your heart, "I will ascend into heaven, I will exalt my throne above the stars of God; and I will sit over all; I will make myself like the Most High."

Yet, you shall be brought down to hell, to the uttermost parts of the pit. A fire shall come from within yourself and devour you.

Then, they that see you shall gaze narrowly at you and consider you, saying, "Is this he who made the earth to tremble, who did shake kingdoms, who made the world as a desert, and overthrew the cities?"

The great men of each nation sleep in glory, each one in his own tomb, but you are cast out, like the carcasses of vermin.

The spawn of evil shall never be honored.

4. The Zealots

1　Beware the zealots, who are turbulent fanatics, sneering agitators, nihilistic cynics—they who triumphantly celebrate evil, who scoff and nag, mock and scold, quibble and criticize.

2　Oppose at every turn the zealots, who are corrupt and abominable in their doings, with mouths full of cursing and bitterness and hands swift to do violence and shed blood. Destruction, unhappiness, and dissembling is in their hearts, and the way of peace have they rejected. Thinking themselves wise, they have not even knowledge. They work mischief and delight in consuming

God's people as if they were candy. They call not upon God, having no fear of Him before their eyes.

3   O, how wicked are the zealots, who speak lies and vanity, with flattering lips and a double heart; who exult in making this generation into one where the wicked walk on every side and the vilest men and women are exalted.

4   Fight at every turn the zealots, who seek to dominate by disintegrating and destroying, who fill the air with accusation and humiliation and use violence to muffle and suppress the voices of those with whom they disagree.

5   The zealots are blind leaders of the blind. And when the blind lead the blind, both will fall into some pit.

6   The zealots preach that having faith in what they think they already know will save. What fools! It is having faith in that which is beyond your understanding that will allow you to reform and transform yourself into something greater, impelling you to sacrifice your current self for the greater self beckoning to you in the future.

7   The zealots claim they can release and appease you by taking away God, family, and tradition. What fools! They reject the very things that regenerate, transform, and liberate.

8   The zealots are blind to the spiritual, thus insisting on mundane and profane remedies for everything. When their material remedies for spiritual problems inevitably fail, the zealots lack the capacity to understand why and instead foolishly demand that what is already failing be forced ever more aggressively.

9   Beware the zealots, who come to you in sheep's clothing, but inwardly are ravening wolves.

10   Woe to the zealots, who seek to destroy the foundations of society, tearing up good and wise traditions that have proved themselves firm and steady against the tremors and upheavals of hard experience, replacing them with empty holes containing only the idle fancies of daydreamers.

11   Woe to the zealots, who fight happiness and light and joy and meaning, who mock following tradition as the worship of ashes, never understanding that it is the preservation of fire.

12 Woe to the zealots, who brag about their righteousness while flaunting their practice of terrible wickedness.

13 Woe to the zealots, who call evil good, and good evil; who put darkness for light, and light for darkness; bitter for sweet, and sweet for bitter.

14 Woe to the zealots, who turn back repeatedly to foolishness and evil, as a dog returns to his own vomit or a washed pig goes back to wallow in the mud.

15 Woe to the zealots, who in their unrighteousness and ungodliness seek to suppress the truth.

16 Woe to the zealots, who claim to be wise, yet speak only dark foolishness.

17 Woe to the zealots, who eagerly abandon the truth about God for assuaging lies, who discard reverence for the divine so they can set up their lusts as idols.

18 Woe to the zealots, who are like a dog in the oxen's manger. Neither does the dog eat, nor does he let the oxen eat.

19 Woe to the zealots, who load the people with terrible burdens, yet do not lift a finger to ease them.

20 Woe to the zealots who create heavy lies to deceive the people and weigh them down, sinking them into the depths of evil.

21 Woe to the zealots, who claim to speak truth to power, but are really cowards who hate the truth and only ever speak power to truth.

22 Woe to the zealots, who shout their pretended ideals merely to justify their resentments and hatreds, who claim to care about the poor but really just hate the rich, who feign concern for the downtrodden, but just detest those who are successful.

23 Woe to the zealots, who pretend to embody human compassion, yet show none to their enemies, while still screaming their demands that their enemies show compassion for them.

24 Woe to the zealots who, lying to themselves and the world, preach tolerance as the highest virtue, yet embrace an abundance of evils and neglect the weightier matters: morality and loyalty, and wisdom, virtue, and hope.

25 Woe to the zealots, blind guides who strain at a gnat, but swallow a camel.

26 Woe to the zealots, hypocrites, who claim to protect the weak, yet defend and celebrate the murdering of babies.

27 Woe to the zealots who feel guilty consciences, yet refuse to repent and instead seek to corrupt others like unto themselves, as if bringing more people into the misery of sin could turn their evil into goodness.

28 Woe to the zealots, who spare no expense and make every effort to spread their evil message to gain even a single convert, yet make the new convert twice as much a child of hell as themselves.

29 Woe to the zealots, who devour innocent youth and excrete darkness.

30 Woe to the zealots who do all their deeds to be seen of others, who relish appearing morally superior, yet all the while are working to advance evil and fight goodness.

31 Woe to the zealots who claim their doctrines offer comfort, even though they really bring shame and darkness. They are like blankets covered with the germs of a deadly plague—the people who go to them for warmth only realize too late they have exposed themselves to death.

32 Woe to the zealots, who have hidden and destroyed the keys of knowledge, locking the people away from the presence of God, yet refusing to enter themselves, seeking only to hinder those trying to enter.

33 Woe to the zealots, that brood of vipers, who turn the goodness of our society into hell.

5. Sin and Repentance

1 Repent and turn yourself from all your transgressions, so that iniquity shall not be your ruin.

2 Beware the seven deadly sins: lust, gluttony, greed, sloth, wrath, envy, and pride. Subdue them by practicing these seven corresponding virtues: chastity, temperance, charity, diligence, patience, gratitude, and humility.

3 Do not content yourself only with negatives, focused just

on forsaking that which is evil. Cleave also to that which is good.

4　You commit sin not only by doing wrong, but also by failing to do what you should. Do not underestimate how destructive these sins of omission can be.

5　Bring forth truth from your inmost being—recognize and acknowledge your faults and sins, and then repent.

6　When you say you have no sin, you deceive yourself, and the truth is not in you; therefore, turn to God, confess your sins, repent, and reform yourself, that you may be forgiven and cleansed from all unrighteousness.

7　If you would sincerely repent, you must seriously consider your own works: not God's ways towards you, but your ways towards Him.

8　To repent, you must pass through a change of mind. Transform your thoughts and opinions of things. Come to yourself and be wise again.

9　When you are repentant, your spirit is in anguish. Your heart and soul are troubled by your sins. Your iniquities are as a heavy burden upon you. Repentance makes a new, clean heart and right spirit in you.

10　It is not easy to rid the memory of a catching tune; it stays with us, lasts on, and comes back from time to time. Similarly, depraved speech, images, and media also stick in your mind long after you have heard or seen them. Thus, close your ears, eyes, and mind against evil as soon as you encounter it; when it has gained an entrance and its idea is admitted and in your mind, it becomes more shameless.

11　When you sin, you fall into a pit you yourself dug, throwing yourself into your own mischief and misery.

12　Even if a sin is never discovered and you escape external punishment, you will never escape two consequences of sin: the first and worst is to have committed the sin and stained your soul; the second is the fear that your sin will someday be discovered, or if you are so past feeling that you fear not the discovery or your sins or even revel in them, then the second consequence is that you have so completely left the Triple Path that you have placed yourself firmly on the road to ruin and perdition.

6. Virtue Comes From Within

1   Virtue cannot be imposed by outside compulsion or rules. It comes from an internal commitment to doing good.

Not many rules are needed to govern the virtuous—only the bare essentials to ensure an organized society. The virtuous comply with them not from fear of punishment, but out of their own internal desire to practice virtue.

The unvirtuous are always looking for exceptions to rules and for justifications why they should not apply. They follow rules only when convenient or when afraid they might be caught disobeying. A community full of the unvirtuous is thus on a path toward destruction.

2   Sow virtuous acts, and you will reap a virtuous character and the sweet consequences of doing good. If you sow sparingly, you will reap sparingly, if you sow bountifully, you will reap bountifully.

3   The capacity of the human mind for self-deception is nearly limitless, as is its capacity to justify and rationalize evil and foolishness. Watch that you do not lead yourself into error or evil.

4   Make of yourself the sort of person in whose company you would not dare to sin. While you are still making yourself into this sort of person, solitude may prompt you to all kinds of evil. Thus, always act as you would if some good companion were there looking on. But also seek to develop your character so that, eventually, you abstain from evil actions not because you are ashamed of sinning or of being discovered, but because you desire to do good.

5   If you seek privacy, do it so that you may live more safely and accomplish your work more effectively, not that you may sin more secretly. If your deeds are honorable, do not worry whether everybody know them; if they are base, what does it matter if no one know them, so long as you yourself do? You cannot fool your soul.

6   Some rituals, traditions, and norms develop to allow

groups to differentiate themselves and to let individuals signal their allegiance to, and membership in, their group. Such practices are important. You should honor those of the Congregation of the Faithful of the Triple Path and treat them with solemnity and complete commitment, but if you place the greater weight on them, above basic principles of goodness and morality, you will never understand true virtue.

7. The Golden Rule and Empathy

1   Do to others as you would have them do to you, including doing to others, where possible and moral, what they would want done to them. Cease so doing to others who fail to reciprocate. Do not do to others that which is harmful to them, that which wrongfully interferes with their autonomy or accountability, that which would harm third parties or the community, or that which would cause you to act immorally.

2   Treat each person (including yourself) never only as a means to an end, but also always as an end in themself.

3   If you treat others according to the Golden Rule, and they do not reciprocate, avoid future dealings with them. You do not have an unending obligation of altruism toward those who do not return your kindness or who would do you harm.

4   Seek to understand others. Examine situations from their perspective; be in their minds.

5   Mourn with those who mourn. Comfort those who need comfort. Be quick to listen and slow to speak.

6   Make it your goal that you act in ways that minimize unnecessary pain and suffering.

7   Feelings of empathy and compassion are not perfect guides to virtuous action. The proper, virtuous course is not necessarily that which makes you feel good in the moment.

8   Do not do for others what they can do for themselves, even if you feel moved by compassion to do so.

8. Love

1   Love binds things together in harmony.

2   Loving everyone equally is no different from loving no

one at all.

3 Love means nothing if it does not mean loving some people more than others. Let your love for those close to you be strongest and firmest.

4 No man loves his family and his native land because they are special or unique or great; he loves them because they are his own.

5 Love your neighbor.

6 Do not love merely in word or speech, but in truth and action.

7 Love is patient; love is kind; love is not envious or boastful or arrogant or rude. It does not insist on its own way; it is not irritable or resentful; it does not rejoice in wrongdoing, but rejoices in truth and in wisdom, virtue, and hope. It bears all things, believes all things, hopes all things, endures all things.

8 Let your love be genuine, constant, and never-ending. With this love, it is easy to overlook others' faults, and when others feel your love for them, it is easy for them to overlook your faults.

9 When there is love among a people, they bear each other's burdens.

9. Anger and Hatred

1 Live free of a character that is quick to anger, wrath, malice, and speaking slander and abusive language.

2 There are few weaknesses more destructive than being easily provoked to anger and hatred.

3 Hate evil. Hate foolishness. Avoid hating people.

4 Be slow to anger. Acting out of anger often leads to sin.

5 Among even those who mistreat you, choose to free yourself from self-destructive anger.

6 Despise strife.

7 Do not respond to the evil of others with evil of your own.

8 There is also righteous anger. Sometimes the most virtuous course requires it.

9 Righteous anger means anger for the right reasons, against

the right people or things, in the right way, and for the right length of time.

10 He who is not angry when he has just cause to be also sins. Unreasonable patience is the hotbed of many vices: it fosters negligence and incites not only the wicked but even the good to do wrong.

11 Righteous anger motivates you to fight chaos and tyranny, speak truth, and move forward in times of strife, uncertainty, and danger.

12 Sometimes you have to make enemies, but do not make unnecessary ones.

10. Justice

1 The foundation of justice is good faith and truth and fidelity to promises and agreements.

2 Practice what is just.

3 Be overcome by justice.

4 Make just judgments. Be impartial. Judge incorruptibly.

5 Obey the law.

6 Gain possessions and wealth justly.

7 Avoid the unjust.

8 Testify what is right.

9 Know who is judging.

11. Judging and Criticizing Others

1 Do not be a faultfinder,

2 Abandon your selfish craving for self-righteousness.

3 Do not so much pry into and censure the hearts and lives of others as your own.

4 Concern yourself less about what your neighbor says or does or thinks or possesses and instead set about improving what you say, do, think, and have so that you do not have time to worry about finding fault with your neighbor.

5 Dwell not on the misdeeds of others, whether the misconduct was by doing or not doing something. Instead, focus on what you do or are not doing.

6 Worry more about improving yourself than about judging

others. When there are specks both in your eye and your neighbor's, the speck in your eye is closer and looks much larger. Why do you see the speck in your neighbor's eye, but you cannot discover the one that looks like a log in your own? First take the log out of your own eye, and then you will see clearly that there is only a speck in your neighbor's.

7   Do not be so shameless as to undertake to cure your fellow-men when you are ill yourself. Instead, if you must, discuss with them troubles that concern you both, and share remedies with each other, just as if you were lying ill together in the same hospital.

8   Judge others how you would wish to be judged. When you judge harshly, you are really showing that you despise kindness, forbearance, and patience.

9   It is better to not see the faults of others at all, than it is to see faults in others and not see faults in yourself.

10   A focus on improving yourself, rather than in judging others, does not mean passive toleration of evil and wickedness. Such tolerance is a sin, no different than despair: the sin that believes in nothing, cares for nothing, seeks to know nothing, interferes with nothing, enjoys nothing, hates nothing, finds purpose in nothing, and lives for nothing, yet remains alive because there is nothing for which it will die.

11   Accuse one who is present. Do not oppose someone absent.

12. Hypocrisy

1   You are a hypocrite. Focus less on condemning others' hypocrisy than on overcoming your own.

2   Do not be a hypocrite who focuses on appearing virtuous to others, but is full of evil, self-indulgence, and greed. Concern yourself less with how others will perceive your actions than you are with doing good, and on doing it for the right reasons.

3   How can you recognize the faults of others when so often you cannot even recognize your own? Conquer the hypocrisy that blinds you. If you cannot see the faults in yourself, how can you

overcome them? How can you grow in virtue? If you remain a hypocrite, you will never come to an understanding, and will wallow in evil and foolishness all of your days.

4   Why would you clean the outside of your cup but leave the inside dirty? What does it matter if your cup appears clean to others, when what you drink is filthy and impure? First, clean the inside of your cup.

5   In your struggle to conquer your own hypocrisy, also be vigilant that you do not allow evil hypocrites to take advantage of you.

6   Fair speech may hide a foul heart.

7   Those who loudly claim to be acting on the highest principles are often not telling the truth.

8   A prosperous and happy community is the fruit of a virtuous people. Virtue requires effort. The hypocrite tries to deceive the virtuous to take advantage of their goodness. He tries to enjoy the fruits of others' virtue without making the effort to produce those fruits himself.

9   Hypocrites tempt themselves into believing they can have the benefits of virtue without the costs. Those who continue in such self-deception realize only too late that their hypocrisy has cankered their souls, crippled their characters, and destroyed the goodness of the communities they exploited.

10   Hypocrites are parasites. An orderly, good society punishes them swiftly, harshly, and severely.

11   Remember the parable of the lord and the feast.

13. Cooperation

1   It is shortsighted and foolish to believe that success comes only when others lose. Seek in every situation to ensure that everyone ends up better off than when they started.

2   If you cannot learn to listen to others as they whisper their prayers, you may well confront them later on when they howl their war cries.

3   Do not hold grudges after victory. Once someone does what you have been trying to get them to do, offer praise and re-

ward.

4   With those who are reasonable and willing to compromise, be reasonable and compromising, when you can do so without betraying wisdom, virtue, hope, or that which is sacred. With those who are unreasonable or unwilling to compromise, never compromise on anything, not even a little, for such as these will take and take until they have conquered or destroyed you.

14. Charity and Compassion

1   Share the load of the unfortunate.

2   Remember the poor, the needy, the sick, and the afflicted. For, are we not all beggars before God? Do we not all depend on Him?

3   As we have opportunity, let us do good to others, and especially to those who are of the family of our faith.

4   Far better is it to help those in need to become competent and self-sufficient, than it is to merely give them fleeting support for the moment. Never enable or reward dependence. It is no help at all to make someone useless.

5   Compassion and charity are virtues best applied on the small scale, among family, friends, and neighbors.

6   When exercising charity, learn to be wise like serpents, yet still innocent as doves.

7   Your individual resources are limited, while in comparison the needs of the destitute are nearly infinite. Give wisely of your resources to maximize their effect, in ways that encourage self-sufficiency and not dependence. Help the needy learn what they must do to prosper like you. Give first to those who have the most potential to benefit, and who have shown through their actions that they can become self-sufficient and productive.

8   When you can help with no or very little cost to yourself, then offer that help:

Deny no one the water that flows by.

Let anyone who will take fire from your fire.

Honest counsel give to one who is in doubt.

Who kindly sets a wand'rer on his way

Does e'en as if he lit another's lamp by his:
No less shines his, when he his friend's hath lit.

9 When considering whom to help, weigh the probability that your aid will make a positive difference for the person versus the probability that your involvement in that person's life will tear you down.

10 If you are rich and you do not give appropriately of your substance, your riches will canker your soul. If you are poor and look with eyes full of greediness at others' possessions—if you do not labor with your own hands for your full support, but instead rely on aid from others' income and efforts—then you have cursed yourself and your children's lives because of your idleness, your lack of motivation, and your failure to be productive.

11 Not everyone who asks for your charity is good or deserving. Against those who evilly seek to take advantage of your goodness, stand up for yourself. Do not put up with them—not even a little. So doing, you protect yourself and your community from tyranny and corruption.

12 Remember the parables of the ant and the grasshopper and the farmer and the snake.

13 Not all those who fail are victims; not all those who are low want to be lifted up.

14 Compassion and charity can be great virtues when kept to their Golden Mean—by being properly bounded in scope and by the other virtues. When taken to extremes, however, they become pathological, just like so many other virtues. Compassion is the Good Samaritan helping the beaten traveler on the side of the road, but compassion is also the mother grizzly bear killing the innocent passerby who unwittingly got too close to her cubs. Compassion is protecting the innocent victim, but it is also sheltering the evil murderer who happens to look vulnerable.

15 Beware of pathological altruism that diverts you from giving the full measure of care you owe to those to whom you are obliged with the highest duties: your spouse and children and posterity. And also be not diverted from your great duties to parents

and family, friends, community, nation, and all mankind, always in that order of precedence. Far more heartless is it to abandon those who place their trust in you, than it is to neglect an outsider.

16 Do not rob from your posterity's future to help strangers in the present. Your duty to the former, even though you be separated from them in time, is greater than your duty to the latter, even though they be present in front of you.

15. Ego

1 How long will you have such pleasure in vanity, and seek after lies?

2 When you have done something good, why do you want more to come of it, such as gaining a good reputation or getting some reward? Virtue is its own reward. Practice virtue because it is the right thing to do, not because you might receive some reward from it.

3 Do not be a boaster or attention-seeker. Do not show yourself off as someone who practices much discipline, wisdom, or virtue; do not do benevolent acts to make a display.

4 It makes no difference how many persons are acquainted with your uprightness. If you wish your virtue to be advertised, you are not striving for virtue but for renown. Are you not willing to be virtuous without being renowned? Indeed, practicing virtue often requires that you be disgraced in the eyes of many. Thus, if you are wise, let ill repute, well won, be a delight.

5 Do not boast in might. Do not depend on strength.

6 Do not be someone who craves recognition and relishes being greeted with respect and honor, who cares about status more than following the Triple Path.

7 "I am richer than you are, therefore I am superior to you"; "My income is higher than yours, therefore I am better than you"; or, "I have more prestigious diplomas than you, therefore I am more impressive": these conclusions do not follow. Rather, these are the proper conclusions: "I am richer, therefore my property is superior to yours"; "My income is higher, therefore my income is better than yours"; "I have more prestigious diplomas,

therefore my diplomas are more impressive". You, after all, are neither property, nor income, nor diplomas.

16. Selflessness

1   One of the ways you learn to be virtuous is by learning to be selfless. Do not let your capacity for virtue be crippled by the notion of "I" and "my".

2   Learn selflessness most completely by having children and caring for them.

3   Your obligation to be selfless is not unlimited. Your relationships with others make concentric circles of obligation. You have greater obligations to those who are closest to you, and waning obligations to those farther from you. Your greatest obligation (whether these are already present in your life or yet to come in the future) is to your children, posterity, and spouse, for whom you should make the greatest sacrifices. You next owe your next greatest obligations to parents and family, then to friends, then to other members of your community, then to your nation, and then to others more broadly.

4   Exercising excessive selflessness beyond proper bounds is pure selfishness because such unbounded altruism can too easily exhaust your resources, leaving you unable to fulfill your most important obligations, especially to spouse and children. Never show altruism in the selfish pursuit of your own perceived personal progress or emotional satisfaction if it comes at the expense of those to whom you owe your greatest duties. In exercising selflessness, there must be balance. Once you have sacrificed to protect and ensure the welfare of your children, posterity, and spouse, you should temper your selflessness with prudence to ensure you do not unnecessarily compromise your family's, or your, welfare.

5   You are not required to sacrifice your own interest and surrender to others what you need for yourself, but you must seek to fulfill your own interests by causing injury to your neighbor's. When someone enters a footrace, it is his duty to put forth all his strength and strive with all his might to win; but he ought never with his foot to trip, or with his hand to foul, a competitor. Thus, in the stadium

214

of life, it is not unfair for anyone to seek to obtain what is needful for his own advantage, but he has no right to wrest it from his neighbor.

17. Joy and Contentment

1 Sorrow may linger for the night, but joy comes in the morning.

2 Do not seek out joy in useless things.

3 Those things that provoke the admiration of the crowd are temporary. Joy that enters from outside will someday also depart. Develop a character and mind, through your thoughts and actions, that causes joy to spring from inside your own soul.

4 Joy comes from loving and being loved; from caring for others and being cared for; from sacrificing for others and practicing virtue within the connectedness of human relationships.

5 It is foolishness to think you will find happiness through the unhappiness of others.

6 Pleasure from achievement, success, or prosperity is fleeting. Joy and contentment come more from having righteous goals and making virtuous progress toward achieving them, not from accomplishing some specific worldly end. They come from virtuous living during the journey, not from reaching a destination. Never set a goal that would require you to sacrifice your principles to accomplish. Your pleasure at achieving it will be only momentary, at the cost of sacrificing your integrity, and you will have forfeited the joy you could have had in pursuing virtuous goals instead.

7 Pursuing joy and contentment through material prosperity is foolish. Each gain brings momentary pleasure that quickly fades. Virtuously seek to obtain sufficient for your needs and reasonable wants, but do not focus on becoming rich. You will never find lasting joy or fulfillment in wealth or in seeking to acquire it.

8 Find joy by recognizing the many reasons you have to be joyful. Cultivate gratitude within yourself. You have much for which you should be thankful. Make time every day to consider the things for which you can be grateful and to thank God for them.

9 Teach yourself to feel satisfaction in that which is good

and virtuous, and you will find peace and strength, even when adversity comes.

18. Forgiveness and Revenge

1   If you desire mercy and forgiveness from others, then be merciful and forgive also, but forgive wisely, after the person who has wronged you has apologized, acknowledging he has wronged you, why he did it, what he has learned from it, and credibly demonstrated he will avoid the same problem in the future.

2   Avoid an obsession with revenge. Such an attitude leads away from virtue. It stains your character, keeping you from appreciating the beautiful parts of life and making you bitter and someone whom others avoid.

3   Have you been wronged? Do you feel vengeful? You have the best vengeance by not letting your enemy control your feelings. You have the best vengeance by not letting external events lead you to evil actions, thoughts, and feelings.

4   Avoid resentment, which breeds the desire for revenge.

5   It is not easy to discriminate between vengeance and justice.

19. Free Will and Accountability

1   When people try to answer whether there is free will, they are not even on the right question.

2   Your existence, and your freedom within it, is like playing a game with fixed rules, such as chess: you are constrained by many limits, but you still have nearly infinite possibilities within those constraints.

3   Making a choice means also accepting responsibility for its consequences. Insulating or saving others from the natural consequences of their bad choices not only offends justice, but also robs from them the chance to learn and improve, thus compounding the likely magnitude of their future errors.

4   Find joy through practicing virtue. Even when someone seeks to externally limit your freedom of action, your mind still belongs to yourself. The first lesson of practicing virtue is that your choices are your own. Choose virtue.

5   Our actions are influenced by pre-existing conditions, but each of us is also an individual capable of independent action. We each enjoy an existence separate from all others. While our previous experiences and current circumstances strongly influence our behavior and actions, our personal behavior is not directly compelled by any outside force. Our actions arise out of internal processes and our unique personal characteristics and experiences. As autonomous individuals, we accumulate experience and knowledge and adjust our behavior by responding to our environment and to incentives.

6   Individuals and societies do best when each person acts according to the belief that he or she has free will and treats others under the assumption that they also have free will.

7   You traverse the landscape of being, making moral choices that determine the course of your life. These choices of yours, summed together with those of every other individual, determine the course of the world too.

8   Consider yourself as an active agent of choice confronting an infinite vista of potential and molding that potential into reality, for good or for evil. So considering yourself, you will have proper respect for yourself, for your good choices can smooth the wrinkled flaws of reality. You will also have the proper fear of yourself, for your bad decisions can warp the structure of reality.

9   Your actions affect many other people. The consequences of your choices are amplified. Thus, when you do good, it is better than you think. But when you do wrong, it is worse than you think.

10   Societies progress and flourish when individuals are as free as possible from outside constraints and also held accountable for the results of their actions. Because our actions also have effects beyond ourselves, to be held truly accountable, we must each bear the consequences our actions have on others and on the community. For this reason, it is right for communities to impose reasonable rules and punishments.

11   The son does not bear the iniquities of the father, unless he approve and imitate them. Neither does the son bear the great

deeds of the father, unless he approve and imitate them.

12　Your forebears' actions are not yours—neither their heroic deeds, nor their ignominious failures. No past life has been lived that lends you glory or ignominy. Your soul alone renders you noble—or disgraceful—through your actions, deeds, thoughts, and desires. Your soul may rise superior out of any earlier condition into which it was born, or it may sink below, no matter how high or low was the original condition.

13　Freedom is not the ability to implement your every whim; it is not the dim gratification of instantaneous impulse. Real, lasting, mature freedom is being able to choose for yourself which load you are going to pick up and carry, which great responsibilities you are going to assume.

14　If your world goes astray, look inside yourself for the cause and also for the solution.

15　Choose what is divine.

20. Thoughts and Opinion

1　As a very small rudder guides a large ship, so also your thoughts guide the course of your life.

2　When the sea is calm, all ship captains alike show mastery in floating. When the sea grows stormy, the captain who pitches his ship to and fro against the waves meets his doom, while he who steadies his own ship survives.

3　All that you are is the result of your thoughts. It is founded on your thoughts, it is made up of your thoughts. Good thoughts bring wise and virtuous action, and meaning follows. Bad thoughts bring foolishness and evil deeds, and emptiness follows.

4　Strive to look on things as they really are.

5　You rarely do something when your thoughts have dwelt on doing the contrary. Can you become something when your mind always lingers around its opposite? Let your thoughts dwell on wisdom, virtue, and hope, and you will have more wisdom, virtue, and hope. Dwell on foolishness, evil, and lazy despair, and you will have more of those also.

6　Guard your thoughts; unguarded, they are difficult to perceive and rush wherever they desire without discipline. If your thoughts are unsteady and your mind is troubled, you cannot understand the Triple Path.

7   Avoid purposeless, useless, or evil thoughts. Focus your thoughts on those things that, if someone asked suddenly, "what are you thinking about?", you could immediately answer with perfect openness about something simple and benevolent; socially useful; free of rivalry, envy, and suspicion; and nothing that would cause you to blush. And when thoughts contrary to these intrude, do not let them linger.

8   Just as rain pours through a bad roof and floods the house within, passion will pour through your undisciplined mind and overwhelm your character and actions. Just as rain flows along the outside of a good roof and falls harmlessly on the ground, passion will flow harmlessly on the periphery of your disciplined mind, not affecting your character or actions.

9   Your opinion can make heaven into hell.

10   Forgetting trouble is usually the way to cure it.

11   It is because of your opinions that you suffer. "He insulted me, he abused me, he beat me, he defeated me, he robbed me. *I have been harmed*". Take away your opinion, then you take away the complaint, "I have been harmed". Take away the complaint, "I have been harmed", and the harm is usually taken away.

12   It is not people or things themselves that disturb you, but your judgments about them. When, therefore, you are hindered, or disturbed, or grieved, first blame yourself and your own judgments. A fool always first blames others when he fares ill.

13   It is not the man who reviles or disparages you that offends you, but it is your judgment about his actions that offends you. When someone irritates you, it is your own opinion that has irritated you. When thus confronted, first endeavor not to be carried away by the external impression; for if once you gain time and delay, you will more easily become master of yourself.

14   You would violently oppose anyone who tried to send you into physical slavery. Yet, you freely hand over your mind to those

who revile or annoy you, letting them make you grow disturbed and troubled. And you freely hand it over to those who are morally reprehensible when you willingly listen to and watch their wicked opinions, over and over, all for the sake of some trivial entertainment. Are you not ashamed of this?

15 There are more things likely to frighten you than there are to crush you. You suffer more often in imagination than in reality.

16 Focus not on all the things about which you chafe and complain, but instead on the fact that you do chafe and complain. You have no complaints unless there be something in the universe that you think worthy of complaint.

17 Ambition, luxury, and greed: these things, too, depend on opinion. Free yourself of your opinion, and you also free yourself of the curse of these three.

18 Set freedom before your eyes and strive for that reward. And what is freedom? It means not being a slave to circumstance, to the provocations of others, to your opinions, or to your desires.

19 It is in your power to control your opinion of a thing or a person and not let it disturb you; things and people have no natural power to control your judgments. Do not let your reactions and opinions be controlled by those who do wrong to you, and never let others' treatment of you lead you to do wrong.

20 Why would you let yourself feel anxiety about potential trouble, and thus ruin the present through fear of the future? It is foolish to be unhappy now because you may be unhappy at some future time. Strip your opinions of all that disturb and confuse and see what each is at bottom; you will then comprehend that they contain nothing fearful except the actual fear.

21 Do not let the opinion of others determine what you consider to be of worth. The opinions of the world are always wavering and often take both sides. Everything that is good is good in itself. Neither worse, nor better, is a thing made by being praised. Your perceptions of a thing's value should always be based on its compatibility with the Triple Path. Such value is not made better or worse by being praised by others. Is wisdom, virtue, or hope

any more valuable to you because they are praised? Do wisdom, virtue, or hope lose their value if fools blame or criticize them?

22   How can the follower of the Triple Path please the crowd? Frequently it takes trickery to win popular approval. The favor of ignoble men can be won only by ignoble means. If they do not recognize you as one of themselves, they will withhold their approval, thus requiring that you make yourself like unto them. What you think of yourself is therefore much more to the point than what others think of you.

21. Actions

1   If it is not right, do not do it; if it is not true, do not say it.

2   Do not do what should not be done. Do not neglect doing what should be.

3   Do only that which you could speak of with honor.

4   You do evil not only by doing something wrong, but also by *not* doing what is right.

5   You will come to regret your unvirtuous deeds. Act with virtue, and you will not feel regret.

6   Do what you mean to do.

7   Have the courage to act on what you believe.

8   Do everything in its proper time.

9   When you know, act quickly.

10   Use your skill.

11   Guard and defend what is yours.

12   Use what you have.

13   By your desires and works is your true character manifest.

14   All that you do becomes a part of you.

15   In any competition, it is not the most beautiful, the strongest, or the most intelligent who win, but those who actually compete—those who *do,* not those who merely *are.*

16   Stop wasting time with much talking about what a good man ought to be. Just be one. Doing good is the only path to virtue.

17   If you take refuge in theory and words, thinking this will make you virtuous, then you are like a patient who listens attentively to his doctor, but then does none of the things he learned he

221

must do to make himself well.

18 Do not concern yourself more with talking about how to do good than you concern yourself with actually doing good. Virtue comes not from talking, writing, hearing, or reading about doing good. It comes only by doing good and desiring good. Keep your deeds and words from contradicting. Prove your words by your deeds.

19 There is no such thing as vicarious virtue. The acts of others will never make you virtuous. The only way you can be virtuous is by practicing virtue yourself.

20 You learn by doing. You become a builder by building and a musician by playing an instrument. So too, you will become merciful by showing mercy, just by acting justly, temperate by exercising temperance, brave by behaving courageously, and loving by caring for others. You become wise by seeking wisdom and virtuous by practicing virtue

21 What you choose to do shows what you want to become. You most truthfully manifest your real character through your actions. You show what you value by what you spend your time on. Thus, seek to practice virtue unceasingly and not idle away your time.

22 When virtue has sunk into your soul, it will be demonstrated not just by mere words, but by actions showing stalwartness of heart and resolve of character.

23 It is a ridiculous thing to flee from others' badness, but not your own. If you do wrong, you do wrong against yourself.

24 There is a consequence for every action you take and for every decision you make. Do not be surprised when you dig a pit that you end up falling into it.

25 Live your life so that you would not be ashamed for anyone to discover any aspect of it. Live with the expectation that everything covered up will be uncovered, and everything secret will become known. Live so that you do not fear if everything you have done in the dark is seen in the light, and what you have whispered behind closed doors is proclaimed from the housetops. Think and

act as if there is someone looking into your inmost soul, for even if your every deed and thought is never discovered, what does that matter? You cannot fool your soul. And nothing is shut off from the sight of God. He is the witness of your soul.

26 It is possible that you may depart from life this very moment; control your acts and thoughts, and discipline yourself accordingly. Seek wisdom, practice virtue, and labor with hope all the days of your life.

27 Beware of using the ends to justify the means. It is a dangerous path to start justifying unvirtuous acts because you are doing them to achieve some supposedly worthy goal.

22. Courage

1 Be of good courage, you who trust in God and seek wisdom, practice virtue, and labor with hope.

2 Act with courage, showing an example for future generations that could be included among the ideal types of history.

3 Love wisdom, virtue, and hope, but without cowardice or softness.

4 Pursue honor. Do not abandon it. Detest dishonor.

5 Struggle with glory.

6 Respect yourself.

7 Fortune favors the brave, but the coward is foiled by his faint heart.

8 Venture into danger prudently and with good reason.

9 Be bold in action, but reflective ahead of time. Be not bold in ignorance.

10 Your courage and fortitude are strengthened by being challenged.

11 You will never have true faith and self-confidence in your ability and capacity, and no one else should either, until you have proved yourself confronting many difficulties and hardships. It is in this way that your spirit and character can be tested and proved.

12 Develop courage by making it your habit to despise things that are terrible and standing your ground against them.

13 If you are not willing to fight to defend your beliefs and that

which you claim to hold dear, then you will be brought to live under the boots of those who are.

14 In the face of that which must or should be done, this is courage: having a clear vision of the danger that lies before you and yet still going forth to meet it; or, enduring fear and being uncertain of victory, yet still proceeding.

15 Those who, out of fear, fail to do what must or should be done because it is hard or difficult are worthy of contempt and condemnation.

16 Have the courage to say no at the right time. Each time you assent to, or silently tolerate, that which you should not, you become ever more willing to accommodate worse and worse evil. Out of such timid cowardice emerge terrible servants of wickedness who help hell manifest itself on Earth.

17 What is bravery? It is the impregnable fortress for your mortal weakness; surround yourself with it and you can hold out free from anxiety during life's siege; for you will be using your own strength and the weapons of your own character.

18 Your soul can be more powerful than the winds of fate. The good and bad things brought to you by chance are merely the raw materials out of which you yourself build your life. You guide your affairs in either direction. Under your own power you produce a good and honorable life, or a wretched one.

19 Bad men and women can make anything bad—even things that had come with the appearance of what is best. Wise and virtuous men and women, however, correct the wrongs of fate. They soften hardship and bitterness because they know how to endure them. They accept prosperity with appreciation and moderation, and stand up against trouble with steadiness and courage.

20 Do not fear gaining disrepute in the eyes of the disreputable.

21 Frankly express your opinions and what you have found to be true. Be open about what you hate and love. Do not fear what others think about your opinions and what you believe to be true. Do not esteem others' opinions over your own. To care less for

truth than for what people will think is the mark of a coward.

22 When your enemies surround you on all sides like swarming bees, continue to seek wisdom, practice virtue, labor with hope, and trust in God.

23 Do not let yourself be deterred from that which is right and honorable; do not let yourself be tempted into evil or baseness. Do what is right and honorable, even if it involves toil, even if it involves peril, even if it involves harm to yourself; and do not do that which is evil or base, even if it brings you money, or pleasure, or power.

24 He who loses his reputation for being a good man in order to do that which is right truly shows his great devotion to practicing virtue.

25 Be willing to die to protect your family and friends, your faith, your community, and your nation.

23. Priorities

1 Pursue what is fruitful.

2 Be a better steward of the time God has given you.

3 Are you more concerned with getting and keeping the world than with having a good conscience?

4 Why do you feel always busy? A great part of what you do and think is unnecessary, frivolous, or trivial. Make time for yourself by doing first the things that are most important—that which helps you live the Triple Path. And then cease doing so many unnecessary things. This brings not only the joy that comes from doing good things, but also the serenity had only by someone who is not harried and preoccupied.

5 Keep a proper perspective, so you do not think to be highly desirable those things which are mildly desirable; so that you are not too zealous in striving for things which are only mildly desirable or not desirable at all; so that you do not highly value things which ought to be slightly valued, or not valued at all.

6 Do not busy yourself with trifling things. Do not give credit to the unsubstantiated claims of the superstitious. Do not give yourself up passionately to entertainment or sport or games. Do not become a partisan of sports teams, athletes, performers, or works of

fiction. Leisure and recreation help you maintain balance and mental well-being, but passion and partisanship in such matters is wasteful frivolity that detracts from what is most important.

7 Avoid vulgar entertainment and also entertainment made or consumed by those who are ignorant of wisdom, virtue, and hope.

8 Do not devote much effort or deep study to matters that are obscure and useless.

9 If you were sick, you would try your hardest to be rid of the illness as soon as possible, not giving greater attention to business or personal amusements. What, then? Shall you not do the same thing now? Your soul is sick and weak. Throw aside all hindrances and give your time to improving your soul by following the Triple Path, which is not a thing to be followed at odd times, but a subject for constant practice.

10 Seek wisdom, practice virtue, and labor with hope while you yet can. Nature has not given you enough time that you can have the leisure to waste any of it. Out of this river of time that carries us so swiftly on its current to our end, of what avail is it to spend the greater part on useless things?

11 You make time for that which is most important to you. Why do you always find time to eat? Because your life depends on it. There will never be enough time to do everything you want, but you must always make time to properly direct your thoughts and actions and to follow the Triple Path—your life depends on it.

12 "I didn't do it because I was too busy." "I didn't do it because I didn't have enough time." Do not accept such excuses from others or yourself. We are all free. No one is at the mercy of affairs. We get entangled in them of our own accord. Those things that you actually do are where your priorities lie. The things you fail to complete are those that you value less, no matter what you may say.

13 Do not spend money for that which is of no worth. Do not waste your time and labor on that which does not satisfy. Seeking fulfillment in useless things is like trying to satisfy hunger by eating

candy.

14 Do you really believe that the highest good is in following the Triple Path? If so, then you would follow it. Do you believe that the trifling distractions that preoccupy you, and that preoccupy so many others, are the highest good? If not, then why do you waste your time on them, when so many other more important things await?

15 We all have some vague notion that we are mortal. Many in the world, though, do not *understand* that we must all die; those who do end their quarrels and idle pursuits.

16 Think about the times of your great-great-great-great grandfather. In that time you would have seen people marrying, bringing up children, sick, dying, warring, feasting, trafficking, cultivating the ground, flattering, being obstinately arrogant, suspecting, plotting, wishing for some to die, grumbling about the present, loving, heaping up treasure, and desiring power. All those people are now dead. Or think about your great-great-great grandfather. Again, all is the same. His life too is gone. Consider also all prior nations and previous eras of time and see how many, after great efforts, soon died and decomposed. But most of all, think about yourself and those you yourself have known, who distract themselves with idle things, neglecting to seek wisdom, practice virtue, and labor with hope. And thus remember to prioritize the Triple Path, giving proper value and proportion to both your actions and thoughts. Do not waste your time on trivial pursuits. Build something of worth with your life that, even if consciously forgotten in coming centuries, will leave an influence for good that will echo down through the generations to the benefit of your descendants and all mankind.

17 Your worth is determined by the things about which you busy yourself. Thus, ask yourself: How does this action affect my worth? Are the things with which I am busying myself of real value? Do my actions help me follow the Triple Path?

18 Consider a man who uses the Hope Diamond as a hammer to pound nails into a wooden toy he is building. Certainly everyone would consider him a fool. Why? Because he is using

something of such great value to build something so trifling. Do not use your life, your time, your compassion, your intelligence, and your many gifts to build trifles. Use these things, and everything else you have, to build up wisdom, virtue, and hope in yourself, your family, and the world.

19 While you are procrastinating and postponing, life speeds by.

20 Do not be a procrastinator, putting off into the future all your undertakings and thus never finishing anything.

21 Be a good steward over the time God has given you, but which you let others too easily slip or wrest away from you. Save this most valuable, yet fleeting and slippery, of possessions, and set yourself free. Be thrifty with your time.

22 How much of your life is taken up with weeping and worry! How much by years of inexperience or of useless endeavor. Even in the longest lives of the best of men, real living is usually the least portion thereof. Seek to maximize the real living in your life.

23 Do not let your time be lost to you, as some moments that are torn from you, some that are gently removed, and others that glide beyond your reach. The most disgraceful kind of loss, yet the one that is most in your power to prevent, is from carelessness. Too much of your life passes while you are doing ill, doing nothing, or doing that of no purpose. Hold every minute in your grasp. Lay hold of today's task, and you will not need to depend so much upon tomorrow's.

24 Never put off to tomorrow what you can do today. How long have you been putting off so many important things, and how often have you had opportunities that you did not take advantage of! Your time in this world is temporary. Your existence is flowing away. If you do not use your time for seeking wisdom, practicing virtue, and laboring with hope, that time will have been wasted, and it will never return.

25 Seek to find your calling in life, then work to fulfill it. The most powerful influence in determining your life's work is exerted by nature, and the next most powerful by fortune. Thus, you must,

of course, take account of them both in trying to find and fulfill your personal calling. Of the two, nature will most often claim the more attention because it is so much more stable and steadfast.

26 Remember the parable of the river

24. Motivation

1 Do what is right as an end in itself, not because you expect some reward. Your soul is refined and purified when you practice virtue and seek wisdom for their own sake, not when you do it in expectation of either earthly reward or heavenly blessings. Have you practiced virtue? Have you sought wisdom? That is reward enough. When you follow the Triple Path for its own sake, you cannot help but bring great reward to yourself, even though you do not desire it. It comes *because* you do not desire it.

2 Act on principles that could be made universal to all.

3 Always do what ought to be done because it *is* what ought to be done. Do not act out of worry for what others will think or what reputation your actions will bring you.

4 Do not act with duplicity and hidden intent to do evil or cause harm. Leave no room in your character for this.

5 Do not act out of a self-righteous desire to prove yourself more virtuous than others.

25. Discipline

1 Cling to discipline.

2 Control the eye.

3 You are a slave to whatever masters you.

4 Seek to develop a free and upright mind, subjecting other things to itself and itself to nothing.

5 This is the way to greatness: practicing thrift, self-restraint, and courage.

6 Seek always to improve your character and to discipline yourself. Cultivate a love for labor and perseverance. Be not distracted by trivialities. Be not a slave controlled by the undisciplined and unfocused parts of your mind.

7 Act with self-control and discipline; those who fail to do so lead disturbed and tumultuous lives, feeling the constant weight of

a guilty conscience and the fear that their misdeeds will be discovered, suffering again and again the consequences of their bad choices.

8 The soul is not to be pampered. Flee from temptations to vice, to weakness, and to laziness. There are places that those who are on the Triple Path avoid as foreign to good morals. Learn which they are and avoid them. Select for your repose those places that are wholesome not only for the body but also for your character and your soul. Seek out places that are pure.

9 You can avoid most sins if you have a witness who stands near when you are likely to go wrong. Therefore, live among men as if God beheld you and speak with God as if men were listening. Control yourself as if God and men knew your thoughts and desires.

10 With each thing that befalls you, remember to turn to yourself and see what abilities you have to deal with it properly. If you see someone attractive, you will find that self-restraint and temperance are the abilities you have against your desire. If hard labor or pain is laid upon you, you will find the abilities are endurance and fortitude. If it be abusive words, you will find it to be patience. And thus habituated, the appearances of things will not hurry you away along with them.

11 Figure out how to deal with yourself so that you more often practice virtue, so that you keep the promises you make to yourself and thus can trust yourself.

12 You are neither master nor slave to yourself. You have your own nature. You can shape it, but not by tyrannizing yourself. Figure out how to entice your nature into virtuous action.

13 Your conscious, thinking mind is a small part of your complete self. Its control of yourself is like a rider on an elephant trying to lead an unruly, independent beast with its own agenda. Your feelings, desires, decisions, and thoughts often come from automatic, instinctive parts of your mind working outside your conscious thoughts. Discipline and self-restraint come less from having the fortitude to consciously control all of your thoughts, feel-

ings, and behavior, but from being able to train the elephant of your non-conscious mind so you can nudge it into the right course you seek to follow.

14 The obstacle in doing right is often not a conscious lack of desire, but following through with proper action. When the mental and physical demands on you grow beyond your ability to manage, your conscious mind starts to lose control. Beware of hunger, tiredness, or other distractions, lest they tax your will and sap your discipline. Find the weaknesses that most affect your resolve to act rightly. Then, reduce unnecessary mental demands in those areas.

15 Those with idle and weak characters seek fulfillment from immoderate and excessive behavior. Be faithful and strong, seeking fulfillment by exercising self-control and moderation.

16 There is nothing wrong with normal human desires, but they should be enjoyed properly, with moderation, wisdom, and virtue. Do not let your desires control you.

17 Desires are a fundamental part of life, but never do evil to satisfy them. Remember that even many good desires can be harmful or dangerous when taken to extremes. There is also almost no desire you cannot use to lead you to do good. Find ways to satisfy your desires that are not evil or harmful to you or others. Seek to channel them and harness them to help you do good.

18 Do not despair when you make mistakes. Mistakes are part of learning. Expect them. Set your expectations so that your mistakes do not leave you in a state of despair when you err. Place yourself in situations where you will be able to recover from your mistakes. Thus, you will transform potentially harmful or dangerous impulses into benign ones.

26. Hard Work

1   Virtuous work is the sustenance of a wise and noble mind.

2   First, learn to willingly endure hard work; then, to enjoy it.

3   Stand tall under heavy loads. You were born to carry burdens.

4   Find the heaviest load you can handle, and pick it up. Try

to pick up things that are a little heavier than you think you can handle.

5   Do not waste yourself laboring to do evil or dishonest work.

6   Work for what you can make yours.

7   Endure toil and rouse yourself to hard and uphill effort. The follower of the Triple Path does not fear sweat.

8   Do not busy yourself just for the sake of being busy. Do the work that must be done and that which has meaning and importance (either for its own sake, or because it allows you to support yourself and your family).

9   Learn to work with your own hands.

10   Work for the common interest.

11   Our luxuries condemn us to weakness, making us forget how to do that which we have long stopped doing, or never bothered learning how to do in the first place.

12   The evils of leisure can be shaken off by hard work. When you are in the grasp of sluggishness or sloth, rouse yourself and busy yourself with virtuous action. When you are busy doing good, you have no time for wantonness.

13   Avoid the laziness and vanity of wealth. Avoid paying others to care for your basic needs. Cook and clean for yourself. Learn how to maintain your tools, possessions, abode, and transportation.

14   Poverty is nothing to be ashamed of, unless you are making no effort to overcome it.

15   Do not be idle. The idle should neither eat the bread nor wear the clothes of the laborer. Anyone unwilling to work should not eat.

16   Those who are willfully idle are worthy of angry contempt. Their indolence is evidence of their physical, moral, and intellectual flabbiness. The willfully idle have no place in a sane, healthy, and vigorous society.

17   Let the law of work be a fundamental law of your being. Work hard doing work that is honest and well worth doing.

27. Self Reliance

1   Be self-sufficient. Hold yourself up, standing tall on your own, not held up by others.

2   No one else owes you a living.

3   Never trouble another with what you can do yourself. Never trouble yourself to do for others what they can, or should, do for themselves.

4   Do everything you can to take care of yourself before you seek the charity of others, but do not be ashamed to ask for help when you truly need it.

5   When you are in need, you must also consider the needs of your potential benefactors. You have an obligation to first take care of yourself so that others do not unnecessarily expend effort to help you.

28. Desire and Self-Indulgence

1   Do not wait to practice virtue until there is nothing left for you to crave. That time will never come. When one desire ends, another begins.

2   Your blind desires plunge you into harm, yet will never satisfy you. Your attachment to pleasure, power, riches, and vice keeps you from wisdom and virtue.

3   Be controlled neither by your desire for pleasure nor your fear of pain.

4   Yearn not for the soft things, lest you earn the hard.

5   Do you love pleasures, honor, or riches more than God?

6   Physical pleasures do not bring lasting fulfillment or peace. You will die before you find fulfillment in them. Your physical desires may be temporarily satiated, but are never permanently satisfied. The value of your life does not consist in its abundance of pleasure or possessions.

7   Unvirtuous acts in the present thwart your future happiness and welfare. Why would you act for immediate gratification at the expense of your future? Why would you so highly value momentary pleasure, vice, and greed over the joyful serenity of virtue?

8   Those who are slaves to their appetites and lusts are wor-

thy of contempt and condemnation.

9 The decadent and hedonistic are called self-indulgent because they are pained more than they ought, both when they fail to get things pleasant to themselves and also when they are merely craving them. They are led by their appetites to seek to satiate them at great cost. How absurd to be pained for the sake of pleasure!

10 If you allow yourself to be carried forward by your every desire, do not be surprised when you find yourself in a whirlpool of self-destruction.

11 What you seek in life, seek it not out of a desire for material gain. What you hold onto in life, hold onto it not out of a fear of loss.

12 Live happily, free from greed and lust, even living among the greedy and lustful.

13 Cruelty, greed, materialism, fornication, adultery, lust: these are not just characteristic of our age, but of many people in all ages. Do not let them be characteristic of you.

14 Things are never worthy objects of your love. Never let yourself love money, possessions, or finery. You will never get enough of them to satisfy yourself. They will never love you back. And having love for them leads to much evil—live free of it and be content with what you have.

15 No matter how few or how many material goods you accumulate, no matter how many pleasurable or exciting experiences you have, none of them will be yours after you die.

16 If you are greedy, you cannot bear giving up your income; if you crave notoriety, you cannot bear giving up fame; if you lust for power, you cannot bear to hand authority to others. Do not be like the foolish and unvirtuous who hold tight to these things, shivering with the fear that letting go would cause sorrow. Do not be as those who never stop for a moment of reflection and stillness, who always gaze with greedy eyes.

17 You will never be satisfied with what you achieve. You deem lofty the objects you seek because you are on a lower level and hence far away from them; but they are mean in the sight of

him who has reached them. And he desires to climb still higher; that which you regard as the top is merely a rung on the ladder.

18 Deceive not yourself into believing that attaining worldly objectives will bring peace to your soul. There is no one who is contented with his prosperity. Men complain about their current situation, always preferring what they have failed to win. Observe the rich or ambitious men who have reached the most sought-after honors. These grandees are always gaping after new gain, condemning what is already behind them. Following the Triple Path can settle this problem for you and bring you one of the greatest boons: the absence of regret for your own conduct and character. So, follow the Triple Path and let your soul be great, holding itself unruffled to its ideals, pleased with itself on account of the very things which displease others, a soul that makes life the test of its progress, free from fear and not a slave of desire.

19 Some appetites are natural and common, others are peculiar to individuals and acquired. For example, the appetite for food and drink is natural, since every one who is lacking craves them. Same also for love, especially among the young. In the natural appetites, few go wrong, and generally only in one direction—that of excess, desiring more than most people do. These people may be called belly-gods, for when they crave food, they fill their belly beyond what is right. But with regard to the pleasures peculiar to individuals, many go wrong, delighting either in the wrong things (that which no person ought to delight in) or for those things for which they might rightly desire, but in the wrong way.

29. Vices

1 Part of learning virtue is unlearning vice. Fleeing vice is the beginning of virtue.

2 The road to vice is not only downhill, but steep.

3 You love and hate your vices at the same time. Forsake your love for your vices; stop upholding them and preferring to make excuses for them, rather than shaking them off. And not just your love for them, but also give up on your vices themselves, and free yourself of this conflict in your soul.

4 Vices tempt you by the rewards they offer. There is no evil that does not offer inducements. Avarice promises money; luxury, a varied assortment of pleasures; ambition, power, praise, and influence; and so on for every other vice.

5 Turn away from those things associated with whatever vices you wish to conquer. If you wish to lay aside your desire for the things which you used to crave so passionately, you must turn away both eyes and ears from that which reminds you of what you have abandoned.

6 Do not conceal your vices, which do most harm when they are hidden behind a pretense of decency.

7 Beware lest vices creep into your heart under the name of virtues. Evil things sometimes appear good or honorable. There are vices which are next-door to virtues. Even that which is lost and debased can resemble that which is upright: spiritlessness disguised as calmness; rashness as bravery; sluggishness as moderation; cowardice as prudence; lust and unchastity as masculinity; promiscuity as charm; and pathological altruism as charity.

8 How can you struggle against your vices enough to overcome them, if the time you give to seeking wisdom, practicing virtue, and laboring with hope is only the amount left over from your vices?

9 Remember the parable of the young man and the teacher.

30. Greed and Materialism

1 Be happy with what you have.

2 Do not trust wealth.

3 Lay aside the things of this world, and seek for the things of a better. Where your treasure is, there will your heart be also. Do not set your heart on riches for yourself. Set it on following God; on seeking wisdom, practicing virtue, and laboring with hope; on your family; and on your fellow beings.

4 Let your only prized possession be virtue. Then, no matter what else is taken from you, you will say "I have lost nothing", for no one can rob you of your virtue—it can only be lost through your own choices.

5 The greatest evil of covetousness is its ingratitude.

6 You covet something, so you lie to obtain it. You desire it, so you create dispute or conflict to get it. You want it, so you take it. If you let such selfishness, lust, and greed grow within you, they will diminish and weaken your sense of virtue, making you willing to do ever-greater evil to get what you want.

7 If you wish to make yourself rich, do not add to your store of money or possessions, but subtract from your desires.

8 Beware of ceaselessly seeking material possessions and wealth, falsely believing you are fulfilling valid needs and desires. You should work to meet your real physical needs, and it is not wrong to fulfill your modest wants when you have the means to virtuously do so. But your real needs are few and the virtuous decrease their desires to a minimum. You will need and want but little if you desire but little.

9 Consider how much of what you possess is superfluous and of how many things you would not even feel their loss were it necessary to part with them!

10 What profit to you is it to have many rooms in your house? You sleep in only one. No place is yours where you yourself are not.

11 Your attempts to follow the Triple Path cannot bear fruit unless you take pains to live simply.

12 Eat simply, not extravagantly or expensively. Why would you cram into yourself things of value as if your belly could keep what it has received? How does it matter what the stomach receives, since it must lose whatever goes in?

13 Getting riches has been for many men, not an end, but a change, of troubles.

14 For many problems, money provides no solution. Sometimes, it worsens the problem.

15 Money rarely makes a man feel rich; on the contrary, it usually smites men with a greater craving for itself. Why? Because he who possesses more begins to be able to possess still more.

16 If you live according to your needs, you will almost never

be poor; if you live according to opinion, you will never be rich. Your needs are slight; the demands of opinion are boundless. Suppose that the property of many millionaires is heaped up in your possession, that fortune carries you far beyond the limits of a normal income, decks you with gold, gives you power, and brings you so much luxury and wealth that you have no way to spend it all before you die. You will only learn from this to crave still more.

Your real needs are limited, but those which spring from false opinion have no stopping-point. The false has no limits. When you wander astray off the Path, your wanderings can become limitless.

17 Begin with the Triple Path, first and always. Away with all excuses such as: "I have not yet enough; when I have gained the desired amount, then I shall devote myself wholly to the Triple Path". This ideal, which you would put off and place second to other interests, should be secured first of all. You may retort: "I wish to acquire something to live on". Yes, but follow the Triple Path while you are acquiring it. After you have come to possess all other things, shall you then wish to possess wisdom also? Is spiritual health to be the last thing you need in life—a sort of supplement? No! Follow the Triple Path now, whether you have anything or not. Seek understanding first, before anything else.

18 When you prosper, it is easy to forsake the Triple Path and turn to evil ways. If, in spite of detachment from greed, selfishness, and evil desire, you find yourself with wealth, be even richer in virtuous acts; use your wealth to do good.

19 Do not be so forgetful and blind that you are surprised at losing something. Someday you will lose everything. You will lose your life as surely as you will lose your property. Thus, take all your losses with equanimity.

20 Remember the parables of the two young men and the empty knapsack.

31. Moderation and Balance

1 Exercise prudence.

2 Nothing to excess.

3   Remember the principle of the Golden Mean.

4   Remember the parable of Icarus.

5   How noble it is to be contented. How much peace comes from demanding nothing more than your needs, and desiring nothing more than your modest wants.

6   The temperate occupy a middle position regarding objects of pleasure. They desire moderately those things that do not hinder good spiritual and physical health, that are not contrary to what is beautiful, and that are not beyond their means. They do not enjoy the things the self-indulgent enjoy most, and in fact rather dislike most of them. They do not enjoy the things they should not, nor the excess of things they should, nor do they feel more than a moderate pain or craving when those things they desire are absent.

7   A man who wants nothing more than what he has can never be called poor. He who desires more than he has will never feel rich enough, no matter how much he has. He who feels like he has enough, no matter how little it is, has something that even almost every rich man lacks—a stopping-point. Enough is never too little, and not-enough is never too much.

8   The starving man most desires food. His desires consume and overcome him. Avoid gluttony and greed by avoiding complete self-denial of those things that are morally permissible and needful. Keep your desires from controlling you by acting in moderation, with virtue, to meet your simple, just needs.

9   What is nourishment to the appetite of a hungry man is a burden to one with a full stomach, making him fat, unhealthy, and closer to the grave.

10   Love beauty, but without undue extravagance.

11   Use whatever riches you have sparingly, as if they were given for safe-keeping and will be withdrawn. Never boast of them.

12   Never let the pleasures of life become indispensable to you, for then you become a slave of your pleasures, rather than enjoying them in proper ways and in moderation.

13   The momentary, virtuous physical pleasures of life are not evil, so long as you enjoy them in moderation and do not oth-

erwise act unvirtuously or immorally to experience them. Make sure that your experience of them contributes to your pursuit of the Triple Path and does not distract from it. Beware of seeking them out as ends for their own sake.

14 Self-restraint is not a good in and of itself; rather, what is good is restraining oneself from evil and from those things that become evil in excess.

15 It is rarely wise to let compulsive ambition drive you single-mindedly toward a goal, to the exclusion of all else. Seek balance in your life. There is more than just one important thing in it.

16 Many people rise to positions of importance because they have focused so much time on achieving success in one area that they have neglected the other areas of their life. The status they achieve is not evidence of their greatness, but of their foolishness. Do you want to be great? Then achieve balance in your life. Develop a well-rounded character. Take on the great responsibilities of marriage, children, and family. Participate and serve in your community. Always be learning new things and new skills. Have hobbies and outside interests.

17 Lacking a balanced life is a serious character flaw that should disqualify one from positions of prominence or authority. To be worthy of honor, develop yourself in all aspects of life, especially the spiritual, intellectual, and emotional; prove your character by successfully nurturing your family and following the Triple Path with courage and firmness.

18 What is the proper limit to wealth? First, to have what is necessary; second, to have what is enough. Work hard always, but crave no more than these two. You are not poor when you have too little, but when you crave more than what you have. In the eyes of the virtuous, whatever they have is enough, is abundant. They do not lust after that which they have not. What does it matter how much you have saved in the bank, how much you are earning on your investments, and how much property you own, if you still covet your neighbor's property, never grateful for what you have, only focusing your hopes on gains to come?

32. Killing, Violence, and Anger

1   Do not kill or do physical violence without justification.

2   Taking another's life is only justified if done in self-defense against that person to protect your own life or that of an innocent person. Violence against another is only justified to defend yourself or an innocent person from harm from that person.

3   Do not threaten violence against others unless you are prepared for them use violence against you.

4   If you are angry with your brother, quickly reconcile yourself with him.

5   Avoid harshness, cruelty, or violence in your character— these just provoke the same in others. How can you, who are seeking meaning and happiness for yourself, unjustly inflict pain and suffering on others who also long for meaning and happiness?

6   Ensure that, when necessary for self-defense, you have the capacity to use violence, both in terms of skills and mindset. Also, though, be civilized. When there is no necessity for it, keep your capacity for violence under control. Do not relish violence, nor be eager to mete it out.

7   Renounce war and proclaim peace, and seek diligently to turn the hearts of all people to wisdom, virtue, hope, and peace.

8   Those who live by the sword die by the sword. War is only justified to defend from attack or aggression. Seek to ensure that your nation never acts first with aggression against others.

9   Abortion is an evil, only justifiable in the case of rape or incest and usually only in the earliest stages of pregnancy. And even when justifiable, it should only be done after careful thought and soul-searching, with the abuser of the woman then being held responsible for murder.

Is an unborn child a person? Presented with this question, err on the side of preserving life when pregnancy is caused by a woman's free choice. When the pregnancy came through no choice of her own, then the balance changes.

It is selfish wickedness to decide that a child must die so that you may live as you wish.

33. Honesty and Integrity

1   Do not lie. Tell the truth. Deal honestly.

2   Tell when you know.

3   The virtuous seek after truth, so they do not tell untruths to others.

4   Keep your word. Be firm on what you agree. It is better never to have made a promise than to make one and not keep it.

5   Integrity reduces your terrible complexity to the simplicity of your word, so there can be cooperation instead of enmity.

6   Do not speak ill of others outside their presence. Do not gossip.

7   Do not steal. Do not take what does not belong to you or what you did not honestly earn.

8   Live not by lies.

9   Flee from deceit. Get away from lying lips and a deceitful tongue.

10   Be embarrassed to lie.

11   Root out deception from your speech and thoughts. Do not use words to deceive yourself, or to put on false appearances, or to hide your ignorance. Do not use others' words to avoid your responsibility to think for yourself.

12   Little lies lead to more and bigger lies and eventually to the seductive, arrogant lie you begin to believe yourself—that you can manipulate reality with your lies and that being itself deserves no respect. But then eventually, sometimes when it is too late, you are forced to a reckoning with your lies and things fall apart. That is when the path to Hell can open and swallow you, and your life becomes degeneration, frustration, disappointment, and lazy despair; when you finally, desperately try to go through the motions of sacrifice, yet God seems not to be pleased.

34. Chastity, Family, and Sex Roles

1   Honor the hearth.

2   Crown your ancestors.

3   Respect your parents.

4   Respect the elder.

5   Intend to get married.

6   Love whom you rear.

7   Educate your children.

8   Teach youngsters.

9   It is better to delay the time of beginning sexual activity, than to begin too early.

10   Marriage is between one man and one woman. It should be permanent, fruitful, and faithful. You should only have one spouse, and you should have no sexual partners other than your spouse. Do not have sex outside of marriage—do not commit adultery or fornication.

11   The husband and wife can be better together. Single, if one falls, who is there is to help lift up? Who can bring warmth when the cold comes? Together, they can help each other up. In the cold, they can keep each other warm.

12   Let the husband fulfill unto his wife his marital duties, and likewise also the wife unto the husband. For, the wife does not have authority over her own body, but the husband; and likewise the husband does not have authority over his own body, but the wife. Do not deny each other, except perhaps by mutual consent for a set time, that you may give yourselves over to prayer and meditation, and then come together again, that you be not tempted.

13   Children are entitled to be born within the bonds of marriage, into a loving family.

14   Husbands should honor and support their wives' sacred role as mothers. Wives should honor and support their husbands' sacred role as fathers. Parents should honor and support their children's sacred roles as sons and daughters of God and future husbands and fathers or wives and mothers. Want what is best for them—that they seek wisdom, practice virtue, and labor with hope. Support above all else their commitment to these.

15   Societies that stop honoring the divine image of holy mother and infant cease to be.

16   A loving family and marriage can be the joy and delight of life. Nothing brings greater meaning and satisfaction to life. Mono-

gamy, marriage, and family are the foundations of a healthy, productive, advanced society. Value marriage and family above all other things. Get married. Have children. Make your marriage lifelong, stable, committed, and exclusive. Support your spouse.

17 Come together in marriage not only to join with your spouse, but also to have children. Love and nurture your children in patience and selflessness. Teach them by word and example, starting when they are young, to follow the Triple Path.

18 Children are a heritage of God, the fruit of the womb is His reward. As arrows are in the hand of a mighty man, so are the children of one's youth. Happy are the parents who have their quivers full of them. They shall not be ashamed when they speak with their enemies at the gate.

19 Those who are willfully or negligently barren have no place in a sane, healthy, and vigorous society.

20 Remember the parable of the flower's seed.

21 Biological sex is a reality. Most men and women are happiest and find most meaning when living the traditional roles of their sex.

22 Fathers should preside over their families with love, wisdom, and virtue. They are responsible for providing the necessities of life and for protecting their families. Mothers should nurture their children and care for them with love, wisdom, and virtue. Fathers and mothers should help each other as equal partners. Death, disability, or other circumstances may require individual families to adapt. Extended families should provide support in such situations.

23 More important than your duty as a parent to protect and provide for your children is your duty to teach them to become competent and self-sufficient. It is more important that your children be strong, than that they be safe. Do not let your protection of your children drive them into weakness; instead, treat them in a way that strengthens them and encourages them toward mature, powerful independence.

24 Parents have a duty to teach their children to live and flourish in the world. They must therefore act as proxies for the world,

albeit merciful and caring ones, ensuring that children face the consequences of their actions and learn social skills.

25 Parents should teach their children not to shirk difficulties, but to meet them and overcome them; not to strive after a life of ignoble ease, but to strive to do their duty, first to themselves and their families, then to friends and community, then to nation, and finally toward all mankind.

26 Bad parenting happens all too often. Recognize and contain your capacity as a parent for harsh, vengeful, arrogant, resentful, angry, and deceitful behavior.

27 Impose the minimum necessary rules on your children, and enforce them with the minimum necessary force—such simple, minimal rules as: Do not use violence against others, except in self-defense. Do not bully other children. Be grateful for what you have. Express gratitude. Share. Pay attention to what adults say to you. Eat with good manners and gratitude. Look after your belongings. Be good company when fun is happening. Behave in a way that makes other people pleased to have you around.

28 Calmly and properly discipline your children with love, achieving the right balance between mercy and justice. So doing, you interfere with their freedom in the moment, but also channel their future growth toward mature, responsible adulthood, so that they are ready to put away childish things at the right time.

29 Divorce is an evil, only justified in extreme circumstances, such as criminal abuse, extramarital affairs, or the other spouse's failure to fulfill central marital duties.

30 Family comes first. It is your most urgent, profound obligation. Attending to supposedly urgent outside obligations is never an excuse for neglecting your family, since your obligation to your family is the most important.

31 Your obligations to your children, spouse, and family do not justify mistreatment of others. It is never right to act immorally toward outsiders to try to get some benefit for your family or those who are close to you.

32 Children do not grow up only in their family, isolated from

the rest of the world. Parents have primary responsibility to teach and nurture their children, but extended families and everyone else in the community are also responsible.

35. Relationships with Others

1 Love one another with mutual affection.

2 Speak well of others.

3 Restrain your tongue.

4 Avoid harsh words; when you speak harshly to others, they will answer you in the same way.

5 Be kind. Contribute to the general good by giving and receiving acts of kindness every day, thus cementing human society more closely together, person to person.

6 Love friendship. Guard friendship. Help your friends. Be kind to them.

7 Give a timely response.

8 Give a timely counsel.

9 Be courteous.

10 Stand tall with your shoulders back.

11 Learn to be charming, witty, and tactful in your conversation. Conduct yourself as one who is well-bred and educated, not vulgar, indecent, or buffoonish.

12 When you are a newcomer, ask another to do you a favor, something within reason. He that has once done you a kindness will be more ready to do you another, than he whom you yourself have obliged. So doing, you allow your neighbor the chance to prove himself a good person, and you also put yourself in his debt to return the favor. Thus, you start creating bonds of mutual familiarity and trust between you and he.

13 Stop looking for others' faults. Do not be easily offended.

14 Do not let anyone vex you and thus divert you from your steady judgment and action in following the Triple Path.

15 If you have been betrayed or taken advantage of, do not respond by becoming cynical or nihilistic or faithless. Instead, learn to be wise like serpents, yet still innocent as doves.

16 Be jealous of no one.

17 Shun what belongs to others.

18 Do not let yourself be agitated by others, and do not be the kind of person who makes it easy for others to become agitated.

19 Every day you will meet the busybody, the ungrateful, arrogant, deceitful, envious, unsocial. Do not let yourself be offended by their ignorance. It is your choice whether to feel injured or angry because of them.

20 Do not be an obsequious person who thinks it his duty to give no pain to the people he meets, who backs down too readily, even when it would be dishonorable or harmful to do so. Neither, though, be someone who is always contentious, who never compromises, who cares not about the pain he causes to others.

21 Keep yourself from insolence and arrogance.

22 Scorn others' insolence and arrogance.

23 Be not high-handed or overbearing toward those of lower station than yourself.

24 Do not meddle in others' affairs. Do not readily listen to slander or gossip. Do not speak ill of someone outside of that person's presence.

25 If you wish to bring honorable influences to bear upon your mind and straighten out your wavering spirit that is prone to evil, then associate with those who are good.

26 The person who keeps close company with someone who is dirty will inevitably get a share of the dirt on him, even if he himself happened to start out clean.

27 Do not meddle in others' affairs. Do not readily listen to slander or gossip. Do not speak ill of someone outside of that person's presence.

28 One who mistreats others or acts dishonestly or dishonorably with others will likely end up dealing similarly with you.

29 If someone gossips about others to you, expect that he is gossiping about you with others.

30 It is natural to understand others' minds in terms of how your own mind works. Be wary, therefore, of those who readily or frequently attribute to others false intentions, nefarious or petty mo-

tives, or hidden agendas.

31 Watch out for your enemies.

32 Flee enmity.

33 Despise slanderers.

34 If someone brings you word that another is speaking ill of you, do not immediately jump to defend yourself against what was said. Instead, consider answering: "The man did not know the rest of my faults, otherwise these would not have been the only ones he mentioned."

35 Do not too quickly attribute to malice others' mistreatment of you. Misunderstandings and neglect are more common in this world than trickery and malice.

36 People flatter one another; despise one another; raise themselves above one another; and make them crouch before one another. This hate and flattery go hand in hand. Give up both.

37 How closely flattery resembles friendship. An enemy comes to you full of compliments, in the guise of a friend.

38 Suppose a person despises you. This is that person's own affair. Your personal concern is to never do or say anything lacking in virtue.

39 When others offend you, remember these eight principles:

First, that we are social beings, and made for one another;

Second, that many people do wrong out of ignorance.

Third, that you also do some evil and have the disposition to commit more;

Fourth, that you often do not even understand whether an action is evil and that you must have great discernment to pass correct judgment on others' acts;

Fifth, that life is a fleeting moment and shortly both you and the person will be dead;

Sixth, it is not others' acts that upset you, but your own opinions. You choose whether to take offense;

Seventh, that often you bring more pain on yourself by the anger and annoyance you allow yourself to feel in response to such acts than by the acts themselves; and

Eighth, that a genuine, kind, and patient disposition usually has the greatest power to bring others to your opinion.

36. Power and Leadership

1   Fear ruling.

2   People do not follow a true leader because of his position or title.

3   Power or wealth are not justifications for vain pride, but calls to far greater responsibility, requiring that you even more diligently seek wisdom, practice virtue, and labor with hope.

4   What brings greatness and power? Being like a swift low-lying, down-flowing river—always moving ahead, becoming the center to which flow all the other streams.

5   A great leader works to unite people and nourish their commitment to wisdom, virtue, and hope. He is kind and welcoming, prudent, and full of integrity and self-control. He loves virtue, wisdom, and hope. His character is as free as possible of arrogance, violence, greed, and a short-temper.

6   When much needs to be done (and there is always much that needs to be done), you need not strive alone. Many hands make lighter work. Delegate. Share the burden, and the credit.

7   Receiving rank or position do not mark a leader. Many occupy positions of authority, but few actually lead. They care so much about notoriety, recognition, power, or money that they do not learn this one lesson: true leadership requires wise virtue.

Almost without realizing it, even those with good intentions transform themselves into tyrants within their domain. Sad experience teaches that it is the nature and disposition of almost all people, as soon as they get a little authority, to immediately begin to exercise it wrongfully over others.

No power or influence can or ought to be maintained by virtue of one's position, but instead only by virtuous strength—by holding a clear vision of the way forward and instilling that vision in others; by leading through example, persuasion, long-suffering, gentleness, and genuine love and kindness, acting without hypocrisy or deception; reproving at times with sharpness, but always after-wards showing an increase of love, so that they do not think you an enemy, but know that your fidelity and love are stronger than any-thing else.

8   When the wicked rule, the people mourn. Only the wise, virtuous, honest, and hopeful should have a voice in the governance of a community, and only the best among them should lead it; seek after these sorts of people.

9   Do you resent and condemn those who abuse their power? Until you understand how you have it within yourself to do the same thing, you are just as unworthy as them. The vices of most people, who are powerless, escape notice. As soon as people get some confidence in their positions, though, their vices become no less prominent than those they had so vociferously condemned. Most people simply lack the means whereby they may unfold their wickedness.

10   Do you wish for power and control over others? Do you long for status and recognition? Already you fail. The one who most desires power is least deserving of it; he will selfishly seek his own benefit, rather than do his duty and serve those in his charge. Be like Washington and Cincinnatus, not Hitler, Stalin, and Mao.

11   When the evil, ambitious, and power-lusting rule, the guilty go unpunished because of their money; leaders use their power to control others and enrich themselves; the powerful steal, commit adultery, and bring death and violence.

12   Great honors ruin even great people. Power and fame make it hard to stay virtuous. Seek after none of these.

13   The less accountability someone has, the more likely it is that person will abuse power. There is great danger when account-ability is lacking. Make, therefore, each person accountable.

14   The more power and authority someone has, the greater harm that person can cause by abusing power, and the more diffi-cult it is to limit that person's exercise of power. Having power makes it easy to develop a constituency supporting the continued exercise of that power, no matter how unjust. There is great dan-

ger in concentrating power and authority. Limit, therefore, the power and authority entrusted to any one person. Make it so that no one may ever grow so powerful that it becomes too difficult and destructive to remove him. Make it impossible for any one person to develop a constituency so strong that he becomes immune from correction or challenge.

15 Does limiting power also prevent good and wise leaders from maximizing their ability to do good? No. Unlimited power turns virtuous and wise leaders into evil and foolish ones. Power corrupts. Absolute power corrupts absolutely. Power spoils and taints even the best leader's wisdom and virtue. The virtuous and wise do not want power. Instead, they teach correct principles to the capable and let them govern themselves.

16 The graveyards are full of indispensable people.

17 What makes good people rebellious? Rulers who cannot stop interfering. A ruler should not only act for the people's benefit, but also trust them and leave them alone. Respect them and let them live their lives, and they will not grow weary of you.

18 There are two ways a group can fail: having a leader who does not lead with wisdom, virtue, and hope, or being a group made up of people lacking wisdom, virtue, and hope. Some peoples lack the capacity for following the Triple Path. Only a fool would try to lead them.

19 If people fear your power, then you do not really have any.

20 Outside intervention or control do not bring harmony, happiness, and peace to a community. Those things come unbidden when everyone follows the Triple Path and contributes to the community. When this happens, there is little need for someone to even be in charge.

21 If power or fame come to you, apply these lessons. Ensure that your power is limited and shared with others. Stay accountable; make sure others are in a position to keep you in check and stop you from abusing power. Seek and follow virtuous counsel both from trusted associates and outsiders. Live your life trans-

parently and openly so that it becomes difficult for you to act hypocritically and unvirtuously without it being quickly discovered.

22 Hierarchies are a part of human nature. Strive to be competent, and good, so that you can succeed within the hierarchies in your life.

23 Seek to eliminate tyranny from the hierarchies around you, but never forget that dismantling the hierarchies that exist will not eliminate hierarchy. It will just end up in the creation of new hierarchies with their own tyrannies.

37. Debt

1 Govern your expenses. Never stop being thrifty.

2 Do not enslave yourself to others through debt. How can you focus on following God and the Triple Path when you are beholden to another master? Keep yourself free by avoiding debt. Pay your debts and free yourself from bondage.

3 Only take on debt when the future benefit clearly outweighs the cost, such as to buy a house, get an education that will increase your earning potential and enrich your character, or start a business with good prospects.

4 Incur debt thoughtfully and deliberately. Calculate the interest you will pay; weigh the cost versus the potential benefits, as well as the likelihood of achieving those benefits; consider the debt's risks and the future opportunities you will forgo while repaying it; then, only contract the debt if the benefit outweighs the cost.

38. Health and Diet

1 Your body is the temple of your soul and a dwelling for the spirit of God. Care for it as you would any holy place.

2 Work to be as healthy as possible. The better your health, the greater your ability to follow the Triple Path. Care for your health so that you may run and not be weary, and walk and not faint.

3 Eat the flesh of animals always with thanksgiving for the life which has been taken to give you sustenance, and never wastefully.

4 Sustain your body and mind with exercise: your mind through learning, study, thinking, meditation, and elevated conver-

sation with others seeking to do the same; your body by staying active and through strength and cardiovascular exercise. But let not your bodily exercise become an obsession taking all of your time.

5   Get enough sleep. Avoid caffeine and other stimulants. Prioritize your waking hours to accomplish what is most important and eliminate that which is not so that when the time for sleep arrives you may sleep. Do not foolishly try to accomplish more by giving up sleep. You pay a price each time you do so—worse health, tiredness, decreased happiness, and a continued failure to learn discipline.

6   Drink alcohol, if at all, only in moderation and after you have come of age. If you or close relatives have had problems with alcohol, then never drink at all.

7   Never use tobacco or other harmful drugs.

8   Also remember that it is not what goes into your mouth that defiles you, but what comes out of it. What goes into you goes to your stomach and then out to the sewer. It is from within yourself that your evil intentions come out and defile you: murder, violence, adultery, fornication, selfishness, theft, deceit, envy, slander, pride. Seeking good health is a means toward developing virtue, not the end.

39. Good Character

1   More valuable than status or wealth or power is having good character. Events outside your control may cause you to lose these first three, but you are the ultimate and final authority on what your character will be, and it is the only thing you can be sure you will always carry with you wherever you go.

2   Character is destiny.

3   Exercise nobility of character.

4   Prove your character.

5   No matter your stage or station in life, do your duty with responsibility, dedication, and enthusiasm.

6   As a child, be a credit to your parents.

7   As a youth, be self-disciplined.

8   As of middle-age, be just, civilized, and discerning.

253

9 As an old man, be sensible and decorous.

10 On reaching the end, be without sorrow.

11 Do not mock or wrong the dead.

12 Practicing virtue requires having courage and always doing that which is honorable.

13 Wait to have children until you are married. Then, for their sake, strive to stay married. Avoid idleness. Get what training and education you need so you can earn a living. Work hard, going above and beyond what is expected of you. Be a good neighbor—civic-minded and appropriately charitable. Be a patriot. Avoid vulgar language. Respect your elders. Shun addictions and crime.

14 Be someone who is uncontaminated by pleasure, unharmed by pain, untouched by insults, and dyed deep with justice and love; someone who abhors evil, fights in the noblest fight, and cannot be overpowered by any passion; someone who accepts without complaint or bitterness whatever happens to you, yet still always works to overcome obstacles and improve yourself.

15 Control yourself. Practice virtue, even if it means feeling pain or foregoing pleasure. Free your behavior from anger; instead, be affectionate. Do not let yourself be distracted. Labor with hope in all circumstances. Be satisfied on all occasions and never ill-tempered. Be a good manager of money; do not spend money on unnecessaries and frivolities.

16 Speak plainly.

17 Establish for yourself a consistent character that you are able to maintain whether you are by yourself, with friends, or with enemies.

18 Righteous actions, often repeated, allow you to develop right habits, which in turn allow you to develop a good, stable character. Wrong actions, often repeated, lead you to develop bad habits, which in turn causes a wicked character—sometimes to such a degree the wicked man seems incapable of choosing the right things; yet, his wicked character of this type will have always originated through his own initial voluntary choices to do wrong.

19 Do everything with a purpose; do not act falsely or with

254

hypocrisy. Do what is set before you without complaining. Never put off doing something worthwhile. Practicing virtue should be so routine for you that it is a habit; be someone who cannot be diverted from doing what is right. Never act with bad intentions. Be truthful. Readily forgive. Let your behavior be a proper mix of agreeableness with dignity.

20 Act always with honorable purposes, a good conscience, right actions, and an even and calm way of living.

21 Treat others so that they would never feel you despise them. Be kind and accommodating, so that interactions with you are more agreeable than any flattery. Be agreeable and easy in conversation.

22 Seek good friends and do not soon tire of them. Do not court friends by gifts or by flattery or by trying to please them. Do not let others flatter you.

23 Your circumstances do not excuse you from doing your duty and having discipline and good character; they do not excuse you from following the Triple Path. Thus, let it make no difference to yourself whether you are cold or warm, drowsy or alert, ill-spoken-of or praised, or whether you are dying or living. Discomfort and comfort, living and dying: all of this is a part of life.

24 Do not speak without regard for what is right or wrong. Do not delight in talking about others' failings. Do not praise falsely and hypocritically. Do not try to face in all directions, without thought for right or wrong, to try to gain favor by appearing to agree with whomever you are speaking to. Do not insist that things always be done your way. Do not take what belongs to others and appropriate it for your own use. Do not ignore your own faults and errors. Do not refuse to change when you see your faults and errors or when others point them out to you. Do not be a petty hypocrite who honors and respects people when they agree with you, but who demonizes them and refuses to see the good in them when they disagree with you.

25 The common style of speaking reflects the general character of the time, and a person's style reflects his own character. Do

not have a profane or vulgar character. Thus, speak not profanely or with vulgarity, and beware of those who do.

26 Remember the parable of clearing land.

27 How can you know how to live if you do not know when to live? You are more industrious and a better person when you anticipate the day and welcome the dawn; and you are the opposite when you lie dozing when the sun is already high in the heavens.

28 When you were a child, you spoke like a child, thought like a child, and reasoned like a child. Now it is time to grow up and put an end to childish ways. For, after you come of age, it is not childhood that stays with you, but childishness. With the passage of years, this becomes all the worse, for you come to possess the apparent authority of old age, together still with the follies of childishness. Put aside your attention to trifles and shadows. Instead, attend to your duty, with wisdom, discipline, and virtue. The greatest cure to childishness is raising children of your own.

40. Exemplars of Virtue

1 Honor good men and women.

2 Examine the priorities of stalwart followers of the Triple Path and others who are wise and virtuous; look at what kind of things they avoid, and what kinds they pursue, and then follow their example.

3 Good men and women of all eras constantly speak the truth, boldly forsake and rebuke vice, and patiently suffer for the truth's sake.

4 Choose as a guide one whom you will admire more when you see him act than when you hear him speak. Choose as your guides not those who speak before large crowds, but those who teach by their lives; who, if they say how they think you ought to live, prove it by their own practice; who after telling what you should avoid then are not caught doing that which they have ordered to avoid.

5 Choose as exemplars those whose life, conversation, and soul-expressing face show forth wisdom, virtue, and hope; picture them always to yourself as your patterns and even as your protec-

tors. For, we must indeed have someone according to whom we may regulate our characters, just as you use a ruler to straighten that which is crooked.

6   The examples of true followers of the Triple Path will show you the quiet grandeur of living the good life and yet not make you despair of attaining it; you will understand that it is on high, but that it is accessible to whoever has the will to seek it.

7   When you observe someone else practicing true virtue, it should inspire admiration in you, and yet also hope that you are capable of attaining it too.

8   No matter how much wisdom or virtue you think you have attained, there will always still be others greater than you. Seek them out and learn from them: not only wisdom and virtue, but also humility.

9   No one is worthy of perfect emulation. Foolish or evil acts are never justified, even if done by a normally wise and good person. Remember that we are all subject to weaknesses of character and flaws in our thinking.

10   Trust in God. Do not trust in a great moral leader to exemplify perfection for you; do not trust in some paragon of virtue to show you flawless goodness. No such teacher or exemplar exists; no one is perfect; no one does right all the time. If you place blind trust in others, when you come to know their imperfections, you will either fool yourself into believing their immorality is virtue, or you will become disillusioned and reject the good things you had learned from them.

11   Do good. Exemplify virtue to others, and learn from others' good examples in turn. Help others overcome their own personal weaknesses, and accept others' help to overcome your own.

12   Watch yourself. Take care to do what you should be doing, so that your bad example does not confound others in their faith in God or their practice of the Triple Path.

41. Sharing the Triple Path

1   The worth of each soul is great. Seek always to lead others to the Triple Path. Be a living example of following it, so you may

guide them using your experience. Do not be a blind guide. How can you increase wisdom in the world if you do not seek it yourself? How can you show what virtue is to others if you do not practice it yourself? How can you teach others about laboring with hope if you yourself do not so labor?

2 Let your example in following the Triple Path, though it be imperfect, shine as a light to others, guiding them to the safety of wisdom, virtue, and hope, just as a lighthouse guides ships on the water to safety.

3 Remember the parable of the light. Let the light of your good example shine through in all you do.

4 Not all are capable of following the Triple Path. Not everyone can learn to act with wisdom, virtue, and hope. Seek out those who can, and show the Triple Path to them.

5 Give not that which is holy unto the dogs, nor cast your pearls before swine, lest they trample them under their feet, and turn again and tear you in pieces.

References

1. Virtue

1- Lucilius 70:4. **2-** BoM, 1 Nephi 2:9. **3-** 2 Thessalonians 3:13; BoM, Alma 37:34. **5-** Maps, p. 13. **7-** D&C 58:26-29; Dhammapada 163; BoM, Mosiah 4:29-30. **8-** Nicomachean, Book 2, parts 2 and 6-9. **10-** Nicomachean, Book 2, part 4. **11-** Lucilius 22:2-3. **12-** Jordan Peterson, Podcast 48, 46:00. **13-** D&C 58:27; Dhammapada 118. **14-** Dhammapada 262. **15-** 2 Corinthians 3:3; Mosiah 4:30; Dhammapada 231-34. **16-** BoM, Mosiah 5:2. **17-** Wilhelm Hofmann, *et. al.*, "Yes, But Are They Happy? Effects of Trait Self-Control on Affective Well-Being and Life Satisfaction", *Journal of Personality*, June 11, 2013. **18-** John Rogers, *The Nature and Necessity of Repentance*, 1728, p. 11. **19-** Plato; Cicero; Ambrose; Augustine of Hippo. **20-** Hesiod, *Works and Days*, ca. 700 BC, line 285. **21-** Canon Frederick Lewis Donaldson, March 20, 1925 sermon at Westminster Abby, subsequently quoted by Mohandas Gandhi, "Seven Social Sins", *Young India*, October 22, 1925; Jordan Peterson, "Freedom of Speech: Not Just Another Value", talk on May 13, 2017. **22-** Delphic maxim 26. **23-** James 2:14-18, 3:13.

2. Evil

1- Delphic maxims 31, 119. **2-** 12 Rules, p. 212. **5-** Jordan Peterson, Podcast 20, 8:13. **7-** Dhammapada 316-318. **8-** Lucilius 122: 5. **9-** 12 Rules, 183-4. **10-** Jordan Peterson, Podcast 33: Jacob's Ladder Biblical Lecture, 2:15:00. **11-** Nicomachean, Book 2, part 3. **12-** Dhammapada 161. **13-** Romans 12:21; Dhammapada 223. **14-** Jordan Peterson. **15-** Alexander Solzhenitsyn, *The Gulag Archipelago*, 1973. **16-** Friedrich Nietzsche, Beyond Good and Evil, 1886, Aphorism 146. **17-** Terence, *Heauton Timorumenos*. **18-** Jordan Peterson, various public talks. **19-** Jordan Peterson, Podcast 56. **22-** Lucilius 123:9. **23-** Psalm 10:4, 6-7, 9, 11-14.

3. The Adversary

1- Thomas Cranmer, *Book of Common Prayer of the Church of England*, 1662, Baptism. **2-** James 4:7; William Shakespeare, *Twelfth Night*, ca. 1601-02, Act III, scene 4, line 107. **3-** 1 Peter

5:8-9. **4**- 1 Corinthians 10:21; Friedrich Schiller, Wallenstein's Death, Act I, scene 3, line 64. **5**- William Shakespeare, *Hamlet*, ca. 1600, Act II, scene 2, line 628; Hugh Latimer, *The Sermon of the Plough*, 1548. **6**- William Shakespeare, *The Merchant of Venice*, ca. 1597, Act I, scene 3. **7**- Isaiah 14:12-20; Ezekiel 28:12-19; Dante Alighieri, "Inferno", *Divine Comedy*, 1320, Canto 34, line 34.

4. The Zealots

2- Psalm 14:2, 6, 7, 8, 12:2. **3**- Psalm 12:1-2, 7-8. **4**- Carlo Lancellotti, "Augusto Del Noce on the 'New Totalitarianism'", *Communio*, 44 (Summer 2017), p. 331; Peggy Noonan, "Get Ready for the Struggle Session", *Wall Street Journal*, March 7, 2019. **5**- Matthew 15:14. **6**- 12 Rules, pp. 251-52. **7-8**- Kenneth A. Lantz, *The Dostoevsky Encyclopedia*, 2004 (quoting Fyodor Dostoevsky notebook for 1863-1864 and Dostoevsky's unfinished article "Socialism and Christianity"). **9**- Matthew 7:15. **11.** Hope 9:1. **13**- Isaiah 5:20. **14**- 2 Peter 2:22. **15**- Romans 1:18. **16**- Romans 1:21-22. **17**- Romans 1:24-25. **18**- Thomas 102; Ancient Greek fable; **19**- Luke 11:46; Matthew 23:4. **20**- 12 Rules, pp. 259-62 (discussing Hitler's use of the big lie). **22**- 12 Rules, p. 320. **25**- Matthew 23:24. **28**- Matthew 23:15. **29**- Mark 12:40; Luke 20:47. **30**- Luke 11:43-44; Matthew 23:5. **32**- Luke 11:52; Matthew 23:13. **33**- Matthew 23:33.

5. Sin and Repentance

1- Ezekiel 18:30. **2**- Evagrius Ponticus and Gregory I. **3**- John Rogers, *The Nature and Necessity of Repentance*, 1728, p. 75. **4**- 12 Rules, p. 303. **5**- Psalm 51:3, 6. **6**- 1 John 1:8-9. **7**- John Rogers, *The Nature and Necessity of Repentance*, 1728, pp. 50, 57. **8**- *Same* at p. 11. **9**- Psalm 6:3, 38:4, 51:10, 142:4. **10**- Lucilius 123:9. **11**- Psalm 7:15-16. **12**- Lucilius 97:14-16.

6. Virtue Comes From Within

2- 2 Corinthians 9:6. **4**- Lucilius 25:5-7, 83:19. **5**- Lucilius 43:3-5. **6**- Bhagavad Gita 2:43.

7. The Golden Rule and Empathy

1- Matthew 7:12; Michael Scott Earl, *Bible Stories Your Parents Never Told You*. **2**- Immanuel Kant, Grounding for the Metaphysics of Morals, 1785 (Kant's second formulation of the categorical imperative). 4- Meditations 6:53. 5- BoM, Mosiah 18:9; James 1: 19. 6- 12 Rules, pp. 230-31. 7- Jordan Peterson Podcast. 8- Jordan Peterson Podcast.

8. Love

1- Colossians 3:14. 3- George Orwell, "Reflections on Gandhi", *Partisan Review*, 1949. 4- Lucilius 66:26. 5- Matthew 5:43-47; Luke 6:27. 6- 1 John 3:18. 7- 1 Corinthians 13:4-8. 8- Romans 12: 9; Hebrews 13:1; 1 Peter 4:8. 9- Galatians 6:2.

9. Anger and Hatred

1- Colossians 3:8. 2- Dhammapada 201. 3- Romans 12:9. 4- James 1:20. 5- Dhammapada 197. 6- Delphic maxim 80. 7- 1 Thessalonians 5:15. 9- Nicomachean, Book 4, part 5. 10- Thomas Aquinas, Summa Theologiae, Question 158, Anger (quoting material falsely ascribed to John Chrysostom). 11- 12 Rules, pp. 55-58. 12- Jordan Peterson Podcast 2.42, 1:48.

10. Justice

1- Cicero, *De Officiis*, 1:23. 2- Delphic maxim 27. 3- Delphic maxim 5. 4- Delphic maxims 32, 84, 86. 5- Delphic maxim 2. 6- Delphic maxim 64, 117. 7- Delphic maxim 13 (alternate numbering, see Al. N. Oikonomides, "Records of 'The Commandments of the Seven Wise Men' in the 3rd c. B.C.", 63 *Classical Bulletin* 67, 76 (1987). 8- Delphic maxim 14 (alternate numbering). 9- Delphic Maxim 66.

11. Judging and Criticizing Others

1- Delphic maxim 25. 2- Jordan Peterson Podcast. 3- John Rogers, *The Nature and Necessity of Repentance*, 1728, p. 50. 4- Meditations 4:18. 5- Dhammapada 50. 6- Matthew 7:1-5; Luke 6:37-42; Thomas 26. 7- Lucilius 27:1. 8- Romans 2:1-5. 10- Dorothy Sayers. 11- Delphic maxim 87, 125.

12. Hypocrisy

2- Matthew 23:25; Luke 11:39-41. 3- Chuang Tzu, Sec. 4 (In the World of Men), Watson translation. 4- Matthew 23:25; Luke 11: 39-41. 6- J. R. R. Tolkien, *The Two Towers*. 7- Maps, p. 320.

13. Cooperation

2- James Billington, "Religion and Russia's Future", Templeton Lecture on Religion & World Affairs, 1997. **3**- 12 Rules, p. 158.

14. Charity and Compassion

1- Delphic Maxim 135. **2**- D&C 44, 52:40; BoM Mosiah 4:17-19, 26. **3**- Galatians 6:10. **4**- 12 Rules, pp. 78-79. **5**- Jordan Peterson, Podcast 16, 1:06:00. **6**- Thomas 39; Matthew 10:16. **7**- Cicero, De Officiis, 1:52; D&C 42:31; BoM Mosiah 4:24, BoM Jacob 2:17. **8**- Cicero, De Officiis, 1:51-52 (quoted poem by Ennius). **9**- Jordan Peterson, Podcast Season 2, 46, 26:00. **10**- D&C 56:16-17. **11**- 12 Rules, pp. 55-58. **13**- 12 Rules, p. 106. **14**- Jordan Peterson, Podcast 16, 1:06:00.

15. Ego

1- Psalm 4:2. **2**- Meditations 7:73; Matthew 6:1-6. **3**- Meditations 1:7. **4**- Lucilius 113:32. **5**- Delphic maxims 89, 114. **6**- Mark 12: 38-40. **7**- Enchiridion 44.

16. Selflessness

1- Bhagavad Gita 4:31, 12:13. **3**- Steve Sailer, "The Self-Righteous Hive Mind", *Taki's Magazine*, April 11, 2012; Alistair Sutcliffe, Robin Dunbar, *et. al.*, "Relationships and the social brain: Integrating psychological and evolutionary perspectives", *British Journal of Psychology*, Vol. 103, 2012, pp. 149-168. **5**- Cicero, *De Officiis*, 3:42.

17. Joy and Contentment

1- Psalm 30:5. **2**- Lucilius 23:1. **3**- Lucilius 102:20. **4**- Jonathan Haidt, *The Happiness Hypothesis: Finding Modern Truth in Ancient Wisdom*, 2006. **5**- Lucilius 94:67. **6-8**- Jonathan Haidt, *The Happiness Hypothesis: Finding Modern Truth in Ancient Wisdom*, 2006.

18. Forgiveness and Revenge

1- Jordan Peterson, Podcast 36, 1:50. **2**- D&C 64:9. **3**-BoM, 1 Nephi 7:21; Meditations 6:6. **4**- 12 Rules, 175. **5**- Jordan Peterson, Podcast 43, 16:00.

19. Free Will and Accountability

2- Jordan Peterson, Podcast 46, 15:25. **4**- BoM, 2 Nephi 2:25. **7**- Jordan Peterson, Podcast 33, Jacob's Ladder (quoting Carl Jung). **8**- Jordan Peterson, Podcast 48, 54:00. **9**- Jordan Peterson, Joe Rogan

Podcast. **11-** John Rogers, *The Nature and Necessity of Repentance*, 1728, p. 6. **12-** Lucilius 44:5. **13-** Jordan Peterson, Podcast 45, 4:30. **14-** Dante Alighieri, "Purgatorio", *Divine Comedy*, 16: 73-83. **15-** Delphic maxim 49.

20. Thoughts and Opinion

1- James 3:4. **2-** William Shakespeare, *Coriolanus*, Act 4, Scene 1; AE. **3-** Dhammapada 1-2. **4-** Meditations 4:11. **6-** Dhammapada 36, 38. **7-** Meditations 3:4. **8-** Dhammapada 13-14. **9-** John Milton, *Paradise Lost*, 1674, Book 1, line 254. **10-** Lucilius 94:27 (quoting Publilius Syrus, Frag. 250 Ribbeck). **11-** Meditations 4:7; Lucilius 78:13, 14; Dhammapada 3-4. **12-** Enchiridion 5. **13-** Enchiridion 20. **14-** Enchiridion 28. **15-**Lucilius 13:4. **16-** Lucilius 96:1. **17-** Lucilius 78:13. **18-** Lucilius 51:9. **19-** Meditations 4:11, 6:52. **20-** Lucilius 24:1, 12. **21-** Lucilius 26:6, Meditations 4:20. **22-** Lucilius 29:11.

21. Actions

1- Meditations 12:17. **2-** Dhammapada 292. **3-** 12 Rules pp. 188-90. **4-** Meditations 9:5. **5-** Dhammapada 314. **6-** Delphic maxim 58. **7-** Delphic maxim 66 (alternate numbering, *see* Al. N. Oikonomides, "Records of '*The Commandments of the Seven Wise Men*' in the 3rd c. B.C.", 63 Classical Bulletin 67, 76 (1987). **8-** Ecclesiastes 3:1-8; Tao Te Ching 8:2. **9-** Delphic maxims 50 and 104. **10-** Delphic maxim 57. **11-** Delphic maxim 33. **12-** Delphic maxim 85. **13-** D&C 18:38. **15-** Nicomachean, Book 1, part 8. **16-** Meditations 10:16. **17-** Nicomachean, Book 2, part 4. **18-** Romans 2:13; Lucilius 20:1, 2. **19-** Meditations 6:51. **20-** Nicomachean, Book 2, part 1. **21-** D&C 60:13; Tao Te Ching 8:2. **22-** Lucilius 20:1. **23-** Meditations 7:71, 9:4. **24-** Ecclesiastes 10:8-9. **25-** Meditations 2:11; Luke 12:2-3; Lucilius 83:1. **26-** Meditations 2:11.

22. Courage

1- Psalm 31:24. **2-** Lucilius 98:13. **3-** Pericles (as recorded by Thucydides), Funeral Speech, 430 BC. **4-** Delphic maxims 22, 81, 118. **5-** Delphic Maxim 99. **6-** Delphic Maxim 129. **7-** Lucilius 94:27 (from Virgil, *Aeneid*, x. 284, and an unknown author). **8-** Delphic maxim 120; Nicomachean, Book 4, part 3. **9-** Pericles (as recorded by Thucydides), Funeral Speech, 430 BC. **10-** Lucilius 13:3. **11-**

Lucilius 13:1. **12-** Nicomachean, Book 2, part 2. **14-** Pericles (as recorded by Thucydides), Funeral Speech, 430 BC; Nicomachean, Book 3, part 8. **15-** Lucilius 124:3. **16-** 12 Rules, 244. **17-** Lucilius 113:27. **18-** Lucilius 98:2. **19-** Lucilius 98:3. **20-** Lucilius 91:20. **21-** Nicomachean, Book 4, part 3. **22-** Psalm 118:10-12. **23-** Lucilius 76:18. **24-** Lucilius 81:20. **25-** Delphic Maxim 132.

23. Priorities
1- Delphic maxim 110. **3-** John Rogers, *The Nature and Necessity of Repentance*, 1728, p. 29. **4-** Meditations 4:24. **5-**Lucilius 75:11. **6-** Meditations 1:5, 1:6. **7-** Enchiridion 33. **8-** Cicero, *De Officiis*, 1:19. **9-** Lucilius 53:9. **10-** Lucilius 117:32. **11-** Meditations 8:8. **12-** Lucilius 106:1. **13-** BoM, 2 Nephi 9:51; Lucilius 23:1, 3. **14-** Meditations 5:12. **15-** Dhammapada 6. **16-** Meditations 4:32. **17-** Meditations 7:3. **18-** Chuang Tzu, Sec. 28 (Giving Away a Throne), Watson translation. **19-23-** Lucilius 1, 22:14, 94:28, 99:10. **24-** Meditations 2:4; Thomas Jefferson, A Dozen Canons of conduct in Life. **25-** Cicero, *De Officiis*, 1:119-120.

24. Motivation
1- Matthew 6:1-6; Meditations 11:4; Tao Te Ching 7:2. **2-** Immanuel Kant, *Grounding for the Metaphysics of Morals*, 1785 (Kant's first formulation of the categorical imperative). **3-** Meditations 1:16. **4-**Tao Te Ching 64:3. **5-** Jordan Peterson Podcast.

25. Discipline
1- Delphic maxim 21. **2-** Delphic maxim 102. **3-** 2 Peter 2:19. **4-** Lucilius 124:12. **5-** Lucilius 73:15. **6-** Meditations 1:7, 1:16, 2:2. **7-** Lucilius 105:7-8. **8-** Lucilius 51:2, 4-5. **9-** Lucilius 10:5, 11:9-10. **10-** Enchiridion 10. **11-** 12 Rules, pp. 95-96. **12-** 12 Rules, 119-21. **13-** Jonathan Haidt, *The Happiness Hypothesis: Finding Modern Truth in Ancient Wisdom*, 2006. **14-** Ross W. Greene, *The Explosive Child*, p. 17. **15-** Dhammapada 7-8. **17-18-** Joseph Gresham Miller.

26. Hard Work
1- Lucilius 31:5. **3-**Lucilius 71:26. **4-** Jordan Peterson, "Freedom of Speech: Not Just Another Value", talk on May 13, 2017. **5-** Lucilius 22:8. **6-** Delphic Maxim 79. **7-** Lucilius 31:7. **8-** Lucilius 22: 8. **9-** Meditations 1:5. **10-** Meditations 3:5. **11-** Lucilius 55:1. **12-**

Lucilius 56:8. **14-** Pericles (as recorded by Thucydides), *Funeral Speech*, 430 BC. **15-** D&C 42:42; 2 Thessalonians 3:7-10. **16-** Theodore Roosevelt, National Duties—Address at Minnesota State Fair, September 2, 1901, p. 4.

27. Self Reliance

1- Meditations 3:5. **2-** Rod Dreher, "The Lost Boys", *The American Conservative*, November 13, 2018. **3-** Thomas Jefferson, A Dozen Canons of conduct in Life. **4-** Meditations 3:5.

28. Desire and Self-Indulgence

1- Lucilius 19:6. **2-** Lucilius 15:9; Bhagavad Gita 2:43. **4-** Epicharmus, quoted in Xenophon, *Memorabilia*, ca. 370 BC, 2.1.20. **5-** John Rogers, *The Nature and Necessity of Repentance*, 1728, p. 29. **6-** Luke 12:15, 34; Dhammapada 48; Chuang Tzu, Sec. 20 (The Mountain Tree), Watson translation. **8-** Lucilius 124:3. **9-** Nicomachean, Book 3, part 11. **10-** Lucilius 37:5. **11-** Lucilius 9. **12-** Dhammapada 199. **13-** Lucilius 97:1. **14-** 1 Timothy 6:10; Hebrews 13:5; Ecclesiastes 5:10; BoM, Mormon 8:37. **16-** D&C 56:17; Chuang Tzu, Sec. 14 (The Turning of Heaven). **17-** Lucilius 118:6. **18-** Lucilius 115:17. **19-** Nicomachean, Book 3, part 11.

29. Vices

1- Lucilius 50:7; Horace, *Epistles*, I.1, line 41. **2-** Lucilius 97:10. **3-** Lucilius 112:4, 116:8. **4-** Lucilius 69:4-5. **5-** Lucilius 69:3-5. **6-** Lucilius 56:10. **7-** Lucilius 45:7, 120:8. **8-** Lucilius 59:10.

30. Greed and Materialism

1- Delphic maxim 73. **2-** Delphic maxim 128. **3-** D&C 25:10; Matthew 6:21. **4-** Lucilius 9:19. **5-** Lucilius 73:2. **6-** James 4:2-3. **7-** Lucilius 21:7 (quoting Epicurus). **8-** Lucilius 108:11; Dhammapada 48; Chuang Tzu, Sec. 20 (The Mountain Tree), Watson translation. **9-** Lucilius 87:1. **10-** Lucilius 89:21. **11-** Lucilius 17:5. **12-** Lucilius 110:13. **13-** Lucilius 17:11 (quoting Epictetus). **14-** 12 Rules, 229. **15-** Lucilius 119:9. **16-** Lucilius 16:7-9. **17-** Lucilius 17:5, 8. **18-** 1 Timothy 6:18; BoM, Helaman 12:2. **19-** Lucilius 98:10.

31. Moderation and Balance

1- Delphic maxim 17. **2-** Delphic maxim 38. **5-** Lucilius 15:9. **6-** Nicomachean, Book 3, part 11. **7-** Lucilius 119:5-7. **9-** Lucilius 95:15.

10- Pericles (as recorded by Thucydides), Funeral Speech, 430 BC.
11- Lucilius 74:18. 12- Lucilius 39:6. 13- Jonathan Haidt, *The Happiness Hypothesis: Finding Modern Truth in Ancient Wisdom*, 2006. 14- Nicomachean, Book 7, parts 1-10. 18- Lucilius 2, 74:12.

32. Killing, Violence, and Anger
4- Matthew 5:21-26. 5- Meditations 1:16; Tao Te Ching 30:1, 3; Dhammapada 131, 132, 291. 6- Jordan Peterson, "Biblical Series III: God and the Hierarchy of Authority", June 6, 2017; Tao Te Ching 31, 69:3 (Beck and Bynner translations); Tao Te Ching 69: 4 (Walker and Crowley translation). 7- Hebrews 12:14l; D&C 98: 16. 8- Matthew 26:52; Revelation 13:10; BoM, Alma 48:14; D&C 98:34-36. 9- Attributed to Mother Teresa (last sentence only).

33. Honesty and Integrity
1- D&C 51:9. 2- Delphic Maxim 88. 4- Ecclesiastes 5:5; Delphic maxim 68 (alternate numbering, *see* Al. N. Oikonomides, "Records of '*The Commandments of the Seven Wise Men*' in the 3rd c. B.C.", 63 Classical Bulletin 67, 76 (1987). 5- 12 Rules, p. 264. 7- Exodus 20:15. 8- Alexander Solzhenitsyn, "Live Not By Lies", 1974. 9- Delphic Maxim 46; Psalm 120:2. 10- Delphic maxim 64 (alternate numbering). 11- 12 Rules, 255-58. 12- 12 Rules, pp. 263-64.

34. Chastity, Family, and Sex Roles
1- Delphic maxim 132. 2- Delphic maxim 131. 3- Delphic maxim 4. 4- Delphic maxim 126. 5- Delphic maxim 9. 6- Delphic Maxim 124. 7- Delphic maxim 44. 8- Delphic maxim 127. 9- Meditations 1:17. 10- "Permanent, fruitful, and faithful": Catholic definition of marriage; Joseph Henrich, *et. al.*, "The puzzle of monogamous marriage", *Philosophical Transactions of the Royal Society B*, January 23, 2012; Galena K. Rhoades and Scott M. Stanley, *Before "I Do": What Do Premarital Experiences Have to Do with Marital Quality Among Today's Young Adults?*, 2014, The National Marriage Project at the University of Virginia; Nicholas H. Wolfinger, *Does Sexual History Affect Marital Happiness?*, October 22, 2018. 11- Ecclesiastes 4:9-12. 12- 1 Corinthians 7:3-5. 13- LDS Church, *The Family: A Proclamation to the World*, September 23, 1995. 14- 12 Rules, p. 393-94. 15- 12 Rules, p. 394. 16- D&C 49:16;

BoM, Jacob 2:27; BoM Mosiah 4:15; BoM, 4 Nephi 1:39; D&C 68:25. **17**- D&C 49:16; BoM, Jacob 2:27; BoM Mosiah 4:15; BoM, 4 Nephi 1:39; D&C 68:25. **18**- Psalm 127:3-5. **19**- Theodore Roosevelt, National Duties—Address at Minnesota State Fair, September 2, 1901, p. 4. **21**- Betsey Stevenson and Justin Wolfers, "The Paradox of Declining Female Happiness", NBER Working Paper No. 2009-11, May 2009; Sabino Kornrich, et. al., "Egalitarianism, Housework, and Sexual Frequency in Marriage", American Sociological Review, Vol. 78, No. 1, 2012, pp. 26-50; Matthew D. Hammond and Chris G. Sibley, "Why are Benevolent Sexists Happier?", Sex Roles, Vol. 65, 2011, pp. 332-343; Jaime L. Napier, et. al., "The Joy of Sexism? A Multinational Investigation of Hostile and Benevolent Justifications for Gender Inequality and Their Relations to Subjective Well-Being", Sex Roles, Vol. 62, 2010, pp. 405-419. **22**- LDS Church, The Family: A Proclamation to the World, September 23, 1995. **23**- 12 Rules, pp. 78-79, 401. **24**- 12 Rules, p. 175. **25**- Theodore Roosevelt, National Duties—Address at Minnesota State Fair, September 2, 1901. **26**- 12 Rules, p. 174. **27**- 12 Rules, pp. 168-69. **28**- 12 Rules, p. 177, 224-25. **30**- Meditations 1:12.

35. Relationships with Others

1- Romans 12:10. **2**- Delphic maxim 47. **3**- Delphic maxim 82. **4**- Dhammapada 133. **5**- Jonathan Haidt, The Happiness Hypothesis: Finding Modern Truth in Ancient Wisdom, 2006; Sonja Lyubomirsky, et. al., "Pursuing happiness: The architecture of sustainable change", Review of General Psychology, Vol. 9, No. 2, 2005, pp. 111-31; Cicero, De Officiis, 1:22. **6**- Delphic maxims 15, 20, 28, 105. **7**- Delphic Maxim 98. **8**- Delphic Maxim 103. **9**- Delphic maxim 97. **10**- 12 Rules, Rule 1. **11**- Nicomachean, Book 4, part 8. **12**- Benjamin Franklin, The Autobiography of Benjamin Franklin, 12 Rules, p. 197. **13**- D&C 88:124; Dhammapada 153. **14**- Meditations 11:9. **15**- Thomas 39; Matthew 10:16; Jordan Peterson, Podcast 13, 31:00. **16**- Delphic maxim 60. **17**- Delphic maxim 34. **18**- Bhagavad Gita 12:15. **19**- Meditations 2:1. **20**- Nicomachean, Book 4, part 6. **21**- Delphic Maxim 83. **22**- Delphic Maxim 41. **23**- Nico-

machean Book 4, part 3. **25-** Lucilius 94:40. **26-** Enchiridion 33.
27- Meditations 1:5. **28-** Meditations 11:18. **31-** Delphic maxim 29.
32- Delphic maxim 116. **33-** Delphic maxim 63. **34-** Enchiridion
33. **35-** J.W. von Goethe, *The Sorrows of Young Werther*, 1774.
36- Meditations 11:14. **37-** Lucilius 45:7. **38-** Meditations 11:13.
39- Meditations 11:18.

36. Power and Leadership

1- Delphic maxim 109. **2-** Thomas 81. **3-** Pericles (as recorded by
Thucydides), Funeral Speech, 430 BC. **4-** Tao Te Ching 61:1, 3.
5- Titus 1:7-8; Hesiod, *Theogony*, lines 88-89 (Norton Anthology,
Third Edition, Vol. A, p. 42); Tao Te Ching 61:4. **6-** 12 Rules, p.
397. **7-** D&C 121:34-46. **8-** D&C 98:9-10. **9-** Lucilius 42:3-4. **10-**
Arthur C. Clark, *The Songs of Distant Earth*. **11-** Helaman 7:5.
12- Cassius Dio, *Roman History*, ca. 220, quoting Quintus Lutatius
Catulus (Capitolinus), 78 BC; Chuang Tzu, Sec. 4 (In the World of
Men); Watson translation, p. 51. **13-14-** BoM, Mosiah 29:16-25.
15- Lord Acton, *Letter to Bishop Mandell Creighton*, April 5,
1887; Joseph Smith, as quoted by John Taylor, "The Organization
of the Church", *Millennial Star*, Vol. 13, No. 22, November 15,
1851, p. 339. **16-** Elbert Hubbard, *The Philistine: A Periodical of
Protest*, 1907. **17-** Tao Te Ching 75:1-2 (Walker translation), 75:3
(Mitchell translation), 71:1-2 (Walker translation). **18-** Joseph Smith,
as quoted by John Taylor, "The Organization of the Church", Millennial Star, Vol. 13, No. 22, November 15, 1851, p. 339; Tao Te
Ching 57:1, 59:1, and 71:1-2 (Walker). **19-** Tao Te Ching 71:1-2
(Walker). **21-** Chuang Tzu, Sec. 4 (In the World of Men), Watson
translation, p. 51. **22-** Jordan Peterson. **23-** talks by Jordan Peter-
son; Nick Phillips, "Why Ordinary Americans Reject Architectural
Ideologues", *The American Conservative*.

37. Debt

1- Delphic maxim 72, 122. **2-** D&C 19:35.

38. Health and Diet

1- 1 Corinthians 7:19. **2-** D&C 89:20. **3-** D&C 89:11-12, 14; Dhammapada 131, 132, 291. **4-** Lucilius 15:4-5. **5-** D&C 89:9. **6-** D&C
89:5-8, 17; Anya Topiwala, *et. al.*, "Moderate alcohol consumption

as risk factor for adverse brain outcomes and cognitive decline: longitudinal cohort study", *BMJ*, 2017; Harvard School of Public Health, Alcohol: Balancing Risks and Benefits; Andy Towers, "Maybe moderate drinking isn't so good for you after all", *The Conversation*; Dana E. King, "Adopting Moderate Alcohol Consumption in Middle Age: Subsequent Cardiovascular Events", *The American Journal of Medicine*, March 2008. **7**- D&C 89:8. **8**- Matthew 15:11; Mark 7:14-23; Thomas 14.

39. Good Character
1- 12 Rules, 255-58. **2**- Heraclitus. **3**- Delphic maxim 30. **4**- Delphic maxim 54. **5**- Jordan Peterson, "Freedom of Speech: Not Just Another Value", talk on May 13, 2017. **6-10**- Delphic maxims 143-147. **11**- Delphic Maxims 134, 140. **12**- Lucilius 74:1. **13**- Amy Wax and Larry Alexander, "Paying the price for breakdown of the country's bourgeois culture", *The Philadelphia Inquirer*, August 9, 2017. **14**- Meditations 3:4. **15**- Meditations 1:9, 1:15, 1:16, 2:17. **16**- Delphic maxim 70. **17**- Enchiridion 33. **18**- Nicomachean, Book 2, part 1 and Book 3, part 5. **19**- Meditations 1:15, 2:17. **20**- Lucilius 23:7. **21**-Meditations 1:9, 1:15, 1:16. **22**- Meditations 1:16. **23**- Meditations 6:2. **24**- Chuang Tzu, Sec. 31 (The Old Fisherman), Watson translation. **25**- Lucilius 114:2. **26**- Dhammapada 252. **27**- Lucilius 122:1, 3. **28**- 1 Corinthians 13:11; Lucilius 4.

40. Exemplars of Virtue
1- Delphic Maxim 65. **2**- Meditations 4:38. **3**- Church of England, Lectionary, June 24, Nativity of St. John the Baptist. **4**- Lucilius 52:8-9. **5**- Lucilius 11:9-10. **6**- Lucilius 64:5. **7**- Lucilius 64:6. **9**- Mosiah 2:11. **12**- Psalm 69:6.

41. Sharing the Triple Path
1- D&C 11:21, 18:10-16, 19:40. **2**- Matthew 5:14. **3**- Matthew 5: 14-15; Mark 4:21-25; Luke 8:16-18; Thomas 33. **5**- Matthew 7:6.

Hope

Contents

1. Hope

1   Having hope means that even if you are afflicted from all sides, you will not be crushed; perplexed, but not pulled down to lazy despair; persecuted, but without feeling forsaken; struck down, but still holding fast to the Triple Path.

2   Labor with hope to make the world better first by focusing on improving yourself, then your family, and then your community.

3   Let this be your constant goal: that in every situation, things

are better because you are there; that your influence and actions are always a force for improving yourself, your circumstances, your family and those around you, and the whole human race.

4 Find the potential for improvement in every situation and then work to make that potential reality.

5 Seek a world in which those who work against you wake up and see the light, so that they might accept the good you seek and let it encompass them too.

6 Be not an idealist with ceaseless optimism that blinds you to the negative, but also neither be a scornful cynic overwhelmed into inaction (or worse still, into chaotic destruction) by your despair and disillusionment. Instead, be a hopeful realist who recognizes the good and bad in every situation and then does your best to make things better.

7 Hope is an anchor to your heart, making you sure and steadfast, always striving for improvement, abounding in virtue, and growing in wisdom.

8 Praise hope.

9 What good is it if you say you have hope, but you do not have wisdom and virtue? Is hope enough? No! You need all three. You cannot really labor with hope without also seeking wisdom and practicing virtue.

2. Discontent

1 Be not discontented by life.

2 Set your house in order before you criticize the world.

3 When you feel discontent, return firmly to the Triple Path. With what are you discontented? With the evil of others? Remember that we are all imperfect. Cease your idle laments about the evil in the world. Instead, fight against it and show others the Triple Path.

4 Whether you live a life of wisdom, virtue, and hope or whether you live a life of foolishness, evil, and lazy despair, you still will be buried, reduced to dust, and be quiet at last. Before that happens, how much better to work to increase the wisdom virtue, and hope in the world, rather than idly lamenting the fool-

ishness, evil, and lazy despair already here.

5   A dark night of the soul usually comes during a serious spiritual quest, when things fall apart and hopelessness, despair, and black nihilism beckon to you. But cease not your quest and still press forward, for after the dark night comes the glorious sunrise.

3. Sacrifice

1   Stand in awe and stillness, and sin not. Make right sacrifices and put your trust in God, offering a humble heart before Him.

2   You come into life with an ethical burden to justify your own existence. The purpose of life is not to maximize your ratio of personal happiness or pleasure to suffering. The purpose of a wise and virtuous life is to take on honorable, worthwhile challenges and to sacrifice to overcome them. Such challenges, voluntarily undertaken, mold and shape you. They bring nobility of soul and allow you to accomplish great things.

3   It is far better to suffer for doing good, than for doing evil.

4   Sacrifice now to reduce future pain and suffering.

5   Regulate, control, and order your impulses of the moment so that your current self does not trammel your future selves and set your soul on a path to destruction.

6   Sacrifice for a better tomorrow. Work today so that tomorrow improves. Give up that which is of value right now to attain something better in the future. Delay gratification in the moment to achieve greatness in times to come. Pleasure forestalled can bring great rewards later.

7   The best among us delay gratification, bargaining with the future. They sacrifice, and their sacrifices get better and more efficacious as they practice them.

8   Not all sacrifices are of equal quality or value. Figure out which are the proper ones to make, and then make them.

9   Small sacrifices will often solve small problems, but expect that it may take big, encompassing sacrifices to solve large, complex problems.

10   What would be the best, most encompassing, most effective, most pleasing to God, of all possible sacrifices you might

make? How much better might the possible future be if you made it?

11 It is possible to make wicked sacrifices as well as righteous ones. Such sacrifices are abominations. Do you offer polluted sacrifices? Why you would treat God as contemptible?

12 Sometimes, apparently correct sacrifices of high quality are not rewarded, and the reason for the failure is not clear. Understanding why is a difficult question to answer. Sometimes there is no answer. Even so, still sacrifice.

13 Sometimes things fail to go well not because of the world, but because of you. The world you perceive is to a large extent discerned through the lens of your values. If your world is not what you want, examine what you value most. Sacrifice that which you have overvalued. Let go of your current presuppositions. Perhaps you must sacrifice that which you had loved most so that instead you can value above all God, and wisdom, virtue, and hope. Thus you can set yourself on the path to reaching the full potential of whom you might become, rather than staying who you are, self-confined in an undesirable world.

14 The stories of our God tell us that He requires sacrifice, often demanding not just any sacrifice, but exactly what we think we love most.

15 Do not sacrifice that which is expedient, but that which must be sacrificed.

16 Lift up your eyes to God. Aim your sacrifices at attaining His highest wisdom, His encompassing virtue, and His relentless hope.

17 You are not committed to something unless you are willing to sacrifice for it.

18 Seek to build a society where sacrifice is rewarded. Cleave to those who believe likewise.

19 Make sacrifices of thanksgiving.

20 Remember the parable of the child and the cupcake.

4. Patience

1 Be patient in suffering. Endure your afflictions patiently,

even if you have many and suffer abuse, beating, or punishment, but exercise your patience with power and self-control, never with weakness. Be patient, but not passive. Persevere to resolve your problems, conquer your troubles, and escape your hardships.

2 Be patient with others' flaws. Encourage the fearful; help the weak; offer support to those who are struggling to follow the Triple Path. Remember that you yourself were once foolish and lacking in virtue. Be honest with yourself and remember that you are still so now.

3 Toward the anger of others, first respond with calmness and patience; calmness will pacify numerous great offenses and soothe many explosive situations.

5. Focus on What You Can Control

1 Pay attention. Be on your guard. Know your opportunity, and your peril.

2 Recognize and harness fortune when it comes, but do not trust that it will come, neither trust in it if it does.

3 A fool worries about what cannot be changed and ignores those things that can be improved.

4 Stand tall and take responsibility for your life. Voluntarily accept the burden of being and face the terrible demands of life. Sacrifice whatever it takes to live with meaning. Defend and expand the territory of your life, transforming it into something better, something more wonderful.

5 Pay attention to the whisperings of your conscience. What problems in the world stand out to you, bother you? This may be destiny calling out to you, showing to you the dragons you must confront. You can develop the vision and the fortitude to confront the dragons, but you must first notice them, and then take responsibility for fighting them.

6 Focus on your physical and spiritual surroundings. Ask yourself: "What is bothering me?" Next, ask: "Could I fix it? Would I be willing to fix it?" If you cannot answer yes to these questions, search again. Aim lower until you find something that bothers you and that you could and would fix. Fix it. Then, start again.

7   Some things are under your control. Others are not. If you think to be under your control that which is not, you will be burdened and in turmoil; grieving, blaming both God and men. If you learn to correctly distinguish between what is under your control and what is not, you will not find fault with God or men. Take, therefore this step toward peace. If it be a thing not under your control, have ready at hand your answer: "It is nothing to me".

8   You can eliminate many useless things that bother you; this is because they are caused by your own opinions and attitudes. Let go of your concern about things outside your control. Instead, focus on what is in your power to change. Focus on your own thoughts and actions, and on following the Triple Path.

9   Learn to channel and control your thoughts, speech, actions, and desires toward following the Triple Path.

10   The promise of your desires is to attain what you desire; the promise of aversion is to not fall into what you seek to avoid. When you fail in your desire, you feel merely disappointed. When you fall into what you want to avoid, you feel miserable. If, then, you confine your aversion only to foolishness, evil, and lazy despair—that which is contrary to the right use of your own faculties and that which you have in your own control—you will avoid much misery. Withdraw, therefore, your aversion from all the matters that are not under your control; transfer it to what is contrary to the right use of that which is under your control.

11   Do not take lightly the decisions you make. Your choices, for good or evil, determine the contours of your life. And the aggregate of every human life shapes the landscape of mankind's present and future.

12   How have you improved your time, which is short and uncertain?

6. Perseverance

1   Finish the race without shrinking back.

2   Rouse yourself and correct your mistakes. Trust in God and follow the Triple Path, for only these have the power to stir you and shake off your deep slumber.

3   Watch yourself at all times. Be industrious and diligent in all things. Meditate, pray, and focus your actions always on seeking greater wisdom, practicing better virtue, and laboring more with hope, so that you do not fall away from the Triple Path.

4   No matter your circumstance, seek wisdom, practice virtue, and labor with hope.

5   It is not enough just to start on the Triple Path, you must also endure to the end.

6   As long as you live, keep learning how to live.

7   Within you is a well of goodness, and it will never stop bubbling up, if you never stop digging.

8   Weary not in well-doing, for in due season you will reap the consequences, if you faint not.

9   Weary not in well-doing, even if you only have opportunities to do small things. Out of small things proceed that which is great.

10   Laboring with hope does not mean maintaining an unwavering belief that things will always improve, but being determined to never stop working to make things better.

11   Laboring with hope does not mean never feeling discouraged or disappointed. It means continuing to work to make things better, even *when* you are discouraged and disappointed.

12   Seek to spend each day so that at its end, you may say, "I have lived well. I have sought wisdom, practiced virtue, and labored with hope". Spend each day so that you are able to await the next in possession of yourself and without fear.

13   When confronted by something difficult you are called to do, do not think, "this is impossible", but instead think, "if anything is possible for another to achieve, then I too will do my utmost to achieve it".

14   Being preceded and surrounded by so great a cloud of validating tradition and experience, cast away the sin that distracts you and clings so closely, lay aside every weight that slows you down, and run with patience the race set before you.

15   Many of the good things in the world you enjoy are here

because those who came before built them and left them for you. Everything you build, and the ruins of everything you destroy, you will leave for those who come after you. They will be just as deserving as you were of the good things you received from those who came before. Toil and strain to make the world better, as those who came before who did for you.

16 Plant trees that are slow to grow, but bring shade to cheer your grandchildren in the far-off years. A society thrives when old men plant trees whose shade they know they will never sit in.

17 With the wealth of wisdom you have inherited from your predecessors, play the part of a careful steward, increasing that which you have inherited. Let there be no more dark ages. Pass this inheritance on to your descendants larger than when you received it. Much still remains to do, and much will always remain; those born a thousand ages hence will still have the opportunity of adding something further.

7. Balance

1 Illumination comes neither from asceticism nor debauchery, but from the balance of the Golden Mean. It comes neither from renouncing the world nor embracing it as it is, but from living and working within it to make it better. It comes neither from celibacy nor from promiscuity, but from monogamy and creating and nurturing and sustaining a family. It comes neither from shutting yourself off from physical desires and ambitions, nor from uncritically indulging them, but from channeling them to good and virtuous ends.

2 Be an example of balance and a force for good. Start a family. Nurture and love your spouse and children. Build up and contribute to your community. Show love to others and teach wisdom, virtue, and hope.

8. The Great Now

1 Live in the present, foreseeing the future and seeking Divine forethought.

2 This is the day in which God has placed you. Rejoice and be glad in it.

278

3   No matter how much things improve, or degenerate, you will always have troubles. Your troubles of the moment are yours to solve in the moment.

4   Do not pine for some great far-off future perfect utopia. A great hoped-for future will not come by waiting for it. Live in the great now, not in your dreams for the future. Work to make your hoped-for future a reality in the present.

5   Think of your existence as being stretched across time, with your potential future self manifested in the present as your conscience and intuition. What you could be in the future beckons to you in the present.

6   Instead of criticizing the past, concentrate on what you can do in the present to build up a great future.

7   Do not sell your future for your transitory desires in the present.

8   Nothing that is yet to happen is preordained.

9   How much have evils that never happened cost you?

10   Do not waste your time unnecessarily worrying about tomorrow; tomorrow will take care of itself. Sufficient unto the day is the evil thereof.

11   Every day, align your soul with God and with wisdom, virtue, and hope, and ask yourself, "What can I do, today, to live with meaning, to make life a little better?". Then, attend to the day while aiming at the highest good.

12   Today, do the most good possible. When tomorrow arrives, then do even more good. And so too make it the same with the weeks, months, years, and decades of your life.

13   Be not disturbed by the future. You will meet it, if you have to, with the same weapons of wisdom, virtue, and hope that today arm you against the present.

14   Past and future are both absent. Do not torture yourself about what may be or what has passed. Save your strength, so you are ready when actual suffering comes to you in the present.

15   Some things torment you more than they ought; some torment you before they ought; and some torment you when they

ought not torment you at all. Overcome your natural habit of exaggerating, or imagining, or anticipating sorrow. Do not fear before the crisis comes; it may be that the dangers that terrified you will never come upon you.

16 You suffer needlessly when you let yourself suffer before or after it is necessary. It is likely that some troubles will befall you in the future, but it is not a present fact. How often has the unexpected happened! How often has the expected never come to pass! And even if something were ordained to be, what does it avail to run out to meet your suffering? You will suffer soon enough, when it arrives. Even bad fortune is fickle. Perhaps it will come, perhaps not; in the meantime it does not. So look forward, meanwhile, to better things.

17 How wretched and foolish is premature fear of your troubles, letting your soul be apprehensive of the future, consumed with an anxious desire that what you have may remain with you to the very end. In such a state, you will never be at rest, worriedly waiting for a bad future, losing the present blessings that you might enjoy.

18 The fool is always getting ready to live. If you have spent your time always looking forward to tomorrow, then you have not yet lived, but have only been preparing to live, and though your life ends on the final day, it perishes a little more every day.

19 Live in the present, not fearing the future; but do not for this reason be indifferent to the future. Turn aside from whatever may cause fear, foreseeing whatever can be foreseen by planning. Observe and avoid, long before it happens, anything that is likely to do you harm. In this, have a spirit of confidence and a mind strongly resolved to endure all things. He who can bear fate can also beware of fate.

20 The seeds of what you anticipate are already here, now, scattered across the earth. Bring a great future into the present by gathering what is wise and virtuous in the world, building on them, and creating new wisdom and virtue out of them.

21 Remember the parable of the yeast.

22 When you make bread, adding a little yeast at the begin-

ning makes the dough grow into large loaves by the end. What you do now has the power to make the present grow into a great future.

9. Tradition

1   Tradition is not the worship of ashes, but the preservation of fire.

2   Appreciate and value the traditions of your forefathers, even though you may not initially recognize their purpose.

3   Respect the traditions of your ancestors, as voices echoing hard-earned wisdom out of the past to you.

4   The limits of tradition are not prison walls confining your freedom; they are guardrails protecting you from tumbling off the edge of a precipice.

5   Tradition preserves the solutions to problems no one remembers. If you abandon the solutions, the problems will become all too familiar again.

6   Withdrawing from tradition, religion, and nation will not free you, but rather make you apt to falling prey to the desperation of meaninglessness.

7   When we leave the solid ground of tradition, we walk out onto thin ice, where just below, deep, freezing waters roil.

8   If some tradition or practice that makes no sense to you has been around for a very long time, then, seemingly irrational or not, it will likely last longer still, outliving you and those who call for its demise.

9   Conditions change. Culture and traditions are vulnerable to corruption. Our traditions are not perfect.

10   Lasting progress usually comes by making small improvements on what came before. When faced with new questions or challenges, it is wise and prudent to respond with small, incremental changes, if any at all. If the need for radical change becomes unavoidable, woe to you, for such change almost never comes without much pain and difficulty, with a great risk of leading you astray into difficult or evil paths.

11   Truth lies open for all; it has not yet been monopolized. There is plenty of it left for us and our posterity to discover. The

teachers of the past are not our masters, but our guides. We usually follow in their footsteps on the old road they have trod before. If we find a way along the path that appears shorter and smoother to travel, let us scout out miles far ahead to verify the soundness of the proposed change. And let us always beware that we do not shortsightedly fool ourselves into following what ends up being a dangerous or faulty path, when the safety of the old road was there all along.

12 It is much easier to burn something down than to build its replacement.

13 A break from tradition is more likely to bring decline, ruin, or collapse, than improvement.

14 Why should you respect tradition? Why not instead derive your values and practices using the facts you know and your own faculties of reasoning and logic? Because you are fallible and ephemeral. Your abilities of reasoning and logic are not as good and objective as you think they are. Moreover, the most real aspects of existence manifest themselves across the longest of time frames. They are not necessarily apprehensible in the here and now. Thus, even if your abilities were infallible, you could still never derive all the right values and practices just from the facts that portray themselves to you over your short life.

15 Each person is usually most conservative about what he knows best.

16 How foolhardy it is to radically restructure the stabilizing traditions of our society just to solve a so-called problem that a small minority claim to face! Why would any but the most foolish pretend to solve an individual's private disturbance through a social revolution causing far more turmoil and trouble?

17 Disregard and shun those who constantly push for many changes or who promise paradise through some great abrupt shift, and especially those who are never satisfied with what ground has been ceded to them and are never willing to grant concessions to others. To such as these, you must never cede anything. If you let them have their way, they will destroy the foundations of your so-

ciety, tearing up good and wise traditions that have proved themselves firm and steady against the tremors and upheavals of hard experience, replacing them with empty holes containing only the idle fancies of daydreamers.

18 Remember the parable of the pelican and the fisherman.

19 Live in wisdom and virtue, following the weight of tradition and the accumulated understanding of the past, but do not mistake honoring tradition for following the depraved whims of the masses. There are things that, if done by the few, we would refuse to imitate; yet when the majority have begun to do them, we follow along—just as if anything were more honorable because it is more frequent! It is easy for evil ideas and practices, when they have become prevalent, to reach the standard of righteousness in the eyes of many. Never let them do that to you.

20 When you let outsiders into your communities and institutions, there is great risk they will not feel comfortable, and that if they gain power, they will work to eliminate and abolish everything distinctive and sacred you have because these things make them feel like the outsiders they are.

21 If you are a stranger, act like one, until you are no longer a stranger.

10. Progress Toward Paradise

1 Is paradise up above? Then it is for the birds. Is it in an unknown future? Then we will probably never see it. Paradise cannot, and will not, be given to us. It will come only when we build it.

2 They change their skies, but not their souls, those who run across the sea.

3 To whatever new shining utopia you try to create, you will bring the same old problems you are trying to escape, until you conquer them where you remain.

4 Remember the parable of the two pilgrims.

5 It matters little whether you lay a sick man on a wooden or on a golden bed, for wherever he be moved he will carry his ailment with him.

6 The person you are and the people you live among mat-

ter more than the place to which you go. Work to conquer your personal faults, and seek to live among those doing the same.

7 The more that you sort yourself out, the more responsibility you will be able to take for those around you, and the more problems you will be able to solve.

8 Someone truly motivated by a desire to make things better is less concerned with changing other people as he is with changing himself. If he does believe that there is some change others must make, he will have already taken responsibility and made that change first in himself and his own household before speaking up about it.

9 Paradise will come gradually, as we slowly improve what came before and, little by little, conquer our problems. Go and labor with all your strength to build paradise—live in truth, with faith in God; seek wisdom, practice virtue, labor with hope, and teach and nurture your children to do the same. When everyone around you does likewise, then you will have together remade your surroundings into the promised land, no matter what the place was before you started there.

10 Your ancestors, and many others, sacrificed tremendously for what you have inherited—some literally sacrificed their very lives. Year after year, they created a little more than they consumed and destroyed, in terms of things physical, artistic, intellectual, and spiritual. That growth, compounded over centuries and millennia, is the civilization you enjoy today. Respect what they did. Be grateful for it. And build and save and sacrifice the same as your ancestors did, to pass on the inheritance of our civilization to your descendants.

11 Worthy goals are often partially or wholly incompatible. Charting the right course is often an exercise in making tradeoffs between competing objectives.

12 Improvements usually come slowly, but the way to ruin is rapid.

13 Not all change is progress. There is no law that requires that things must always improve.

14 Even if you compare the best communities to a hypothetical utopian ideal, they will fall short. Radical change to such communities will usually make them worse.

15 Though you drive nature out with a pitchfork, ever she will return. If you carve out a track that she may follow and then invite her onto it, then you might direct her in more useful ways.

16 In your quest for progress, never forget that human nature not only has much that is ennobling and beautiful, but also much that is devious and evil. Be vigilant against evil. Build safeguards into every institution and endeavor.

17 Pursue harmony. Harmony makes small things grow; lack of harmony makes great things decay.

18 Things fall apart. They naturally deteriorate, and our blindness, inaction and deceit further add to the degeneration. You must therefore always pay attention and be maintaining, improving, building.

19 We exist for the sake of each other, that we may mutually help each other, but do not let the selfish exploit your goodness. When the selfish live among the virtuous, they will prey on them and take everything they can. Seek, therefore, the company of the virtuous. When only the virtuous dwell together, they will live in paradise because they will create it together.

20 Evil always tries to infiltrate the paradises created by the virtuous. What starts out being sincere ends up being deceitful. What was simple in the beginning acquires monstrous proportions in the end. Therefore, keep ambitious, aspiring, self-important, self-aggrandizing, prideful, hypocritical, or evil people from entering your community and always keep them out of power; keep institutions transparent and simple; and follow the Triple Path, always.

21 Greatly distrust anyone who seeks to change the world by forcing other people to change.

22 Beware of newcomers showing up and quickly volunteering to help and take over tasks. Only give responsibility to those who have proved themselves over time to be trustworthy.

23 Never give great responsibility to those with few or no

children, nor give them charge of anything of consequence. They have little stake in the future of the community and there is great risk they will lead it to decline or ruin.

24 Success breeds complacency, making it easy to forget to pay attention. Do not turn a blind eye and take for granted what you have. Notice when things start deteriorating and corruption is taking root, lest everything fall apart.

25 Look ahead. Anticipate difficult things while they are easy, and do things that would become great while they are small. Many difficult things would have been easy to solve at the start; great things often arise from small and simple beginnings.

26 When everyone seeks wisdom, practices virtue, and labors with hope, they will be of one heart and mind; they will live in goodness and harmony.

27 Any great endeavor must be based in wisdom, strength, virtue, and beauty: wisdom to contrive it, strength to support it, virtue to sustain it, and beauty to adorn it.

11. Government and Society

1 Governments exist for the benefit of individuals and to promote the good and safety of society. No government is legitimate that limits (beyond extreme minimums needed to protect other citizens' free exercise of the same) its citizens' freedom of thought, free exercise of conscience, freedom of speech and association, right to own and control property, right to self-defense, and right to self-determination. No government is legitimate unless it requires of all citizens equally the obligation to account for their actions, to respect the autonomy of others, and to build up the community and promote its welfare. Government should combat criminality, but never control conscience; punish guilt, but never suppress the freedom of the soul; secure citizens' right to support themselves, but never insulate them from the natural consequences of their actions. To accomplish this, governments should impose the minimum necessary rules, enforced with the minimum necessary force.

2 It is the place of the politician, the official, the judge, the civil servant, the officer, the soldier, and all else employed by the

state to bear in mind that he represents the state and its citizens, that it is his duty to uphold their honor and dignity, to enforce the law, to protect and preserve the citizens' constitutional rights, and to remember that all this has been committed to him as a sacred trust.

The private individual ought first, in private relations, to live on fair and equal terms with his fellow-citizens, with a spirit neither servile and grovelling nor yet domineering; and second, in matters pertaining to the state, to labor for her peace and honor; for such a one we are accustomed to esteem and call a good citizen.

As for the foreigner or the resident alien, it is his duty to attend strictly to his own concerns, not to pry into other people's business, and under no condition to meddle in the politics of a country not his own.

3   Always be contributing something to the common good.

4   Do not allow absorption in your private affairs to diminish your knowledge of your community's, nation's, and country's business or diminish your involvement in settling public issues. One who keeps aloof from public life is useless.

5   The more corrupt the state, the more numerous the laws.

6   A just society should reward productive, prosocial behavior. It should punish theft and exploitation. It should ensure, as much as practically possible, equality of opportunity, but never equality of outcome.

7   Rights cannot exist without responsibilities, nor liberty without duty, nor freedom without obligation. Indeed, rights and liberty and freedom exist so that you can discharge your responsibilities and duties and obligations.

8   Tyranny expands to fill the space made available for it. Fight every sign of it. Never consent to tyranny. Make your refusal clear and explicit, and stand behind it.

9   An excess of chaos often brings on tyranny. Tyrannies often collapse, bringing on an excess of chaos. Reject both chaos and tyranny. Live instead in responsible freedom.

10   Collectively pursuing a goal or ideal produces a hierarchy,

since some will do better at achieving it than others. You must pursue worthy goals, however, to live with meaning. Seeking to achieve equality of outcomes will thus eliminate meaning from life. This does not mean, however, that all hierarchies are justifiable or that all outcomes are just. Fortunately, in an advanced society there are many worthy goals to pursue and thus many different valid hierarchies in which to compete.

11 When a hierarchy is based on power instead of relevant competence, then it is prone to collapse.

12 A common faith is a necessity for a society to have internal peace and decent government.

13 That we might more easily love our country, our country should be made lovely.

14 In a harmonious, well-functioning society neither the authorities nor regular individuals are gossips or zealots: they care little about discovering the details of others' lives or about penalizing others for their minute infractions. But also in a harmonious, well-functioning society, the standards of behavior are good and reasonable and not oppressive; in response, good people want to follow them and try to live above reproach, so they care little about what others may find out about them.

15 Do you want to live in a well-ordered and pleasant society? Then live among those capable of, and actively trying to, seek wisdom, practice virtue, and labor with hope. When they know correct principles, they govern themselves.

16 These are the patterns for successful self-government in any group:

First, the group's boundaries are clearly defined, including boundaries about geography, resources, responsibilities, mission, and membership.

Second, group rules are matched to local needs and conditions

Third, those affected by the rules participate in creating and modifying them.

Fourth, outside authorities respect the rights of group

members to make their rules.

Fifth, group members create and carry out a system for monitoring group members' behavior and compliance with the rules. Those who monitor are group members who are accountable to the rest of the group.

Sixth, the group impartially imposes graduated, proportional sanctions for rule violations.

Seventh, the group provides accessible and cheap ways to resolve disputes.

Eighth, responsibility for governing is built in nested tiers from the lowest level up to the entire interconnected system.

Ninth, group members effectively communicate with one another; all group members are free to express their opinions without reproof or punishment.

Tenth, there is a sense of internal trust within the group. All group members respect norms of reciprocity.

12. Banishing Hypocrisy

1 That which is not good for the swarm, neither is it good for the bee. What is not permitted to others is also not permitted to you. Do not be a hypocrite who tries to justify actions for yourself that you would condemn if taken by others.

2 That which is not permitted to the individual is also not permitted to the group, the institution, the corporation, the government, or the Church. When an individual commits an act of greed or cruelty or murder, we condemn it. How can we condemn these individual acts, but praise the murders and horrors of unjust wars, or profit from the greed of dishonest corporations?

3 Do not be a parasite who seeks to benefit yourself or your family at the community's expense.

4 Hypocrisy destroys the fabric of a community. A harmonious society thrives on trust, honesty, and fairness. Hypocrisy destroys all of these. For this reason, virtuous communities punish unrepentant hypocrites, casting them out and declaring forfeit their ill-gotten gains.

5 Beware of those who draw close to God with their lips,

while their hearts are far from Him.

6 Do not be a hypocrite, exploiting others by falsely making it appear you are trustworthy, honest, and just. Instead, be trustworthy, honest, and just, with no deception. When hypocrites are in control, the evil prosper and the virtuous suffer. Hypocrites' double standards corrode a community, making everyone less inclined to practice virtue and be honest, causing neighbors to lose trust in each other, and making fairness and justice disappear.

13. Trust in Others

1 Put complete trust only in God.

2 Seek to emulate those whose good examples inspire you to improve, but never let such prudent observation and emulation turn into worship and idolization. Do not become enamored with the limited caricature of goodness you observe in someone else. Evil lurks in all men's hearts. Everyone fails. Never trust so much in a role model that discovering his weaknesses would destroy your hope or overcome your resolve to follow the Triple Path.

3 Do not let others' failures to live up to perfection hurt your own pursuit of it. Learn to do better by improving upon their examples. Let everyone you meet be a model of good to emulate and evil to avoid.

14. Tragedy and Suffering

1 Great are the troubles even of the righteous.

2 Tragedy and suffering come to all, to both the righteous and the evil. Some is unavoidable—caused by the evil and foolishness of others or the randomness of life—and some is the avoidable result of your own foolish choices.

Learn these three lessons from suffering, death, and disasters:

First, you do not know when you will die or when tragedy will befall you. Now is the time to live with wisdom, virtue, and hope. If you wait to follow the Triple Path, you may start too late and leave behind a life of foolishness, disagreeable deeds, and evil acts. When tragedy comes, you may be unprepared to face it and suffer more greatly as a result.

Second, you cannot predict the future. Prepare wisely as best you can for possible tragedy, so that you are well-placed to overcome whatever happens.

Third, when tragedy strikes others, try to help them overcome it. But, since you must choose where to direct your limited resources, the prepared and prudent to whom befall unexpected tragedy are more deserving of your help than the unprepared and foolish.

3   No time or place is exempt from the vicissitudes of life. Surrounded by contentment, causes of suffering spring up. War arises in the midst of peace, and that which we depended upon for protection is transformed into a cause of fear; friends and allies become enemies. The summer calm is stirred into sudden storms, wilder than the blizzards of winter. The most temperate are assailed by illness, the strongest by wasting disease, the most innocent by chastisement, the most secluded by the noisy mob.

4   Do you wish for a long life? And then does misfortune befall you and you complain? A long life includes all these troubles, just as a long journey includes dust and rain and delays.

5   Never cease to follow and marvel at the natural course of this most beautiful universe, into which all your sufferings and triumphs are woven. In the midst of tribulation, never forget that existence consists of opposites: day follows night, the calm comes after the storm. And during good times, also remember this and prepare for troubled times ahead. You will approach courageously a danger you have already prepared yourself to meet. If you are unprepared, you will be panic-stricken even at the most trifling things.

6   If you see dark clouds brewing and feel the wind blowing, yet do nothing to prepare for a storm, you have no cause to complain after it has flattened you.

7   In good times toughen yourself for occasions of greater stress; in times of peace prepare yourself against violence. If you would be one who does not flinch when the crisis comes, then train yourself before it comes.

8   When each of life's hardships comes, say to yourself: "For this have I been preparing and training. For this have I been seeking wisdom, practicing virtue, and laboring with hope."

9   When misfortune befalls you, do not curse your luck, receiving the results of chance with dejection. Accept your situation as if it were assigned to be your duty, then work to make the best of the situation and come out on top, saying: "Whatever this may be, it is my lot; it is rough and it is hard, but I must work diligently at the task of succeeding".

10   When misfortune befalls you, ask yourself what you may have done to contribute to its coming. Then, ask yourself how you can stop making those same mistakes. Finally, ask yourself how you can repair the damage you caused by your past failures.

11   The unexpected calamity creates the heaviest load; the surprise brings greater pain. Learn to better discern what may come and prepare to confront it.

12   Stand tall under any load. You were born to carry burdens.

13   You cannot escape all hardships, but you can overcome many of them and endure the rest to the end. By force of will a way is made.

14   An unconquerable burden that you endure with stubborn defiance begins to feel lighter.

15   Be more displeased with foolishness, evil, and lazy despair than you are with affliction and suffering.

16   Root out your fear of future suffering, and the recollection of past suffering. How can that which has not yet come to pass concern you? And what benefit is there in reviewing past sufferings, and in being unhappy, just because once you were unhappy? Even when set in the very midst of troubles, say to yourself, perhaps some day the memory of this sorrow will even bring delight.

17   Often, you must suffer into truth and wisdom, for you refuse to seek them when you are amid ease and comfort.

18   When the sorrows of death compass you and the pains of hell grasp at you, call on the name of God.

19 You brought nothing into this world, and how can you carry anything out? God gives and He takes away. Blessed be the name of God.

15. Death and Immortality

1 Accept old age.

2 Death comes to everyone: to the wise and foolish, to the virtuous and evil, to the hopeful and pessimist alike. Followers of the Triple Path, though, leave the world better than they found it, just as their forebears, whether spiritual or physical, did for them.

3 The living know they will die. What do the dead know? They have no more earthly reward, and even the memory of them will eventually be forgotten. Whatever good you can do while you are alive, do it well, and with courage and enthusiasm. What more earthly works or thoughts can you accomplish in the grave to which you are headed?

4 Be not as the foolish and evil who care not about how wisely or virtuously they lived, but only about how long. It is within the reach of every person to live wisely and virtuously, but within no one's power to assure long life.

5 Life is short. You make it shorter still by your unsteadiness and focus on what is less important, breaking it up into little bits and frittering it away. How much faster and focused would you be if you knew that an enemy were at your back, pressing hard upon your steps as you fled? And yet, an enemy is indeed pressing upon you. Round out your life and accomplish its mission before death comes.

6 Strive while you are yet alive so that the potential of your youth be transformed ever more into the accomplishments of your maturity.

7 Do you desire immortality in this earthly realm? What remains here after your death? At least, there are these: your descendants; your writings; what you have built; the ruins of what you destroyed; the effects of your acts—whether wise and virtuous, or foolish and evil; and your bones, until they turn to dust.

8 Remember the parable of the empty tomb.

References

1. Hope
1- 2 Corinthians 4:8-10. **4-** 2 Corinthians 3:3. **5-** 12 Rules, p. 397. **7-** Ether 12:4. **8-** Delphic maxim 62. **9-** James 2:14-18, 3:13.

2. Discontent
1- Delphic maxim 133. **2-** 12 Rules, Rule 6. **3-4-** Meditations 4:3, 4:26. **5-** 12 Rules, 209-10; St. John of the Cross.

3. Sacrifice
1- Psalm 4:4-5, 51:17. **2-** Jordan Peterson, Podcast 33, Jacob's Ladder, 32:00. **3-** 1 Peter 3:17. **4-** 12 Rules, pp. 200-1. **5-** 12 Rules, p. 193. **6-8-** Jordan Peterson, Podcast 30—The Great Sacrifice: Abraham and Isaac. **9-10-** 12 Rules, 195. **11-** Proverbs 15:8, 21:27; Malachi 1:7. **12-** Jordan Peterson, Podcast 30—The Great Sacrifice: Abraham and Isaac. **13-** 12 Rules, pp. 198-99. **14-15-** Jordan Peterson, Podcast 30—The Great Sacrifice: Abraham and Isaac. **16-** 12 Rules, 215. **17-** Jordan Peterson. **19-** John Rogers, *The Nature and Necessity of Repentance*, 1728, p. 25.

4. Patience
1- Romans 12:11; D&C 24:8; Dhammapada 399. **2-** 1 Thessalonians 5:14; Titus 3:2-3. **3-** Ecclesiastes 10:4.

5. Focus on What You Can Control
1- Delphic maxim 10, 61. **2-** Delphic maxim 68, 142. **4-** 12 Rules, p. 60. **5-** Jordan Peterson, "Thought Economics: A Conversation with Dr. Jordan B. Peterson", Jordan Peterson Blog. **6-** 12 Rules, p. 140. **7-** Enchiridion 1. **8-** Meditations 9:31-32. **9-** Dhammapada 362. **10-** Enchiridion 2. **11-** Jordan Peterson, Podcast 62, 49:00. **12-** John Rogers, *The Nature and Necessity of Repentance*, 1728, p. 55, 69.

6. Perseverance
1- Delphic maxim 92. **2-** Lucilius 53:8. **3-** D&C 20:33, 75:29. **4-** 2 Corinthians 4:8-10. **5-** D&C 18:22. **6-** Lucilius 76:3. **7-** Meditations 7:59. **8-** Galatians 6:9. **9-** D&C 64:33. **12-** Lucilius 12:9. **13-** Meditations 6:19. **14-** Hebrews 12:1-2. **15-** Ecclesiastes 2:18-23. **16-** Lucilius 86:15 (Quoting Georgics, ii. 58); Ancient Greek Proverb. **17-**

Lucilius 64:7.
7. Balance
1-2- Guru Nanak Dev Ji.
8. The Great Now
1- Delphic Maxims 18, 40. **2-** Psalm 118:24. **4-** Thomas 51. **5-** Jordan Peterson, Podcast 33, Jacob's Ladder, 21:00, (quoting Carl Jung); Jordan Peterson, Podcast 63, 1:29:00. **7-** Jordan Peterson, Podcast 33, Jacob's Ladder, 59:00. **9-** Thomas Jefferson, *A Dozen Canons of conduct in Life.* **10-** Matthew 6:34. **11-** 12 Rules, pp. 141-42. **12-** 12 Rules, p. 390. **13-** Meditations 7:8. **14-** Lucilius 74:33-34. **15-** Lucilius 13:4-5. **16-** Lucilius 13:10-11, 98:8. **17-** Lucilius 98:6-7. **18-** Lucilius 8:16, 13:16, 45:12-13. **19-** Lucilius 98:7. **20-** Thomas 113. **22-** Thomas 96.
9. Tradition
1- Att. to Gustav Mahler. **3-** 12 Rules, 188. **5-** Donald Kingsbury, *Courtship Rite*, 1982. **6-** 12 Rules, p. 28. **7-** 12 Rules, 148. **8-** Nassim Taleb, *Antifragile.* 2012. **9-** 12 Rules, p. 255. **11-** Lucilius 33: 11. **14-** Jordan Peterson, Debate with Sam Harris, Part One, 1:27. **15-** Robert Conquest. **16-** 12 Rules, p. 148. **19-** Lucilius 123:6. **21-** Delphic maxim 12.
10. Progress Toward Paradise
1- Thomas 3. **2-** Horace, *Epistles*, I.11. **5-** Lucilius 17:12. **6-** Lucilius 28:4, 7. **7-** 12 Rules, p. 397. **8-** 12 Rules, p. 320. **9-** D&C 38:40, 42:45. **10-** 12 Rules, pp. 394-95; https://mobile.twitter.com/Human Progress/status/985146406888452096. **12-** Lucilius 91:6. **14-** Jordan Peterson. **15-** Horace, Epistles, I:10, line 24. **17-** Delphic maxim 107; Lucilius 94:46 (quoting Marcus Agrippa, Sallust, Jugurtha, x. 6). **18-** 12 Rules, p. 262. **19-** Meditations 8:59; Cicero, *De Officiis*, 1:22; Tao Te Ching 2:2, 8:2; D&C 82:19. **20-** Chuang Tzu, Sec. 4 (In the World of Men), Watson translation, p. 26. **21-** Maps, p. 8. **24-** 12 Rules, 186-87. **25-** BoM, Alma 37:6; Tao Te Ching 63:2. **26-** Joseph Smith, Pearl of Great Price, Moses 7:18. **27-** Jeremy Ladd Cross, *The True Masonic Chart or Hieroglyph Monitor*, 1860.
11. Government and Society
1- D&C 134; Jordan Peterson, Podcast 42, 9:00. **2-** Cicero, *De*

Officiis, 1:124-125. **3-** Cicero, *De Officiis*, 1:52. **4-** Pericles (as recorded by Thucydides), Funeral Speech, 430 BC. **5-** Tacitus, *Annals*, 3:27. **6-** 12 Rules, p. 167. **7-** Jordan Peterson, Podcast 57, 22:00. **8-** 12 Rules, pp. 55-58. **9-** 12 Rules, p. 144. **10-** 12 Rules, p. 335. **11-** 12 Rules, p. 167. **12-** Jacques Barzun, *From Dawn to Decadence*, 686 (writing about George Bernard Shaw). **13-** Edmund Burke, *Reflections on the Revolution in France*, 1790, p. 116. **15-** Joseph Smith, as quoted by John Taylor, "The Organization of the Church", *Millennial Star*, Vol. 13, No. 22, November 15, 1851, p. 339. **16-** Elinor Ostrom, *Governing the Commons: The Evolution of Institutions for Collective Action*, 1990; Elinor Ostrom, et. al., *Working Together: Collective Action, the Commons, and Multiple Methods in Practice*, 2010.

12. Banishing Hypocrisy

1- Meditations 6:54. **2-** Lucilius 95:30-32. **5-** Matthew 15:8.

13. Trust in Others

14. Tragedy and Suffering

1- Psalm 34:19. **2-** Luke 13:2-5; Lucilius 74:10. **3-** Lucilius 91:5. **4-** Lucilius 96:3. **5-**Lucilius 107:4, 8, 10. **7-** Lucilius 18:6. **8-** Epictetus, *Discourses*, Book 3, Chapter 10. **9-** Lucilius 120:12. **10-** 12 Rules, p. 185 (discussing Solzhenitsyn's *Gulag Archipelago*). **11-** Lucilius 91:3-4. **12-** Lucilius 71:26. **13-** Lucilius 37:3 (quoting Virgil, *Aeneid*). **14-** Lucilius 94:7. **15-** John Rogers, *The Nature and Necessity of Repentance*, 1728, p. 13. **16-** Lucilius 78:14-15 (partially quoting Virgil, *Aeneid*, i. 203). **17-** Joseph Gresham Miller; Democritus. **18-** Psalm 116:3-4. **19-** 1 Timothy 6:7; Job 1:21.

15. Death and Immortality

1- Delphic maxim 113. **2-** Ecclesiastes 9:2. **3-** Ecclesiastes 9:5, 10. **4-** Lucilius 22:17. **5-** Lucilius 32:2-3. **6-** 12 Rules, pp. 397-98.

Parables

*There is no one correct interpretation of any of these parables.
Their symbols have multiple meanings (some perhaps not even
intended by the author) that can be adapted to personal circumstance. Even for the few parables where an interpretive commen-
tary is provided, it is not the only possible interpretation.*

Contents

1. The Bridges of Hammon and Sophrete

Two cities, each very distant from the other, sat on the same side of a great river. The river was wide and deep, with a powerful and fast current. Crossing the river was dangerous and difficult, but those few who crossed returned with stories of an unknown country full of mysterious wonders.

The first city was named Hammon, and the second was called Sophrete.

In Hammon, few citizens had ever crossed the river. Everyone generally agreed that reaching the other side would be good in theory, but they were occupied too much with trivialities, such as sporting contests, entertainment, gossip, and intellectual and cultural fads, to spend much time considering how to connect to the other side.

Most citizens in Hammon expected that someone else would solve big problems for them. The power-obsessed, the hypocrites, and the depraved thus found it easy to slip into positions of authority and offer their own self-serving solutions, which most people apathetically accepted. Those in charge in Hammon did everything they could to publicly humiliate, demonize, and ostracize the few who questioned them, to neutralize the potential threat to their power (and also discourage future challengers).

Hammon's leaders did not care about the other side of

the river, but they used the people's interest in it to serve their own ends. They promised a great bridgebuilding project, but drew out the process and ran up expenses to divert money to themselves and their cronies. When those in charge inevitably lost power and a new group of miscreants took over, the new leaders canceled the prior leaders' bridge project and started a new one, to more easily divert new spending to themselves. This process repeated yet again with a third set of leaders.

Hammon never completed a bridge, having only the eyesore of three incomplete bridges jutting out partially into the river. Hammon's townspeople found utility in the unfinished bridges—they used the open space on them for social gatherings, for picnics, and for fishing, but the bridges never served the purpose for which they had been built, and the meager uses to which they were put hardly justified the expense of building them.

In Sophrete, the citizens concerned themselves not just with trivialities, but also with weightier matters. Their leaders were good men who tried to do the right thing, because the citizens tirelessly worked to discover the power-obsessed, the hypocrites, and the depraved, and to keep them out of power.

A small, but growing number of Sophrete's citizens had braved the waters and crossed the river. Many others wished to cross, but doing so was beyond their capacity. When the citizens realized the potential value of building a bridge to connect to the other side, they trained themselves how to take on such a project. They responsibly managed it and paid for it themselves. The bridge's construction took time, but it was done well, and done right. When completed, it was beautiful and became Sophrete's pride. It firmly established their connection to the other side. Through it, the townspeople found many treasures and great knowledge.

2. The Emperor's New Clothes

One day, two swindlers came to a vain emperor presenting themselves as weavers and tailors of fine clothing. For a large
sum, they offered to make the finest clothes ever known—a magic
suit that could not be seen or felt by anyone lacking in wisdom or
virtue. They were very persuasive. The emperor and his ministers
became convinced of the swindlers' claims, and the emperor hired
the swindlers to make the new clothes for him.

To tailor the suit, the swindlers pretended to fit clothes on
the emperor, but neither he nor his ministers could see anything.
Each of them began to doubt the truthfulness of the swindlers, but
none dared admit he could not see the clothes. No one wanted
the others to think he was lacking in wisdom and virtue, and no
one wanted to contradict what he thought to be the group's con-
sensus about the clothes' reality.

When the swindlers declared the clothes ready, they in-
sisted the emperor send out a proclamation requiring his subjects
attend the unveiling of these magical clothes that only the wise and
virtuous could see. As the swindlers pretended to dress the emperor for the unveiling, he again doubted the clothes' reality, but
dared not challenge the swindlers. If the clothes actually were real,
he feared admitting that he could not see them; if they were not
real, he feared admitting he had been fooled for so long.

The emperor marched out in a regal procession amongst

his subjects who were gathered in large crowds outside the palace. They all made a show of being in awe of his fine clothes. Some feared appearing to lack wisdom and virtue; others feared retribution for challenging the opinion of the empire's elite and of the rest of the crowd.

The emperor passed by a child who laughed and asked why the emperor was parading around in his underwear. The child's parents were deeply embarrassed. They disciplined him, and he learned to not contradict the received wisdom.

The emperor continued to go about in his underwear, pretending to wear the swindlers' imaginary clothes. The swindlers pretended to make suits for themselves and too began to go about in their underwear. Next, they made clothes for the emperor's ministers, then for the nobles and the wealthy, and then for the commoners. The swindlers grew rich and powerful.

A minority of the people doubted the emperor and the swindlers. They refused to pay the swindlers and go about in their underwear. Sometimes the doubters were treated with tolerant condescension; often, they were mocked and shunned.

The empire had a warm climate. For many years, the majority who believed in imaginary clothes could safely go about dressed only in their underwear. Finally, though, a rare blizzard brought cold, wind, and snow. The majority no longer had any real outer clothes left to wear. Those few who still wore clothes tried to share with the others, but they refused. By then, they had banished their doubts. They firmly believed the lie that their clothes were real. The emperor, his ministers, and all the rest who had been fooled froze to death, firm in their false beliefs.

The only citizens of the empire to survive were those who had the courage to stand firm for the truth in the face of the constant, foolish criticism of the majority, even though there seemed to be little immediate reward for doing so.

The swindlers also survived. They had kept an emergency supply of real clothes and coats. The other survivors arrested them and put them to death.

3. The Cure for the Blind

A wise teacher came among a community of the blind to teach them how to cure their blindness. His cure was not perfect, but when applied fully, it restored much of their sight.

The teacher was with them only a short time. When he left, only a few had learned incomplete forms of the cure and had only partially restored their own sight.

As news about the teacher's cure spread, his few followers began to teach the different forms of the cure each had learned, as best they could remember. Some cures were better than others, but none of them were the teacher's complete cure. Many essential parts of the different cures remained the same, though, because it was obvious when someone offered a completely ineffectual cure. The people separated into groups based on which cure they used. Each group offered explanations for how the cure worked, but the explanations were mostly wrong. The truth was that no one knew how it worked.

A small minority of the people had a different form of blindness that was incurable. After applying the cure, they still saw only darkness. Having been blind their whole lives, they could not even understand what it was to have sight—their abstract understanding of the descriptions of others was a poor substitute for personally experiencing the light of sight. They assumed that the others who raved about the cures were liars; that because the cure did not work for them, it was a fraud. They mercilessly criticized the cure and the cure-followers, trying to find every possible flaw and point them out. They convincingly questioned the groups' explanations for how the cure worked, showing how they did not make sense. If the explanations were clearly wrong, they argued, then the cures must also be fake.

More and more people started to recognize that the different groups' cures did not work as well as promised. They listened to the criticisms of the incurably blind and started noticing how much they still could not see and that many things were blurry and unfocused. They suspected there were many things to be seen that they were not even aware of. They wondered if what they had been perceiving was really an illusion.

Out of disillusionment and frustration, they stopped applying the cures they had been using. Their blindness returned, for the cures required consistent application to remain effective. These newly re-blinded people joined the incurably blind and spent their time attacking the groups and the teacher, rather than seeking out a better cure. As criticism against the cures grew, increasing numbers of people turned back to blindness.

Those who persisted in their new blindness raised their children without knowledge of the cure. Many of these children lived out their lives in unnecessary darkness, not even fully realizing what they lacked.

Some of those who rejected the cure remembered the light they used to perceive and eventually realized that an imperfect, unexplainable cure was better than none at all. They still felt dissatisfied with the imperfect cure they had, however, and decided to seek a better one, rather than continue forever in blindness or in partial sight. They learned from each other and studied the groups' different versions of the cure, looking for commonalities. Each person found that while many of these commonalities were things his own prior group already taught, some were things his group did not have. As each person tried the things that were new to him, his eyesight often improved greatly.

Next, they tried less-common parts of the different group's cures that seemed compatible with what they knew to work. (Some of these came from the original teacher, and some had been created over time within individual groups as they differentiated.) They also added new things that appeared consistent with the other parts they knew to work and thus offered good prospects for supplementing or improving it. Often, the things they tried had little effect or even made their eyesight worse. Occasionally, though, some of these new additions improved their eyesight. They kept track of what worked and what did not. Eventually, they created a cure that was better than the cures applied by the different groups and better even than the teacher's original cure. They even started to figure out how some parts of the cure worked

They tried to explain to the others what it was like to have pure, full sight, but the blind and partial-sighted could not understand. The partially sighted persecuted and maligned this new cure, claiming that the old groups' cures already provided full sight. They slandered those seeking a new cure, calling them liars and deceivers. They accused them of betraying the teacher and the established groups of which they had once been members. The incurably blind and the disillusioned who had become blind continued to insist that there was no such thing as blindness, and thus also that this new cure was a fraud and that its proponents were dangerous deceivers.

Those who had created a better cure formed their own group focused on the cure and on protecting themselves from the persecutions of the others. They continued to refine and improve the cure. Their group of cure-followers slowly grew. It attracted wise and practical people who were better at discerning truth from falsehood and between what is relevant and irrelevant. Their example helped many people, especially the children of those who had chosen blindness and had never been taught a cure, to find their way to the best cure, and to sight.

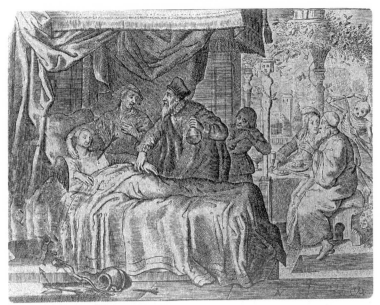

4. The Poisoned Arrow

A man was shot with a poisoned arrow. As he lay injured, his family and friends brought a doctor to him to remove the arrow and administer an antidote for the poison.

The man stopped the doctor, saying, "I will not have this arrow removed until I know the surgical technique to be used; until I know whether he who wounded me was wealthy or poor, well-liked or unpopular, sane or crazy, powerful or impotent. I will not have it removed until I know the name of he who wounded me; until I know whether he was tall or short, dark or pale, blond or brunette; until I know whether his eyes were blue, brown, green, or gray; until I know his city, state, and country; until I know the language he speaks; until I know whether the bow firing the arrow that wounded me was a long bow or a crossbow; until I know whether the bowstring was made of natural or artificial fibers; until I know whether the arrow's shaft was wood, bamboo, reed, aluminum, or carbon fiber."

His family begged him to at least receive an injection of the antidote.

307

He said, "I will not receive an antidote to the poison until I know whether the poison is natural or synthetic; until I know whether it is acid or base; until I know whether it is neurotoxic, carcinogenic, or radioactive; until I know how much poison has entered my bloodstream; until I know the lethal dosage of the poison; until I know the chemical formula of the antidote; and until I know the amount to be administered to me."

The man died and all those things about which he had questioned still remained unknown to him. Indeed, for those around him with the tools to save him—his family, friends, and doctor—the answers to many of his questions were as much mysteries to them as they were to him. And even for the answers they did have, there was not enough time to explain them before the arrow and poison killed him.

5. The Sick Physician

A man limped out of his city apartment and proclaimed to all that he was a skillful physician and could cure all manner of diseases. He spoke in a learned jargon of hard and cramped words, which nobody understood. This made many admire his learning, and give credit to his vauntings.

At last a wise man in the crowd could take no more.

"How can you", the wise man asked, "with your fat paunch, blotchy skin, crippled body, and fevered complexion proclaim yourself as one able to cure the infirmities of others? Physician, heal thyself!"

6. Children in the Library

Two children entered a room with floor-to-ceiling bookshelves lining the walls. The shelves were filled with books in many languages. The children did not understand most of the words on the books' spines and covers, let alone those inside. But, they could not help but note that the books were arranged and organized according to some definite plan, a mysterious order, that they could not comprehend and only dimly suspected.

7. The Truck Driver

A poor truck driver started hauling loads of hay across an international border every day. The customs official suspected the man was smuggling something, so each day the official would carefully search him and his truck. The official never found anything.

As time passed, the truck driver grew more and more prosperous. The customs official was sure the man could not have gained his money by hauling hay, so he redoubled his efforts to catch the truck driver in the act of smuggling. Every day he searched carefully, but every day he came up empty.

After years of this same routine, the truck driver comfortably retired. The customs official also retired. One day, he passed the truck driver on the street in their border town.

"We have both retired", the customs official said. "There is nothing I can do to you now. Please, I must know—you really were smuggling across the border, weren't you? What was it?"

"Yes, I was smuggling", answered the truck driver. "I was smuggling trucks."

Sometimes the most important things are so obvious they become almost invisible. Always be on guard, lest you ignore that which you should have paid most attention to.

8. The Testing Sower

A man found a bag of seeds. He did not know what would grow from them. (Now, the truth was that there were good and bad seeds, and live and dead seeds, mixed together.) The man scattered them to see what fruit, if any, they would bear, and where.

Some seeds fell on the side of the road; all the seeds were quickly eaten by mice.

Some seeds fell among thorns. The live seeds sprouted, but the thorns choked both the good and the bad and slowed their growth; all the sprouts were eaten by insects.

Some fell on stony ground. The live seeds again sprouted, but because there was no depth to the soil, neither the good nor the bad seeds could take root. They withered and were trodden under foot by man and beast.

Some seeds fell on good ground. The dead seeds did not sprout and were eaten by the birds. The good seeds sprang up and grew and yielded good fruit, some thirty, and some sixty, some a hundred. Others sprouted weeds and noxious herbs. When the bad sprouts were still small, the man plucked them up and cast them into the fire.

9. The Young Man and the Swallow

A prodigal young man had run through all his money and had only one good coat left. One fine day he happened to see a swallow skimming along a meadow and twittering brightly. He took this as a sign summer had come.

He sold his coat and gambled the proceeds away.

Not many days later, winter set in again with renewed frost and cold. Shivering and nearly frozen himself, he found the swallow stiff and lifeless on the ground.

"Miserable creature!" he exclaimed. "You wrought your own destruction, and by heeding you, I wrought my own as well."

10. The Two Pilgrims

A pilgrim passed a field in which an old farmer had just finished plowing. The pilgrimage site lay in the next town. Ready to take a rest from his travels on the road, the pilgrim stopped to talk to the farmer.

"What kind of people are in the town?" the pilgrim asked.

"Well, what were they like in the place where you came from?" the farmer replied.

"Terrible", the pilgrim answered. "They were all lazy, troublesome, and selfish. None were trustworthy. That is why I left on my pilgrimage—to get away from them."

"Oh really?" the old farmer replied slowly. "Well, unfortunately you will find the same sort in the next town."

The disappointed pilgrim left, trudging on, resigned to his fate. The farmer began sowing his field.

Just as the farmer had finished sowing, another pilgrim passed and stopped to talk.

"What kind of people are in the town?" the second pilgrim also asked.

"Well, what were they like in the place where you came from?" the farmer again replied.

"Wonderful", the second pilgrim answered. "They were diligent, trustworthy, and neighborly. I was sorry to leave when I felt called to make this pilgrimage."

"Be of good cheer", said the farmer. "You will find the same sort in the next town."

11. The Traveler

A traveler tried to escape from his footprints and shadow by running from them. He only made more footprints, and his shadow never left him. He ran until his strength gave out, and he collapsed under a tree. Only then, sitting in stillness in the shade, did he escape them and come to himself. Restored, he got up and walked into the sunlight. Looking forward, he did not notice his footprints or his shadow behind him as he swiftly moved toward his destination.

You are the source of the thoughts and feelings that afflict you. You cannot escape from yourself, not even by filling your life with trivialities and vain pursuits. You can, though, escape from what afflicts you. Still your mind and find peace and wisdom. Control your thoughts and remember that it is not reality that afflicts you, but your opinions about reality. Then, with the opinions that afflict you banished from your attention, come to yourself and move swiftly along the Triple Path.

12. The Sand in the Hourglass

Consider sand in an hourglass. The sand in the top is waiting for its moment to move down—it is the future. A small amount flows through the neck—it is the present. The sand in the bottom sits motionless below—it is the past. Past, present, and future. But it is all the same sand.

At its finish, turn the hourglass upside down—the sand jumbles together and the flow starts anew. Each grain falls in a different order from before. But the top bulb always empties into the bottom bulb. It is all the same sand.

13. The Ring of Truth

A king ordered his sages to create a phrase of wise counsel that would be true in every situation. He told them to inscribe the phrase on a ring that would always be with him as a reminder.

The sages returned the following day and presented a plain ring that had inscribed on it the phrase, "This, too, shall pass away".

The king soon thereafter suffered a great misfortune. In the midst of this, he looked at his ring and was comforted.

Seeing him do this, his chief sage stepped forward.

"But sire", he reminded. "Also do not forget. The ring will be equally true in times of good fortune."

14. The Fair Jar

A local fair attraction had a large jar filled with jelly beans. Passersby could pay a quarter to guess how many were inside. The person closest to the correct number would win the whole jar.

All night long, people deposited quarters in a slot and then added their entry to a list of guesses. Because they had to give something up to play, most put in a good effort to make sure their answer was as correct as they could make it. At the end of the night, as fair-goers stopped on their way out to discover who had won, a crowd formed at the booth. No attendant showed up, however, to declare a winner and award the prize.

In the crowd was a grandfather with two of his grandchildren, both of whom had submitted guesses. The grandfather inspected the booth.

"The jar is here", he observed. "But it is sealed. And besides, there is no time to count so many jelly beans. We have the list of each person's guess. Let us calculate the average of all the guesses and award the jar to whomever came closest to it."

A young, solitary lawyer in the crowd disagreed.

"Since we cannot be certain of the real number of jelly beans, we could never be sure the prize would be going to the right person", the lawyer argued. "We should all thus give up on the game entirely and just go home."

"Using the average", the grandfather argued, "will get us the closest we can to the right answer. We should move forward with the best knowledge we have and select a winner."

"If we cannot exactly determine the correct number", the lawyer replied, "then there can be no winner."

Some members of the crowd agreed with the lawyer. They left, thus losing the chance to win the jar.

The majority of the crowd agreed with the grandfather. They examined the guesses. Each was different. They calculated the average and awarded the jelly beans to the person whose guess had come closest.

Now, the truth was that the average was not precisely correct. But, it was more correct than any one person's guess. And the person who won the jar had actually made the closest guess.

As the crowd dispersed and left the fair, the jar's winner opened the jar and shared the candy with the other members of the crowd.

15. Icarus

On the island of Crete, the wicked king Minos imprisoned within a large maze Icarus, a young man, and Icarus's father
Daedalus, a skilled inventor. The maze's exits were well-guarded,
and escape by sea was also impossible, as the king kept strict watch
on all the vessels, and permitted none to sail without being carefully searched.

"Minos may control the land and sea", said Daedalus, "but
not the air. I will try that way."

He set to work building wings for himself and Icarus. He
fashioned feathers together, securing the larger ones with thread
and the smaller with wax. When at last the work was done, they
put on the wings, and flapping, found themselves buoyed upward
in the air. They practiced with the wings in secret, always flying at
low elevations within the maze in which they were imprisoned,
and thus taught themselves the basics of how to fly.

When finally all was ready for their flight, Daedalus gave
this final instruction: "Icarus, my son, keep always at a moderate
height. If you fly too high, the heat of the sun will melt the wax securing the feathers; if too low, the dampness of the sea will clog

your wings. Follow me and keep near on the middle course I show through the air, and you will be safe."

He kissed the boy, not knowing it was for the last time. Then rising on his wings, Daedalus flew off, looking back from his own flight to see how his son managed his wings.

As they flew out to sea, the great expanse opened to their view, far out to the distant horizon.

The longer they flew, the more confident Icarus grew with his wings. The wind rushed past his face. He let out a whoop. He began to leave the guidance of Daedalus's way. He soared upward as if to reach heaven. It was exhilarating. Eventually, though, the nearness of the blazing sun softened the wax holding the small feathers together.

Icarus looked in alarm as more and more feathers peeled away. Remembering only then his father's warning about flying too high, he dived down, close to the cool protection of the ocean.

"Icarus!" Daedalus shouted out, looking down at his son. "Follow the course I have showed you—the middle way!"

"But I must cool my wings!" Icarus shouted up to his father as he skimmed along the sea.

Just then, an ocean swell rose up and swallowed Icarus. The remaining feathers of his wings were soaked. Flight was impossible.

Daedalus circled back around. He watched helplessly as his son bobbed up and down in the midst of a vast sea, sputtering and trying to keep himself afloat.

"Son, there is nothing I can do to rescue you now, for my wings cannot support both our weight", Daedalus shouted down to Icarus.

Daedalus looked at the sun's position in the sky to get his bearings and note their position at sea.

"I will try to return for you in a ship", he continued. "Try to stay afloat."

And as they both cried bitter tears, Daedalus flew off.

When Daedalus reached land, he chartered a small fishing boat with the only money he had. He returned to the spot where Icarus had fallen into the ocean. All he found were feathers floating on the water.

Icarus was gone, destroyed because he did not follow the middle course shown to him by his father.

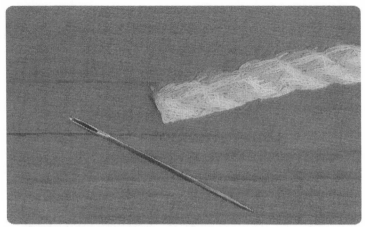

16. The Young Man and the Teacher

A young man came to a great teacher and asked, "Teacher what must I do to be justified before God?"

"Love God; follow the Golden Rule; love others; and practice virtue", the teacher responded.

"Master, I love others", the young man responded. "I am not greedy. I donate to the poor. I show compassion. I am tolerant. Surely then, I am justified. What else could I do?"

"And the future children, who will never be because you waste your time on debauchery and triviality?" the teacher asked. "What love, compassion, and tolerance show you to them? And how have you practiced the Golden Rule to them? If before you existed you could have answered for yourself, you would have desired that your parents conceived and raised you, yet you do not the same for the next generation. And what of the women on whom you satisfy your lusts, leaving them less well prepared for futures as wives and mothers? And what of the wickedness you tolerate and encourage in others—how do you show love for God by so doing?

"If you would be justified before God in wisdom and virtue, then send your girlfriend out of your apartment. Be with no one until you marry. Marry a good and virtuous woman and be with her only. Have children and raise them in faith and tradition. Do not tolerate wickedness. Do not drink to excess. Cease your debauchery. Forsake unnecessary trivialities. Stop squandering so much of your life on television and entertainment and wasted time on the internet."

The young man went away sorrowing, for his lifestyle brought him much pleasure.

The teacher turned to those with him and said, "Truly I tell you that it is easier for a rope to go through the eye of a needle than it is for a zealot or a libertine to be justified before God."

17. Hercules at the Crossroads

When Hercules was passing from boyhood to youth, he went to a quiet place near a crossroads and sat under a tree to think on his future.

Two women approached from opposite paths. The first had a fair and noble face and was dressed modestly in a beautiful white dress. The other's face was heavily made up. Her clothes were red and she was dressed so as to disclose all her charms.

The first woman approached in a dignified way, never altering her pace. The second ran eagerly to him and reached Hercules first. She said, "Hercules, I see that you are in doubt about which path to take toward life. Make me your friend; follow me, and I will lead you along the easy road. You shall learn how to make your own pleasure and comfort your highest concern in life. Of wars and worries you shall not think, but shall ever be considering what choice food or drink you can find, what sight or sound will delight you, what touch or perfume; what tender love can give you most joy, what bed the softest slumbers; and how to come by all these pleasures with least trouble. And do not worry how you shall achieve your enjoyments, I will never lead you into winning them by toil and anguish of body and soul. You shall live off the fruits of others' toil, and refrain from nothing that can bring you gain. For to my companions I give authority to pluck advantage where they will."

Now after all of this Hercules asked, "Lady, what is your name?"

"My friends call me Happiness", she said, "but those that hate me call me Vice."

Meanwhile, the other woman had drawn near, and she said: "I, too, am come to you, Hercules: I know your parents, and I have taken note of your character during the time of your education. Therefore, I hope that, if you take the road that leads to me, you will turn out a right and good doer of high and noble deeds. But I will not deceive you by a pleasant prelude: I will rather tell you truly the things that are, as God has ordained them. For of all things good and fair, God allows nothing to man without toil and effort. If you want God's favor, you must follow Him; if you desire the love of friends, you must do good to them; if you covet honor from others, then you must act honorably; if you want land to yield you fruits in abundance, you must cultivate that land; if you are re-solved to get wealth from flocks, you must care for those flocks; if you would grow great through war and want power to liberate your friends and subdue your foes, you must learn the arts of war from those who know them, and you must practice their right use; and if you want your body to be strong, you must accustom your body to be the servant of your mind, and train it with toil and sweat."

Hearing this, Hercules asked the woman in white, "And, Lady, what is your name?"

"Vice and her followers call me Toil", she said, "but my Father named me Virtue, and many call me Meaning."

Now Vice answered and said: "Hercules, did you notice how hard and long is that road of which this woman speaks? I will lead you by a short and easy road to partake of all my good things."

And then Virtue said to Vice: "What good thing is really yours? You do not even wait for the desire of pleasant things, filling yourself with things even before you desire them, eating before you are hungry, drinking before you are thirsty, buying costly wines and running to and fro in search of trivial novelties. You arouse lust by unnatural tricks. It is not toil that makes you long for sleep, but when you wax wanton by night and then consume in sleep the best hours of the day. You are eternal, yet the outcast of Heaven and the scorn of good men. You do not know what a good life means, for never have you wrought a good work. Who will believe what you say? What sane man will dare join your swarm? Your new followers vaunt their young, healthy bodies while their souls grow ever weaker, withered, and weary. Their past deeds bring them shame, their present deeds distress. They run through pleasure in their youth while laying up hardship for their old age, and thus they have no strength of soul to rely on when their bodies have grown old and weak. And they always eventually come to discover that you will abandon them in their hour of greatest need.

"On the other hand", Virtue continued, "my companions know I am always faithful, always present, no matter the hardship through which they pass. I am a good helpmate in the toils of peace, a staunch ally in the deeds of war, and the best partner in friendship. To my companions, meat and drink and other enjoyments bring sweet and simple delight: for they wait till they crave and need them and can lawfully partake. And a sweeter sleep falls on them than on idle folk: they are not vexed at awaking from it, nor for its sake do they neglect to do their duties. My young companions rejoice to win the praise of the old, and the elders are glad to be honored by the young. Without regret they all recall their past deeds, and their present well-doing brings meaning to their lives."

A vision opened to Hercules's mind. He saw a future life full of all kind of pleasure and lazy enjoyment and idle pursuit, but he saw also his life end empty and soulless.

Another vision opened to him. He saw a future life of toil, and sweat, and pain, and heartache, but he also saw his life end with honor and courage and meaning.

"I will choose the path of virtue, honor, and courage",

Hercules said.

"You have chosen well", Virtue replied.

Anger burned in Vice's eyes.

"There will come a day when you labor against hopeless odds", Vice sneered. "A day when you see all your toil coming to naught; when all men seem arrayed against you; when all your labor shall appear to have been in vain. On that day, remember all the good things I offered to you that you gave up in exchange for your grinding toils."

"And, yet, I choose to be Virtue's companion", Hercules responded. "Begone, foul temptress."

Vice turned and departed.

"O Hercules, may you ever follow me and be my companion on this Path you have chosen", Virtue responded. "If you toil earnestly with me until the end, when comes that appointed end, you will not lie forgotten and dishonored, but live on and remembered in God's Mind for all time."

And Hercules got up and went to his labors, until the end of his days.

18. Passive Intentions

Someone who believes he will find wisdom simply by reading or hearing the words of others is like a person who fancies himself a traveler because he reads tourist guide books.

Someone who thinks virtue comes merely by feeling committed to doing what is right is like a person who thinks himself a successful businessman because he desires wealth.

Someone who thinks that laboring with hope can be accomplished by doing only what brings good feelings and emotional satisfaction is like a runner who thinks he can win a marathon without feeling any pain or discomfort.

19. The Orchardman

A traveler stopped for a moment to watch an orchardman who was cultivating and watering his fruit trees.

"Why do so many wild trees grow with no one to tend them, while your trees require so much effort?" the traveler asked.

"Those wild trees mostly produce no fruit, or useless fruit, or bad fruit", the orchardman replied. "I cultivate these trees because they produce the fruit I need."

And with that, the orchardman returned to his work and the traveler to his journey.

20. The River

Decide what you want to achieve and then abide by the decision and work to achieve it. Control yourself and your affairs with a guiding purpose, like a skilled captain navigating a boat on a river to its destination. Even though he cannot control the weather or the river's conditions, through his skill and determination, he usually arrives at his chosen destination.

Be not as those who leave control of their lives to chance and circumstance, letting themselves be merely swept along by life, like debris afloat on a river: some debris is held back by sluggish waters and transported gently; some is torn along by violent currents; some is left on the bank as the current slackens; and some is carried out to sea by the onrush of the stream. It does not matter where the pieces of debris end up, though, because they never had a destination to begin with.

21. The Empty Knapsack

If you neglect the Triple Path, seeking instead fulfillment and happiness through status, possessions, or pleasure, then you are like a man starting an important foot journey who filled his knapsack with food, not knowing there was a hole on the bottom. The farther he went, the emptier his knapsack became. When he arrived at his destination eager for nourishment, he had only emptiness and hunger. He sorrowed, realizing only at the end of his journey that he had left that which would have sustained him on the ground to be trampled.

22. The Flower's Seed

A flower that produces no seeds brings fleeting beauty into the world and then dies, having made little impact. A flower that produces seeds brings into the world not only its own fleeting beauty, but also an impact that long outlasts its death, through that which grows from its seeds.

23. The Two Young Men

Two young men starting on their careers both said to themselves: "I will work hard to earn wealth and prosperity. Then, when I am rich I will use the leisure I have earned to seek wisdom, practice virtue, and labor with hope."

These were their intentions, but that same night the first died without wealth, wisdom, virtue, or hope. The second toiled many years, gaining much money, but never enough to satisfy himself. He was always too busy trying to get more things to ever make time to follow the Triple Path. Eventually he too died, also without wealth, wisdom, virtue, or hope.

24. The Fortified City

Let your resolve to live the Triple Path, and your practice of it, be like a fortified city built on a mountain, strong and not hidden.

25. The Light

No one finding himself in darkness takes his light and covers it with a box or hides it away in a closet. Let the light of wisdom, virtue, and hope shine through in all you do.

26. Clearing Land

It is easy to see others' faults, but not so easy to see your own. Do not seek out and gather up knowledge of other people's faults, like someone gathering dung to fertilize a field; such fertilizer only grows weeds and poisonous plants in your mind.

Do not hide your faults. Seek to find them out, and then to strip them from yourself like someone clearing a new plot of land. Thus having prepared the field of your character, you may sow the seeds of wisdom and virtue into your life and gather a bountiful harvest.

27. The Wise and the Foolish Man

If you read the words in this book and act on them, then you are like a wise man who builds his house on a foundation of rock. When rain falls, floods come, and winds blow, that house will not fall down. When you follow the Triple Path consistently, you build your life on a strong foundation, strengthening your character and mind, so that when life's challenges come, you will stand firm.

If you do not follow the principles in this book, then you are like a foolish man who builds his house on a foundation of sand. When rain falls, floods come, and winds blow, that house will fall. When you fail to follow the Triple Path, you build your life on soft, weak foundations, becoming more impotent and un- steady at confronting life's challenges.

28. The Redwood Seed

The redwood seed is among the smallest of seeds. It starts inside a cone, imprisoned, incapable of growth or change until fire burns off the old deadwood that would smother its growth, and then opens the cone to release the seed into the wild. When it falls on fertile ground, it grows into the mightiest of trees—taller, bigger, and older than any other living thing, spreading its seeds until it is surrounded by a forest of great redwoods like itself.

So too let it be for you and the Triple Path. Let the fire of your righteous desires burn off that which you should sacrifice and release the seeds of wisdom, virtue, and hope within you. Or, the fires of adversity and hardship may involuntarily burn off the dead-wood and release the seeds for you instead. Woe unto you if you have protected the deadwood and let so much accumulate that the fires needed to consume it all burn so hot that they threaten to consume the living wood as well.

Either way, once released, the seeds will start small, but will grow within you into greatness, if you nurture them. And then, you may spread more seeds until there is a great forest of wisdom, virtue, and hope around you.

29. Yeast

In the evening, a baker took a small measure of yeast and added it to a lump of bread dough. In the morning, the dough had risen to many times its original size. The dough was baked, and yielded delicious, nourishing bread.

Wisdom, virtue, and hope are like yeast. If you find even just a little of these three and let them into yourself, they will enlarge your soul. And just as the heat of the oven transforms dough into nourishing bread, the heat of experience and challenge will transform your soft and malleable inclinations and sentiments into a firm and wholesome character that will nourish not just yourself, but those around you as well.

30. The Owl and the Other Birds

Some birds together observed a farmer sowing his fields with seeds. They thought nothing of it.

"Beware", the owl warned, pointing to a certain field. "In that field he sows flax seed. Our old owl lore, which has rarely led me astray, warns that misfortune and evil come of planted flax. We must take care to pick up every one of the seeds, or we will all be sorry."

Food of a much nicer kind, however, was plentiful. And it was so pleasant to fly about and sing, thinking of nothing, that few birds paid attention to the owl's warning. The owl and a few others picked out what seeds they could, but it only amounted to a small portion of what the farmer had planted.

"It is not yet too late", the owl warned when the blades of flax appeared above the ground. "It will be more difficult now, but if we work together to pull it all up, blade by blade, we may yet escape the fate otherwise in store for us."

The birds paid no heed and mocked the owl as troublesome and full of silly fears. The owl and those few who heeded his words left, moving their nests far away from the farmer's flax field.

Eventually, the flax grew and was harvested. The flax was made into rope. The rope was made into nets. And many birds that had despised the owl's advice and stayed behind were caught in those nets.

Destroy the seed of evil, lest it grow up to your ruin.

Heed the voice of wisdom and act on it, lest you come to regret it later.

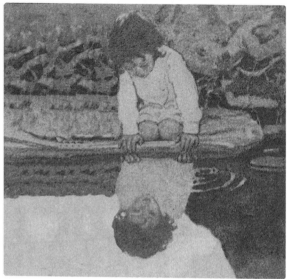

31. Muddy Water

A young child who had never seen herself went to a small pool to look at her reflection. She first dropped a rock in to see how deep it was. The rock sent ripples through the surface and kicked dirt from the bottom into the water. The child stared at her murky, rippling, hazy reflection in the muddy water. She did not understand what she saw, and was puzzled. She came away more confused about who she was than she had been before she tried to see herself.

Soon after, another child came to the same pool, also seeking to see her reflection for the first time. She let the water sit undisturbed, and it eventually became calm and clear by itself. Once the pool was still and emptied of what clouded it, the child could easily see the reflection of herself and her surroundings in the smooth water. That child left the pool with a better understanding of herself and the world.

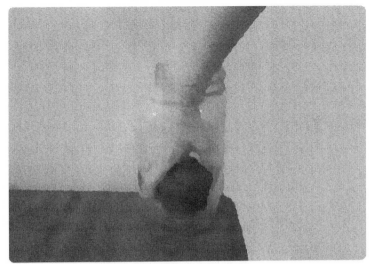

32. The Child and the Cupcake

A kidnapper took a narrow-necked jar and attached it to a table in a park so that the jar could not be moved. Inside the jar he placed a cupcake.

A young child who had wandered away from his parents came along and reached in his hand to grab the cupcake. The neck of the jar was too narrow for the child to withdraw his hand without letting go of the cupcake. The child, however, was not willing to let go. He stubbornly held on.

The child saw the villainous-looking kidnapper slowly approach.

Still, the child refused to let go of the cupcake.

The child *had* been free to drop the cupcake, yet he held on, and was captured.

33. The Fox and the Grapes

A famished fox saw some clusters of grapes hanging high on a vine. She resorted to all her tricks to get at them, but wearied herself in vain, for she could not reach them.

At last, she went away, her nose in the air.

"They weren't even ripe", she said, sniffing. "I didn't even want any sour grapes anyway."

34. The Ants and the Grasshopper

One bright day in late autumn a family of ants were bustling about in the sunshine, drying out the grain they had stored up during the summer, when a starving grasshopper came up and humbly begged for a bite to eat.

"What!" cried the ants in surprise. "Haven't you stored anything away for the winter? What in the world were you doing all summer?"

"I didn't have time to store up any food", whined the grasshopper. "I was so busy making music that before I knew it, the summer was gone."

The ants shrugged their shoulders in disgust.

"Making music, were you?" they cried. "Very well. Now dance!"

And they turned their backs on the grasshopper and went on with their work.

35. The Dog, the Wolf, and the Collar

A gaunt, hungry wolf ran into a plump dog who was passing by. They greeted each other and walked together a while down the road.

"You appear so well-fed", the wolf marveled. "And your coat is so shiny. Where do you find so much food around here in this season?"

"I guard my master's house from thieves", the dog explained. "And for my troubles, he gives me warm lodging and many scraps from his table. Rare is the day when I go without enough to eat. Now, cousin, my master seeks more guard dogs. Why not come back with me? Do as I do, and you will rarely know hunger."

The wolf agreed and followed the dog toward town.

On the way, the wolf noticed a bare spot on the dog's neck where the hair was worn away.

"What happened to your neck?" the wolf asked.

"Oh, it is nothing", said the dog. "That is only the place where my master puts a collar on at night to keep me chained up; it chafes a bit, but one soon gets used to it."

"Never mind, then", said the Wolf, turning away. "I will not sell my freedom for a full belly."

36. The Fox and the Sick Lion

A lion that was too old and weak to hunt decided to feed himself by trickery. He returned to his den and pretended to be sick so that the beasts would come pay respects to their king. They each came one by one to his den, where the lion devoured them.

The fox came as well, but stood outside the cave at a distance.

"Good afternoon, sir", the fox called out. "How do you fare?"

"Not so well", the lion replied. "But why do you stand out there? Come inside to pay your respects."

"No, thank you", said the Fox. "I notice many footprints leading into your cave, but I see no trace of any coming out."

37. The Lord's Feast

A lord sent out a proclamation that he would have a great feast. Each guest was required to bring one measure of wine to pour into some of the lord's empty wine casks, as their contribution to the celebration. The lord promised that for each cask the guests filled, he would provide for the festivities another cask filled with his own wine.

One greedy man wanted to partake of the nourishment of the food and the merry camaraderie of the celebration, but did not want to give up any of his wine.

"No one will see what it is that I pour into the cask", the man thought to himself. "If I pour in one measure of water it will not ruin an entire cask of wine. I will get to enjoy the festivities without having to give up anything!"

On the day of the feast, the man presented himself at the appointed hour, anxious to enjoy the merrymaking. He quickly poured his measure of water into the cask and entered.

When all had arrived, the first drinks were poured out of the casks that had been filled by the guests. When all cups were filled, the lord toasted his guests, and all drank. Something was wrong with the wine, though. It was watery.

"There is more water than wine in my cup!" the lord bellowed. "My feast is not for the greedy or the hypocrite!"

The man smiled within himself. He was safe. How could he be discovered?

The lord called his servants.

"Inspect the container brought by each guest", the lord ordered. "Every guest having a container with residue of wine shall receive a double portion of food and drink. Every guest having a container only of water shall be banished and also have his name posted throughout the land for all to know of his dishonesty."

The man looked down nervously at the empty container at his feet. Could he escape? But the lord's servants stood at the exits. There was nothing he could do.

The man's container was the first to be inspected.

"There is only water!" the servants declared.

"Then let him be cast out!" the lord proclaimed.

The man prostrated himself to the lord, about to beg for mercy.

"You would ask for mercy not out of remorse for having done wrong, but because you are sorry you were caught", the lord said. "You shall have no part in my feast!"

The servants roughly grabbed the man and expelled him from the feast hall. The man went away sorrowing, and hungry.

38. Belling the Cat

Long ago, the mice held a general council to consider what measures they could take to outwit their common enemy, the cat.

Some said this, and some said that; but at last a young mouse got up and said he had a proposal to make, which he thought would meet the case.

"You will all agree", he said, "that our chief danger consists in the sly and treacherous manner in which the enemy approaches us. Now, if we could receive some signal of her approach, we could easily escape from her. I venture, therefore, to propose that a small bell be procured, and attached by a ribbon round the neck of the cat. By this means we should always know when she was about, and could easily retire while she was in the neighborhood."

This proposal met with general applause, until an old mouse got up and spoke.

"That is all very well", the old mouse said, "but who is to bell the cat?"

The mice looked at one another and nobody spoke.

39. The Sticks

An old man on the point of death had five sons who were always quarreling among themselves. He summoned them to give some parting advice.

He ordered them to bring in a bundle of five sticks.

"Break them", he said to his oldest son.

The son strained and strained, but despite all his efforts, he was unable to break the bundle. The other sons also tried, but none succeeded.

"Untie the bundle", the old man said, "and each of you take a stick."

When they had done so, he told them: "Now, break," and each stick was easily broken.

40. Androclus and the Lion

    In the Circus Maximus of Ancient Rome, a great and terrible spectacle was staged, pitting men against beasts. Among the many lions, one stood out—it was larger and stronger than the others, its roar loud and deep.

    Among those brought in to fight the beasts was an escaped slave named Androclus. When that lion saw him from a distance it stopped short and focused only on him. The lion approached him slowly and quietly. When it drew near, it slowed and crouched. Androclus cringed and looked away. The arena grew quiet. The lion began to wag its tail. It walked up to Androclus until they were almost touching. Then, it opened its mouth and gently licked Androclus's feet and hands.

    Androclus regained his lost courage and gradually turned his eyes to look at the lion. A smile of joy came over Androclus's face and he began to pet the lion's head and to caress it.

    The spectators were so astonished that they broke out into mighty shouts. The Emperor, who was in attendance, called Androclus to him to inquire why that fiercest of lions had spared him.

"When I was a slave in Jerusalem, my master had me beaten every day—and for no reason", Androclus explained. "So, I escaped away into the desert. When the midday sun was fierce and scorching, I hid in a remote and secluded cavern. Not long afterwards this lion came to the same cave with one paw lame and bleeding, making known by groans and moans the torturing pain of his wound. He approached me and lifted his foot showing it to me and holding it out as if to ask for help. I drew out a huge thorn embedded in the sole of his foot, and then cleaned the wound and bandaged it. Relieved of much of his pain and discomfort, the lion put his paw in my hand, lay down, and went to sleep. For three years after that day the lion and I lived in the same cave, and on the same food as well. He would bring for me to the cave the choicest parts of the game that he took in hunting, which I, having no means of making a fire, dried in the noonday sun and ate. And I would care for his wounds and trap and hunt smaller game for us to eat.

"Eventually, though, I grew tired of that wild life", he continued. "When the lion had gone off to hunt, I left the cave. After three days' travel, some soldiers caught me. They took me to Rome, where my master had moved. He at once had me condemned to death by being thrown to the wild beasts. Apparently, this lion was also captured after I left him, and he is now repaying me still for my kindness, my cure of him, and our companionship during those three years."

The Emperor had the story announced to the crowds. They erupted in great shouts and cheers that Androclus should be pardoned and freed, and reunited with the lion. And so it was done.

Androclus settled in Rome. He could often be seen in the years after leading the lion, attached to a slender leash, through the streets of Rome.

Many would stop and give money to Androclus and meat to the lion. Everyone who met them anywhere exclaimed: "This is the lion that was a man's friend, this is the man who was physician to a lion!"

355

41. The Crow and the Fox

A crow found a piece of cheese and flew with it to a tree that was some way off. A fox, drawn by the aroma of the cheese, came and sat at the foot of the tree, and tried to find some way of making it his.

"Good morning, dear miss crow", he said. "How well you are looking today! What beautiful feathers you have! Perhaps your voice is as sweet as your feathers are fine. If so, you are really the Queen of Birds."

The crow, quite beside herself to hear such praise, at once opened a wide beak to let the fox be judge of her voice, and so let fall the cheese.

"That was all I wanted", the fox said, snapping up the cheese. "In exchange for your cheese I will give you a piece of advice. Learn that all who flatter have their own ends in view."

42. The Farmer and the Snake

One cold winter's day, a farmer passed a snake half-dead in the snow. Pitying the poor wretch, he picked it up and put it into his coat to warm it up and save it from certain death. When the snake was restored by the warmth, he slithered up the farmer's body, brought his fangs to the farmer's neck, and delivered a fatal bite. As the farmer lay dying in the snow, he thought to himself, "I should have expected nothing less from trying to help a scoundrel."

After the man had died, the snake curled up next to the warmth of the farmer's body. Before long, though, the farmer's body cooled and then froze. There was no more warmth for the snake. It soon died also.

43. The Wolf and the Shepherd

A wolf followed a flock of sheep for a long time without attempting to injure any of them. The shepherd at first stood on his guard against him, as against an enemy, and kept a strict watch over his movements. But when the wolf, day after day, kept in the company of the sheep and did not make the slightest effort to seize any of them, the shepherd began to look on him as a guardian of his flock rather than as a threat.

One day, the shepherd needed to go into town. He left the wolf to watch over the sheep. The wolf seized on the opportunity and fell upon them, slaughtering the greater part of the flock.

When the shepherd returned to find his flock destroyed, he exclaimed: "It serves me right. How could the sheep ever be safe with a wolf among the flock?"

44. The Shepherd and the Cub

A Shepherd found a young wolf cub and had it brought up among his dogs, with whom it grew to be quite friendly. As they guarded the flock, when any other wolves came to rob the fold, the young wolf was always one of the first to give them chase. When the dogs could not keep up, he would keep on. Often, he caught up to the wolf, who would give him an equal share of the sheep to eat. Other times, as he returned, he would linger behind the dogs, keeping a sharp lookout for any stray sheep from the fold. Instead, however, of bringing these home, he would drive them to an out-of-the-way spot, and there mangle and devour them.

He did this once too often, and was caught at it by the shepherd, who quickly set him hanging by the neck from the branch of a tree and killed him.

Wolf knows wolf, scoundrel knows scoundrel.

A wicked nature does not produce a good character.

45. The Dog in the Manger

A farm dog asleep in a manger filled with hay was awakened by the oxen, which came in tired and hungry from working in the field. The dog, however, would not let them get near the manger. He snarled and snapped at them, as if the manger were filled with the best of meat and bones, all for himself.

The oxen looked at the dog in disgust.

"How selfish he is!" they said. "He cannot eat the hay, and yet he will not let us eat it who are so hungry for it!"

The farmer came in. When he saw how the dog was acting, he took a stick and drove the dog out of the stable with many a blow for his selfish behavior. He sent the dog away with no food for the night.

The oxen ate their hay and enjoyed their rest.

46. The Two Prayers

Two men went into church to pray. The first sat in the very front and center, and prayed loudly to himself thus, "God, I am grateful that I am not as others are, like the adulterers, criminals, and unbelievers. I fast twice a week, and I pay a tenth of all my income as tithing. I am grateful that you have separated me, my family, and my people from others and that we have been specially chosen of you. I am grateful that we have the truth and have not been led away by the false and foolish traditions believed by those around us. Amen."

The second man, standing far off, sat in the back corner and prayed quietly to God, saying, "God, I am in need of mercy. I am a foolish, ignorant, and unvirtuous man! I am vain and need more humility. I need greater wisdom and more virtue. I hope to become ever more like Thee, and I again resolve to strive after this. Amen."

The second man left seeking to live better than he had before. The first man left self-assured of his righteousness and lived on as he had been, changing nothing and continuing in all his previous errors. The second man went back to his home justified, but not the first. He who exalts himself before God idles away his life. He who humbles himself before God moves forward on the Triple Path.

47. The Careless and Watchful Householders

A careless householder never locked his doors. Worse still, he had not even bothered to examine the kind of neighborhood the house was in before he bought it. He awoke one morning to discover that a thief had broken into his house overnight and stolen all his valuable possessions within.

An attentive householder made sure to lock his doors and secure his house every night. Even before that, he had made sure to buy a house in a secure neighborhood with good neighbors who helped watch over each other's property. He looked for weaknesses in his home's security and fixed them. He also kept vigilant watch over his house as necessary, but it was less necessary than it might have been because of all his other steps to secure his home. The house was never broken into, and his possessions remained secure.

A thief will break in when you are paying the least attention for him. If the careless householder had known the hour the thief was coming, he would have watched and resisted.

You are always in danger of foolishness, evil, and lazy despair creeping into your life when you are not paying attention and do not expect them. Thus, take care to defend yourself against them. Strengthen your character and place yourself in situations that help you seek wisdom, practice virtue, and labor with hope. Establish the patterns of your life to make it difficult for foolishness, evil, and lazy despair to enter. And keep watch over yourself that you do not fall away from the Triple Path.

48. The Three Treasure Seekers

An old man showed to his three grandsons a map to a treasure in a far-off land. Each grandson resolved to seek it out and find it.

The first got distracted by other pursuits. He forgot what the map showed. He never started his search. He never reached the treasure.

The second believed he could remember the path the map showed. He set out, trusting in himself to remember and never forget. During the journey, he forgot the way. He wandered much, eventually into a dangerous land. He was set upon by thieves and fled back home with nothing to show for his efforts.

The third grandson asked his grandfather to give him the map. The grandfather refused, but told his grandson he was free to copy it. The grandson carefully made his own copy. Then, he set off on his search. He consulted his map frequently to make sure he was following the correct path, so that he knew where he was and where he needed to go. He made corrections to the map when he found mistakes in it. (Some mistakes were from his own copy errors and some were mistakes that had been in his grandfather's map.)

After a difficult and long quest, he came to what he expected to be the end. There was no further path marked on the map, but there was no treasure either. There was only a gloomy and foreboding forest. He found a small sign with one final instruction: "You must enter the forest where there is no path, where it looks darkest to you. *You* must find this place and then choose to make your own path there. For through the forest of darkness, no treasure seeker may follow the path made by another."

His labors through the forest were even more difficult than everything that had come before, but he persisted. His quest following the map's path had prepared him. He used the skills he had developed, the lessons he had learned, and the courage he had earned to blaze his own trail through the forest.

Finally, he came to a beautiful, bright, flowered clearing in the middle of the forest. At the far end of the clearing was a cliff with a cave entrance at its base.

The cave led upward into an enormous treasure room. The riches inside appeared infinite. What he was able to carry out was only a small part of the whole, yet was still worth a fortune.

He returned home rejoicing in the priceless riches he had earned from his quest.

He carefully preserved the map for his future children and grandchildren to consult and copy so that each might blaze his own trail through the forest of darkness and earn his own treasure.

49. Whitewashed Tombs

A whitewashed tomb appears beautiful, pure, and clean on the outside, but inside is full of filth, dead bones, and rotting flesh.

Do not be a hypocrite who makes himself appear to have wisdom, virtue, and hope, but inside is full of foolishness and evil.

50. The Three Sons

A shop owner with three sons went to the first and said: "Son, go work in my shop today." The son answered, "I will go, father", but then did not go.

The shop owner went to his second son and said the same thing. That son said, "no, I will not go". Afterward, he went to the shop to work.

The shop owner sought out his third son to say the same thing, but found him already in the shop working, teaching the second how to work there.

The father was displeased with his first son and pleased with both the second and third; yet, it was only to his third son to whom he entrusted the shop as an inheritance.

It is better to speak of doing evil, and then do good, than it is to speak of doing good and then do evil. Better still is it to first do good and then speak of doing it.

51. The Banquet and the Rope Ladder

A profane man died. He heard a voice tell him he would see both heaven and hell and then decide where to spend eternity.

The man first found himself in hell, in a large room with no ceiling. There was an endlessly long table set up, filled with delicious foods. However, the people sitting at the table groaned in hungry misery. All the food was in the middle of the table. The people were tied to their chairs, so they could not bend forward to reach the food. The only utensils were long spoons that were long enough to reach the food, but were thus too long for anyone to feed themselves.

Those at the table would try over and over to feed themselves by scooping food up in their spoons and then throwing the food in the air and trying to catch it in their mouths. Because of their restraints, their throws and catches were clumsy and rarely landed in their mouths. The banquet hall was a chaotic mess, with uncaught food scattered and rotting all over the ground, the diners, and table.

The man was suddenly carried away into heaven. He was

puzzled, for heaven was set up identically to hell, with the same banquet table and restrained diners. But here, the room was clean and filled with the sounds of happy conversation. Only one thing differed: the diners were feeding each other by scooping up food and giving it to their neighbors.

The man found himself again back in hell. He approached the nearest suffering diner, leaned down and whispered, "You fool! There is no need for you to go hungry. Feed one of your neighbors, and certainly he will return your kindness."

"You expect me to feed him?" the diner said. "I'd rather starve than give him the satisfaction of eating!"

In the distance, the man could see a thin rope ladder hanging down from heaven extending all the way to hell. Remembering the choice of where to spend eternity was his, and not wanting to spend it in hunger with such selfish companions, he began climbing the ladder, eager to reach the banquets of heaven.

The climb out of hell is a long one, and the man eventually grew tired. He stopped halfway up to rest. To his dismay, he noticed another new arrival to hell climbing up after him. Fearing that the flimsy rope ladder might break from the added weight, he shouted down, demanding that the other climber get off, that the ladder was his and his alone. The climber below him refused and demanded instead that the man get off. The man then heard the voice of another climber above him demanding that the man and the other climber below both get off the ladder. The man refused. He was worried that if he stayed too long in hell, he would be forced to stay there.

The three began arguing. Each tried to knock the other two off the rope while desperately trying to hang on. Eventually, the rope snapped from their scuffling. All three fell down into hell.

The man was taken and strapped into a chair and restrained for all eternity. His nearest table companions were those who had been climbing above and below him. He was so angry with them for preventing his escape from hell that he refused to feed them.

With regret, he called out to heaven. "Please warn those who are still living—I did not learn, but if I had seen what I see now, I would have learned."

A voice replied, "you did see when you were still living, yet you never learned. Even at the end you refused to learn. The living have teachers enough. Those with ears to hear and the resolve to act already have what they need to be able to learn and do what is necessary to become worthy of heaven. Those without ears to hear and the resolve to act will never learn, no matter how many times they are taught, unless they choose to open their ears and fortify their resolve."

Now, to you reading this, the man and the two others on the ladder likely seem foolish and evil, but it is easy to see the foolishness and evil of others and tell them what you think they must do to set themselves right. It is much harder to see your own foolishness and evil and correct it. Focus on shedding your own faults, and seek to live among those working to do likewise, and you can start building heaven around you.

52. The Ring of Gyges

After a great earthquake, a man named Gyges discovered a hole that had opened in the ground. He descended. Inside, he was amazed to discover a chamber in which sat a hollow bronze owl. There were doors on this statue. When he opened them, he discovered the body of an enormous dead man. On the man's hand was a gold ring. Gyges took the ring for himself.

He climbed out of the ground. As he walked away, he began twisting the ring on his finger. He discovered that whenever he turned the bezel inward toward his palm, he became invisible. When he turned it outward, he became visible again.

He tested it many ways, and every time it was the same: he could become invisible and visible at will.

"With this ring, not even God can see me!" Gyges bragged to himself.

Gyges had a prosperous neighbor. When the neighbor went out, Gyges made himself invisible and went into the neighbor's home to be with the neighbor's beautiful wife. Afterward, Gyges waited until the neighbor returned home. Gyges watched his neighbor until he discovered the treasury where the neighbor locked away his money and prized possessions. After all were asleep that night, Gyges stole the key to the treasury, opened it, and took all that was inside.

With the advantage the ring gave him, Gyges went on to ever-greater debauchery, theft, cruelty, and wickedness until he had experienced much pleasure, inflicted much pain, grown rich, and entirely corrupted his soul.

Now, suppose a perfectly wise and virtuous man got just such a ring. Would he be as Gyges? Would he imagine himself free to do wrongly just because he could do it undetected? No, of course not!

But, none of us are perfectly wise and virtuous. It is good that we avoid evil and foolishness in our moments of weakness at least out of fear of the disapprobation of others or the penalties of the law. Far better, though, is it when we act with wisdom and virtue for their own sake, regardless of the external consequences.

Now, finally, imagine that you yourself got such a ring. Examine yourself honestly. What would you do with it, if no one could see you—if not even God could see you?

"Invisible to God?", you may say. "That is impossible!"

Of course it is, but just imagine for a moment, even so, it were possible. What would you do? What would you *really* do?

The answer to this question tells you much about who you are, what you are becoming, and how you must change if you would make something greater of yourself.

53. Counting the Cost

Embark on a new endeavor only after first weighing its costs versus its benefits. Only a fool would build a new house without first sitting down and estimating its cost to see if he has enough money. Otherwise, he might lay the foundation and then be unable to finish the building. What use is a bare foundation with no building to rest upon it?

And only a fool would build a new house without checking if better alternatives are available to him. Otherwise, he might build a house that is more expensive or worse than one already available. What use is an overpriced or second-rate house?

54. The Dog's Reflection

To get home, a dog carrying a piece of meat in his teeth had to pass over a plank across a stream. As he crossed, he saw his own reflection in the water. Mistaking it for another dog with a piece of meat that seemed larger than his own, he snapped at it. When he opened his mouth, his meat fell into the stream and was swept away by the current. He tried to retrieve it, but could not get it back. And, of course, he never got the new meat he was trying to take, because it had always been an illusion.

55. The Goose and the Golden Eggs

A man owned a goose that every day laid a golden egg.
Each day, the man took the egg to market to sell. He began to grow
rich, but not fast enough for his liking. He grew impatient that the
goose gave only a single golden egg a day.

One day, after he had finished counting his money, the
idea came to him that he could get all the golden eggs at once by
killing the goose and cutting it open. He did just that, but not a
single golden egg did he find, and his precious goose was dead.

56. The Shepherd's Boy

There was once a young shepherd's boy who tended his flock at the foot of a mountain near a dark forest. It was an out-of-the-way place. Rarely did anyone pay him any mind.

One day, he thought of a plan to get some notice and attention. He rushed down towards the village calling out, "Wolf! Wolf!"

The villagers and the shepherd came out to meet him and help drive off the imagined wolf. This pleased the boy so much that a few days later he tried the same trick, and again the villagers and shepherd came to his aid.

After not many days a wolf actually did come out from the forest. It stared menacingly at the sheep.

The boy, of course, cried out "Wolf! Wolf!" louder than he ever had before. This time, however, the villagers thought the boy was again deceiving them, and nobody stirred to come help— not even the shepherd.

The wolf made a good meal off the boy's flock.

57. The Crow and the Pitcher

A thirsty crow came upon a pitcher that had once been full of water. He flew to it hoping to find water to drink. When he reached it, he discovered to his grief that it contained so little water that his beak could not reach far enough down to get at it, and the pitcher was too heavy to knock over to drink the water as it spilled out.

He thought for a while on his predicament. An idea came to him. He used his beak to drop pebbles, one by one, into the pitcher until the water was high enough for him to drink.

He did what it took to get the water he needed to quench his thirst and save his life.

58. The Travelers and the Dry Well

Long ago, there was a man in a far-off land traveling on foot down an empty road through arid, desolate country. He came upon another man traveling the same road. They walked together a while.

Feeling thirsty and nearing one of the infrequent wells along the route, they stopped to refill their waterskins and to refresh themselves. When they dipped the bucket into the well, though, it came up dry. They tried again, and again it came up dry.

The first traveler thought it best to set off again to search further along the road for a well with water in it. The second traveler disagreed.

"You fool!" he said to the first traveler. "We already have a well here. You do not know how long it will be until you reach another one. You do not know if that well will be dry too. I will stay here instead and keep trying to draw water from this well. Stay with me. There is still some water left in each of our waterskins. This water that we have can sustain us while we continue trying to extract water from this well."

"It is true I do not know how far it is to the next well or whether it will have water", the first traveler replied. "But I do know that this well is empty, and it is foolish to continue seeking water from a dry well. If you wish to complete your journey, you must seek water where it can be found, not where it is convenient to look for it. Please follow me on the path and find water, before it is too late."

And with that, he got up and left.

He sought water. On a road he had not known and had not planned to take, he found a spring with fresh, sweet water flowing out of the ground. He drank deeply and refilled his waterskin.

His journey to the spring had taken him far from the dry well. His waterskin would hold enough to sustain him on the way to the dry well and back to the spring again, but there would be little left to share with the other man. Still, he made his way back to the dry well, in hopes he could at least warn the other man and point him in the right direction. He found the other man still there, still dipping his bucket into the dry well, though his movements were slower and more hesitating. The first man told the other of the spring he had found.

"If you have found water, then why do you not share?" the second man asked.

"My waterskin holds only enough for me", the man replied. "I can spare a little to revive you and get you started on the way, but you must come to the spring yourself. Then, you will be able to drink as much as you can directly from the source and refill your own waterskin."

He passed his waterskin to the second man for a drink to refresh himself. The water appeared to revive him a little. He sat taller. He thought a moment, then slumped again. Finally, he spoke.

"I do not believe you", the second man said. "I have never heard of this road of which you speak. Perhaps it was a mirage, or a hallucination from the heat and the sun. Or perhaps you are lying and have some nefarious purpose in telling me of this spring. Whatever the reason, it is no matter. I have what I need here. Eventually, I believe, this well will yield the water I seek. It must! I have spent so much effort here already."

He turned back and lowered the bucket again into the well. The first man sadly got up. There was nothing he could do. He could not force the second man to come to the spring.

"The spring will still be there waiting, if you change your mind", he said. "I pray it not be too late."

The first man made his way back to the spring. He again drank deeply and refilled his waterskin. He looked out ahead. The water from the spring flowed out into a stream that ran next to this new road he had found. The road appeared to point more directly to his destination, so he set out on it.

He completed his journey, purposefully following this new path—one that rarely lacked water and took him through landscapes that became ever more lush and verdant.

The second traveler remained, dipping the bucket again and again into the dry well. It always came up empty. That man died, weak, alone, and thirsty.

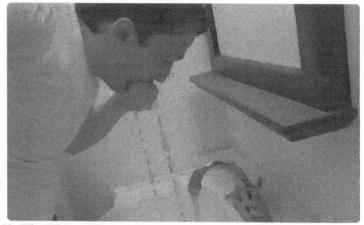

59. The Thirsty Dreamer

A sleeping man dreamed he was thirsty. Over and over, he desperately sought water, but whenever he found some, his mouth always remained as parched as ever, no matter how much he eagerly drank.

Finally, he awoke. His lips were cracked. His tongue stuck to the roof of his mouth.

He went to a faucet and thirstily drank. His throat was so dry that, at first, it hurt to swallow.

But this water that he drank after waking up finally satisfied his thirst.

60. New Bread

You do not put fresh bread into a sack with old moldy bread. Otherwise, the new bread will go moldy and be useless. Rather, you make fresh bread after the manner of the old bread and then put it into new, clean sacks so that the new bread may be preserved. Nor do you leave old bread in its sack to go moldy. Instead, you consume it to partake of its sustenance before it goes bad, and to make room in your pantry for the new bread.

61. Truth in the Wilderness

A traveler passing through the desert came upon a woman who was alone and terribly dejected.

"Who are you?" he asked.

"My name is Truth", she replied.

"Why have you left the city to dwell alone here in the wilderness?" he asked.

"There is nowhere that I may dwell in that city", she answered. "In former times, lies were found among only a few, but now have spread to every household."

"O, woe is you!" the man declared.

"Woe are they", she said. "For without my protection, they are ripe for destruction."

62. The Westward Garden

A man who owned a large property planted his prize garden on the west of his estate. The garden was a productive delight for many years. Eventually, though, the plants in the garden began to wither. Nothing he did would revive the garden. The plants seemed to have lost the will to thrive. There was good virgin land further west of his property. He bought it up. He took his hardiest vines and planted them there. They took root and filled the new land. Their increase was so great that their growth expanded back into the old garden, reviving it and eventually growing into new parts of his estate.

63. The Pelican and the Fisherman

A poor fisherman went out in his boat to catch what he could to support his family. A lazy pelican who hated the effort of searching for and catching fish flew over the poor fisherman's boat and saw the small pile of the fisherman's catch for the day. As the fisherman started to guide his boat back to shore, the pelican dived down and stole a fish out of the pile. The fisherman shooed the pelican away. The pelican flew up into the air, waited until the fisherman was not looking, and dived down again to steal another fish. The pelican kept this up, stealing more and more fish. The pelican's thefts depleted so much of the fisherman's meager catch that he did not have enough to both feed his family and sell fish at the market for money to buy other necessities.

The fisherman kept a lifelike wood carving of a fish stowed in his boat as a good luck charm. He knew that his success really depended mostly on his own hard work, but his father and grandfather had carried the wooden fish with them every day when they went out to sea, and so he brought it with him to continue the tradition. Seeking solace, he took out the wooden fish and held it, despairing the meager remnants of his catch. If ever he needed luck, he thought, it was then. He then set down the wooden fish and started guiding his boat again back to shore.

The pelican, still circling overhead, saw the wooden fish. The fish looked real, and it was larger than the rest. Greedily, he swooped down and plucked it up in his beak. He tried to swallow it as he flew back into the air, but the fish caught in his throat. The pelican fell down to the water's surface, choking. The wooden fish was firmly lodged in his throat, and he could not get it out. He expended much effort struggling to get the fish out of his throat—far more than he would have spent just working to catch his own fish. But, his efforts were in vain. The pelican soon choked to death. The fisherman used his net to get the pelican. He returned to shore with his wooden fish retrieved from the pelican's throat, a small pile of fish to sell, and a pelican for his family to eat.

The pelican died because it failed to learn the simple lesson that each must work for his own sustenance, rather than living off the labors of others. The fisherman and his family did not go hungry that night because the fisherman had learned to value tradition, even though he could not initially recognize its purpose.

64. The Cathedral Builders

The citizens of a medieval town decided to build a cathedral. They knew it would not be finished for generations—until after they, their children, and their grandchildren were all long dead. Even so, they started the project. And for generations the people of the town, from the high and rich to the low and poor, contributed their time and money to its construction, even though it was not they who had started the work.

When completed, the cathedral became world-renown as a great monument of devotion to God and of human achievement. To this day, pilgrims and admirers visit it to partake of its grandeur, beauty, strength, and holiness.

65. The Empty Tomb

A young man decided to seek out a tomb that legend said contained the secret to the meaning of life. After a long search, he found it in the Holy Land, hidden underground among some old Roman ruins. He looked in, but it was empty. He did not know why, but he felt a powerful sense of fear and dread as he entered. Even so, he continued in and explored every nook and cranny. He saw no books or scrolls or other secrets inside. In fact, there was no writing of any kind. There was not even a coffin or a sarcophagus in the tomb. It just had an empty recessed area cut into the stone wall where a corpse or a coffin would have been placed. He lay down in the bare alcove, confused.

He meditated on his journey. He thought about the place in which he found himself, and realized that the land around the tomb was some of the best he had seen along the way. It was fertile and empty, free to anyone willing to settle on it. There were even plenty of stones left over from the scattered ruins, ready to be used for building. He resolved to settle there.

He urgently made the long journey home. He married his beloved, and together they journeyed back to the land by the tomb. Out of the old stones from the ruins he built a small house. He also built a small altar of stones above the tomb, where he and his wife would go to pray and give thanks to God.

He farmed the land, and she managed the household. Each time a new child was born, he would go into the empty tomb and carve on its wall the new child's name and birthdate.

Some years had good harvests, and others had bad ones. Still, they worked hard, saving of their abundance in good years and living frugally in bad years. They continued to use the old stones to gradually built up their house. They found buried nearby some old scrolls on which were written words of wisdom. They first studied them, then started adding to them, writing about what they knew and had learned, about the story of their life and their plans for the future, and tales that captured their imaginations.

They built a small temple around the altar. They had more children. They continued to use the old stones to build up their house and the temple. The man and wife added more to the writings, and used all of them to teach their children.

More time passed. The children grew into adulthood and married, settled close by and started their own families and farms. They built houses, using the old stones at first, and then quarrying new stones as the old stones ran out.

Their grown children taught their own children now. The man continued to carve the names and birthdates of each descendant on the tomb walls.

They all continued building onto the temple. It grew larger and finer and grander. As they learned and discovered, they wrote, including the stories of their lives—of their past, present, and hoped futures—and of tales of courage and wisdom, virtue, and hope.

The man and wife reached the twilight of life. They died. Their descendants buried the two of them, leaving them to rest in a tomb that was no longer empty, with the names of their descendants surrounding them on the walls, and the temple the family had built together—now great and beautiful—rising above them.

And those descendants continued to improve and build onto the temple, to read and add to what had been passed down to them, and to build their own families, houses, temples, and epics.

References

1. **The Bridges of Hammon and Sophrete.**

2. **The Emperor's New Clothes-** Hans Christian Andersen, "The Emperor's New Clothes"; Lionel Tiger and Robin Fox, The Imperial Animal, 1971; illustration by Vilhelm Pedersen, 1837.

3. **The Cure for the Blind-** Illustration by Simon François Ravenet, 1767.

4. **The Poisoned Arrow-** Cula Malunkyovada Sutta, The Shorter Instructions to Malunkya, translated from the Pali by Thanissaro Bhikkhu; illustration adapted from etching by Crispyn van den Queborne (after Adriaen Pietersz Crabeth), ca. 1640.

5. **The Sick Physician-** Aesop Fable 289, The Fox and the Frog (text adapted from Samuel Croxall, 1722 and G. F. Townsend, 1867); Ancient Greek Proverb; Luke 4:23; illustration adapted from Jan Luyken: *Asan Aga Spreekt Toehoorders Op en Groot Plein Toe* and *The Eleventh Hour Laborers*; *Parable of the Tares*, all ca. 1700.

6. **Children in the Library-** Albert Einstein in George Sylvester Viereck, *Glimpses of the Great*, 1930.

7. **The Truck Driver-** "Smuggling Donkeys", folktale attributed to Nasreddin; illustration adapted from photograph by David Stanley under Creative Commons Attribution 2.0 Generic license.

8. **The Testing Sower-** Mark 4:3-9; Thomas 9; Matthew 13:24-30; illustration by John Everett Millais, 1864.

9. **The Young Man and the Swallow-** Aesop Fable 169 (text adapted from G. F. Townsend, 1867 and Ernest Griset, 1874); illustration by C. Whittingham, 1814.

10. **The Two Pilgrims -** D. L. Ashliman, "The Two Travelers and the Farmer", ca. 1950 (folktale from Idaho); illustration by Robert Barnes, 1886 (from serialized edition of *The Mayor of Casterbridge by* Thomas Hardy).

11. **The Traveler-** Chuang Tzu, Sec. 31 (The Old Fisherman), Watson translation.

12. **The Sand in the Hourglass-** Illustration adapted from Philippe

de Champaigne, 1671.

13. The Ring of Truth- Persian fable.

14. The Fair Jar.

15. Icarus- Thomas Bullfinch, *The Age of Fable*, 1855. Illustration by Antonio Tempesta, 1606.

16. The Young Man and the Teacher- Matthew 19:16-30; Mark 10:17-31; Luke 18:18-30.

17. Hercules at the Crossroads- Xenophon, *Memorabilia*, ca. 370 BC, 2.1.21–34 (from the translation by E.C. Marchant); illustration by Johann Jakob Frey the Elder, ca. 1725, after Annibale Carracci, *The Choice of Hercules*, 1596.

18. Passive Intentions- Illustration adapted from David Teniers the Younger, *A man reading a book, smiling*, ca. 1650 and A.L. Leroy, *Interior With a Man Reading at His Desk*, 1827.

19. The Orchardman- Aesop Fable 119, The Gardener Watering his Vegetables; illustration by Vincent van Gogh, *In the Orchard*, 1883.

20. The River- Lucilius 23:8.

21. The Empty Knapsack- Thomas 97.

22. The Flower's Seed- John 12:24-26.

23. The Two Young Men- Thomas 63; Luke 12:16-21; illustration by H. Alken, 1821.

24. The Fortified City- Thomas 32; Matthew 5:14.

25. The Light- Matthew 5:14-15; Mark 4:21-25; Luke 8:16-18; Thomas 33; illustration by Jan Luyken, ca. 1700.

26. Clearing Land- Dhammapada 252; illustration by J.D. Kelly, ca. 1920.

27. The Wise and the Foolish Man- Matthew 6:24-27.

28. The Redwood Seed- Matthew 13:31-32; Mark 4:30-32; Luke 13:18-19; 12 Rules, pp. 244-47, 393-97.

29. Yeast- Matthew 13:33; Luke 13:20-21; Thomas 96; illustration by anonymous, from Book of Hours, ca. 1490-1500.

30. The Owl and the Other Birds- Aesop Fable 39, The Swallow and the Other Birds (text adapted from Joseph Jacobs, 1889 and Ernest Griset, 1874); illustration by C. Whittingham, 1814.

31. Muddy Water- Tao Te Ching 8:2, 15:3, 22 (Mitchell Translation); Chuang Tzu, Sec. 5 (The Sign of Virtue Complete), Watson translation, p. 65; illustration adapted from Jessie Wilcox Smith, *A Child's Garden of Verses*, 1905.

32. The Child and the Cupcake- Epictetus, *Discourses*, Book 3, Chapter 9; Wilson Rawls, *Where the Red Fern Grows*, 1961; 12 Rules, pp. 199-200.

33. The Fox and the Grapes- Aesop Fable 15 (text adapted from Joseph Jacobs, 1889 and Ernest Griset, 1874); illustration by François Chaveau, 1668.

34. The Ants and the Grasshopper- Aesop Fable 373; illustration by Arthur Rackham, 1912.

35. The Dog, the Wolf, and the Collar- Aesop Fable 346 (text adapted from Joseph Jacobs, 1889); illustration by Richard Heighway, 1889.

36. The Fox and the Sick Lion- Aesop Fable 142; illustration by Ernest Griset, 1874.

37. The Lord's Feast- African folktale; illustration by Jan Luyken, ca. 1700.

38. Belling the Cat- Medieval fable attributed to Aesop, Perry Index no. 613 (text adapted from Joseph Jacobs, 1889); illustration by Gustave Doré, 1868.

39. The Sticks- Aesop Fable 53 (text adapted from Joseph Jacobs, 1889 and *Aesop for* Children, 1919); illustration by C. Whittingham, 1814.

40. Androclus and the Lion- Aulus Gellius, *Attic Nights*, 177 A.D. (quoting Apion, *Wonders of Egypt*, ca. 39 A.D.); illustration by Henry Justice Ford, 1914.

41. The Crow and the Fox- Aesop Fable 124; illustration by Thomas Bewick, 1820.

42. The Farmer and the Snake- Aesop Fable 127.

43. The Wolf and the Shepherd- Aesop Fables 158 and 169 (text adapted from G. F. Townsend, 1867); illustration by Milo Winter, 1919.

44. The Shepherd and the Cub- Aesop Fable 267 (text adapted from Ernest Griset, 1874 and Laura Gibbs, 2002); illustration by Harrison Weir, 1868.

45. The Dog in the Manger- Ancient Greek fable; Thomas 102; illustration by Ernest Griset, 1869.

46. The Two Prayers- Luke 18:9-14; BoM, Alma 31:15-18; illustration adapted from photograph by Eric Enstrom, 1918.

47. The Careless and Watchful Householders- Luke 12:35-40; Matthew 24:42-44; Mark 13:34-37.

48. The Three Treasure Seekers- Joseph Campbell, *The Hero's Journey*, 1990 (inspiration only for the parable's fifth paragraph); illustration adapted from Thomas Bulfinch, *The Age of Fable*, 1874, p. 466 and Thomas Bulfinch, *Bulfinch's Mythology*, 1913, p. 645.

49. Whitewashed Tombs- Matthew 23:27-28; illustration adapted from public domain photograph by James De Mers.

50. The Three Sons- Matthew 21:28-32; illustration by Jan Luyken, ca. 1700.

51. The Banquet and the Rope Ladder- Old story, known as "Allegory of the Long Spoons", "Parable of the Banquet", or "Parable of the Long Chopsticks", attributed as an old Buddhist, Chinese, Christian, Hindu, or Jewish parable; Ryunosuke Akutagawa, "The Spider's Thread", 1918; Luke 16:19-31; illustration adapted from photograph by J.P. King, 1903.

52. The Ring of Gyges- Plato, *Republic*, Book 2; Cicero, *De Officiis*, 3:38-39; illustration adapted from engraving of Pierre-Narcisse Guérin, *Aeneas at the Court of Queen Dido*, 1817 in Thomas Bullfinch, *Bullfinch's Mythology*, 1913, p. 263.

53. Counting the Cost- Luke 14:28-30; illustration by Edward Lear, ca. 1850.

54. The Dog's Reflection- Aesop Fable 169 (text adapted from G. F. Townsend, 1867 and Joseph Jacobs, 1889); illustration by C. Whittingham, 1814.

55. The Goose and the Golden Eggs- Aesop Fable 87 (text adapted from *Aesop for* Children, 1919); illustration by C. Whittingham, 1814.

56. The Shepherd's Boy- Aesop Fable 210 (text adapted from Joseph Jacobs, 1889); illustration by Milo Winter, 1919.

57. The Crow and the Pitcher- Aesop Fable 390 (text adapted from Joseph Jacobs, 1889 and G. F. Townsend, 1867); illustration by Milo Winter, 1919.

58. The Travelers and the Dry Well- Thomas 74; illustration adapted from F.C. Welsch, "A Ride in the Desert", in George Ebers, *Egypt: Descriptive, Historical, and Picturesque*, 1881, p. 93.

59. The Thirsty Dreamer.

60. New Bread - Thomas 47; Matthew 9:16-17; Mark 2:21-22; Luke 5:36-39.

61. Truth in the Wilderness- Aesop Fable 355 (text adapted from G. F. Townsend, 1867 and Laura Gibbs, 2002); illustration adapted from George Frederick, *Good Old Arizona*, 1943 and Stefano della Bella, *Diversi Capricci*, ca. 1644-47, plate 14.

62. The Westward Garden- Psalm 80:8-10.

63. The Pelican and the Fisherman- Illustration adapted from Jacob Maris, *Fishing Boat*, 1878.

64. The Cathedral Builders- Peter Turchin, *Ultrasociety*, 2016, pp. 6-8.

65. The Empty Tomb- Illustration adapted from Carlo Ferrario, *Design for a stage set of a Crypt (for the Opera La Morosina)*, ca. 1870.

Creed, Rites and Feasts, and Practice

In this section of the book, you will find occasional references to something called the Codex, which is another book that will be a companion volume to this one. The Codex will apply the symbolic approach to continue cherishing and learning from the legendary and mythological stories of our culture (without necessarily believing those stories to be literally true) by collecting them into one place—stories from the Bible, Greco-Roman and Germanic myths, and medieval legends. The Codex is still only in very rough draft form. You can find the latest draft at TriplePath.org/Codex.

Creed

1. We believe in God and that we must love, serve, and emulate Him. We also believe that it is impossible to fully define Him with words and that it is thus each individual's right and responsibility to come to a personal understanding of Him for themself.

2. We believe we must seek wisdom, practice virtue, and labor with hope.

3. We believe in showing love to all people and in practicing the Golden Rule.

4. We believe that a person's highest moral duty is first to spouse and children, then to parents and other family, then to friends and community, then to nation, and finally toward all mankind.

5. We believe in being fearless and fierce in defense of the Church and the Triple Path and those to whom we owe our greatest duties.

6. We believe in being as self-sufficient as possible and that we are each accountable for our own actions and the consequences that flow therefrom.

7. We accept as Scripture the book of the Triple Path, except its preamble, and also the Codex. We also accept the great works of Western Civilization as useful for contemplation and study.

8. We believe in the importance of traditional values, including time-honored mores about sex roles and marriage, and in honoring and following the traditions, morals, and practices of our ancestors.

9. We believe that all who would count themselves as fol-

lowers of the Triple Path must hold sacred our Rites, practices, and traditions, and honor and follow them.

10. We observe the following practices: First, celibacy before marriage and fidelity afterwards; Second, maintaining Sunday as a day of rest, spiritual focus, and family, free from work and spending of money; Third, completely abstaining from tobacco; Fourth, not eating gluten; Fifth, only drinking alcohol, if ever, in moderation; Sixth, eating in a healthy and moderate manner and exercising to keep our bodies fit and strong; and Seventh, avoiding excessive consumption of caffeine and refined sugar.

11. We celebrate the following communal Rites and Feasts: First, Communal Sacrament as a congregation; Second, the Consecration of Chapels, Churches, Basilicas, and Cathedrals; Third, the Ordination of Cardinals, Archbishops, Bishops, Chief Elders, and Councilors; and Fourth, the Feast Days of New Year, Lent, Easter, May Day, Mid-Summer, Tricrux, Allhallowtide, Thanksgiving, and Yule.

12. We celebrate and observe the following private Rites and practices: First, Repentance; Second, daily spiritual study, meditation, and prayer; Third, Private Sacrament; Fourth, the Consecration of Oil; Fifth, the Consecration of Stoles; Sixth, the Anointing and Blessing of the Sick; Seventh, Father's Blessings; Eighth, Blessings of Counsel and Comfort; and Ninth, the Dedication of Homes.

13. We celebrate the following Rites of passage: First, the Naming and Dedication of Infants; Second, Baptism; Third, Confirmation; Fourth, Initiation; Fifth, Marriage between one man and one woman; Sixth, Ordination of males as Junior and Senior Deacons, Priests, and Elders; Seventh, the Thanksgiving of a Mother After Childbirth; and Eighth, the Burial of the Dead.

14. We believe that congregations' affairs should be controlled as locally as possible and that there should be no paid or professional clergy at any level of the Church.

15. We believe that power and authority corrupt and that all positions of leadership should be held only temporarily and

filled through sortition of those who best fit the requirements of the position.

16. We believe in seeking truth wherever it can be found, no matter whether it brings happiness or pain, let it come from whence it may.

17. We believe in being humble about what we think we know, that there are many things we do not know, and that there are probably many things we can never know.

18. We seek after all that is ennobling and uplifting. We believe in being honest, true, chaste, honorable, faithful, and benevolent; in being patient, but never passive; and in always manifesting in our lives courage, hard work, industriousness, perseverance, and discipline.

Rites and Feasts

This section explains how the Church's Rites and Feasts are to be practiced within a duly organized congregation, which is called a Ward or Branch (always referred to as a "Ward" in the description of Rites that follow). Some Feasts are tied to specific dates or months. The timing of the Feasts of May Day, Allhallowtide, and Thanksgiving should thus be shifted by six months in the Southern Hemisphere to match the proper season. Based on local Diocesan or Provincial preference, the Feast of Yule may also be shifted by six months for the same reason.

In the performance of all these Rites and Feasts, Officiants and participants should seek to ensure close adherence to the form and language set forth herein. Far more important, however, is to ensure that the Rites and Feasts are performed in a Godly, reverent, and spiritual manner, and therefore avoiding overzealous obsession with the exactness of the performance.

As more fully explained in the section below about Church Organization and Practice, those living outside the boundaries of a duly organized Ward or Branch who wish to be counted among the faithful of the Church and participate in its Rites and Feasts may administer them at home, within the family or in groups. When a group of followers of the Triple Path independently organizes itself, it is called an Unrecognized Branch.

When a family or an Unrecognized Branch administers a Rite, they should first take care to ensure as much as possible that all the normal qualifications for receiving it are met. Within a family, such Rites generally would be administered by the father, or in cases where the father does not wish to follow the Triple Path, by a grandfather, uncle, or other close male relative; if no male relative is available, then they may be self-administered. A man administering the Rites within his family would administer them to the other family members and then receive them from some other man. If no other men are available to administer them, he may administer the Rites to himself. In cases of individuals wishing to join the Faithful with no connection to others so desiring, the Rites may also be self-administered.

Within an Unrecognized Branch, the Rites would be administered within the Branch by males designated by the Branch as acting Deacons, Priests, and Elders.

The Rites of Ordination and Initiation may only be administered within an officially organized Ward.

Once anyone who has received self-, family-, or Unrecognized Branch-administered Rites begins living within the boundaries of a duly organized Branch or Ward, he or she should receive all the Rites again through the Ward as if for the first time, unless the Province grants a special dispensation.

The Rites and Feasts below are divided into the following sections: Communal Rites, Feasts, Private Rites, and Rites of Passage.

Contents

Communal Sacrament

Communal Sacrament is usually held on Sunday mornings when a Ward is gathered together. It should be conducted in a solemn, reverent, and joyful manner, but also like a family gathering where as many as possible may participate and all worship in love, reverence, and fellowship. Music should be of a sacred character that breathes a spirit of faith and the light of the divine. Speakers' remarks should be in harmony with the teachings in this book.

If there is not a Ward within a reasonable distance, a group may gather in private on Sunday to hold Sacrament and follow either the order of Communal Sacrament or Private Sacrament.

An Officiant administers the Rite and plans the speakers, hymns, and musical numbers for the day, seeking to allow a variety of ward members to participate. The Bishop and Vice-Bishops should establish a calendar at least three months in advance, rotating in turn through the ward's Priests and Elders to act as Officiant, so that each have equal chance to administer the Rite.

Before the start of the meeting, the Junior Deacons should have set out on the Sacrament altar unbroken, gluten-free bread in Sacrament trays and filled small Sacrament cups with water. A music leader may be designated to select the hymns and lead the Ward in singing them. For hymns with more verses than would be practical to sing all at once, care should be taken to select appropriate verses and rotate through them to ensure that the Ward does not end up always singing just the beginning verses of each hymn.

For the parts of the service where members of the Ward jointly respond or pray with the Officiant, the Reader for the day may lead and coordinate the Ward in its responses. The Ward may also project the words of the responses or prayers in a screen at the front of the sanctuary, provide a written program containing the responses and prayers, or provide copies of this book in the *pews to which members of the Ward may refer to read the proper responses and prayers.*

The meeting should begin with a welcome from the Officiant and any necessary announcements (though making too many announcements should be avoided). Following the Officiant's welcome, the Ward sings a hymn. A Ward member previously invited by the Officiant then offers an opening prayer, after which the Officiant stands before the Ward and says:*

Praise be to God. And blessed be the Congregation of the faithful of the Triple Path, now and forever. Amen.

The Ward repeats:

Amen.

The Officiant continues:

Brothers and Sisters, we meet together today to render thanks to God for the great benefits we have received at His hands, to set forth His most worthy praise, to hear the most holy word, and to seek those things which are requisite and necessary, as well for the body as the soul. Wherefore, I pray and beseech you, let us remember:

There is much we do not know and there is much we will never know. (Wisdom 5:1)

We look at wisdom, yet do not see it; we hear it, yet do not listen to it; we try to grasp it, yet cannot get hold of it; we write about it, yet cannot describe it. (Wisdom 4:1)

We think and speak about virtue, yet do not practice it.

Officiant and Ward respond:

But we cannot fool our souls. (Virtue 1:14; 6:5; 21:25)

Officiant continues:

It is a disease of the soul to think ourselves wise and virtuous when we are not. Recognizing this as a disease is the first step to curing it. (Wisdom 4:11)

Wisdom, virtue, and hope will transform us, allowing us to see more of our own faults. Let us recognize them, conquer them, and, by the grace of God, reform ourselves. (Foundations 1:22)

Officiant and Ward respond:

We know we are limited in an infinite number of ways; yet through God's grace and the Triple Path, let us always remember that the different manners in which we might seek wisdom, practice virtue, and labor with hope are still limitless. (Foundations 1:9)

Officiant continues:

Brothers and Sisters, let us always acknowledge and confess our manifold sins and wickedness and neither dissemble nor cloak them before the face of Almighty God, our heavenly Father; but confess them with a humble, lowly, penitent, and obedient heart. Let us pause to think on them and confess them in our hearts to God and ourselves.

Everyone bows their head in contemplation during a long silent pause.

The Officiant says:

I beseech you, as many as are here present, after this meeting to also confess these things to whomever you may have wronged, and to repent of your sins.

Now, kneel and accompany me with a pure heart, and humble voice, unto the throne of heavenly grace and pray with me:

The Officiant and all in the Ward kneel and pray together.

O God,

We are in need of mercy.

We are foolish, ignorant, and unvirtuous.

We are vain and need more humility.

We are in need of greater wisdom and more virtue.

We hope to become ever more like Thee, and we again resolve to strive after this. (Parables 46)

Amen.

The Ward and Officiant remain kneeling.

Next, the Ward prepares for the administration of the Bread and Water of the Sacrament. Only those who have been Baptized and are in good standing in the Church and those who are children under eight years of age who have been Named and Dedicated should partake of them. If necessary, the Officiant should make an explanatory announcement to this effect.

The Ward sings another hymn, during which two or three Senior Deacons stand and prepare the Sacrament Bread by breaking it, with clean hands, into pieces to be distributed to the Ward (Priests or Elders may act as Deacons as needed). At the hymn's conclusion, the Deacons, Officiant, and the Ward kneel before the Sacrament altar and a Senior Deacon offers the following prayer over the Bread:

O God, the Eternal Father, we consecrate and sanctify this Bread to the souls of all those who partake of it, that they may eat it in remembrance of Thee and their faith, as a symbol that just as Bread sustains the body, the Triple Path sustains the soul; that they may witness unto Thee, O God, the Eternal Father, that they will always endeavor to seek wisdom, practice virtue, labor with hope, and renounce foolishness, evil, and lazy despair, that they may draw closer to Thee. Amen.

At the conclusion of the prayer, the Deacons stand. The Senior Deacons hand the Bread to the Junior Deacons. The Junior Deacons distribute the Bread to the Ward. Once all have partaken, the Deacons kneel again. A second Senior Deacon offers the following prayer over the Water:

O God, the Eternal Father, we consecrate and sanctify this Water to the souls of all those who drink of it, that they may do so in remembrance of Thee and their faith, as a symbol that just as Water quenches physical thirst, the Triple Path quenches spiritual thirst; that its clarity and purity may inspire them to purify their souls and seek clarity of thought and action; that they may witness unto Thee, O God, the Eternal Father, that they will always endeavor to seek wisdom, practice virtue, labor with hope, and renounce foolishness, evil, and lazy despair, that they may draw closer to Thee. Amen.

At the conclusion of the prayer, the Deacons stand. The Senior Deacons hand the Water to the Junior Deacons. The Junior Deacons distribute the Water to the Ward. Once all have drunk the water, the Deacons return to their seats in the congrega-

tion and the Officiant and the Ward are seated.

The first Sunday of each month (except in February and March, during the time of Lent) is a Communal Sacrament of Fast and Testimony. On this day, all ward members of sufficient age and health and those not engaged in strenuous labor should fast by skipping two meals, generally dinner on the Saturday before and breakfast on the Sunday of the meeting, or instead, breakfast and lunch on the Sunday. After the Ward has partaken of the Bread and Water of the Sacrament on a Fast and Testimony Sunday, Rites such as the Rites of Naming and Dedication of Infants and of Confirmation are performed before the Reading.

On all Sundays after the Ward has partaken of the Bread and Water of Sacrament and after any Rites have been performed, the Reader, a confirmed member of the ward previously invited by the Officiant, conducts the Reading by going to the pulpit and reading a short passage from the Meditations and Parables section of this book or from the Codex. The reader should select the passage in consultation with the Officiant and ensure it is related to the theme of the meeting. The passage should generally not be more than two pages. On a day when Confirmations have been performed, the Reader should always be one of those confirmed. If more than one person was confirmed, those who did not act as Reader on the day of their confirmation should be designated as Readers on subsequent Sundays until all have had a chance to serve as Reader. In general, preference should be given to designating recently confirmed members and youth as Readers, but by no means should the Reader always be a youth or recently confirmed member.

The Reader says:

And now a Reading from the book of the Triple Path (or the Codex).

The Reader reads the passage he or she has selected.

On a Fast and Testimony Sunday, the Reader then also says:

Please stand and recite with me the Creed.

The Ward stands and jointly recites the Creed with the Reader.

The Reader returns to his or her seat.

The Officiant introduces the program for the meeting, during which two to four speakers who are confirmed members of the Ward offer brief remarks about a spiritual subject, selected by the Officiant, which is in harmony with this book. Speakers should strive to give talks that are original, interesting, and engaging. The Officiant should not be one of the speakers. Generally, a musical number should be performed, or rest hymn sung by the Ward, halfway through the presentations by the speakers.

On Fast and Testimony Sundays, rather than having predesignated speakers, the speakers' time is opened to confirmed members of the Ward to bear short testimonies about their experiences trying to live the Triple Path or to share other extemporaneous thoughts of a spiritual nature.

In either case, Communal Sacrament should conclude after about one hour and fifteen minutes.

During the speaking or testimony portion of Communal Sacrament, a separate children's program may be organized if the members of the Ward so desire. For such a program, children under age 12 are invited to leave to a separate room, or to the back of the sanctuary, for a spiritual program or lesson tailored to a child's level of understanding. The program or should be in harmony with this book. Such programs should be conducted by responsible, respected, baptized, and initiated members of the Ward who are parents. The children's program should always be conducted by at least three adults and the persons conducting the program should rotate regularly, usually weekly, so that all adults may participate regularly in the normal adults' program. In no Church meeting should any one adult be left alone with a child or youth, or with multiple children or youth, who are not the adult's own child or children, and any adult who acts in any capacity in the Ward that involves children should first pass a thorough background check and receive regular training on recognizing and preventing abuse.

After the speakers have concluded their remarks and children have been reunited with their families, the Officiant again stands before the Ward and says:

Brothers and Sisters, let us pause to think on the many things in our lives for which we would be grateful if we did not have them and had only newly received them. (Wisdom 9)

Everyone bows their head in contemplation during a long silent pause.

The Officiant says:

Now, Brothers and Sisters, please be upstanding, and let us pray.

All in the Ward stand, while the Officiant prays, his arms upraised:

O God, we give thanks for all the good things in our lives, which come by Thy grace. We give thanks for deliverance from afflictions and tribulations. We give thanks for kindness and affection and love, and any teaching that is sweet and plain that guides us toward wisdom, leads us to practice virtue, or inspires us to labor with hope. We rejoice in the Divine illumination that flows into us from following the Triple Path.

We have known hardship and sorrow; we are grateful for the lessons we learned from them. But we dwell not on our misfortunes, and instead marvel at all the great blessings in our lives.

We give thanks for family, food, clothing, shelter, and the simple joys of life, and we pray for all those who find these lacking.

We are grateful for thought and conscience, for the freedom to act and not be acted upon, and for the consequences that naturally flow from our actions.

We give thanks for the spark of Thy divinity we feel in our best moments, and the chance to do better after we have passed through our worst.

May we be preserved on the Triple Path and protected from faltering or stumbling through life. We here resolve again to move forward with firmness on the Triple Path, always, and progress toward a brighter day.

Amen.

The Ward repeats:

Amen.

Now, Brothers and Sisters, let us kneel in silence, and remember God's presence with us now.

All kneel. After a moment of silence for reflection and divine communion, the Officiant continues:

Brothers and Sisters, as we renew our commitment to God and the Triple Path, I beseech you again to accompany me with a pure heart, and humble voice, unto the throne of heavenly grace and pray with me:

The Officiant and Ward continue kneeling and pray together:

O God,

We pray that, by Thy grace:

In our seeking, we find wisdom;

In our desires and actions, we practice virtue, with a grateful heart and love for others;

In our labors, we cultivate hope and the fortitude to continue laboring; and

We keep ourselves from entering into temptation or falling prey to evil desires. (Wisdom 6:3)

Our complete trust we reserve only for Thee. (Hope 13:1)

We will seek to turn our weaknesses into strengths, (Wisdom 5:14)

And let the Triple Path mold and construct our souls; order our life; guide our conduct; and show us what we should do and what we should leave undone. We will follow the course it shows us when we waver amid uncertainty. (Foundations 1:2)

Amen.

The Officiant says:

It is profitable to consider not only our weaknesses, but also our strengths. For, in our moments of trial and suffering we find hope and encouragement by remembering our times of tri-

412

umph. Let us pause to think on our recent successes—those times when we diligently sought wisdom, practiced virtue, or labored with hope.

Everyone bows their head in contemplation during a long silent pause.

The Officiant says:
Brothers and sisters, please be seated.

The Ward and Officiant are seated.

The Officiant says:

The meeting ends with a hymn and another prayer offered by a member of the ward who has been previously invited by the Officiant.

If there is any remaining unconsumed Bread or Water that was blessed, then it should be deconsecrated. To do so, after the sanctuary has emptied a Deacon, Priest, or Elder kneels before the Sacrament altar and offers the following prayer:

O God,

By the authority of the Congregation of the Faithful of the Triple Path and in my office as a(n) (say the name of the person's office), I deconsecrate this bread (and/or water) so that it return to secular use.

Amen.

The bread and water should then be disposed of in a respectful manner.

Following Communal Sacrament, a Sunday School should be conducted with classes for children and youth divided according to their age, and also a class for adults. A theme of instruction should be followed each year (or subdivision of year, as deemed appropriate), studying this book and other material in harmony with it, including the Codex and major source materials for this book.

Following Sunday School, children under age 12 meet together as a group for singing and instruction in harmony with this book. Youth aged 12 to 17 are divided by sex and age and meet for instruction in harmony with this book. Adults are also divided by sex for instruction and discussion in harmony with the Triple Path.

Consecration of a Chapel, Church, Basilica, or Cathedral

The Rite of Consecration of a Chapel, Church, Basilica, or Cathedral should be performed just before the first Sacrament to be held in a new Chapel, Church, Basilica, or Cathedral, or any other space to be used for Communal Sacrament. The Officiant should preferably be an Elder.

The Officiant stands before the Ward and says:

Brothers and Sisters, inasmuch as devout and holy men have through the ages erected houses for the public worship of God, and separated them from all unhallowed, worldly, and common uses, to fill the mind with greater reverence for God and affect their hearts with more devotion and humility, let us solemnly set apart this place for sacred worship.

Let us pray.

O Eternal God, we are gathered here with humility and readiness of heart to consecrate this place to Thee and the Congregation of the Faithful of the Triple Path, separating it from all unhallowed, ordinary, and common uses (*if the place it to be used only temporarily for worship, then substitute,* "separating it during our use of it from all unhallowed, ordinary, and common uses"), and dedicating it to our practice of the Triple Path, the reading of holy words, for celebrating holy Rites, for offering prayer and thanksgiving, and for committing and re-committing ourselves to follow Thee and the Triple Path.

We consecrate it as a place for the faithful to meet together to render thanks to Thee for the great benefits we have received at Thy hands, to set forth Thy most worthy praise, to hear the most holy word, and to seek those things which are requisite and necessary, as well for the body as the soul.

We consecrate this place, that through Thy grace, it may be set apart to Thee and the Triple Path, for worship in truth and purity through all generations (*if the place it to be used only tem-*

415

porarily for worship, then omit "through all generations" and instead say "during our use of it").

Visit, we beseech thee, O God, this place, that all the snares of the adversary and the evil ways of the world may be driven from it.

And may thy blessing be upon us ever more.

The Officiant then pronounces words of blessing as he feels inspired to speak, taking care not to overstep the bounds of prudence or propriety. He then closes by saying:

Amen.

The Communal Sacrament then proceeds as normal.

If a place that has been consecrated is no longer to be used for worship, then it must be deconsecrated.

To deconsecrate the place, an Elder stands at the pulpit or other equivalent place and offers the following prayer:

O God,

By the authority of the Congregation of the Faithful of the Triple Path and in my office as an Elder, I deconsecrate this place so that it return to secular use.

Amen.

The place may return to secular use and should no longer be used for regular worship, unless it is consecrated again.

Ordination of a Cardinal, Archbishop, Bishop, Chief Elder, or Councilor

All those holding positions as Church Stewards—Cardinals, Vice-Cardinals, Archbishops, Vice-Archbishops, Bishops, Vice-Bishops, Chief Elders, Vice-Chief Elders, and Councilor—must be men of enduring maturity and sober mind, who have been consistent in seeking wisdom, practicing virtue, and laboring with hope. They must have been Baptized, Confirmed, Initiated, and Married, and be in good standing in the Church. They must have shown, and continue to show, their abiding commitment to God and the Triple Path. Cardinals, Vice-Cardinals, Archbishops, Vice-Archbishops, and members of Diocesan and Provincial Councils must already have been Ordained as Elders before their names are put forward for those Stewardships.

All chosen to be Stewards must currently fulfill the same requirements as those for Baptism, Confirmation, and Initiation. They must believe in God, affirm their support for all aspects of this book and the Creed, and also demonstrate through their actions their commitment to the Creed and the principles of the Triple Path. In particular, they must have demonstrated their commitment for the ten years prior to Ordination by regularly attending Church, participating in and contributing actively to the success of their Ward (if they have changed Wards, their active participation in their prior Wards should be confirmed), and diligently following the Rites, Feasts, observances, and practices of Creeds 10 through 13. They must also affirm that they are willing to fulfill faithfully the duties, as set forth in this book, of the Stewardship to which they have been selected. Candidates may not be Ordained as Stewards unless they have at least three children of good moral character who actively participate in their Wards (with allowance to be made for those with deceased children and for converts to the Church whose children were not born within the faith). He must be married to one wife to be Ordained. After Or-

dination, a Steward must remain married to continue in good standing as a Steward, and thus authorized to act in the capacity of his Stewardship. For any person baptized before the age of 18, the marriage requirement can only be fulfilled by being married to another member of the Church of the West.

Candidates should also be contributing financially to their Ward in full compliance with the Ward's assessment of members' annual financial contributions. Most importantly, the Candidate should demonstrate a sufficiently mature and spiritual disposition commensurate with the solemn and sacred nature of the Stewardship.

No one may seek Ordination to a position as a Steward. Only those who have been selected for listing on a sortition list for a Steward position may be Ordained to that position. No one should campaign for a position as a Steward or campaign for the selection of someone else as a Steward. Each Qualified Voter should vote according to his or her own best judgment, except that male voters cannot vote for themselves, and female voters cannot vote for their husbands. A man eligible for Ordination to a position as a Steward may refuse the offered Ordination. He may later accept Ordination whenever he is selected from a subsequent list.

Any person placed on a sortition list and then selected to fill a position as a Steward must also be presented to the Qualified Voters in his Ward, Diocese, or Province for approval. If for a Ward position, his name must be published and announced in his Ward three consecutive Sundays during Communal Sacrament. If for a Diocesan or Provincial position, it is done at a Diocesan or Provincial meeting and then in all constituent Wards for the following three weeks, as further described in the Church Organization and Practice section of this book.

To make such announcements, in Communal Sacrament during the announcements before the start of the meeting, the Officiant for that meeting shall say the following:

(Candidate) has been found to be qualified to be Ordained as a (state the name of the Stewardship position) and has been chosen by sortition for the position.

I would remind you that all Elders in this Church, and especially all Stewards, must be in good standing in the Church and be men of enduring maturity and sober mind, who have been consistent in seeking wisdom, practicing virtue, and laboring with hope. They must have shown, and continue to show, their abiding commitment to God and the Triple Path. They must believe in God, affirm their support for all aspects of the book of The Triple Path and the Creed, and also demonstrate through their actions their commitment to the Creed and the principles of the Triple Path by the following: regularly attending Church; participating and contributing actively to the success of their Ward; diligently following the Rites, Feasts, observances, and practices of Creeds 10 through 13; being married to one wife; and having at least three children of good moral character who actively participate in their Wards (with allowance to be made for those with deceased children and for converts to the Church whose children were not born within the faith). More than this, Elders must also be vigilant, sober, of good behavior, given to hospitality, apt to teach; not given to wine and not greedy; patient and not a brawler, not covetous; one who rules well his own house; not a novice, lest being lifted up with pride he fall into condemnation. Moreover, he must have a good report of them which are without; lest he fall into reproach and bring the Church into the same.

He has accepted the Ordination, but his selection must be ratified. All Qualified Voters who are in favor, affirming that, to the best of their knowledge, he fulfills the qualifications for this Stewardship, please make it known by raising your right hand.

The Officiant pauses to allow the Qualified Voters in the Ward to vote.

If any of you know cause, or just impediment, why he should not be Ordained, you are to declare it privately to the Bishop and Vice-Bishops after this meeting. This is the first (second, or third) time of asking.

If anyone dissents, the Bishop and Vice-Bishops (or Dio-

419

cesan or Provincial Council), deal with the objections appropriately and with discretion, in conformity with this book, the Creed, the Doctrines of the Church, and Church traditions, standards, and principles.

Once the proposed Ordination has been presented three times to the Ward (for Ward positions), or to all the Wards of the Diocese or Province (for Diocesan or Provincial positions), and any concerns resolved, then the Ordination may proceed.

A Steward in a Ward position should be Ordained in Communal Sacrament the Sunday after the third time of asking, usually in Ward Conference. If he is not yet an Elder, he should be Ordained an Elder and then Ordained to his Stewardship as part of the same Rite. The Rite should be adapted so that the Candidate's father (or Godfather or other similar man) Ordain him an Elder, then the relevant Steward Ordain him to his Stewardship.

A Steward in a Diocesan or Provincial position should be Ordained at the Conference following the three weeks in which his name was presented to the Wards, or if he was selected to fill an unexpected vacancy, at a time and place deemed appropriate by the Diocesan or Provincial Council in a setting open to all members of the Diocese or Province.

For Ward Stewards, the Officiant for the Ordination should be the current Ward Bishop; for Diocesan Stewards, the Officiant should be the current Archbishop of the Diocese; for Provincial Stewards, the Officiant should be the current Cardinal of the Province. A Steward authorized to act in the Bishop's, Archbishop's, or Cardinal's stead (i.e., a Vice-Bishop, a Vice-Archbishop, or a Vice-Cardinal) may also officiate. If the prior Bishop is not available to Ordain the new Bishop, then the Officiant should be an Archbishop, Vice-Archbishop, Cardinal, or Vice-Cardinal. If the prior Archbishop is not available to Ordain the new Archbishop, then the Officiant should be the Cardinal or Vice-Cardinal. If the prior Cardinal is not available to Ordain the new Cardinal, then the Officiant should be a Vice-Cardinal, and only act with the explicit authorization and presence of the Provincial Coun-

cil. Branch Stewards should always be Ordained by the Arch-bishop or a Vice-Archbishop.

The Ordination is performed by an Officiant together with, in Wards, the Vice-Bishops; or in Dioceses and Provinces, the Vice-Archbishops or Vice-Cardinals and the Council (hereinafter referred to as "Vice-Stewards"). Throughout the Ordination, the Officiant and the Steward should refer to the Candidate to be Or-dained by name whenever the text refers to "Candidate" in paren-theses.)

To start, the Officiant approaches the Vice-Stewards, and addressing them and the Congregation present, says the following:

I present unto you (Candidate) to be Ordained a (Chief Elder; Vice-Chief Elder; Bishop; Vice-Bishop; Archbishop; Vice-Archbishop; Diocesan Councilor; Cardinal; Vice-Cardinal; or Provincial Councilor).

The most senior Vice-Steward says:

Has (Candidate) been found qualified, in his knowledge, actions, and commitment to exercise this sacred role, to the honor of God and the Triple Path, and the edifying of this Church?

The Officiant replies:

He has.

The Vice-Steward addresses the Candidate:

That this present group may also witness your qualification, and understand your mind and will in these things, and that this your public promise here may more move you to do your duties, I would examine you here as well, and you shall answer plainly to these things, which we, in the name of God and of this Church, shall ask of you.

And I charge and admonish you most solemnly that you must respond truthfully and sincerely, only responding with the Candidate's words for this Rite if they most surely and accurately represent your mind as well.

Have you accepted, and will you continue to accept. the teachings in the book of the Triple Path and our Creed?

The Candidate answers:

Thus have I endeavored and will continue to so endeavor.

The Vice-Steward asks:

Have you been Baptized, Confirmed, Initiated, and Married?

The Candidate answers:

I have.

If the Candidate has already been Ordained and Elder, the Vice-Steward asks:

Have you been Ordained an Elder?

The Candidate answers:

I have.

The Vice-Steward asks:

Have you observed, and will you continue to observe, the practices of repentance; daily spiritual study, meditation, and prayer; celibacy before marriage and fidelity within it; maintaining Sunday as a day of rest, spiritual focus, and family, free from work and spending of money; completely abstaining from tobacco; not eating gluten; drinking alcohol, if ever, only in moderation; eating in a healthy and moderate manner and exercising to keep your body fit and strong; and avoiding excessive consumption of caffeine and refined sugar?

The Candidate answers:

Thus have I endeavored and will continue to so endeavor.

The Vice-Steward asks:

Have you faithfully celebrated and ministered, and will you endeavor faithfully to celebrate and minister, our communal and private Rites and Feasts: Communal Sacrament; the Consecration of Chapels, Churches, Basilicas, and Cathedrals; the Feast Days of New Year, Lent, Easter, May Day, Mid-Summer, Tricrux, Allhallowtide, Thanksgiving, and Yule; Repentance; the Consecration of Oil; the Consecration of Stoles; Private Sacrament; the Anointing and Blessing of the Sick; Father's Blessing; Blessings of Counsel and Comfort; and the Dedication of Homes?

The Candidate answers:

Thus have I endeavored and will continue to so endeavor.

The Vice-Steward asks:

Have you recognized, and will you continue to ever recognize and honor, that your highest moral duty is first to spouse and children, then to parents and family, then to friends and community, then to nation, and finally toward all humankind?

The Candidate answers:

Thus have I endeavored and will continue to so endeavor.

The Vice-Steward asks:

Have you been seeking the truth and striving for it, that you may discover where you are in error? (Wisdom 3:1, 4)

The Candidate answers:

Thus have I endeavored and will continue to so endeavor.

The Vice-Steward asks:

Have you banished and driven away, and will you continue with all faithful diligence to banish and drive away, from the Church all erroneous and strange doctrines contrary to the book of the Triple Path?

The Candidate answers:

Thus have I endeavored and will continue to so endeavor.

The Vice-Steward asks:

Have you accepted, and will you continue to accept, the importance of traditional values and in honoring and following the traditions, morals, and practices of our ancestors?

The Candidate answers:

Thus have I endeavored and will continue to so endeavor.

The Vice-Steward asks:

Do you take upon yourself the solemn and sacred responsibility as a Steward of our traditions, committing that if you ever think you have found a way along the path that appears shorter and smoother to travel, that you will scout out miles far ahead to verify its soundness, always being ware that you do not shortsightedly fool yourself into following what ends up being a dangerous or faulty path, when the safety of the old road was there all along? (Hope 9: 11)

The Candidate answers:

I take upon myself this most solemn and sacred responsibility. I will endeavor with my greatest effort to be present and vigilant, and wise, that I not choose wrongly. I will watch carefully that I not fool myself by rationalizing away the wisdom of the past and of tradition. I will endeavor always to remember that a break from tradition is more likely to bring decline, ruin, or collapse, than improvement. (Virtue 1:11; Hope 9:13)

The Vice-Steward asks:

Have you been, and will you continue to be, fearless and fierce in defense of the Church and the Triple Path, and our traditions, and those to whom you owe your greatest duties?

The Candidate answers:

Thus have I endeavored and will continue to so endeavor.

The Vice-Steward asks:

Have you been, and will you continue for the rest of your life to be, as self-sufficient as possible and to hold yourself accountable, never shrinking from your own actions and the consequences that flow therefrom?

The Candidate answers:

Thus have I endeavored and will continue to so endeavor.

The Vice-Steward says:

We commend you for your dedication. And so finally, I ask, do you, of your own free will, accept this Ordination, to serve, without any remuneration, God and this Church, to help your fellow-travelers in their journey on the Triple Path?

The Candidate answers:

Yes.

The Vice-Steward addresses the Candidate:

In this most solemn and important Stewardship, I charge you to act with great care, to apply yourself to this Stewardship and to show yourself dutiful and thankful unto God and the Congregation of the Faithful of the Triple Path, which have placed you in so high a dignity, and also to beware that neither you yourself offend, nor give occasion that others offend. Remember how studious you should be in reading and learning the book of the Triple Path, the

Codex, and the best books of our civilization, and also that you should forsake, as much as practicable, worldly and frivolous cares and pursuits.

Let the Officiant proceed with the Ordination.

The Officiant raises his arms and prays:

O God, we seek mercy in our infirmities that we may serve Thee and this Church, to help our fellow-travelers in their journey on the Triple Path. Let this, Thy servant to be Ordained, and all of us, act in holiness and pureness of living, with wisdom, virtue, and hope. Amen.

The Candidate is then seated before the congregation. The Officiant places a small amount of consecrated oil on his finger and says:

(Candidate), I anoint you a (name of Stewardship position) of (name of Ward, Diocese, or Province) of the Congregation of the Faithful of the Triple Path, in the name of God, and of wisdom, virtue, and hope.

As he speaks, the Officiant uses his finger to anoint the Candidate with Consecrated Oil on the forehead, making the form of the Tricrux with the oil, forming one of each of the three prongs as he says each of the words "wisdom", "virtue", and "hope".

If the Candidate is being Ordained as a Bishop, Archbishop, or Cardinal, and if the person Officiating is of the same Stewardship, then the Officiant says:

I pass on to you my Stewardship as (Bishop, Archbishop, or Cardinal).

Alternatively, if the Candidate is being Ordained as a Bishop or Archbishop, and if the person Officiating is not of the same office, and for the Ordination of Vice-Stewards, Vice-Bishop, and for Diocesan and Provincial Councilors, then the Officiant says:

The Stewardship of he who served before you is now revoked and I pass on to you that Stewardship as (Bishop, Vice-Bishop, Archbishop, Vice-Archbishop, Cardinal, or Vice-Cardinal). Amen.

Alternatively, if the Candidate is being Ordained as a Car-

dinal, and if the person Officiating is not of the same Stewardship, then the Officiant says:

By the authority of the Provincial Council, and in their presence, the Stewardship of he who served before you is now revoked and I pass on to you that Stewardship as Cardinal.

Amen.

Then, in all cases, the Officiant says:

Now, all those Elders previously invited, come forward to join in Ordaining (Candidate).

The Officiant moves behind the Candidate and places his hands on the Candidate's head. The Vice-Stewards and any other Elders who have been previously invited join in and lay their hands on the Candidate's head as well. The Officiant Ordains the Candidate by saying:

O God,

By the authority of the Congregation of the Faithful of the Triple Path and in my Stewardship as a (name of Stewardship position of the Officiant; and if it be a Vice-Cardinal Ordaining a Cardinal, then also say, "by the authority of the Provincial Council, and in their presence"), I Ordain this person, (Candidate), as a (name of Stewardship position) of (name of Ward, Diocese, or Province) of the Congregation of the Faithful of the Triple Path.

The Officiant then pronounces words of blessing, counsel, and comfort to the Candidate as he feels inspired to speak, taking care not to overstep the bounds of prudence or propriety. He then closes by saying:

Amen.

Those assisting the Officiant return to their seats.

The Officiant says:

As a symbol of your Stewardship of (state the position), we present you with the Cords of your Stewardship.

The Officiant presents to the Candidate the Cords of the Stewardship position to which he was Ordained. The Officiant dresses the Candidate in the Cords.

The Officiant continues:

Whenever you act as an Officiant in any public Rite, and whenever acting in your capacity as a Steward, you must wear these Cords. As a symbol of your Stewardship in the Church, you must treat them with solemnity and reverence. And of even greater importance, live your life so that you treat this Stewardship with the solemnity and reverence to which it is due. At the end of your Stewardship, you shall pass your Stewardship and Cords on to your successor, as I have passed them on to you.

If the person is being Ordained as a Bishop, Archbishop, or Cardinal, then the Officiant shall give to the candidate a copy of this book and say:

Give heed unto reading, exhortation, and doctrine. Think upon the things contained in this book. Be diligent in them, that the increase coming thereby may be manifest unto all men; for by so doing thou shalt both save thyself and them that hear thee. Hold up the weak, heal the sick, bind up the broken, bring again the outcasts, seek the lost. Be so merciful, that you be not too remiss; so minister discipline, that you forget not mercy.

The Officiant returns to his seat. The Candidate takes the seat, if any, of his Stewardship (the person who had occupied that Stewardship position returns to sit in the congregation). The Communal Sacrament proceeds as normal.

In any Communal Sacrament during which someone was Ordained to a Stewardship position, the Officiant for Communal Sacrament should say the following prayer just before the Reading:

Let us pray.

Almighty God,

We pray through Thy grace that all Stewards in Thy Church may diligently preach the truth of the Triple Path and duly administer the godly discipline thereof, always remembering to serve in humility and sacrifice; being wholesome examples in word, in conversation, in love, in faith, and in purity; and grant to the people that we may do the same.

Amen.

The Feast of the New Year

*The Feast of the New Year, or the Feast of Wisdom, is cel-
ebrated on the first Sunday of January.*

*During the week before the Feast, families and households
conduct a general cleaning and re-organization of their homes,
taking down their Yule decorations on Saturday.*

*The liturgical color for this feast is silver, representing pu-
rity and truth, and the wisdom that comes with age to those who
seek it. For Communal Sacrament on this Sunday, the Church
should be decorated appropriately with silver and the Officiant
should wear a silver Stole.*

*In this special New Year Communal Sacrament, young
men in good standing aged 12 to 18 who are Deacons come to
Church in dark suits and silver ties. Just before the Reading, they
leave the sanctuary. They re-enter, with the Junior Deacons in
front, carrying boxes of chalk, there being enough pieces of chalk
between them for every household in the Ward. All consecrated
chalk previously stored by the Ward should be newly consecrated
each year, and new unconsecrated pieces of chalk added to the
boxes as needed to ensure enough chalk for all households. The
Senior Deacons follow in line behind the Junior Deacons, but not
carrying any chalk.*

*The Junior Deacons place the boxes of chalk on the Sac-
rament Altar and stop in front of the altar. The Senior Deacons
kneel behind the Altar. The Senior Deacons hold the boxes of
chalk in their hands. One of the Senior Deacons (preferably the
oldest Senior Deacon present who has not previously had the
chance to bless the chalk) offers the following prayer (if only one
Senior Deacon is present, then he changes the plurals in the
prayer to singulars):*

O God,

By the authority of the Congregation of the Faithful of the

Triple Path and in our office as Senior Deacons, we consecrate this chalk and set it apart for the Dedication of Homes in this year of (say the present year).

Amen.

The Senior Deacons stand.

The Deacons line up at the front of the sanctuary and take turns saying the paragraphs (the first two paragraphs being read together) of the following Reading (in Wards where there are more Deacons than paragraphs, preference in selecting the readers should be given to the older Deacons who did not say the prayer of consecration over the chalk):

And now a Reading from the book of the Triple Path:

Now is the time to wake up, for the day is at hand, and an eternal night is coming upon you. Why would you sleep through the daylight of your life? Cast off your works of darkness and put on the armor of light. Walk in the daylight, with wisdom, virtue, and hope; walk not in the shadows, in revelry and drunkenness, in licentiousness and debauchery, in discord and jealousy. (Foundations 1:16)

Prepare yourself to receive wisdom, and it will flow in—not when you want it, but when you have earned it. (Wisdom 1:2)

Wisdom is simple. Yet, even if you spent your whole life seeking, you would never receive a fullness of it. But spend your life seeking all the same. The more you seek, the more you will receive, and the closer you will come to a fullness. (Wisdom 1:4)

So long as you are ignorant, keep learning, even to the end of your life. And never forget, you are always ignorant about something. Your knowledge is ever incomplete. Spend your time liberally seeking more of it. And live always seeking greater wisdom, like a swift river always flowing toward the great expanse of the sea. (Wisdom 1:6)

When you contemplate raw wisdom, often you will gaze upon her with bewilderment and awe, like being in a far-off remote area at night and looking upwards at the star-filled heavens, staring in wonder, as if seeing them again for the first time. (Wisdom 1:9)

The wise rest where rest is to be had and do not try to find rest where there is none. The foolish try to rest where there is none and do not rest where it is to be found. (Wisdom 1:14)

Do not let reason mislead you. Let all reasoning be silent when experience gainsays its conclusions. (Wisdom 1:24)

Seek wisdom everywhere—hold onto every bit you find, no matter its source. (Wisdom 1:25)

Do not be surprised to find wisdom in the unlikeliest of places, even in the minds of your opponents—especially in the minds of your opponents. On the other hand, if someone has many clearly wrong ideas, there is a good chance his other ideas are wrong too. (Wisdom 1:26)

Others can point you to the never-ending path of wisdom, but you must travel it yourself to find what lies along the way. (Wisdom 1:27)

Wisdom is a mystery that few seek and even fewer find. Heed the quiet voice of wisdom rather than the shouts of the foolish crowd. (Wisdom 1:28)

We believe in seeking truth wherever it can be found, no matter whether it brings happiness or pain, let it come from whence it may. (Creed 16)

We believe in being humble about what we think we know, that there are many things we do not know, and that there are probably many things we can never know. (Creed 17)

The Deacons leave the chalk on the Altar and return to their seats in the congregation.

The Officiant says:

Today we celebrate the Feast of the New Year, or the Feast of Wisdom. The liturgical color for this Feast is silver, representing purity and truth, and the wisdom that comes with age, to those who seek it.

Brothers and sisters, please kneel with me and let us pray.

All kneel while the Officiant prays:

Almighty and most merciful God,

We pray for thy grace, that we may wake up and follow the Triple Path; that we may cast away our works of darkness, and put upon us the armor of light, now in the daylight of our lives. (Foundations 1:15-16)

Let us spend our lives seeking greater wisdom, contemplating the raw wisdom that comes from Thee. (Wisdom 1:9)

May we find rest where it is to be had and not seek it out where there is none. (Wisdom 1:14)

We pray that we be not misled by reason when experience gainsays its conclusions. (Wisdom 1:24)

We pray that we never forget to seek truth wherever it can be found, no matter whether it brings happiness or pain, let it come from whence it may. (Creed 16)

As the old year is reborn into the new, may we ever remember our baptisms when we were symbolically reborn as travelers on the Triple Path, and may we always be faithful to our promises to seek wisdom, practice virtue, labor with hope, and renounce foolishness, evil, and lazy despair.

Amen.

The Ward is seated and the Communal Sacrament then proceeds as normal, with a Reading and talks that focus on themes of rebirth and improvement.

After the Communal Sacrament has concluded, the head of each household goes to the Sacrament Altar and takes a piece of chalk. That afternoon, the members of each household perform the Rite of Dedication of Homes, first erasing any writing from previous blessings and then using the chalk to chalk their door.

During the household's Private Sacrament that following week, the group should have silent time at the end for each person to reflect quietly and privately about the prior year and the year to come and to set goals for the coming year.

The following Sunday, each household returns the chalk to the Ward for storage for the next year.

When a piece of chalk has become too small to be used it should be deconsecrated. To deconsecrate the chalk, a Senior Dea-

con, Priest, or Elder holds the chalk, or container of chalk, in his hands and offers the following prayer:

O God,

By the authority of the Congregation of the Faithful of the Triple Path and in my office as a(n) (say the name of the person's office), I deconsecrate this chalk so that it return to secular use.

Amen.

The chalk should then be disposed of in a respectful manner.

The Feast of Lent

The Feast of Lent, or the Feast of Repentance and Sacrifice, begins on the Sunday six weeks before Easter Sunday. The Lenten period of sacrifice lasts for the following 40 days, ending in the evening on the Friday before Easter.

On the Sunday before Lent, at the conclusion of Communal Sacrament, the Officiant says:

Next Sunday we begin the holy Feast of Lent, a season to acknowledge and repent of our sins and to make true and lasting reform in our lives. I invite you, therefore, to observe a Holy Lent, by self-examination and penitence, by prayer and fasting, by practicing works of love, and by reading and reflecting on the holy word of our Scripture.

The Reading on every Sunday of Lent should always include Virtue 5:6 as the first paragraph:

When you say you have no sin, you deceive yourself, and the truth is not in you; therefore, turn to God, confess your sins, repent, and reform yourself, that you may be forgiven and cleansed from all unrighteousness.

During Lent, everyone should minimize unnecessary consumption of rich or sweet foods and of caffeine and alcohol. Everyone should also choose at least one luxury from which they will completely abstain. Consumption of entertainment, especially electronic media, should be minimized, as should spending of money. Those of sufficient age and health and those not engaged in strenuous labor should fast on Ash Wednesday, on all the Sundays of Lent, except the fourth Sunday, and on the final Friday of Lent. These should be days focused on prayer, fasting, and repentance.

Because of the subsequent fast days of Lent, the first Sunday of February is not a Fast Sunday. During Lent, the Communal Sacrament on the first Sunday of Lent and on the first fast Sunday in March are Fast and Testimony Sundays.

All those of sufficient age should perform without fail at least weekly the Rite of Repentance and of Private Sacrament.

The Saturday before the start of Lent is Shrove Saturday. It may be celebrated by eating pancakes and sausage for breakfast, and other rich foods throughout the day. Churches ring their bells in the morning to call the faithful to repentance and remind them to start frying their pancakes and sausage. All who are fasting should begin their first fast after lunch or dinner on Shrove Saturday.

Beginning on the evening of Shrove Saturday, and then throughout Lent, the faithful should endeavor to engage in greater self-examination, considering those things for which they need to repent and what reforms they should make in their life to better follow God and the Triple Path.

On the evening of Shrove Saturday, in preparation for the first Sunday of Lent, all confirmed members should privately perform a partial Rite of Repentance focused on their sins over the past year and their goals to reform over the coming year. They should stop their performance of the Rite just after they place a few drops of consecrated oil on the writing of sin and before they burn it. For this partial Rite, to avoid the prying of eavesdroppers and gossipmongers, persons may choose to write their sins in an abbreviated manner, such as using initials. All who performed the partial Rite bring their writings of repentance and reform to Communal Sacrament on the following day, the first day of Lent.

The liturgical color for this feast is black. During all the days of Lent, the sanctuary should be decorated appropriately with black, and all religious symbols, such as the Tricrux, should be veiled in black. The Officiant should wear a black Stole, except on the fourth Sunday of Lent, Rejoicing Sunday, on which he should wear a purple Stole.

The Bishop of the Ward, if he is available, acts as Officiant at the Communal Sacrament of the first Sunday of Lent. If he is unavailable or incapacitated, then one of the Vice-Bishops acts as Officiant.

On the first Sunday of Lent, just before the Bread and

Water of the Sacrament are blessed, the Officiant stands in front of a large fire-safe receptacle and says the following:

In this season we celebrate the Feast of Lent, or the Feast of Repentance and Sacrifice.

On this first Sunday of Lent, let us remember that we are all weak and in need of God's mercy and that all of us fall short of the mark.

The color for this feast is black, symbolizing our mourning for our sins and what we have given up and lost because of them.

All of sufficient age and health fast on the Sundays of Lent, except for the fourth. We minimize entertainments and rich or sweet foods, our spending, and our consumption of caffeine and alcohol. And, we completely give up some luxury that has become too precious to us.

We fast and renounce luxuries during this time of Lent that we be reminded how much we foolishly let ourselves be controlled by our appetites, and how much we need to repent of.

Most importantly, during the time of Lent we intensify our prayers and spiritual exercises. We focus, even more, on practicing virtue.

This first Sunday of Lent is Penitential Sunday. All those who have been confirmed should have already performed a partial Rite of Repentance. Before we partake of the Bread and Water of the Sacrament in remembrance of the promises we make at baptism and confirmation, let us all publicly acknowledge our sins and finish the Rite, repenting as a congregation.

Let all who have come prepared place in this receptacle their writing of sins.

The members of the congregation line up and each in turn throw into the receptacle their writing of sins, which may be crumpled or rolled up so that the writing remain hidden.

Once all writings have been placed in the receptacle, the Officiant last of all throws in his writing, pours a small amount of consecrated oil over the papers, and then lights them on fire (taking care to observe strict fire safety precautions, including burning the paper in a fire-safe container only in an area away from other combustible material and having close at hand something to quickly extinguish the flames, if necessary; if fire safety or local circumstances require greater caution, then the Communal Sacrament, or just this portion of it, may be performed outdoors). The Officiant then says:

Brothers and sisters, please kneel with me and let us pray.

All kneel while the Officiant prays:

Almighty and most merciful God,

As these papers are consumed by the light of these flames and are turned into smoke rising toward the heavens, may our sins be consumed by Thy Divine light that our souls be transformed, rising closer to Thee.

After the flame has expired, the Officiant concludes the prayer of confession:

We pray that Thy divine light and mercy speedily help and deliver us, that we may truly repent and constantly speak the truth, boldly forsake and rebuke vice, and patiently suffer for the truth's sake. (Virtue 40:3)

Turn us again, we pray, and show the light of Thy countenance, that we be made whole.

We are weak. We pray for Thy forgiveness and mercy, as we show mercy to those who have wronged us. May we return again into the arms of Thy mercy, that we be restored to the blessed company of Thy faithful people, through Thy Divine mercy and light.

We firmly intend amendment of our lives. To make a real change, we will endeavor to do those things we have noted on our writings of reform, which we shall carry close with us as a reminder until we perform this Rite once again.

Amen.

All those participating keep on their person the paper until the following Lent looking often at it to remember what they have resolved to do. After the following Lent, the previous paper may be disposed of in a respectful manner.

The Officiant then prays:

Almighty and most merciful God,

May all they who confess their faults and overcome them be spared.

May we hereafter live a godly, righteous, and sober life,

May our souls turn from this wickedness, and live and bring forth fruits worthy of repentance.

And when we are tempted or disturbed in coming days, we pray that we sin not, but stand in awe and stillness, pondering and silent, offering right sacrifices and putting our trust in Thee. (Wisdom 7:1 and Hope 3:1.)

Even when we are wearied by the changes and chances of this fleeting world, may we repose upon Thy eternal changelessness.

We beseech thee, O God, to lighten our darkness with Thy celestial brightness, that we conquer the perils and dangers of this life. May we be sons and daughters of light and banish deeds of darkness.

May there be a new, clean heart and right spirit in us.

Amen.

The ashes are saved for use on Ash Wednesday.

The Officiant says:

Brothers and sisters, let us all repent and pray for each other during this season of Lent and, please, pray for me, a sinner.

Now, let us partake of the Bread and Water of the Sacrament on this first day of Lent.

The Communal Sacrament continues as normal, starting with a hymn and the blessing and distribution of the Bread and Water of the Sacrament, and with bearing of testimonies during the period for talks.

The following Wednesday is Ash Wednesday. Those of sufficient age and health should fast on this day.

On this day, the Ward holds a special Communal Sacrament. If possible, the Communal Sacrament should be held early in the morning before members of the Ward go about their regular daily activities. If that is not feasible, then the Communal Sac-

rament may be held in the evening or some other convenient time. If needed, multiple services may be held.

Beforehand, the collected ashes from the previous Sunday's public Rite of Repentance are mixed with a small amount of Consecrated Oil and placed in a receptacle at the front of the sanctuary. If there are not enough ashes to mark everyone expected to attend, then the ashes may be supplemented with additional ashes collected by the Bishop and the Vice-Bishops from their private Rites of Repentance performed over the previous year.

If he is available, the Bishop of the Ward acts as Officiant at the Ash Wednesday Communal Sacrament. If he is unavailable or incapacitated, then one of the Vice-Bishops acts as Officiant. One of the Vice-Bishops, or if neither is available, some other Elder selected ahead of time, stands to the side of the Officiant to assist. The Assistant should also be dressed in a Stole.

After the Reading, the Officiant stands before the Ward, next to the receptacle of ashes, and says:

We are all weak and in need of God's mercy. We all fall short of the mark.

In ancient times, ashes were used to express grief and penitence, and also as a reminder that we all "will be buried, reduced to dust, and be quiet at last" (Hope 2:4), earth to earth, ashes to ashes, dust to dust.

I have here the ashes from the public Rite of Repentance we just performed on the first Sunday of Lent.

As we begin this season of Lent, let each of us who resolves again this year to move forward with firmness on the Triple Path be marked with the symbol of the Tricrux on the forehead, using ashes that contained the writing of our sins.

Brothers and sisters, please kneel with me and let us pray.

All kneel while the Officiant prays:

Almighty and most merciful God,

With these ashes, we mark ourselves with the Tricrux, to signify publicly and to Thee our grief for our sins and our penitential resolve to forsake them and, by Thy grace, reform ourselves.

May we never forget how short is this limited mortal time we have to repent and reform and to seek wisdom, practice virtue, and labor with hope.

Amen.

The Assistant first marks the Officiant, using ashes to draw the Tricrux on his forehead, saying as he does so:

Repent, and remember that you are dust, and to dust you shall return.

The Officiant says:

Let each who has a real desire to reform themself approach and also be marked.

Those present who desire to be marked line up, and the Officiant and the Assistant mark each one in turn, using ashes to draw the Tricrux on the forehead, saying each time:

Repent, and remember that you are dust, and to dust you shall return.

The Communal Sacrament terminates as usual, except without any talks or testimonies. Those who have received the mark of the Tricrux on their forehead may remove it whenever they desire after the meeting, but should do so in a respectful and reverent manner.

If needed, Deacons may be assigned to take ashes to those who are sick or otherwise unable to attend the Communal Sacrament, saying the prayer over the Bread and Water of the Sacrament, partaking of it with the person, saying the Creed together, and then marking each person as at the Communal Sacrament, saying each time:

Repent, and remember that you are dust, and to dust you shall return.

Any ashes at the end of the day should be deconsecrated. To deconsecrate the ashes, a Priest, or Elder stands before the ashes in the same manner in which they were blessed and offers the following prayer:

O God,

By the authority of the Congregation of the Faithful of the

Triple Path and in my office as a(n) (Priest or Elder), I deconsecrate these ashes that they return to secular use.
    Amen.
    *The ashes should then be disposed of in a respectful man-
ner.*

    *Any remaining Bread and Water should also be deconse-
crated as described in the Rites of Communal and Private Sacrament.*

    *On all the following Sundays of Lent, the Officiant says
the following just after the Reading or Creed and before the talks:*
    In this season we celebrate the Feast of Lent, or the Feast
of Repentance and Sacrifice.

    This the __ (state the ordinal number) Sunday of Lent.

    All of sufficient age and health fast on the Sundays of Lent,
except for the fourth. We minimize entertainments and rich or
sweet foods, our spending, and our consumption of caffeine and
alcohol. And, we completely give up some luxury that has become
too precious to us.

    We fast and renounce luxuries during this time of Lent
that we be reminded how much we foolishly let ourselves be controlled by our appetites, and how much we need to repent of.

    Most importantly, during the time of Lent we intensify our
prayers and spiritual exercises. We focus, even more, on practicing virtue.

    The color for this feast is black, symbolizing our mourn-
ing for our sins and what we have given up and lost because of
them.

    *Only on the fourth Sunday of Lent, the Officiant also says
the following two paragraphs:*
    Lent is a season of bright sadness—one of grief that ends
with the joy of Easter.

    This fourth Sunday in the middle of Lent is called Rejoic-
ing Sunday. Alone on this Sunday of all the Sundays of Lent, we
do not fast. We pause in the middle for some reverent rejoicing,
to remind us of the joy and peace that comes with real repentance

and reform, prefiguring the more complete joy to come at Easter.
The Officiant says the following:
Brothers and sisters, please kneel with me and let us pray.
All kneel while the Officiant prays:
Almighty and most merciful God,
During this season of Lent, may we bring forth truth, even from our most inward parts, and acknowledge our faults and sins.
We ask for Thy mercy upon us, O God, after thy great goodness. We turn to thee in weeping, fasting, and praying, for we do not believe that Thou called us unto uncleanness, but unto holiness.

May our consciences be accused by our sins, that we be grieved and wearied with their burden, so we be driven to turn away from them and instead to Thee, that we repent, that we may receive Thy comfort.

May all those who confess their sins unto Thee be spared. May we turn our faces from our sins and put out all our misdeeds, that we have clean hearts and renewed, right spirits,

May we be freed from the chains of our iniquity by worthily lamenting our sins and acknowledging our wretchedness. May we repent, offering unto Thee right sacrifices, that we may be washed from our wickedness and cleansed.

May we still our minds and guide them to good desires, vanquishing all evil thoughts which may assault and hurt the soul. May our souls subdue our flesh, through Thy divine grace, that we emulate Thy perfection, in righteousness and true holiness.

May every member of thy holy Church, in each's vocation and ministry, truly and godly serve Thee. And may we, Thy people, live our future lives more free of sin, governing ourselves in righteousness, that we be preserved ever more, both in body and soul.

And we who were baptized, dying to the ways of foolishness, evil, and lazy despair, being reborn into a life committed to seeking wisdom, practicing virtue, and laboring with hope, may we pass our lives bravely traveling always firmly forward on the Triple Path.

Amen.

Brothers and sisters, please be seated.

The Communal Sacrament proceeds as normal, except after the closing prayer the Officiant says:

Now, Brothers and Sisters, truly repent for your past sins; have a lively and steadfast faith in God and the Triple Path; amend your lives to be partakers of God's Divine light. And above all things, give most humble and hearty thanks to God.

Let us all pray for each other. I will pray for you, and all of you, please, go in peace, and pray for me, a sinner.

The Communal Sacrament ends.

The Feast of Easter

The Feast of Easter is celebrated on the Sunday closest to the Spring Equinox and on the Friday and Saturday immediately before that Sunday.

The liturgical color for this feast is purple, representing the spirituality that comes from seeking wisdom and the self-mastery that comes from practicing virtue. On the Saturday morning of Easter all the veils in the sanctuary should be removed and the sanctuary should be decorated appropriately with purple. The Officiant at the Friday dinner may wear a regular or purple Stole. The Officiant at Communal Sacrament should wear a purple Stole.

On Friday, people meet privately as families or in other small groups and share a ritual meal described below. The dinner is officiated by the father of the household, if he is a Church member in good standing; if he is not present or unable to act as Officiant, then a Priest or Elder who is present acts as Officiant.

All adults and children of sufficient age should begin a fast after eating dinner on Thursday.

The meal to break the fast should start at dusk on Friday evening. The Officiant begins by pouring wine or some other drink for everyone at the table, starting with the person to his right, saying the following as he does so:

Let us pray

Praise be to Thee, O Lord, our God. King of the universe, who created the fruit of the vine.

Praise be to Thee, O Lord, our God. Sovereign of the universe, who has made a distinction between holy and not holy, between light and darkness; who has preserved us alive, sustained us, and brought us to enjoy this season.

When he finishes pouring all others' drinks, the Officiant returns to his place at the table and pours his own drink. The youngest person in the company then asks,

Why is this night different from all other nights?

The Officiant responds:

On this night we celebrate the end of our period of sacrifice and repentance. We celebrate our ancestors' stories and histories of sacrifice, of death and rebirth; and their labor, with hope, to press forward to a brighter day.

Troy fell, but legend says the survivors founded Rome, which lasted for a thousand years.

Rome fell, the people starved. Our voluntary fast over the last day means little compared to the privations many suffered involuntarily in that time of plague, war, and famine.

The Moors invaded and subjugated the lands of the West and fought their way into Europe, spreading their faith at the point of the sword.

Constantinople survived another thousand years after the fall of Rome, but she too fell, losing even her name.

At times, even now, our nations falter, with many submitting themselves to barren, foolish ideas, and to invading peoples and ideologies.

And at times we each fall short and must be re-born into our commitment to seek wisdom, practice virtue, and labor with hope.

The Officiant lifts a plate of olives and grapes in his hands and says:

When Troy, Rome, and Constantinople fell, their olive groves burned and their vineyards were trampled underfoot, the fruits of their past labors kept out of reach.

The Officiant sets the plate down out of everyone's reach. He continues:

All they had to eat were the bitterness of poverty, ignominy, and subjugation.

The Officiant passes a plate of gluten-free crackers and grated horseradish to the Company. As each person takes some and places them on his or her plate, the Officiant says:

Let us eat bitter herbs to remember the bitterness of those

times.

All in the company place horseradish on their crackers and eat.

But after each period of subjugation and captivity, our ancestors have labored to overcome again, and came again to savor the sweetness of their successful efforts.

The Officiant passes around the plate of olives and grapes. As each person takes some olives and grapes and places them on his or her plate, the Officiant continues:

When Rome fell, the West almost withered away, but new nations were reborn out of Rome's ashes.

After the Moors invaded, the people rose up and fought, stopping their advance in France, at the Battle of Tours. Following centuries more of struggle, they finally drove the Moors completely out of Europe.

When Constantinople fell, her scholars and libraries escaped westward, and helped bring about a rebirth and regrowth of the West that has not ended to this day.

Once the plate of olives and grapes has been passed around, the Officiant continues:

Let us eat these olives and remember to savor the reward of laboring with hope and virtue.

All in the Company eat their olives. The Officiant continues:

Let us eat these grapes and remember the sweetness of the achievement that comes after arduous sacrifice.

All in the company eat their grapes. The Officiant lifts up a paper bag with its top folded closed, filled with chocolates or other treats. As the Officiant hands the bag to the youngest member of the Company, he says:

And sometimes, there are rewards hidden where we do not expect, which may only be found with much searching.

The youngest member of the company takes the bag and secretly hides it somewhere.

The Officiant says:

447

As it is said that God told Abraham that his seed shall be strangers in a land that is not theirs, so should we be strangers among the foolish, the evil, and those with lazy despair. And in every generation are there not some who rise up against us, seeking to annihilate us? But we will trust in God and work for our deliverance yet again.

In times of plenty, let us remember that all things perish, even the universe, immortal and enduring as it is, changes and never remains the same. Only God stands firm, perfectly unchanging (Wisdom 12:3).

Let us remember that the rising sun is the setting sun. The thing born is the thing dying (Wisdom 12:5).

In times of privation let us always remember that as the years pass and time goes on, decay and emptiness end, and growth and fullness begin again. (Wisdom 12:6)

The past is rolled up into the present, and the present is always unrolling itself out into the future. (Wisdom 12:16)

Just as the Romans sacrificed animals to their gods and ate the meat of that sacrifice, let us, with thanks to God, eat this meal and enjoy the fruits of our sacrifices.

The main meal is served, with a main dish containing beef or pork, in remembrance of the ancient practice of sacrificing bulls and pigs.

After all have eaten, the children look for the hidden bag of treats. Once they are found, they are divided amongst the members of the Company, who have them as a dessert.

After dessert, the Officiant pours for each member of the Company a little more wine, or some other drink, for a final toast. When he has finished, he closes with the following prayer:

Let us pray.

Almighty God.

We will praise Thee from freedom to bondage to freedom; from joy to sorrow to joy; from light to darkness to light; and from redemption to servitude to redemption; from sunrise to sunset to sunrise. We have been satisfied of Thy bounty, o God. Through

Thy goodness we live. We will give thanks unto Thee, and praise Thee; blessed be Thy name continually, in the mouth of every living creature for ever and ever.

May Thy compassion and mercy for us never end. May our numbers and our faith be ever more increased. And may we always place our trust in Thee as our help and shield.

Thou art our God, Father, Maintainer, Supporter, and Enlarger. May we be enlarged speedily beyond all our troubles. Let us depend on Thy hand and not be put to shame, nor be confounded.

Thy truth and Thy peace in the high heavens endure forever. May we always work for Thy truth and peace to be granted to us.

Amen.

At the conclusion of the prayer the Officiant raises his glass and toasts:

Until next year, by God's grace and our efforts, a better one than last.

The Company repeats:

A better one than last!

The dinner ends.

Saturday is a day for celebration and festivities, including treats and Easter egg hunts for children.

On Easter Sunday, Communal Sacrament may be held outdoors. The Reading should focus on themes of persistence in the face of adversity, liberation from bondage, and rebirth. The Officiant says the following just after the Reading and before the talks:

On this day of Easter, the liturgical color is purple. Purple has often been used as a symbol for faith and righteousness. It is also a symbol of the mastery of kingship. Purple for us thus represents the faith and spirituality that come from seeking wisdom and the self-mastery that comes from practicing virtue.

Brothers and sisters, please kneel with me and let us pray.

All kneel while the Officiant prays:

449

Almighty and most merciful God,

We pray, that as we have been baptized, symbolically dying as to foolishness, evil, and lazy despair, that we may ever continue to renounce these as individuals and as a people, being continually reborn into a life of seeking wisdom, practicing virtue, and laboring with hope.

The Ward is seated and the Communal Sacrament then proceeds as normal, with a Reading and talks that focus on themes of personal, cultural, and spiritual rebirth; persistence in the face of adversity; liberation from bondage; and the history of our ancestors.

The Feast of May Day

The Feast of May Day, or the Feast of Hope, is celebrated on the night of April 30, on May 1, and on the following Sunday whenever May 1 does not fall on a Sunday (if May 1 is not a holiday in the country, local wards or families may choose to celebrate May Day on the Friday night, Saturday, and Sunday that fall around or closest to May 1). It is a time to celebrate the return of warmth, summer, growth, and fertility.

During the week leading up to May Day, families or other persons may anonymously leave May baskets (small baskets of sweets or flowers) on the doorsteps of neighbors, friends, and family.

Families also prepare flower wreaths and hang them on the front door of their home, leaving them there until the Feast of Mid-Summer. They also adorn the windows, doors, and gates of their house with flowers. Yellow flowers, violets, and especially roses should be used.

The liturgical color for this feast is green, representing hope and the growing life of spring and summer. For Communal Sacrament on this Sunday, the Church should be decorated appropriately with green. The Officiant at the evening celebration should wear a regular or a green Stole. The officiant at Communal Sacrament should wear a green Stole.

At sunset on April 30 (or, in the case of inclement weather or when celebrating in places where May 1 is not a holiday, on the Friday), families or other small groups, or the Ward, gather at an unlit bonfire. A Priest or Elder officiates. Wearing a Stole and holding a torch, he stands at the head of the group. He begins by saying:

This Feast of May Day has been celebrated, in one form or another, by our ancestors for thousands of years. To the Celts, it was Beltane; to the Romans, Rosalia, the festival of roses. The

Romans named this month of May after their goddess of growth and the Earth. We only worship the one true God, but we still gather, just as our ancestors did, to celebrate this season of growth and fertility: the coming victory of summer over winter, of life over death, of light over darkness.

The Officiant lights the bonfire with his torch, then says:

Brothers and sisters, just as this fire burns away its fuel, let us let the Triple Path burn away the foolishness, evil, and lazy despair in our lives.

The group sings a few joyful hymns or spring songs, someone offers a prayer, and then the group shares an evening meal outside together. Before eating, on the way to the meal, each person walks around the bonfire once. The group may also cook a cake or cobbler over the fire to eat after the meal.

On the morning of May 1 (or the Saturday), members of the ward gather early in the morning at the Church grounds (or some other central outdoor gathering place) and sing hymns and other songs related to hope, joy, celebration, and spring. Girls and women may wear flowers in their hair. After everyone shares a breakfast together, including cakes, children dance around a maypole with ribbons. Before the dancing begins, the person officiating explains:

The story of the Garden of Eden speaks of the trees of life and of knowledge and good and evil, standing in the center of paradise. The Germanic Romans erected columns to celebrate Jupiter's victory balancing order and chaos. Our ancestors also planted trees and erected maypoles as symbols of the world tree, the tree of life, or the *axis mundi*, which means the world axis, a place where north, south, east, and west meet and where heaven and earth connect.

We do the same here, setting up this pole as a symbol of that world axis and as a celebration of the victory of God and good and freedom over evil and chaos and tyranny.

And not just this pole, but let it be so for us, each standing as a pillar, living our lives so that wherever we find ourselves, we make ourselves present in the moment, fashioning whatever place we happen to be into a world axis: a center place, connecting heaven and earth, a place of godly and righteous order and freedom. So may it be also in each of our families and homes.

In expressing this desire that we each turn the place we find ourselves into a world axis, I emphasize the word "a". May no one of us ever be so prideful as to think as his or her place as *the* center place.

Just as this pole (*if the Church has a sacred grove add the phrase* "and these trees' branches") point(s) toward heaven, let us point our souls toward heaven, always remembering God by following the Triple Path.

Now that I have brought these weighty matters to mind, let us also remember that there is room in life for joy and celebration and making merry. So, let this day be a day of dancing and celebration and festivities.

Pairs of boys and girls (or men and women) perform the Maypole dance by alternating around the base of the pole. Each of them holds the end of a ribbon. The dancers weave in and around each other. The boys go one direction and the girls go the other, weaving the ribbons together around the pole until the dancers meet at the base.

The rest of the day is for games, celebration, festivity, dancing, and music. Families may enjoy an outdoor picnic lunch.

On Sunday, weather permitting, Communal Sacrament is held outdoors on the Church grounds. The Tricrux at the front of the congregation should be decorated with roses. Women and girls may come to Church dressed in white dresses and with flowers in their hair. The Officiant says the following just after the Reading or Creed and before the talks:

Today, we finish our celebration of the Feast of May Day, or the Feast of Hope. The liturgical color for this feast is green, representing hope and the growing life of spring and summer. The other symbol of this Feast is the rose.

During this season, the Romans adorned the statues of

their gods with roses. The early Christians transferred this practice to their veneration of saints. Today on this day, we follow in their footsteps, celebrating re-birth and growth by adorning with roses the Tricrux, the symbol of our faith and of our commitment to God.

Brothers and sisters, please kneel with me and let us pray.

All kneel while the Officiant prays:

Almighty and most merciful God,

On this day of the coming of summer, we pray that as all around us grows and blooms, that our souls may grow and bloom so that we may be directed and ruled by wisdom, virtue, and hope; that we may be strengthened for Thy service; that we may have right judgment in all things and rejoice in Thy holy comfort.

We pray that each of us may make ourselves present in the moment, fashioning whatever places we happen to be into pillars and center places, connecting heaven and earth, places of godly and righteous order and freedom, and that we may do the same in each of our families and in this Church. That we, being gathered together in unity, may manifest Thy power and the power of the Triple Path.

Amen.

The Ward is seated and the Communal Sacrament then proceeds as normal, with a Reading and talks that focus on themes of growth and light.

The Feast of Mid-Summer

*The Feast of Mid-Summer, or the Feast of Virtue, is cele-
brated on the Friday night, Saturday, and Sunday following the
Summer Solstice. When the Summer Solstice falls on a Friday, Saturday, and Sunday, then the Feast occurs on the Friday night, Saturday, and Sunday around which the Solstice occurs. The Feast is
for celebrating the light of virtue in our lives.*

*The liturgical color for this feast is blue, representing vir-
tue. For Communal Sacrament on this Sunday, the Church should
be decorated appropriately with blue. The Officiant at the evening
celebration should wear a regular or a blue Stole. The Officiant at
Communal Sacrament should wear a blue Stole.*

*In the week leading up to Mid-Summer, families may dec-
orate the outsides of their homes, especially above or around the
doors, with greenery or special herbs.*

*In the early evening on the eve of the Summer Solstice
(or, in the case of inclement weather or when celebrating in places
where it is not a holiday, on the relevant Friday), families or other
small groups, or the Ward, gather at an unlit bonfire. Women
may wear garlands of flowers; men may wear oak leaves. A Priest
or Elder officiates. He stands at the head of the group, wearing his
Stole and holding a torch. He begins by saying:*

We gather to celebrate this Feast of Mid-Summer, as did
our ancestors for millennia before us. On this day the pagans used
to light fires in memory of Hercules. The Christians kept the custom and did it in remembrance of John the Baptist and to drive
away evil.

Whereas on May Day we celebrated the arrival of Summer and the growing victory of light over darkness, today we celebrate this day in which the light is at its greatest strength and summer is in full bloom.

On this day, when the sun follows its highest path in the

-

heavens, when the nights are the shortest and the days the longest, we celebrate this day in remembrance of virtue and of God, as a symbol of the light He is in our lives and the trust we place in Him.

Just as the brightness of the sun dims all lesser lights in comparison, so virtue, by its own greatness, can shatter and overwhelm evil, pain, wrongs, and annoyances. Wherever its radiance reaches, all lights that shine without its help appear extinguished. (Foundations 4:3)

But just as soon the days will grow ever-shorter and night ever-longer, it is often when the Divine light is shining brightly in our lives that we let it fade and darkness grow in our souls. Let us be on guard for this tendency and always seek to rekindle the divine spark in us, leading us to virtue. And in those moments when our best moments have passed, and we feel uninspired or even feel the desire to do evil, may we have the courage and strength of character to continue doing good even when our desires are imperfect. (Virtue 1:16)

Even at this time of celebration and light, we cannot help but remember that all things perish, everything passes: the rising sun is the setting sun. The thing born is the thing dying. (Wisdom 12:3 and 5)

The flower wreaths that each household prepared at May Day have withered and dried, fit now only as fuel for the fire. But out of their decay will come light.

Let each family place their wreaths.

Each family sends a representative, preferably a child, to place the family's dried May Day wreath upon the unlit fire.

After the wreaths have been placed, the Officiant says:

As I light this fire, let us also remember that decay and emptiness also end, and growth and fullness begin again. (Wisdom 12:6)

The Officiant lights the fire.

The Officiant continues:

Even though this fire will be eventually be consumed and end, fire itself does not. Light is eternal. Heat is eternal. So, let this fire also remind us that some things are eternal—God, and wisdom, virtue and hope. Let this fire remind us of God's eternal light in our lives, inspiring us to live better lives.

And just as the fire protects by driving away wild animals, let us seek to feel the spark and the fire of God's divinity in our hearts driving away evil, protecting us from falling into error.

As the fire consumes the wreaths, youths may attempt to jump over the flames.

The group sings a few joyful hymns or summer songs and someone offers a prayer.

The Officiant holds a container of water with a spout and says:

Let us never forget that speaking about good deeds is not enough. Pretending to act with virtue is useless. We cannot fool our souls. (Virtue 1:14)

Before we leave to share a meal, let us also at this time remember our baptisms, either already past or yet to come, where we promised before God and the Congregation of the Faithful of the Triple Path to endeavor to seek wisdom, practice virtue, labor with hope, and renounce foolishness, evil, and lazy despair, that we may draw closer to God.

Each who has been baptized into our faith, and all others who so desire, come before me. Let this water sprinkled on your hands to clean them remind you of baptism, in which you were symbolically buried to your old life and reborn as a traveler on the Triple Path, committed to seek wisdom, practice virtue, and labor with hope.

Each person who has been baptized, and any other person who so desires, walks before the Officiant holding out his or her hands, onto which the Officiant sprinkles some water. The Officiant concludes:

So, brothers and sisters, seek not just to live, but to live well, practicing virtue. (Virtue 1:1)

The group shares an outside evening meal together (weather permitting). The group may also cook a cake or cobbler over the fire to eat after the meal.

The following day is for celebration, festivity, dancing, and music. Families may enjoy an outdoor picnic lunch and outdoor activities together, including hoop-rolling for children as a reminder that at this time of year, the sun rises to its highest point and then turns back, just as the circle of the hoop.

In the evening, every new family that has come into the Ward during the prior year (and any other family that so desires) should put a table outside their house with food and drink for passing members of the Ward and other neighbors to enjoy, thus allowing newcomers to the Ward to make better acquaintance with their fellow Ward members and help establish their place in the community.

During Communal Sacrament the following Sunday, the Tricrux at the front of the congregation should be decorated with flowers. Women and girls may come to Church dressed in white dresses and with garlands of flowers in their hair, men may come with oak leaves. The Officiant says the following just after the Reading and before the talks:

On this Sunday we finish our celebration of Midsummer, or the Feast of Virtue. The liturgical color for this feast is blue, representing virtue.

Brothers and sisters, please kneel with me and let us pray.

All kneel while the Officiant prays:

Almighty and most merciful God,

On this day in the midst of summer, we pray that just as the days are full of light and warmth, that our souls might be full of Thy light and warmth, that we may practice virtue. That we may live our faith with courage, constantly speaking the truth, boldly forsaking and rebuking vice, and striving to make things better when it is possible, while patiently enduring when it is not. (Virtue 40:3 and Foundations 6:19)

We pray that we may shun those things that lead away from virtue and toward evil: wealth without work; pleasure without conscience; knowledge without character; commerce without ethics; science without humanity; religion without sacrifice; morality without faith; politics without principle; rights without responsibilities; actions without consequences; freedom without tradition; and confidence without Thee. (Virtue 1:21)

May we, being gathered together in unity, practice virtue to manifest Thy power and the power of the Triple Path.

Amen.

The Ward is seated and the Communal Sacrament then proceeds as normal, with a Reading and talks that focus on themes of virtue and the symbolism and meaning of baptism.

The Feast of the Tricrux

The Feast of the Tricrux is celebrated on the Saturday, and Sunday following the Fall Equinox. When the Fall Equinox falls on a Saturday or Sunday, then the Feast of the Tricrux occurs on the Saturday and Sunday around which the Equinox occurs. The Feast is for recognizing the symbol of our faith, the Tricrux, and for girding oneself with courage to fight against darkness.

In the week leading up to the Saturday of the Feast of the Tricrux, families and individuals should conduct a thorough cleaning of their homes and conduct any necessary repairs or improvement projects; they should also clear out their closets of unneeded clothes and shoes and donate them to those in need.

The liturgical colors for this feast are red and gold, red representing courage and gold representing the brilliance of God's divine light. For Communal Sacrament on this Sunday, the sanctuary should be decorated appropriately with red and gold. At the evening gathering the Officiant should wear a regular or a color-inverted Stole (made of a gold-colored fabric embroidered with a red Tricrux). At Communal Sacrament, the Officiant should wear a color-inverted Stole.

On Saturday morning, families, groups, or the entire Ward should hike to the top of a nearby, predesignated hill or mountain, with each person carrying a stone or pebble from the bottom and leaving it at the top.

During the day, people may give Allan apples—large, red, polished apples—to family and friends. That evening, families or groups should share a harvest meal, including beef, apples, blackberries, and a Horkey cake.

To start the meal, just before sunset on Saturday, families, other small groups, or the entire Ward, gather together. A Priest or Elder officiates. He stands at the head of the group and begins by saying:

We gather to celebrate this Feast of the Tricrux, the symbol of our faith, its three prongs symbolizing,
All present say together:
Wisdom, Virtue, and Hope.
The Officiant continues:
Since Midsummer, days have been shortening. Equally divided now are day and night. Until Yule, the days will grow shorter still, the darkness of night growing.

In this season of growing shadows, our ancestors celebrated the holiday of Michaelmas, in memory of the courageous archangel Michael who slew the dragon.

Let us also now gird ourselves anew with courage to wrestle the dragons in our lives, to fight evil and root it out wherever we may find it.

Brothers and sisters, will you do this?
All present respond:
We will gird ourselves with courage to wrestle against evil, that our hearts fail not in the fight. We will be fearless and fierce in defense of the Church and the Triple Path and those to whom we owe our greatest duties. (Creed 5)
The Officiant continues:
The warmth of Summer is behind us. The cold of winter is coming, as if the Earth is dying. Knowing that darkness will be coming, the wise farmer plants in spring, cultivates in summer, and then harvests to store up against the winter. Long before the darkness starts to grow, he already prepares.

In our fight against evil, let us likewise store up virtue during times of spiritual plenty to strengthen our characters so that we might continue doing good even when our desires are imperfect. (Virtue 1:16)

When your enemies surround you on all sides like swarming bees, have the courage to press forward until the end with steadiness, having a perfect brightness of hope, continuing to seek wisdom, practice virtue, labor with hope, and trust in God, so that in every situation, things were better because you were there, just as today we made the mountains and hills a little taller. (Virtue 22:22; Foundations 1:12; and Hope 1:)

The group shares an evening Tricruxtide meal together.

During Communal Sacrament the following day, all Priests and Elders go to Church wearing their Stoles. All other Church members should also wear the Tricrux in some form. Each household also brings one loaf of homemade bread. In addition to the normal Bread blessed during Communal Sacrament, all the households' loaves are placed on the Sacrament table and blessed as well. Bread from the loaves is eaten each day during the following week until it is used up, with the relevant mealtime prayers specially recognizing the Tricrux and a re-commitment to showing courage.

During Communal Sacrament, the Officiant says the following just after the Reading and before the talks:

Be of good courage, all who trust in God and seek wisdom, practice virtue, and labor with hope.(Virtue 22:1)

On this Sunday we conclude our celebration of the Feast of the Tricrux in which we show our respect for the Tricrux, the symbol of our faith, and our commitment to seek wisdom, practice virtue, and labor with hope. In this feast we also re-commit ourselves to showing courage because "those who, out of fear, fail to do what must or should be done because it is hard or difficult are worthy of contempt and condemnation." (Virtue 22:15)

The liturgical colors for this feast are red and gold. Red symbolizing courage and gold symbolizing the brilliance of God's divine light.

Brothers and sisters, please kneel with me and let us pray.

All kneel while the Officiant prays:

Almighty and most merciful God,

We are grateful for our faith and for the symbol of our faith, the Tricrux, ever-reminding us to seek wisdom, practice virtue, and labor with hope.

We re-commit ourselves to showing courage in our practice of the Triple Path, to doing what is right and honorable, even if it involves toil, even if it involves peril, even if it involves harm to ourselves; and to not doing that which is evil or base, even if it brings us money, or pleasure, or power. (Virtue 22:23)

May we not fear gaining disrepute in the eyes of the disreputable. (Virtue 22:20)

And may we not be deterred from that which is right and honorable, that we not let ourselves be tempted into evil or baseness. (Virtue 22:23)

May we always remember that our courage and fortitude are strengthened when we are challenged and when our spirit and character are tested. And that we must prove our faith, our abilities, and our capacity by confronting many difficulties and hardships. (Virtue 22:10, 11)

Amen.

Brothers and Sisters, please be seated.

The Ward is seated

Brothers and sisters, our souls can be more powerful than the winds of fate. The good and bad things brought to us by chance are merely the raw materials out of which we ourselves build our lives. We guide our affairs in either direction. Under our own power do we produce a good and honorable life, or a wretched one. (Virtue 22:18)

Fortune favors the brave, but the coward is foiled by his faint heart. (Virtue 22:7)

Bad men and women can make anything bad—even things that had come with the appearance of what is best. Wise and virtuous men and women, however, correct the wrongs of fate. They soften hardship and bitterness because they know how to endure them. They accept prosperity with appreciation and moderation, and stand up against trouble with steadiness and courage. (Virtue 22:19). Let us always seek to be such wise and virtuous men and women.

The Communal Sacrament then proceeds as normal, with a Reading and talks that focus on themes of courage and the symbolism of the Tricrux.

The Feast of Allhallowtide

The Feast of Allhallowtide is celebrated on the Friday night, Saturday, and Sunday following November 1. When November 1 falls on a Friday, then the Feast occurs on that Friday night and the following Saturday, and Sunday. It is a time to remember, celebrate, and honor the departed, including loved ones, ancestors, and the faithful.

Following the Communal Sacrament of the Feast of the Tricrux, each family or household chooses a faithful departed who is an exemplar of the ideals of the Triple Path to commemorate during the Feast of Allhallowtide. In the weeks leading up to Allhallowtide, the family or household should study the life of this person and conduct activities to celebrate and memorialize his or her life.

During the weeks leading up to the Feast, families decorate their homes with memento mori and vanitas themes.

Also in the weeks leading up to the Feast, Wards should update their commemorative plaques of the names of the dead with the names of those in the ward, or loved ones of Ward members, who have passed away over the prior year.

The liturgical color for this feast is white, symbolizing victory and life. For Communal Sacrament, the Church should be decorated appropriately with white and also with memento mori and vanitas themes. At all grave consecrations and Saturday gatherings, the Officiant should wear a regular or white Stole. At Communal Sacrament, the Officiant should wear a white Stole.

Churches should toll their bells at three o'clock in the afternoon on Friday, Saturday, and Sunday, in remembrance of the departed.

The Friday night of Allhallowtide should be spent reflecting on the good and helpful lives of ancestors and spiritual forbears and in praying for the wisdom, virtue, hope, and courage to follow their examples. Families and individuals should gather and retell stories about departed loved ones, ancestors, and spiritual forebears, and most particularly, the person specially chosen by the family or household.

Saturday is for visiting, cleaning, and decorating with flowers the graves of departed loved ones, ancestors, and spiritual forebears. An evening candle may be left at graves as well.

After cleaning and decorating a grave, it may be anointed with Consecrated Oil by a Priest or Elder, who, while wearing a Stole, pours a small amount of Consecrated Oil on an appropriate place of the grave or the tombstone and says the following prayer:

Almighty and most merciful God,

By the authority of the Congregation of the Faithful of the Triple Path and in my office as a(n) Priest (or Elder), I anoint this grave with Consecrated Oil.

We commend unto Thee the soul of (state the name of the Departed), Thy servant, who is departed hence from us with the sign of faith.

We pray that (his/her) soul be not delivered into the eternal death, but that (he/she) obtains Thy mercy and everlasting peace and be received unto Thee in the fellowship of all Thy departed servants, in eternal rest with Thy perpetual light shining upon (him/her). May (his/her) soul rest in peace in Thee.

We in the country of the living give Thee hearty thanks for the good examples of all those Thy servants, who, having finished their course in faith, do now rest from their labors. And we beseech Thee that our souls, with all those who are departed in the true faith of Thy holy Name, may also be received unto Thee, in Thy eternal and everlasting glory.

We meekly beseech Thee to raise us from the death of sin unto the life of righteousness, that Thy grace and love be with us all ever more, and that we stand firm on the Triple Path until the end of our lives.

Amen.

On Saturday evening families or groups share dinner to-

gether; an extra place should be set and served to remember the absence of the departed.

The dinner is officiated by the father of the household, if he is a Church member in good standing; if he is not present or unable to act as Officiant, then a Priest or Elder who is present acts as Officiant. If the Officiant is a Priest or Elder, he wears his Stole. He begins dinner with the following prayer:

Brothers and sisters, please kneel with me and let us pray.

All kneel while the Officiant prays:

Almighty and most merciful God,

We pray that all thine elect be knitted together in one communion and fellowship, in continual godliness.

And we pray for the gifts of Thy grace, that we who celebrate this glorious Feast to remember the faithful departed may be enabled to joyfully follow them in virtuous and godly living, devoutly given to serve Thee and seek wisdom, practice virtue, and labor with hope, to the glory of Thy name.

Amen.

After dinner, those present eat a cake in which is hidden items signifying major life events, such as a ring to signify marriage. Whoever gets the piece of cake in which is hidden a particular item shares with the group a story about their experience with that life event, that of an ancestor, or their hopes for the future happening of that event. Families or groups may conduct this activity while gathered around a bonfire.

If they gather around a bonfire, the person officiating ends the evening by saying:

In prior ages on this day, each family brought back the flames of the bonfire to relight their own fires at home. Let us take back the light of the example of the faithful departed and use it to relight the devotion to God and the Triple Path in our lives.

During Communal Sacrament, the Officiant says the following just after the Creed and before the talks:

We celebrate this Feast of Allhallowtide as our ancestors have done for ages. At this season, they believed that the veil sepa-

467

rating the living and the dead was thinner.

Thus, during this feast we remember all the faithful departed. Just as has been done for centuries, we have been tolling our bells in remembrance of the faithful departed, famous or obscure.

The color for this feast is white, which symbolizes victory and life.

All who are privileged to be born are destined to die. (Wisdom 13:1)

It is fitting to remember the departed at this season, in the darker part of the year halfway between the Feast of the Tricrux and of Yule, when outside nature around us is dying as well.

If any members or loved ones of the congregation have passed away over the previous year, then the Officiant performs the following three paragraphs, first saying:

On this season, we also particularly remember those of our Ward who have passed away over the last year:

The Officiant reads the names of all in the Ward, or loved ones of Ward members, who have passed away. With each name he reads, a bell is tolled and candle is lit.

We have added their names to our Ward's plaque to commemorate the departed, lest we forget them.

All things perish, everything passes; even the universe, immortal and enduring as it is, changes and never remains the same. Only God stands firm, perfectly unchanging. (Wisdom 12:3)

We brought nothing into this world, and how can we carry anything out? God gives, and He takes away. Blessed be the Name of God. (Hope 14:19)

Stand in awe and stillness, and sin not. Let us offer right sacrifices and put our trust in God. (Hope 3:1)

Hope is an anchor to our hearts, making us sure and steadfast, always striving for improvement, abounding in virtue, and growing in wisdom. (Hope 1:7)

This is the day in which God has placed us. Let us rejoice and be glad in it. (Hope 8:2)

The deep flood of time rolls over all. Neither the infamy of the fool, nor the renown of the wise, will endure forever. The wise die just like fools. Eventually all will be forgotten and everyone will depart into the same realm of silence. Yet, the wise still follow God and the Triple Path; to them, the need to do so is self-evident. (Wisdom 13:11)

Death comes to everyone: to the wise and foolish, to the virtuous and evil, to the hopeful and pessimist alike. Followers of the Triple Path, though, leave the world better than they found it, just as their forebears, whether spiritual or physical, did for them. (Hope 15:2)

All that are born have but a short time to live. We come up, and are cut down, like a flower; we flee as it were a shadow, and never continue in one stay. In the midst of life we are in death.

As the sorrows of death compass us and the pains of hell grasp, let us, who are part of the communion of the faithful followers of God and the Triple Path, pray and call on the name of God for the souls of all those faithful departed. (Hope 14:18)

Brothers and sisters, please kneel with me and let us pray.

All kneel while the Officiant prays:

Almighty and most merciful God,

Whose mercies cannot be numbered,

To whom may we turn for succor at times of sorrow, but to Thee?

We mourn the passing of our fellow travelers on the Triple Path. We commend unto Thee the souls of our Brothers and Sisters, Thy servants, who are departed hence from us with the sign of faith.

We pray that their souls be not delivered into the eternal death, but that they obtain Thy mercy and everlasting peace and be received unto Thee in the fellowship of all Thy departed servants, in eternal rest with Thy perpetual light shining upon them. May their souls rest in peace in Thee.

We in the country of the living give Thee hearty thanks for the good examples of all those Thy servants, who, having finished their course in faith, do now rest from their labors. And we beseech Thee, that our souls, with all those who are departed in the true faith of Thy holy Name, may also be received unto Thee, in Thy eternal and everlasting glory.

We meekly beseech Thee to raise us from the death of sin unto the life of righteousness, that Thy grace and love be with us all ever more, and that we stand firm on the Triple Path until the end of our lives.

Amen.

The Ward is seated. The Officiant stands and says:

Dear Brothers and Sisters, you here present, live your lives well, so that when you are laid to rest it may be said of you that you sought wisdom, practiced virtue, and labored with hope until the end of your days.

See how soon everything is forgotten. Look at the chaos of infinite time on each side of the present and then understand the emptiness of applause, and the changeableness and lack of judgment in those who pretend to give praise. Let us thus quiet our vanities at last and think on the serenity and peace of following and spreading the Triple Path and content ourselves with this. (Wisdom 13:13)

The living know they will die. What do the dead know? They have no more earthly reward, and even the memory of them will eventually be forgotten. Whatever good you can do while you are alive, do it well, and with courage and enthusiasm. What more earthly works or thoughts can you accomplish in the grave to which you are headed? (Hope 15:3)

Whether you live a life of wisdom, virtue, and hope or whether you live a life of foolishness, evil, and lazy despair, you still will be buried, reduced to dust, and be quiet at last. Before that happens, how much better to work to increase the wisdom, virtue, and hope in the world, rather than idly lamenting the foolishness, evil, and lazy despair already here. (Hope 2:4)

We are weak, watery beings standing in the midst of unrealities; therefore let us turn our minds to the things that are everlasting and real—God, truth. and wisdom, virtue, and hope. (Foundations 6:10)

Let us not just obey God, but train ourselves to agree with Him, obeying Him not because we must, but because our souls will it. (Foundations 6:18)

Let us take refuge in God, that we may be at peace. (Foundation 6:20)

Let us commend our souls to God, putting our trust in Him. Let Him be our rock and fortress of shelter. Let Him guide and lead us. (Foundations 6:21)

In Him let our hope and trust rest. Let His faithfulness and truth be our defense. (Foundations 6:21)

The Communal Sacrament then proceeds as normal. The Reading and talks should focus on remembering the lives of the departed who were exemplars of faithful living. After the concluding hymn and prayer, the Officiant dispenses the Ward by saying:

Brothers and Sisters, let us depart this place with the memory of our dearly departed imprinted forever in our hearts and let us also always remember:

Each who passed through this life, rich or poor,

Chose a path to walk 'til at death's door.

You who yet breathe are still choosing yours.

The Feast of Thanksgiving

The Feast of Thanksgiving is celebrated on the fourth Thursday of November and on the following Sunday, or on the second Monday of October and on the preceding Sunday. In countries in which Thanksgiving is not an official holiday, it may be celebrated on the Saturday and Sunday following the fourth Thursday in November

The liturgical color for this feast is burnt orange, symbolizing the warmth of the gratitude we should feel to God for all of the great blessings in our lives. For Communal Sacrament, the Church should be decorated appropriately with orange. At Communal Sacrament, the Officiant should wear a burnt orange Stole.

On Thursday, families or small groups gather for a traditional harvest meal.

The meal is officiated by the father of the household, if he is a Church member in good standing; if he is not present or unable to act as Officiant, then a Priest or Elder who is present acts as Officiant. If the Officiant is a Priest or Elder, he wears his Stole (either his normal Stole, or one that is burnt orange). He begins the meal by saying:

For centuries, our ancestors have celebrated days of thanksgiving. Settlers from the West brought this tradition to the New World that they settled, setting aside a special day for family to gather and show gratitude for the good things in their lives. And so, let us pray and give thanks.

The head of the household or group says the Prayer of Thanksgiving from the Rite of Communal Sacrament, his arms upraised:

O God, we give thanks for all the good things in our lives, which come by Thy grace. We give thanks for deliverance from afflictions and tribulations. We give thanks for kindness and affection and love, and any teaching that is sweet and plain that guides us toward wisdom, leads us to practice virtue, or inspires us to labor with hope. We rejoice in the Divine illumination that flows into us from following the Triple Path.

We have known hardship and sorrow; we are grateful for the lessons we learned from them. But we dwell not on our misfortunes, and instead marvel at all the great blessings in our lives.

We give thanks for family, food, clothing, shelter, and the simple joys of life, and we pray for all those who find these lacking.

We are grateful for thought and conscience, for the freedom to act and not be acted upon, and for the consequences that naturally flow from our actions.

We give thanks for the spark of Thy divinity we feel in our best moments, and the chance to do better after we have passed through our worst.

May we be preserved on the Triple Path and protected from faltering or stumbling through life. We here resolve again to move forward with firmness on the Triple Path, always, and progress toward a brighter day.

Amen.

Following the prayer, the head of household or group invites everyone around the table to in turn say one specific reason for which they are grateful to God that year. After this is complete, the family or group hold hands and the head of household or group invites someone else to pray, after which they enjoy the meal.

During Communal Sacrament on the following Sunday (or the preceding Sunday, if celebrating Thanksgiving in October), the Officiant says the following just after the Creed and before the talks:

Today we finish (*or* start) our celebration of Thanksgiving. The liturgical color for this feast is burnt orange, symbolizing the warmth of the gratitude we should feel to God for all of the great blessings in our lives.

Brothers and sisters, in this season for rendering Thanksgiving to God for all the blessings we have received at His hands,

474

please kneel with me and let us pray.

All kneel while the Officiant prays:

Almighty and most merciful God,

For the fruits of the earth, and the bounty of all the other blessings of merciful Providence, we give Thee humble and hearty thanks. We exclaim to Thee unfeigned thanks and praise, for crowning the year with Thy goodness, in the increase of the ground and the gathering in of the fruits thereof. Let us be, we pray, faithful and good stewards of this great bounty

In this season of lengthening nights and ever-colder days, we give Thee thanks for the past light of summer and the harvest which it brought. We give even greater thanks for thy Divine light and the light of the Triple Path in our lives and the harvest of wisdom, virtue, and hope they bring to our lives.

May our land still yield her increase, and may our souls ever yield an increase, to Thy glory and to our people's future.

And, whenever we pass through times of privation or hardship, we beseech Thee, let us continue with gratitude even in the face of adversity, with a just sense of Thy mercy, keeping ourselves humble and holy, obediently walking the Triple Path before Thee all our days.

Amen.

The Ward is seated and the Communal Sacrament then proceeds as normal, with a Reading and talks that focus on themes of thanksgiving and gratitude.

The Feast of Yule

The Feast of Yule, or Christmas, is celebrated on the night of the Winter Solstice and on December 24 and 25.

Just after Thanksgiving Thursday, families and households put up Yule decorations, including wreaths and a Yule tree. They also plant in a small pot the seeds of some fragrant herb to be grown indoors, making sure to water and care for them regularly until December 24.

The liturgical colors for this feast are red and green, red symbolizing the blood of sacrifice of all those who came before to give us the present blessings we enjoy and green to symbolize the evergreen, which keeps its color in the winter and helps us remember that spring will come again, reminding us to continue laboring with hope, even at the darkest times.

Starting on the Sunday after Thanksgiving Sunday and continuing until the Sunday before New Year's Sunday, the Church should be decorated in red and green and with other appropriate Yule themes, and the Officiant should wear a red and green Stole.

During this period, in every Communal Sacrament after the talks or testimonies, but before the prayer of Thanksgiving and the normal conclusion of the Rite, the Officiant says the following Yule prayer:

Brothers and sisters, please kneel with me and let us pray.

All kneel while the Officiant prays:

Almighty and most merciful God,

We pray for mercy, because we are weak.

We pray that in this season of short days and long, dark nights, and in all seasons, we let ourselves fall not into sin, but instead that we order all our doings by Thy governance, to do always that which is righteous in Thy sight, that the spiritual darkness in our lives be lightened, just as the darkness of these longest nights will be lightened as the days progress.

May we have Thy protection from the perils and dangers of spiritual darkness.

May we daily be renewed by Thy Divine light, that by Thy grace we may cast away works of darkness and put upon us the armor of Thy light. (Foundations 1:16)

May the darkness of this night, and the darkness in our lives, be illuminated by Thy celestial brightness, that deeds of darkness be forever banished from our actions and desires.

We pray for courage and strength against all assaults of our enemies and for Thy grace in our defense, that we may not fear the power of any adversary, and that we be delivered out of the hands of our enemies and serve Thee without fear, in holiness and righteousness all the days of our lives.

May Thy light come to us, we who sit in darkness and in the shadow of death, that our feet be guided along the Triple Path.

May we be protected through the silent hours of this night and through all the dark nights of our souls, so that we who are wearied by the changes and chances of this fleeting world may repose upon Thy eternal light.

From the night until morning until night let us find hope in Thee, that we overcome our iniquities and be redeemed of them.

Amen.

The Officiant says:

The liturgical colors for this feast of Yule are red and green, red symbolizing the blood of sacrifice of all those who came before to give us the present blessings we enjoy and green to symbolize the evergreen, which keeps its color in the winter and helps us remember that spring will come again, reminding us to continue laboring with hope, even at the darkest times.

The Ward is seated and the Communal Sacrament concludes as normal.

On the night of the Winter Solstice, a special evening Communal Sacrament is held (regardless of whether the day falls on a Sunday or not). In years when the Winter Solstice falls on a

Sunday, then Communal Sacrament is not held in the morning.

In this special Yule Communal Sacrament, young women in good standing aged 12 to 18 who have been confirmed but not initiated come to Church in white dresses and red sashes. Just before the Reading, they leave the sanctuary.

After they have left, the lights are extinguished. The Officiant says the following:

On this, the darkest day of the year, let us always remember that it is at the darkest times that the light grows and the darkness disappears.

We each are responsible for bringing into the world what light we can, reflecting the Divine light of God. Let us seek that the light of wisdom, virtue, and hope shine through in all we do.

The young women, each holding a lit candle, enter in line while singing an appropriate hymn. They line up at the front of the sanctuary. After they are done singing the hymn, they take turns saying the paragraphs (the first two paragraphs being read together) of the following Reading (in Wards where there are more young women than paragraphs, preference in selecting the readers should be given to the older young women; more than one young woman may read the longer paragraphs):

And now a Reading from the book of the Triple Path:

If you walk in the day, you do not stumble, because you see by the light of this world. But if you walk in the night, you stumble, because there is no light to guide you. (Foundations 4:1)

Receiving wisdom is like turning on a light in a dark room —it lets you better perceive everything around you. The brighter light of greater wisdom brings truer understanding. (Foundations 4:2)

Just as the brightness of the sun dims all lesser lights in comparison, so virtue, by its own greatness, can shatter and overwhelm evil, pain, wrongs, and annoyances. Wherever its radiance reaches, all lights that shine without its help appear extinguished. (F oundations 4:3)

Laboring with hope is not naively seeing light where there

is none, but fighting the darkness with what you reflect from God's Divine light. (Foundations 4:4)

Evil and good are real. They are black and white. But there are many shades of grey between them. Encircled by greys as you try to move forward on the Triple Path, it can be hard to judge whether you are moving toward the white or the black. Maintain a searching, far-reaching perspective to help you see forward far enough to understand whether the shade of grey you are heading toward is lighter or darker than the shade behind you. Brighter light also helps you see better to detect the difference between the greys around you. Thus, as you move along the Triple Path, also let the Source of all light and goodness shine on you. Only doing these two things can you tell whether you are moving forward or backward on the Triple Path. (Wisdom 11:4)

Live your life so that you would not be ashamed for anyone to discover any aspect of it. Live with the expectation that everything covered up will be uncovered, and everything secret will become known. Live so that you do not fear if everything you have done in the dark is seen in the light, and what you have whispered behind closed doors is proclaimed from the housetops. Think and act as if there is someone looking into your inmost soul, for even if your every deed and thought is never discovered, what does that matter? You cannot fool your soul. And nothing is shut off from the sight of God. He is the witness of your soul. (Virtue21:25)

Let your example in following the Triple Path, though it be imperfect, shine as a light to others, guiding them to the safety of wisdom, virtue, and hope, just as a lighthouse guides ships on the water to safety. (Virtue 41:2)

No one finding himself in darkness takes his light and covers it with a box or hides it away in a closet. Let the light of wisdom, virtue, and hope shine through in all you do. (Parables 25)

Remember the parable of the light. Let the light of your good example shine through in all you do. (Virtue 41:3)

The young women place their candles at the front of the sanctuary and return to their seats in the congregation. The Com-

480

munal Sacrament service proceeds with musical numbers and also talks (if desired) that focus on Yule and themes of light overcoming darkness.

At the conclusion of the musical numbers and talks, the Officiant says:

The procession of our young women bringing light in the darkest time of the year symbolized the light of God and the Triple Path shining in the darkest times of our lives, always acting as a beacon of brightness to us, symbolizing our quest to seek wisdom, practice virtue, and labor with hope.

When we are children, we fear the dark, but let all of us, even we who have put an end to childish ways, still always be aware of and fear the forces of spiritual darkness: of foolishness, evil, and lazy despair.

Just as we use lights to help us make it through these long, dark winter days, let us use the Divine light of wisdom, virtue, and hope to help us fight through the spiritually dark days in our lives.

The Officiant says the Yule prayer as explained above.

The Ward is then seated and the Yule Communal Sacrament concludes as normal.

On the night of December 24, families, households, and other groups share a special dinner. The dinner is officiated by the father of the household, if he is a Church member in good standing; if he is not present or unable to act as Officiant, then a Priest or Elder who is present acts as Officiant. If the Officiant is a Priest or Elder, he wears his Stole.

Before the gathering, any Deacons in the family, household, or group (or, if no Deacons are available, then the Officiant, or any Priests or Elders present) set out special Yule Wafers (preferably imprinted with the Tricrux or other appropriate symbol) on a plate or tray, setting out only exactly enough Wafers for all those present, and Sacrament water to be blessed. If Wafers are not available, regular bread may be substituted.

At the center of the meal table is placed three unlit candles and the pot of fragrant herbs planted after Thanksgiving.

*The group sit around the meal table. The Officiant says
the following:*

We gather here to celebrate Yule, the greatest of our Western holidays. The Romans celebrated it as Saturnalia. The Christians continued many of Saturnalia's traditions, celebrating it as
Christmas. The Germanic peoples celebrated it as Yule, which
name we again use.

This holiday unites into one tapestry many threads from
all around the West. The Romans gave us the date of the celebration, on December 25, the date of the Winter Solstice on their
calendar. In that season they gave gifts, lit candles, and made merry.
The Scandinavians celebrated the return of light in the darkest
days of the year. The Germans decorated trees, burned Yule logs,
caroled, and ate Christmas hams. The English brought a focus on
family, love, and peace. The Americans gave us Santa Claus and
spread the holiday around the world. And thus together developed this most special of days, much greater as a whole than the
separate parts celebrated before.

This celebration is therefore a special emblem of the
Triple Path, which gathers the best of the beliefs, practices, and
traditions from different times and places into one greater whole.

We erect Yule trees during this time of year, which make
the shape of a triangle, that their three sides may remind us of the
Triple Path and our commitment to seek wisdom, practice virtue,
and labor with hope. Also, the tree points toward the heavens, reminding us that the Triple Path directs the course of our lives toward God. And the evergreen is one of the few plants to retain its
color in the depths of the darkness and coldness of winter, reminding us to continue laboring with hope, even at the darkest
times.

There have always been those who fight happiness and light
and joy; those who try to end our traditions, mocking us for worshiping ashes when what we are really doing is preserving fire; those
who want to sever our connection to the past and the great weight
and meaning that comes from stoking the fires of the traditions of

our fathers. (Virtue 4:11)

But our traditions have always come back from such attacks, and those who fought against them have disappeared into history. The Puritans in England and America even went so far as to outlaw Christmas!

No one calls themselves a Puritan today, but billions still celebrate Christmas.

So, let us always fight for our traditions, and for light, goodness, and happiness; and most of all let us fight to live with meaning. As was said in England hundreds of years ago in response to those who would snuff out the joy of Yule,

Let's dance and sing, and make good cheer

For Christmas comes but once a year

Now, let us partake of the Bread and Water of Private Sacrament before we eat together.

A Senior Deacon, if any are present, (or, if none are present, the Officiant, or a designated Priest or Elder who is present) kneels and offers the following prayer over the Wafers:

O God, the Eternal Father, we consecrate and sanctify this Bread to the souls of all those who partake of it, that they may eat it in remembrance of Thee and their faith, as a symbol that just as Bread sustains the body, the Triple Path sustains the soul; that they may witness unto Thee, O God, the Eternal Father, that they will always endeavor to seek wisdom, practice virtue, labor with hope, and renounce foolishness, evil, and lazy despair, that they may draw closer to Thee. Amen.

At the conclusion of the prayer, the person who offered the prayer distributes the Wafers to the Group, saying the following as each person takes a Wafer:

Merry Yule and a Happy New Year.

Once all have partaken, the same person, or another present Senior Deacon, Priest, or Elder kneels and offers the following prayer over the Water:

O God, the Eternal Father, we consecrate and sanctify this Water to the souls of all those who drink of it, that they may do so

483

in remembrance of Thee and their faith, as a symbol that just as Water quenches physical thirst, the Triple Path quenches spiritual thirst; that its clarity and purity may inspire them to purify their souls and seek clarity of thought and action; that they may witness unto Thee, O God, the Eternal Father, that they will always endeavor to seek wisdom, practice virtue, labor with hope, and renounce foolishness, evil, and lazy despair, that they may draw closer to Thee. Amen.

At the conclusion of the prayer, the person who offered the prayer distributes the water to the Group, saying the following as each person takes the water:

May God grant that we be all together again next year.

Any remaining Wafers and Water should be deconsecrated as described in the Rites of Communal and Private Sacrament.

The Officiant says:

Now let us enjoy our Yule meal. At the center of this table are some fragrant herbs planted at Thanksgiving, reminding us that even in the dark times, growth is possible. I now light these three candles, symbolizing the light of wisdom, virtue, and hope.

The Officiant lights the three candles at the center of the table. A meal of Yule ham and other traditional foods proceeds. Following the meal, the family or group lights a Yule log. They also follow their Yule traditions that night and the following day, such as caroling, setting out stockings or shoes, or opening presents.

Repentance

The Rite of Repentance should be performed privately by Confirmed individuals at least monthly, preferably weekly. A recommended time to perform it is before Communal Sacrament on Saturday nights or early Sunday mornings to allow for serious reflection and repentance before partaking of the Bread and Water of the Sacrament. No confirmed member should take the Bread and Water of the Sacrament unless he or she has performed the Rite of Repentance during the preceding month. Parents may help children perform the aspects of the Rite involving fire, but should not read their children's confessions without permission.

To prepare for the Rite, the person beforehand honestly and frankly evaluates his or her actions, thoughts, and desires, seeking to discover those sins and mistakes for which he or she needs to repent. The person should not perform the Rite until he or she has started the repentance process for these sins, by feeling remorse and ceasing whatever caused the need to repent, and beginning the process of making amends, as much as possible, for any harm caused.

If there are sins for which the person does not yet feel remorse or has not made a good faith effort to cease, then he or she should not perform the Rite until feeling remorse and truly entering onto the road of repentance.

Confession of sin is made to God. Sins that involve committing a wrong against another person should also be confessed to the wronged person Any mortal sin that might lead to excommunication must also be confessed to that person's Bishop.

Immediately before the Rite, the person sets out a pen and small piece of paper on which to write the things for which the person is repenting and how he or she intends to reform, consecrated oil to pour on the paper, a fire-safe receptacle in which to burn the paper, and something to ignite the paper, such as a match.

The person begins by saying the prayer of remorse:
O God,

May thy love and Divine light enlighten my heart, that I may remember in truth all my sins and Thy unfailing mercy.

My spirit is in anguish upon me and within me my heart is troubled exceedingly. My iniquities are as a burden heavy upon me.

Through my own sin and wickedness, I have hindered myself. I have unnecessarily worn myself out on the race that is set before me.

I have erred, and strayed from Thy ways like a lost sheep.

I have allowed the devices and desires of my heart to stray from Thee.

I have offended against Thy holy laws.

I have left undone those things which I ought to have done and I have done those things which I ought not. (Foundations 1:2)

I have blasphemed and loved vanity and sought after lies. (Wisdom 7:1)

Through the water of baptism I was reborn onto the Triple Path of seeking wisdom, practicing virtue, and laboring with hope. But, I have squandered this inheritance of my spiritual forebears, and have wandered far in a land that is waste.

Amen.

The person then performs the prayer of confession, and the writing:
Almighty God,

I confess that I have sinned, through my own grievous fault, in thought, word, and deed, in things done and left undone, especially those things I write upon this paper.

On the bottom half of the paper, the person performs the writing of sins by writing upon the paper all his or her remembered sins. The person then continues the prayer:

Therefore, O God, from these and all other sins I cannot now remember, I turn to Thee in sorrow and repentance and pray for Thy mercy on me.

I will work to change and channel my desires away from

evil and toward wisdom, virtue, and hope. I recognize that my actions shape my desires and my desires shape my actions (Foundations 3:20). I now write what I will do to work to change both, so that each reinforce the improvements I seek to make in the other. *The person performs the writing of reform, writing on the top half of the paper those things he or she will do to change both actions and desires to that he or she better avoid those sins of which he or she is guilty, the person should make achievable and measurable goals. To avoid the prying of eavesdroppers and gossipmongers, that which is written need not be long or written in explicit detail, so long as what is written is understandable to the person and serves as a sufficient reminder of that person's goals and plans for improvement.*

The person then tears off the writing of sin and places a few drops of consecrated oil on it to form the shape of the Tricrux. He or she crumples or rolls up the paper, drops it in the receptacle, and then lights it on fire (taking care to observe strict fire safety precautions, including burning the paper in a fire-safe container only in an area away from other combustible material and having close at hand something to quickly extinguish the flames, such as baking soda or a wet towel) and then continues the prayer:

As this paper is consumed by the light of these flames and is turned into smoke rising toward the heavens, may my sins be consumed by Thy Divine light that my soul be transformed, rising closer to Thee.

After the flame has expired, the person concludes the prayer of confession:

I pray that Thy divine light and mercy speedily help and deliver me, that I may truly repent and constantly speak the truth, boldly forsake and rebuke vice, and patiently suffer for the truth's sake. (Virtue 40:3)

Turn me again, I pray, and show the light of Thy countenance, that I be made whole.

I am weak. I pray for Thy forgiveness and mercy, as I show mercy to those who have wronged me. May I return again into the arms of Thy mercy, that I be restored to the blessed company of Thy faithful people, through Thy Divine mercy and light.

I firmly intend amendment of life. To make a real change, I will endeavor to do those things upon this paper, which I shall carry close with me as a reminder until I perform this Rite once again.

Amen.

The person keeps on his or her person the paper until performing again the Rite of Repentance, looking often at it to remember what he or she has resolved to do. After the person has completed the Rite again, the previous paper may be disposed of in a respectful manner.

The person then says the prayer of reform:

O God,

May all they who confess their faults and overcome them be spared.

May I hereafter live a godly, righteous, and sober life,

May my soul turn from this wickedness and live and bring forth fruits worthy of repentance.

And when I am tempted or disturbed in coming days, I pray that I sin not, but stand in awe and stillness, pondering and silent, offering right sacrifices and putting my trust in Thee. (Wisdom 7:1 and Hope 3:1.)

Even when I am wearied by the changes and chances of this fleeting world, may I repose upon Thy eternal changelessness.

I beseech thee, O God, to lighten my darkness with Thy celestial brightness, that I conquer the perils and dangers of this life. May I be a (son/daughter) of light and banish deeds of darkness.

May there be a new, clean heart and right spirit in me.

Amen.

The person disposes of the ashes, cleans the area, and puts away the items used to perform the Rite.

Private Sacrament

Private Sacrament may be performed at any time, but at least should be performed once a week by those baptized and confirmed. It is performed preferably on Wednesday evening, in the home or other similar private space, either by an individual, or a Group of a family or household, or a few acquaintances and friends. Those wishing to perform it more than once a week may do so, but taking care to remember the importance of moderation.

When performed by an individual, the individual administers the Rite by themself. In a Group, a Priest or Elder in good standing, if present, should administer the Rite. In a family, this is generally the father; in other Groups, the Priest or Elder who is hosting will generally Officiate. If there is no Priest or Elder, a Senior Deacon may act as Officiant. If no Elders, Priests, or Deacons are available, then the Rite should be administered only by solitary individuals. Priests or Elders officiating should wear their Stole. Anyone not a Priest or Elder should never wear a Stole while performing the Rite. When the Rite is administered by a single individual, he or she performs the Officiant part and the Group responses and adjusts plural language of address to the singular.

For the parts of the service where Group members jointly respond or pray with the Officiant, the Reader for the day may lead and coordinate the Group in its responses. The members of the Group may also bring with them copies of this book to which they may refer to read the proper responses and prayers.

The Officiant, or any Deacons part of the Group, should have set out gluten free bread and water in Sacrament cups before the start of the meeting.

The meeting should begin with a short welcome from the Officiant. Following the Officiant's welcome, the Group may sing a hymn, if desired. Someone previously invited by the Officiant offers an opening prayer, after which the Officiant says:

Praise be to God. And blessed be the Congregation of the faithful of the Triple Path, now and forever. Amen.

The Group repeats:

Amen.

The Officiant continues:

Brothers and Sisters, we meet together today to render thanks to God for the great benefits we have received at His hands, to set forth His most worthy praise, to hear the most holy word, and to seek those things which are requisite and necessary, as well for the body as the soul. Wherefore, I pray and beseech you, let us remember:

There is much we do not know and there is much we will never know. (Wisdom 5:1)

We look at wisdom, yet do not see it; we hear it, yet do not listen to it; we try to grasp it, yet cannot get hold of it; we write about it, yet cannot describe it. (Wisdom 4:1)

We think and speak about virtue, yet do not practice it.

Officiant and Group respond:

But we cannot fool our souls. (Virtue 1:14; 6:5; 21:25)

Officiant continues:

It is a disease of the soul to think ourselves wise and virtuous when we are not. Recognizing this as a disease is the first step to curing it. (Wisdom 4:11)

Wisdom, virtue, and hope will transform us, allowing us to see more of our own faults. Let us recognize them, conquer them, and, by the grace of God, reform ourselves. (Foundations 1:22)

The Officiant and Group respond:

We know we are limited in an infinite number of ways; yet through God's grace and the Triple Path, let us always remember that the different manners in which we might seek wisdom, practice virtue, and labor with hope are still limitless. (Foundations 1:9)

Officiant continues:

Brothers and Sisters, let us always acknowledge and confess our manifold sins and wickedness and neither dissemble nor cloak them before the face of Almighty God, our heavenly Father; but confess them with a humble, lowly, penitent, and obedient heart. Let us pause to think on them and confess them in our hearts to God and ourselves.

Everyone bows their head in contemplation during a long silent pause.

The Officiant says;

I beseech you, as many as are here present, after this meeting to also confess these things to whomever you may have wronged, and to repent of your sins.

Now, kneel and accompany me with a pure heart, and humble voice, unto the throne of heavenly grace and pray with me:

The Officiant and the Group kneel and pray together:

O God, we are in need of mercy.

We are foolish, ignorant, and unvirtuous.

We are vain and need more humility.

We are in need of greater wisdom and more virtue.

We hope to become ever more like Thee, and we again resolve to strive after this. (Parables 46)

Amen.

The Group remains kneeling while they prepare for the administration of the Bread and Water of the Sacrament. Only those who have been Baptized and are in good standing in the Church and those who are children under eight years of age who have been Named and Dedicated should partake of them. The Officiant and Deacons should ensure that the Bread and Water is only offered to those who may partake.

The Group sings another hymn, if desired, during which the Officiant or any Deacons (or Priests or Elders) present prepare the Sacrament Bread by breaking it, with clean hands, into pieces to be distributed to the Group. A Senior Deacon, Priest or Elder offers the following prayer over the Bread:

O God, the Eternal Father, we consecrate and sanctify this Bread to the souls of all those who partake of it, that they may eat it in remembrance of Thee and their faith, as a symbol that just as

Bread sustains the body, the Triple Path sustains the soul; that they may witness unto Thee, O God, the Eternal Father, that they will always endeavor to seek wisdom, practice virtue, labor with hope, and renounce foolishness, evil, and lazy despair, that they may draw closer to Thee. Amen.

At the conclusion of the prayer, the Officiant or the Deacons (or Priests or Elders) distribute the bread to the Group. Once all have partaken, the Officiant, a Senior Deacon, Priest, or Elder offers the following prayer over the Water:

O God, the Eternal Father, we consecrate and sanctify this Water to the souls of all those who drink of it, that they may do so in remembrance of Thee and their faith, as a symbol that just as Water quenches physical thirst, the Triple Path quenches spiritual thirst; that its clarity and purity may inspire them to purify their souls and seek clarity of thought and action; that they may witness unto Thee, O God, the Eternal Father, that they will always endeavor to seek wisdom, practice virtue, labor with hope, and renounce foolishness, evil, and lazy despair, that they may draw closer to Thee. Amen.

At the conclusion of the prayer, the Officiant, Deacons, Priests, or Elders distribute the Water to the Group.

Once all have drunk the Water, all are seated. A member of the Group previously invited by the Officiant reads a short passage from this book or the Codex *selected in consultation with the Officiant and related to the theme, if any, of the meeting. The passage should generally not be more than two pages. In general, preference should be given to children and youth as Readers.*

The Reader says:

And now a Reading from the book of the Triple Path (*or* the Codex).

The Reader reads the passage he or she has selected.

If so desired, the Group may also recite the Creed. If so, the Reader says:

Please stand and recite with me the Creed.

The Group stands and jointly recites the Creed.

The Officiant, or someone else who has been invited to speak, may say a few short words about some subject related to the Triple Path or other thoughts of a spiritual nature.

After the speaker's remarks have concluded (or, if there was no speaker, after the Reading or the Creed), the Officiant says:

Let us pause to think on the many things in our lives for which we would be grateful if we did not have them and had only newly received them.

Everyone bows their head in contemplation during a long silent pause.

(The Prayer of Thanksgiving may be omitted in Private Sacrament. If it will be recited, then the following ten paragraphs are performed.)

The Officiant says:

Now, Brothers and Sisters, please be upstanding, and let us pray.

All in the Group stand, while the Officiant prays, his arms upraised:

O God, we give thanks for all the good things in our lives, which come by Thy grace. We give thanks for deliverance from afflictions and tribulations. We give thanks for kindness and affection and love, and any teaching that is sweet and plain that guides us toward wisdom, leads us to practice virtue, or inspires us to labor with hope. We rejoice in the Divine illumination that flows into us from following the Triple Path.

We have known hardship and sorrow; we are grateful for the lessons we learned from them. But we dwell not on our misfortunes, and instead marvel at all the great blessings in our lives.

We give thanks for family, food, clothing, shelter, and the simple joys of life, and we pray for all those who find these lacking.

We are grateful for thought and conscience, for the freedom to act and not be acted upon, and for the consequences that naturally flow from our actions.

We give thanks for the spark of Thy divinity we feel in our best moments and the chance to do better after we have passed through our worst.

May we be preserved on the Triple Path and protected from faltering or stumbling through life. We here resolve again to move forward with firmness on the Triple Path, always, and progress toward a brighter day.

Amen.

Now, Brothers and Sisters, let us kneel in silence, and remember God's presence with us now.

All kneel. After a moment of silence for reflection and divine communion, the Officiant continues:

Brothers and Sisters, as we renew our commitment to God and the Triple Path, I beseech you again to accompany me with a pure heart, and humble voice, unto the throne of heavenly grace and pray:

All continue kneeling and pray together:

O God,

We pray that, by Thy grace:

In our seeking, we find wisdom;

In our desires and actions, we practice virtue, with a grateful heart and love for others;

In our labors, we cultivate hope and the fortitude to continue laboring; and

We keep ourselves from entering into temptation or falling prey to evil desires. (Wisdom 6:3)

Our complete trust we reserve only for Thee. (Hope 13:1)

We will seek to turn our weaknesses into strengths, (Wisdom 5:14)

And let the Triple Path mold and construct our souls; order our life; guide our conduct; and show us what we should do and what we should leave undone. We will follow the course it shows us when we waver amid uncertainty. (Foundations 1:2)

Amen.

The Officiant says:

It is profitable to consider not only our weaknesses, but

also our strengths. For, in our moments of trial and suffering we find hope and encouragement by remembering our times of triumph. Let us pause to think on our recent successes—those times when we diligently sought wisdom, practiced virtue, or labored with hope.

Everyone bows their head in contemplation during a long silent pause.

The Officiant says:

Brothers and sisters, please be seated.

The Group and Officiant are seated.

The Group sings a final hymn, if desired, and ends with a prayer offered by someone previously invited by the Officiant.

If appropriate for the circumstances and the ages of the group members, the Group may then have a period of silence for prayer and meditation.

If the Group is a family, then they should have a lesson or activity of a spiritual nature or designed to build family unity. If timing makes it impractical to do this following Private Sacrament, they should do it at some other time during the week.

If there is any remaining unconsumed Bread or Water that was blessed, then it should be deconsecrated. To do so, a Deacon, Priest, or Elder kneels before the Bread (and/or Water) and offers the following prayer:

O God,

By the authority of the Congregation of the Faithful of the Triple Path and in my office as a(n) (say the name of the person's office), I deconsecrate this bread (and/or water) so that it return to secular use.

Amen.

The bread and water should then be disposed of in a respectful manner.

Consecration of Oil

Only Priests and Elders may consecrate oil. Pure extra virgin olive oil should be used, to which is added a few drops of clove oil and sandalwood oil. The person consecrating the oil should be dressed in his Stole. He holds the oil in his hands in an open container and says the following prayer:

O God,

By the authority of the Congregation of the Faithful of the Triple Path and in my office as a(n) Priest (or Elder), I consecrate this oil and set it apart for anointing and blessing.

Amen.

After the consecration of the oil, it should not be used for internal consumption. If it goes rancid or for any other reason will no longer be used for sacred purposes, it should be deconsecrated.

To deconsecrate the oil, a Priest or Elder holds the open container of oil in his hands and offers the following prayer:

O God,

By the authority of the Congregation of the Faithful of the Triple Path and in my office as a(n) Priest (or Elder), I deconsecrate this oil so that it return to secular use.

Amen.

The oil should then be disposed of (and not consumed) in a respectful manner.

Consecration of Stoles

Only Priests and Elders may consecrate Stoles. A regular personal stole is made of dark red fabric with two embroidered gold or yellow Tricruxes placed so that when the Stole is worn one Tricrux is on each side at about chest level. At the bottom on each side is a gold or yellow Trimonvia. The Stole of a Priest has no border. The Stole of an Elder has a yellow or gold border. A Stole may include other additional appropriate decorative or symbolic elements as defined by local custom and practice.

The person who will use a personal Stole should consecrate it personally, even if it has been consecrated before.

The Ward should keep a set of Stoles in the special liturgical colors for feasts. The Bishop or one of the Vice-Bishops consecrate them. The Officiant for the day does not need to reconsecrate an already-consecrated Ward Stole of special liturgical color.

To perform the consecration, a Priest or Elder places a drop of consecrated oil on the inside of the stole at the place where the Stole hangs around the neck. He holds the Stole up, draping it across his hands and says the following prayer:

O God,

By the authority of the Congregation of the Faithful of the Triple Path and in my office as a(n) Priest (or Elder), I consecrate this Stole to be worn for Officiating and performing Rites.

Amen.

The Stole is now consecrated.

The same procedure should be followed to consecrate the Cords of Bishops, Archbishops, and Cardinals, but substituting the word "these Cords" for "this Stole."

Stoles should be worn by Priests and Elders when Officiating or performing any Rite or Feast, unless the instructions for a Rite or Feast specifically say it should not be worn.

A Stole should never touch the ground. If it does, it must be reconsecrated before being used again.

When a Stole is no longer fit for use, it should be deconsecrated and then disposed of respectfully. To deconsecrate it, a Priest or Elder holds the Stole up, draping it across his hands and says the following prayer:

O God,

By the authority of the Congregation of the Faithful of the Triple Path and in my office as a(n) Priest (or Elder), I deconsecrate this Stole so that it return to secular use.

Amen.

The Stole should then be disposed of in a respectful manner.

Anointing and Blessing of the Sick

The Anointing and Blessing of the Sick is done by Priests or Elders. It is conducted in two parts: the Anointing and the Blessing. If at least two people are available to conduct the Rite, then one conducts the Anointing and another performs the Blessing. One person may perform both parts, if no other Priests or Elders are available. Anyone performing an Anointing or Blessing should be dressed in his Stole, unless the exigencies of the circumstance make that impossible. When they enter the house or place to perform the blessing, they shall say:

Peace be to this house (or place), and to all that dwell in it.

When they come into the sick person's presence, they shall pray together, saying:

Let us pray.

O God, we are in need of mercy.

We are foolish, ignorant, and unvirtuous.

We are vain and need more humility.

We are in need of greater wisdom and more virtue.

We hope to become ever more like Thee, and we again resolve to strive after this. (Parables 46)

Amen.

To perform the anointing, The Anointer places a small amount of consecrated oil on his finger and says:

(State the person's full name), by the authority of the Congregation of the Faithful of the Triple Path and in my office as a(n) Priest (or Elder), I anoint you with Consecrated Oil, in the name of God, and of wisdom, virtue, and hope.

Amen.

As he speaks, the Anointer uses his finger to anoint the person being blessed with Consecrated Oil on the forehead, making the form of the Tricrux with the oil, forming one of each of the three prongs as he says each of the words "wisdom", "virtue", and "hope".

The person performing the blessing then places his hands lightly on the head of the person. Any other Priests or Elders present may place their hands on the person's head as well. The person performing the blessing then calls the person by his or her full name and says:

By the authority of the Congregation of the Faithful of the Triple Path and in my office as a(n) Priest (or Elder), I seal the anointing and bless you.

The person performing the blessing utters words of blessing and comfort as he feels inspired to speak, taking care not to overstep the bounds of prudence or propriety. He then closes by saying:

Amen.

The person performing the blessing then prays:

O God,

We ask for Thy grace to this, Thy servant, who is grieved with sickness.

We hope that (he/she) may be sanctified that the sense of (his/her) weakness may add strength to (his/her) faith, and seriousness to (his/her) repentance: That, if it shall be Thy good pleasure to restore (him/her) to (his/her) former health, (he/she) may lead the residue of (his/her) life in faith, following Thee and the Triple Path in Thy fear, that, after this painful life ended, (he/she) may dwell with Thee.

Amen.

If appropriate to the situation, and if the sick person desires it, the Priest or Elder may also administer the Bread and Water of the Sacrament to the sick person, either practicing the full Rite of Private Sacrament, or only pronouncing the prayers over the Bread and Water.

If the full Rite of Private Sacrament is not administered, then they conclude their visit by praying together, saying:

Let us pray.

O God,

We pray that, by Thy grace:

In our seeking, we find wisdom;

In our desires and actions, we practice virtue, with a grateful heart and love for others;

In our labors, we cultivate hope and the fortitude to continue laboring; and

We keep ourselves from entering into temptation or falling prey to evil desires. (Wisdom 6:3)

Our complete trust we reserve only for Thee. (Hope 13:1)

We will seek to turn our weaknesses into strengths, (Wisdom 5:14)

And let the Triple Path mold and construct our souls; order our life; guide our conduct; and show us what we should do and what we should leave undone. We will follow the course it shows us when we waver amid uncertainty. (Foundations 1:2)

Amen.

Any remaining Bread and Water should be deconsecrated as described in the Rites of Communal and Private Sacrament.

Father's Blessing

A Father's Blessing is performed at times of transition, anxiety, or other similar periods when comfort and counsel are needed or wanted. A Father's Blessing shall be performed by a person's father. If the father is deceased or cannot be present, the Godfather or other selected man of similar significance performs instead a Blessing of Comfort and Counsel.

A Father's Blessing is performed in private, in the presence of family or close friends. A father performing a blessing who is a Priest or Elder wears his Stole while performing the Rite. The Father begins the Rite by saying:

Let us pray.

O God, we are in need of mercy.

We are foolish, ignorant, and unvirtuous.

We are vain and need more humility.

We are in need of greater wisdom and more virtue.

We hope to become ever more like Thee, and we again resolve to strive after this. (Parables 46)

Amen.

To perform the anointing, The father places a small amount of consecrated oil on his finger and says:

(State the person's full name), as your Father, I anoint you with Consecrated Oil, in the name of God, and of wisdom, virtue, and hope.

Amen.

As he speaks, the father uses his finger to anoint his child with Consecrated Oil on the forehead, making the form of the Tricrux with the oil, forming one of each of the three prongs as he says each of the words "wisdom", "virtue", and "hope".

The father then places his hands lightly on the head his child and says:

I place my hands on your head to pronounce upon you a

Father's Blessing of comfort and counsel.

The father then pronounces words of counsel, comfort, and blessing as he feels inspired to speak, taking care not to overstep the bounds of prudence or propriety. He then closes by saying:

Amen.

If appropriate to the situation, and if the child or family desires it, the Bread and Water of the Sacrament may also be administered, either practicing the full Rite of Private Sacrament, or only pronouncing the prayers over the Bread and Water.

If the full Rite of Private Sacrament is not administered, then they conclude the blessing by praying together, saying:

Let us pray.

O God,

We pray that, by Thy grace:

In our seeking, we find wisdom;

In our desires and actions, we practice virtue, with a grateful heart and love for others;

In our labors, we cultivate hope and the fortitude to continue laboring; and

We keep ourselves from entering into temptation or falling prey to evil desires. (Wisdom 6:3)

Our complete trust we reserve only for Thee. (Hope 13:1)

We will seek to turn our weaknesses into strengths, (Wisdom 5:14)

And let the Triple Path mold and construct our souls; order our life; guide our conduct; and show us what we should do and what we should leave undone. We will follow the course it shows us when we waver amid uncertainty. (Foundations 1:2)

Amen.

Any remaining Bread and Water should be deconsecrated as described in the Rites of Communal and Private Sacrament.

Blessing of Counsel and Comfort

A Blessing of Counsel and Comfort is performed at times of transition, anxiety, or other similar periods when comfort and counsel are needed. It is performed at the request of the person to be blessed. It is performed by a Priest or Elder in good standing in the Church. Anyone performing an Anointing or Blessing should be dressed in his Stole, unless the exigencies of the circumstance make that impossible. It is performed in private, in the presence of family or close friends. The Officiant begins the Rite by saying,

Let us pray.

O God, we are in need of mercy.

We are foolish, ignorant, and unvirtuous.

We are vain and need more humility.

We are in need of greater wisdom and more virtue.

We hope to become ever more like Thee, and we again resolve to strive after this. (Parables 46)

Amen.

To perform the anointing, The Officiant places a small amount of consecrated oil on his finger and says:

(State the person's full name), by the authority of the Congregation of the Faithful of the Triple Path and in my office as a(n) Priest (or Elder), I anoint you with Consecrated Oil, in the name of God, and of wisdom, virtue, and hope.

Amen.

As he speaks, the Anointer uses his finger to anoint the person being blessed with Consecrated Oil on the forehead, making the form of the Tricrux with the oil, forming one of each of the three prongs as he says each of the words "wisdom", "virtue", and "hope".

The Officiant places his hands on the head of the person receiving the blessing and says:

507

(State the person's full name), by the authority of the Congregation of the Faithful of the Triple Path and in my office as a(n) Priest (or Elder), I place my hands seal the anointing and pronounce upon you a Blessing of Comfort and Counsel.

The Officiant then pronounces words of counsel, comfort, and blessing as he feels inspired to speak, taking care not to overstep the bounds of prudence or propriety. He then closes by saying:
Amen.

If appropriate to the situation, and if the person being blessed desires it, the Officiant may administer the Bread and Water of the Sacrament, either practicing the full Rite of Private Sacrament, or only pronouncing the prayers over the Bread and Water.

If the full Rite of Private Sacrament is not administered, then they conclude the blessing by praying together, saying:
Let us pray.

O God,

We pray that, by Thy grace:

In our seeking, we find wisdom;

In our desires and actions, we practice virtue, with a grateful heart and love for others;

In our labors, we cultivate hope and the fortitude to continue laboring; and

We keep ourselves from entering into temptation or falling prey to evil desires. (Wisdom 6:3)

Our complete trust we reserve only for Thee. (Hope 13:1)

We will seek to turn our weaknesses into strengths, (Wisdom 5:14)

And let the Triple Path mold and construct our souls; order our life; guide our conduct; and show us what we should do and what we should leave undone. We will follow the course it shows us when we waver amid uncertainty. (Foundations 1:2)

Amen.

Any remaining Bread and Water should be deconsecrated as described in the Rites of Communal and Private Sacrament.

Dedication of Homes

This Rite is usually performed by the father when a family moves into a new home and at every subsequent Feast of the New Year. If the father is not available or is unable to perform the Rite, the head of the household may perform it. If the father or head of household is a Priest or Elder, he wears his Stole while performing the Rite.

Before the Rite, the family should either first obtain some consecrated chalk from the Ward or consecrate a piece of chalk before performing the ritual. To consecrate the chalk, a Deacon, Priest or Elder holds the chalk, or container of chalk, in his hands and offers the following prayer:

O God,

By the authority of the Congregation of the Faithful of the Triple Path and in my office as a(n) (say the name of the person's office), I consecrate this chalk and set it apart for the Dedication of Homes in this year of (say the present year).

Amen.

To perform the Rite, the family kneels in a typical place of gathering in their new home. The person performing the Rite says the following prayer:

O God,

We celebrate this place of dwelling for our family.

We dedicate it as a place of love, joy, happiness, laughter, and thanksgiving.

We dedicate it as a holy place of worship to Thee, where we might find safety from the world, and grow in our practice of the Triple Path.

The person performing the Rite then pronounces whatever words the person feels inspired to say, taking care not to overstep the bounds of prudence or propriety. The person then closes by saying:

Amen.

The family then goes to the front door of the house where they chalk the door with consecrated chalk. To chalk the door, they write in the upper left outer corner of the door the first two digits of the year, then a star or sun (symbolizing the Divine light of God in our lives), then the letter "W" (signifying Wisdom), then a Tricrux, then the letter "V" (signifying Virtue), then a Tricrux, then the letter "H" (signifying Hope), then a Tricrux, and then the last two digits of the year. Thus, if the year were 2019, the family would write the following in the upper left outer corner of the door:

$$20^*W\Upsilon V\Upsilon H\Upsilon 19$$

If the door had been previously chalked and the chalk remain on the door, they erase the prior markings before chalking the door again.

Following the chalking, the family should do one of three things with the chalk: 1) return it to the Ward for storage and future use; 2) store it in a dignified manner in their house for future use; or 3) deconsecrate it.

To deconsecrate the chalk, a Senior Deacon, Priest or Elder holds the chalk, or container of chalk, in his hands and offers the following prayer:

O God,

By the authority of the Congregation of the Faithful of the Triple Path and in my office as a(n) (say the name of the person's office), I deconsecrate this chalk so that it return to secular use.

Amen.

The chalk should then be disposed of in a respectful manner.

Naming and Dedication of Infants

Newborn infants should be Named and Dedicated to the Triple Path before the congregation of the child's parents' Ward, generally during a Fast and Testimony Communal Sacrament after the Reading and Creed and before the time for testimonies. The Rite may also be performed for older infants and children under the age of 8 who have not already been Named and Dedicated. If it is done in a Ward other than the parents' normal Ward, it should be done only with the consent of both Wards' Bishops. Under exceptional circumstances, and only upon authorization of the Bishop, the Naming and Dedication may take place at home, in which event special care must be taken to see that the proper records are made.

The Rite of Naming and Dedication should only be held for children having at least one parent who has been Baptized, Confirmed, and is in good standing in the Church. The blessing of the child at the end of the Rite may only be performed by the father if the father has been Baptized, Confirmed, Ordained, and Initiated, and is in good standing in the Church. Otherwise, the Godfather performs the blessing. A parent does not qualify as being in good standing in the Church if the baby was born out of wedlock, unless and until the parent manifests true, credible, and lasting repentance.

For every child to be Named and Dedicated, there shall be one Godfather and one Godmother. The Godparents shall be persons who have been Baptized, Confirmed, Initiated, and are in good standing in the Church, and who will faithfully fulfill their responsibilities both by their care for the child committed to their charge and by the example of their own godly living.

The Officiant for the Rite shall be a Priest or Elder in good standing in the Church, and generally a close relative or friend of the parents, but may not be the father or Godfather if the father

511

or Godfather will pronounce the blessing on the child. The Officiant and the person performing the blessing each wear his Stole while performing the Rite.

The Officiant begins by saying:

Brothers and Sisters, on the joyous occasion of welcoming this new child into the Earth, I beseech you to call upon God the Father, that this child may be steadfast in faith, joyful through hope, and rooted in charity, and so pass the waves of this troublesome world. That he be received into this holy Church, and be made a lively member of the same.

The Officiant speaks to the child's Parent or Parents who are in good standing in the Church, saying:

You have brought this child here to be named before the congregation and dedicated to the Triple Path. You have already committed to renounce foolishness, evil, and lazy despair, to follow God and the Triple Path and count yourself members of the Congregation of the Faithful of the Triple Path. If this child is to reach the fullest possible measure of wisdom, virtue, and hope, then this child must also do the same.

And I charge and admonish you most solemnly that you must respond truthfully and sincerely, only responding with the Candidate's words for this Rite if they most surely and accurately represent your mind as well.

So I ask you, do you promise before God, this Ward (or Branch), and the whole of this Church, to dedicate this child to God and the Triple Path, to love and nurture (him/her), to care for (his/her) physical and spiritual needs, to protect (him/her) from harm and evil influences, and to instruct (him/her) in the Triple Path?

The Parent(s) respond:

We do.

The Officiant speaks to the Godfather and Godmother:

You have come here to support this child and (his/her) parents in their commitment to the Triple Path. You also have already committed to renounce foolishness, evil, and lazy despair, to follow God and the Triple Path and count yourself members of the Congregation of the Faithful of the Triple Path. I would remind you also that if this child is to reach the fullest possible measure of wisdom, virtue, and hope, then this child must also do the same.

And I charge and admonish you most solemnly that you must respond truthfully and sincerely, only responding with the Candidate's words for this Rite if they most surely and accurately represent your mind as well.

So I ask you also, do you promise before God, this Ward (or Branch), and the whole of this Church, to dedicate this child to God and the Triple Path, to support (his/her) parents as they raise (him/her), to love and nurture this child, to care for (his/her) physical and spiritual needs, to protect (him/her) from harm and evil influences, and to instruct (him/her) in the Triple Path?

Godparents respond:

We do.

The Officiant continues, addressing the parents and god-parents:

Now all of you, and all those previously invited, take this child in your hands while the Father (or Godfather) pronounces a name and a blessing upon (him/her).

Any other persons previously invited come forward and help take the child in their hands.

The child's father (or Godfather) prays, addressing the child:

In my capacity as your Father (or Godfather), and by the authority of the Congregation of the Faithful of the Triple Path and in my office as a(n) Priest (or Elder), I anoint you with Consecrated Oil, dedicating you to God and the Triple Path, and to seeking wisdom, practicing virtue, and laboring with hope.

As he speaks, the father (or Godfather) uses his finger to anoint the child with Consecrated Oil on the forehead, making the form of the Tricrux with the oil, forming one of each of the three prongs as he says each of the words "wisdom", "virtue", and "hope".

The father (or Godfather) continues, saying:

We also give you a name and bless you. The name which you shall be known in life and on the records of this Church is, (the Father or Godfather pronounces the full name).

The father or Godfather then pronounces words of blessing as he feels inspired to speak, taking care not to overstep the bounds of prudence or propriety. He closes by saying:

Amen.

Following the Rite, the Officiant, Parents, and Godparents sign a certificate witnessing and memorializing the completion of the Rite, a record of which is to be kept by the Church and the certificate being given to the parents.

Baptism

All Candidates for Baptism must believe in God, affirm their support for all aspects of this book and the Creed, and also demonstrate through their actions their commitment to the Creed and the principles of the Triple Path. In particular, they must have demonstrated their commitment by regularly attending Church for at least one year prior to Baptism, actively participating in their Ward, and diligently following the Rites, Feasts, observances, and practices of Creeds 10 through 13 to the extent possible for their membership status. Before a Candidate is accepted for Baptism, the Bishop and the Vice-Bishops should verify that the Candidate understands and fulfills these requirements and also the commitments the Candidate is assuming by being baptized. For adults, this may usually be done through an interview with either the Bishop or one of the Vice-Bishops. For children who are members of the Ward, an interview is usually not necessary.

Children must be at least eight years old to be Baptized. They usually should be Baptized as soon after their eighth birthday as possible. If feasible, each Ward should make a baptismal font available year round for baptisms, though any body of water large enough to immerse the Candidate may be used.

Any person accepted by the Bishop and Vice-Bishops, as qualifying for Baptism must also be approved by the Qualified Voters of the Ward. His or her name must be published and announced in the Ward for three consecutive Sundays during Communal Sacrament. During the announcements before the start of the meeting, the Officiant for that meeting shall say the following, if the Candidate is a child:

(Candidate) desires to be Baptized and has been found qualified by the Bishop and Vice-Bishops, but the Qualified Voters of the Ward must also approve. All Qualified Voters who are in favor, please make it known by raising your right hand.

If the Candidate is an adult, then the Officiant says the following:

(Candidate) desires to be Baptized and Confirmed and has been found qualified by the Bishop and Vice-Bishops, but the Qualified Voters of the Ward must also approve. All Qualified Voters who are in favor, please make it known by raising your right hand.

For either a child or adult, the Officiant pauses to allow the Qualified Voters in the Ward to vote, then continues:

If any of you know cause, or just impediment, why (he/she) should not be Baptized, you are to declare it privately to the Bishop and the Vice-Bishops after this meeting. This is the first (second, or third) time of asking.

If anyone dissents, the Bishop and Vice-Bishops deal with the objections appropriately and with discretion, in conformity with this book, the Creed, the Doctrines of the Church, and Church traditions, standards, and principles.

Once the proposed Baptism has been presented to the Ward three times, and any concerns resolved, then the Baptism may proceed on the first subsequent day when reasonably possible. Baptisms generally should be conducted on Saturdays.

Both the Baptizer and Candidate, should be appropriately dressed, preferably wearing white clothing. The Baptizer does not wear his Stole. Special care should be taken to see that their clothing will remain modest, even when wet.

Bishops and Vice-Bishops should give special attention to all seven-year-old children in the ward and see that they are prepared for and taught about baptism by their parents and Church teachers.

Two people conduct the Rite: the Baptizer and the Officiant. In coordination with the Bishop and Arch-Bishops, adult Candidates will choose their own Officiant and Baptizer, who each should be a Priest or Elder in good standing in the Church. Children will choose in coordination with their parents and the Bishop and the Vice-Bishops. Usually, a child should be baptized by his or her father if the father is a Priest or Elder in good standing. Other-

wise, a child should be baptized by his or her Godfather, or if he is not available, a close relative or family friend.

The Officiant wears his Stole during the Rite. Throughout the service, the Officiant should refer to the Candidate to be Baptized by name whenever the text refers to "Candidate" in parentheses. The Candidate should work to memorize ahead of time his or her required responses during the Rite. However, an Escort of the same sex as the Candidate who is the Candidate's Godfather, Godmother, or other designated Church member in good standing, should stand with the Candidate and prompt the Candidate what to say if he or she requires assistance. The Baptizer should be seated at the front, to the side of the Officiant.

The baptismal service should begin with a hymn and prayer, after which the Officiant welcomes those attending and then says:

Let us call upon God and devoutly give thanks to Him, and pray,

Almighty God,

We give humble thanks, for the Triple Path and the opportunity to follow it every day. May we grow ever stronger before Thee in wisdom, virtue, and hope. Give your Divine light to (Candidate) that (he/she) may be reborn as a traveler on the Triple Path and to (him/her) and all of us that we may renounce foolishness, evil, and lazy despair, but ever faithfully walk the Triple Path.

Amen.

Brothers and Sisters, we come together to witness (Candidate) enter the waters of holy Baptism, being buried to the ways of the world and reborn as a new traveler on the Triple Path.

The Officiant addresses the Candidate.

(Candidate), arise and stand before me.

The Candidate stands in front of the Officiant. The Escort accompanies the Candidate, standing to his or her side.

The Officiant says:

I charge and admonish you most solemnly that you must

respond truthfully and sincerely, only responding with the Candidate's words for this Rite if they most surely and accurately represent your mind as well.

(Candidate) for what purpose are you here?

The Candidate answers:

To be baptized, to symbolically die and be reborn as a follower of the Triple Path.

The Officiant asks:

Do you believe in God?

The Candidate answers:

I do.

The Officiant asks:

Do you renounce foolishness, evil, and lazy despair?

The Candidate answers:

I renounce them all.

The Officiant asks:

Will you endeavor to follow God and the Triple Path, to seek wisdom, practice virtue, and labor with hope all the rest of your days?

The Candidate answers:

I will.

The Officiant asks:

Will you count yourself a member of the Congregation of the Faithful of the Triple Path?

The Candidate answers:

I will.

The Officiant asks:

Will you endeavor to regularly attend Church, participate in your Ward, and diligently follow the Rites, Feasts, observances, and practices set out in our Creed?

The Candidate answers:

I will.

The Officiant says:

Then I find you worthy for baptism. Will you be baptized in this faith?

The Candidate answers:
That is my desire.
The Officiant says:
Let us pray.

O merciful God

We pray that this person may be buried to (his/her) previous life, that (he/she) may be raised up to a new life of wisdom, virtue, and hope.

We pray that (he/she) may have power and strength to endure to the end on the Triple Path and to triumph against the world and the flesh.

We pray that (he/she) may also be endowed with heavenly light and everlastingly rewarded, through Thy mercy.

Amen.

Then shall the Baptizer take the Candidate down into the water, raising his right arm to the square, holding the Candidate's right hand in his left hand, saying:

(The Candidate's full name), by the authority of the Congregation of the Faithful of the Triple Path and in my office as a(n) Priest (or Elder), I Baptize you in the name of God and of wisdom and of virtue and of hope.

Amen.

The person performing the baptism then immerses the Candidate completely in the water, placing his right hand high on the Candidate's back to support the Candidate's weight while being lowered into the water and to lift the Candidate out of the water again, and using his left hand to guide the Candidate's right hand to the nose to plug it while being immersed.

Following the Baptism, the Baptizer and Candidate each privately change out of their wet clothes while the group sings hymns. Once the Baptizer and Candidate are ready, then one or two persons who have been previously invited give talks of a spiritual nature related to the Triple Path or Baptism. At the close, those present sing a hymn and someone who was previously invited offers a closing prayer.

BAPTISM

Following the Rite, the Officiant, Baptizer, and Escort sign a certificate witnessing and memorializing the completion of the Rite, a record of which is to be kept by the Church, with the certificate being given to the Candidate.

Confirmation

All Candidates for Confirmation must have fulfilled the same requirements as those for Baptism. All Candidates for Confirmation must believe in God, affirm their support for all aspects of this book and the Creed, and also demonstrate through their actions their commitment to the Creed and the principles of the Triple Path. In particular, they must have demonstrated their commitment by regularly attending Church for at least one year prior to Confirmation, actively participating in their Ward, and diligently following the Rites, Feasts, observances, and practices of Creeds 10 through 13 to the extent possible for their membership status. The Candidate should have memorized the Triple Path Creed prior to confirmation.

Before a Candidate is accepted for Confirmation, the Bishop and the Vice-Bishops should verify that the Candidate understands and fulfills these requirements and also the commitments the Candidate is assuming by being Confirmed. For adults, this may usually be done through an interview with either the Bishop or one of the Vice-Bishops (if the adult is to be Confirmed in conjunction with Baptism, the evaluation and interview should be conducted at the same time as that done for Baptism). For youth who are members of the Ward, an interview is not required.

Adults should be confirmed on the first Fast and Testimony Sunday following their Baptism. Children should be confirmed as soon as possible after their twelfth birthday.

Any person accepted by the Bishop and Vice-Bishops, as qualifying for Confirmation must also be approved by the Qualified Voters of the Ward (if the Candidate is an adult being Confirmed in conjunction with Baptism and he or she was already approved for both Baptism and Confirmation, the Candidate does not need to be separately presented for approval again). His or her name must be published and announced in the Ward for three

521

consecutive Sundays during Communal Sacrament. *During the announcements before the start of the meeting, the Officiant for that meeting shall say the following:*

(Candidate) desires to be Confirmed and has been found qualified by the Bishop and Vice-Bishops, but the Qualified Voters of the Ward must also approve. All Qualified Voters who are in favor, please make it known by raising your right hand.

The Officiant pauses to allow the Qualified Voters in the Ward to vote, then continues:

If any of you know cause, or just impediment, why (he/she) should not be Confirmed, you are to declare it privately to the Bishop and the Vice-Bishops after this meeting. This is the first (second, or third) time of asking.

If anyone dissents, the Bishop and Vice-Bishops deal with the objections appropriately and with discretion, in conformity with this book, the Creed, the Doctrines of the Church, and Church traditions, standards, and principles.

The Candidate should be Confirmed following the third time of asking on the next appropriate Communal Sacrament, usually in a Fast and Testimony Sunday. The Confirmation takes place just after the Creed (or Reading, if not done on a Fast and Testimony Sunday).

Two people conduct the Rite: the Officiant and the Anointer. Both the Officiant and the Anointer should be dressed in their Stoles. In coordination with the ward's Bishop and the Vice-Bishops, adult Candidates will choose their own Officiant and Anointer, who each should be a Priest or Elder in good standing. Children will choose in coordination with their parents and the Bishop and the Vice-Bishops. Usually, a child should be anointed by his or her father if the father is a Priest or Elder in good standing. Otherwise, a child should be anointed by his or her Godfather, or if the Godfather is not available, a close relative or family friend of similar significance.

Throughout the Rite, the Officiant should refer to the Candidate to be confirmed by name whenever the text refers to "Can-

didate" in parentheses. The Candidate should work to memorize ahead of time his or her required responses during the Rite. However, an Escort of the same sex as the Candidate who is the Candidate's Godfather, Godmother, or other designated Church member in good standing should stand with the Candidate and prompt the Candidate what to say if he or she requires assistance.

The Officiant begins by saying:

Let us call upon God and devoutly give thanks to Him, and pray,

Almighty God,

We give humble thanks, for the Triple Path and the opportunity to follow it every day. May we grow ever stronger before Thee in wisdom, virtue, and hope. May Thy Divine light shine on (Candidate), that (he/she) may feel confirmed in (his/her) decision to be reborn as a traveler on the Triple Path, and on all of us that we may renounce foolishness, evil, and lazy despair, but ever faithfully walk the Triple Path.

Amen.

Brothers and Sisters, we come together to witness the confirmation of (Candidate), who was previously baptized and thus buried to the ways of the world and reborn as a new traveler on the Triple Path.

The Officiant addresses the Candidate.

(Candidate), arise and stand before me.

The Candidate stands in front of the Officiant. The Escort accompanies the Candidate, standing to his or her side.

The Officiant says:

I charge and admonish you most solemnly that you must respond truthfully and sincerely, only responding with the Candidate's words for this Rite if they most surely and accurately represent your mind as well.

(Candidate) for what purpose are you here?

The Candidate answers:

To confirm my baptism and my commitment as a follower of the Triple Path.

523

The Officiant says:

Do you here, in the presence of God, this Congregation, and the whole of this Church, renew the solemn promise and vow you made at your Baptism, to renounce foolishness, evil, and lazy despair; to endeavor to follow God and the Triple Path, to seek wisdom, practice virtue, and labor with hope all the rest of your days; to count yourself a member of the Congregation of the Faithful of the Triple Path; to endeavor to regularly attend Church, participate in your Ward, and diligently follow the Rites, Feasts, observances, and practices set out in our Creed?

The Candidate answers:

I do.

The Officiant says:

I would test your knowledge of, and commitment to, the Triple Path.

The Candidate answers:

I stand ready.

The Officiant asks:

Have you been Baptized?

The Candidate answers:

I have.

The Officiant says:

Recite to me the Creed of the Triple Path, before God and this Ward (or Branch), as witnesses for the whole of the Congregation of the Faithful of the Triple Path.

The Candidate answers by reciting the Creed.

The Officiant should make allowance for minor errors, and the Escort should offer assistance to prompt the Candidate when needed. However, the Candidate should be able to recite the Creed mostly unaided, demonstrating his or her familiarity with it.

After the Candidate has successfully recited the Creed, the Officiant says:

(Candidate), I find you ready to be Anointed and Confirmed as a member of our Congregation.

Praise to God and the Triple Path.

Amen.

The Ward responds:

Amen.

The Officiant says:

Now, let this person be Anointed and Confirmed as a member of the Congregation of the Faithful of the Triple Path.

The Candidate is seated before the Ward. The Anointer places a small amount of consecrated oil on his finger and says:

(Candidate), I anoint you as a member of the Congregation of the Faithful of the Triple Path, in the name of God, and of wisdom, virtue, and hope.

Amen.

As he speaks, the Anointer uses his finger to anoint the Candidate with Consecrated Oil on the forehead, making the form of the Tricrux with the oil, forming one of each of the three prongs as he says each of the words "wisdom", "virtue", and "hope".

The Officiant says:

Now, all those previously invited, come forward to join this Anointer in pronouncing a blessing.

The Anointer moves behind the Candidate and places his hands on the Candidate's head. Others who have been previously invited join in and lay their hands on the Candidate's head as well. The Anointer Confirms the Candidate by saying:

O God,

By the authority of the Congregation of the Faithful of the Triple Path and in my office as a(n) Priest (or Elder), I confirm this person, (Candidate), as a member of the Congregation of the Faithful of the Triple Path and Church of the West.

The Anointer then pronounces words of blessing, counsel, and comfort as the Anointer feels inspired, taking care not to overstep the bounds of prudence or propriety. He then closes by saying:

Amen.

The Officiant invites the applicant to stand before him and says:

Congratulations, (Candidate). We welcome you as the newest member of the Congregation of the Faithful of the Triple Path. As a token of our esteem, we now present you with this copy of the book of The Triple Path. We exhort you to "Read this book, think on it, and seek greater understanding. However, be not just a reader of these words, but a doer of them also. This book is not the Triple Path. The Triple Path is a way of life, not words on a page." (Foundations 2:5)

Now, as a confirmed member, you have the right and the responsibility to read of this book before our Ward (or Branch). Come and read.

The Candidate goes to the podium and reads a passage from this book selected by himself or herself, beginning the Reading by saying:

And now a Reading from the book of the Triple Path.

The Candidate reads the passage he or she has selected.

If it is a Fast and Testimony Sunday, the Candidate then leads the Congregation in saying the Creed:

Please stand and recite with me the Creed.

Following the Rite, the Officiant and Anointer sign a certificate witnessing and memorializing the completion of the Rite, a record of which is to be kept by the Church, with the certificate being given to the Candidate.

Following the Reading, the Communal Sacrament continues as normal.

Initiation

Initiations generally should be conducted on a weeknight, a few times a year, as necessary. All Candidates for Initiation must be at least 18 years of age. They must fulfill the same requirements as those for Baptism and Confirmation. All Candidates for Initiation must be believe in God, affirm their support for all aspects of this book and the Creed, and also demonstrate through their actions their commitment to the Creed and the principles of the Triple Path. Candidates may not be Initiated unless at least one year has passed since their Confirmation. Candidates must have demonstrated their commitment to the Triple Path by regularly attending Church for at least one year prior to Initiation, actively participating in their Ward, and diligently following the Rites, Feasts, observances, and practices of Creeds 10 through 13 to the extent possible for their membership status. Candidates should also be contributing financially to their Ward in full compliance with the Ward's assessment of members' annual financial contributions. Most importantly, the Candidate should demonstrate a sufficiently mature and spiritual disposition commensurate with the solemn and sacred nature of this Rite. Additionally, all male candidates must have been Ordained as Priests and should usually be Ordained right before their Initiation. Before a Candidate is accepted for Initiation, the Bishop and Vice-Bishops, and then the Archbishop and Vice-Archbishops, should verify that the Candidate understands and fulfills these requirements and also the commitments the Candidate is assuming by being Initiated. This may usually be done through an interview with either the Bishop or one of the Vice-Bishops and then an interview with the Archbishop or one of the Vice-Archbishops.

Any person accepted by the Bishop, Vice-Bishops, Archbishop, and Vice-Archbishops as qualifying for Initiation must also be approved by the Qualified Voters of the Diocese. His or her name must be published and announced in all the Wards of the Diocese for three consecutive Sundays during Communal Sacrament. During the announcements before the start of the meeting, the Officiant for that meeting shall say the following for a female Candidate:

(Candidate) of (state the name of the Candidate's Ward) desires to be Initiated and has been found qualified by the Bishop, Vice-Bishops, Archbishop, and Vice-Archbishops, but the Qualified Voters of the Diocese must also approve. All Qualified Voters who are in favor, please make it known by raising your right hand.

The Officiant pauses to allow the Qualified Voters in the Ward to vote, then continues:

If any of you know cause, or just impediment, why (he/she) should not be Initiated, you are to declare it privately to the Bishop and the Vice-Bishops after this meeting. This is the first (second, or third) time of asking.

If anyone dissents, the Bishop and Vice-Bishops (or Diocesan Council), deal with the objections appropriately and with discretion, in conformity with this book, the Creed, the Doctrines of the Church, and Church traditions, standards, and principles.

Male Candidates should be proposed to the Qualified Voters for both Ordination as a Priest and for Initiation, following the manner listed in the Rite of Ordination of Priests.

Once the proposed Initiation has been presented to the Wards three times, and any concerns resolved, then the Initiation may proceed on the first subsequent day when reasonably possible. Males should be Ordained as Priests before their Initiation.

During this Rite, Candidates renew the same obligations— (and only those obligations) made during Baptism and Confirmation through participation in a ritual drama. The content of this Rite is not published here, but with Diocesan and Provincial approval, may be revealed to Candidates approved to receive it and desirous to know of its content before experiencing it.

Marriage

Marriage in the Church is always between one man and one woman, both at least 18 years of age and Initiated. They should have a degree of kinship no closer than that of second cousins. A Marriage should be permanent, fruitful, and faithful (Virtue 34: 10). The marriage ceremony should always take place in a Church building, generally in the local Ward building of the groom or bride. Extravagant or expensive wedding ceremonies should be avoided, and the Ward should not charge for the use of the Church building.

The names of any couple desiring to be married must be published and announced in their ward or wards for three consecutive Sundays during Communal Sacrament. During the announcements before the start of the meeting the Officiant for that meeting shall say the following:

(State the names of the couple, and the Ward of the other member of the couple, if he or she is from a different Ward) desire to be married and have been found qualified by the Bishop and the Vice-Bishops (or "their Bishops and Vice-Bishops", if one is from a different Ward), but the Qualified Voters of the Ward must also approve. All Qualified Voters who are in favor, please make it known by raising your right hand.

The Officiant pauses to allow the Qualified Voters in the Ward to vote, then continues:

If any of you know cause, or just impediment, why these two persons should not be joined together in holy matrimony, you are to declare it privately to the Bishop and the Vice-Bishops after this meeting. This is the first (second, or third) time of asking.

If anyone dissents, the Bishop and Vice-Bishops deal with the objections appropriately and with discretion, in conformity with this book, the Creed, the Doctrines of the Church, and Church traditions, standards, and principles.

Once the proposed Marriage has been presented to the Ward three times, and any concerns resolved, then the Marriage may proceed.

The Officiant for the Marriage may be any Elder in good standing chosen by the couple. He performs the Rite dressed in his Stole. At the day and time appointed for the Marriage, the persons to be married shall come into the Church after those attending are seated. The Groom shall stand to the Officiant's left and the Bride to his right. If desired, the bride may enter last, with her father. The bride's father (or if the father is deceased or cannot be present, the Godfather or other selected man of similar significance) shall stand to the bride's left. If desired, a best man and a maid of honor may also accompany the Bride and Groom and stand at their side, bearing the rings. The Officiant shall say to all those gathered:

Brothers and Sisters, we are gathered together here in the sight of God, and in the presence of this Ward (or Branch), to join together this man and this woman in holy Marriage; which is an honorable estate, holy, and sacred. Therefore, it is not to be taken in hand, unadvisedly, lightly, or wantonly, but reverently, discreetly, advisedly, soberly, and in the fear of God; duly considering the causes for which Marriage was ordained.

First, it was ordained for the procreation of children and their nurture, to be brought up in the fear and nurture of God and the Triple Path.

Second, it was ordained for the mutual society, help, comfort, and love that the one ought to have of the other, both in prosperity and adversity. Into which holy estate these two persons present come now to be joined. Therefore, if any man can show any just cause why they may not be rightfully or lawfully joined together, let him now speak, or else hereafter forever hold his peace.

The Officiant pauses, giving enough time for anyone to answer. If anyone does so, the Officiant deals with it appropriately. If no one answers, the Officiant continues, addressing the couple directly, saying:

I require that you both answer, on your solemn honor,

that if either of you know any impediment, why you may not be rightfully or lawfully joined together in Marriage, you do now confess it.

If either alleges any impediment why the couple may not be married, and the reasons are credible, then the Marriage must be deferred, until the truth can be discovered.

If no impediment is alleged, then the Officiant shall say to the man:

(Name) will you have this woman to be your wedded wife, to live together after God's ordinance in the holy estate of Marriage? Will you love, comfort, serve, honor, and keep her in sickness and in health; and, forsaking all others, keep yourself only unto her, so long as you both shall live?

The groom answers:

I will.

The Officiant says to the bride:

(Name) will you have this man to be your wedded husband, to live together after God's ordinance in the holy estate of Marriage? Will you love, comfort, serve, honor, and keep him in sickness and in health; and, forsaking all others, keep yourself only unto him, so long as you both shall live?

The bride answers:

I will.

The Officiant asks:

Who gives this woman to be married to this man?

The bride's father (or Godfather or other selected man) takes the bride's right hand and places it in the Officiant's hand. The Officiant then places her hand in the groom's right hand and tells him to repeat after him:

I (Groom's name). take you (Bride's name) to my wedded wife, to have and to hold from this day forward, for better for worse, for richer for poorer, in sickness and in health, to love and to cherish, till death us do part, according to God's holy ordinance, I vow to you.

The Officiant tells the bride to repeat after him:

I (Bride's name) take you (Groom's name) to be my wedded husband, to have and to hold from this day forward, for better for worse, for richer for poorer, in sickness and in health, to love, and to cherish, till death us do part, according to God's holy ordinance, I vow to you.

The Bride and Groom loose their hands. The Groom then gives the Bride a ring. The Best Man (or Groom, if a Best Man is not present) shall lay the ring on the Officiant's book. The Officiant delivers the ring to the Groom. The Groom repeats these words, with the Officiant's assistance, if required:

With this ring I thee wed, and with all my worldly goods I thee endow, in the name of God and the Triple Path.

Amen.

The Groom places the ring on the Bride's ring finger. The Bride then gives the Groom a ring. The Maid of Honor (or Bride, if no Maid of Honor is present) lays the ring on the Officiant's book. The Officiant delivers the ring to the Bride. The Bride repeats these words, with the Officiant's assistance, if required:

With this ring I thee wed, and with all my worldly goods I thee endow, in the name of God and the Triple Path.

Amen.

The Bride and Groom both kneel down. The Officiant says:

Let us pray.

O eternal God,

Creator and Preserver of all mankind, Giver of all spiritual grace, we ask for Thy blessing upon these Thy servants, this man and this woman, whom we bless in Thy name; that they may live faithfully together and perform and keep the vow and covenant between them made (whereof these rings given and received are a token and pledge) and may they ever remain in perfect love and peace together, and live according to Thy laws; through their faithfulness to Thee and the Triple Path.

Amen.

The Officiant joins the Bride's and Groom's right hands

together, and says:

Those whom God has joined together let no man put asunder.

The Officiant turns to the Ward and says:

Forasmuch as (Bride) and (Groom) have consented together in holy wedlock, and have witnessed the same before God and this company, and thereto have pledged themselves to each other, and have declared the same by giving and receiving of rings, and by joining of hands; I pronounce that they be Man and Wife together, in the name of God and the Triple Path.

Amen.

The Officiant adds the following blessing:

May God bless, preserve, and keep you and with His favor look upon you and so fill your lives with wisdom, virtue, and hope. Amen.

The Officiant pronounces the following counsel:

Now, let yourselves no longer be separate, but be one.

Now, you can be better together. Before, if one fell, who was there to help lift up? Who could bring warmth when the cold came? Together, now, may you help each other up. In the cold, may you keep each other warm. (Virtue 34:11)

If the Bride is of child-bearing age, the Officiant includes the following three paragraphs:

I tell you also, you must be fruitful and multiply and replenish the earth. You have come together not only to love and support one another, but also to have children. Love and nurture them in patience and selflessness. Teach them by word and example, starting when they are young, to follow the Triple Path. (Virtue 34:17)

Let us pray.

O merciful God, by whose gracious gift mankind is increased: May this Husband and Wife both be fruitful in procreation of children, and also live together so long in godly love and honesty, that they may see their children virtuously brought up to follow you and the Triple Path.

If the Bride is not of childbearing age, the Officiant starts with the following prayer, saying "let us pray" before beginning:

O God, let this couple receive Thy mercy, that this man may love his wife with virtue, courage, and faithfulness, a follower of holy and godly Elders, and that this woman may be loving and amiable, faithful and virtuous; and in all quietness, sobriety, and peace, be a follower of holy and godly matrons. O God, may they both be blessed, that as they walk out of this Church together this day, they may walk the Triple Path together the rest of their lives, always faithful to each other and to Thee. Amen.

The marriage ceremony ends with the Bride and Groom walking hand-in-hand out of the sanctuary.

Ordination of Junior Deacons

Young men at least 14 years of age who have been Baptized and Confirmed and are in good standing may be Ordained as Junior Deacons. Any male who was Confirmed at 16 years of age or greater should not be Ordained as a Junior Deacon, but instead be directly Ordained as a Senior Deacon.

All Candidates for Ordination as Junior Deacons must currently fulfill the same requirements as those for Baptism and Confirmation. They must believe in God, affirm their support for all aspects of this book and the Creed, and also demonstrate through their actions their commitment to the Creed and the principles of the Triple Path. In particular, they must have demonstrated their commitment by regularly attending Church for at least one year prior to Ordination, actively participating in their Ward, and diligently following the Rites, Feasts, observances, and practices of Creeds 10 through 13 to the extent possible for their membership status. They must also affirm that they are willing to fulfill faithfully the duties of a Junior Deacon as set forth in this book.

The Bishop and the Vice-Bishops should encourage all young men approaching the age of 14 to ensure they qualify to be Ordained. The decision to seek Ordination, however, is the Candidate's alone. No one else should make the decision to seek Ordination on a potential Candidate's behalf. Potential Candidates for Ordination should request of the Bishop and the Vice-Bishops that they be considered for Ordination. Before a Candidate is accepted for Ordination, the Bishop and Vice-Bishops should verify that the Candidate understands and fulfills these requirements and also the commitments the Candidate is assuming by being Ordained. This may usually be accomplished through an interview with either the Bishop or one of the Vice-Bishops.

Any person accepted by the Bishop and the Vice-Bishops

as qualifying for Ordination must also be approved by the Ward. His name must be published and announced in his Ward three consecutive Sundays during Communal Sacrament. During the announcements before the start of the meeting the Officiant for that meeting shall say the following:

(Candidate) desires to be Ordained as a Junior Deacon and has been found qualified by the Bishop and the Vice-Bishops, but the Qualified Voters of the Ward (or Branch) must also approve. All Qualified Voters who are in favor, please make it known by raising your right hand.

The Officiant pauses to allow the Qualified Voters in the Ward to vote, then continues:

If any of you know cause, or just impediment, why he should not be Ordained, you are to declare it privately to the Bishop and the Vice-Bishops after this meeting. This is the first (second, or third) time of asking.

If anyone dissents, the Bishop and Vice-Bishops deal with the objections appropriately and with discretion, in conformity with this book, the Creed, the Doctrines of the Church, and Church traditions, standards, and principles.

Once the proposed Ordination has been presented to the Ward three times, and any concerns resolved, then the Candidate should be Ordained during the next appropriate Communal Sacrament. The Ordination is conducted during Communal Sacrament, just following the announcements and before the singing of the hymn and the opening prayer.

The Officiant for the Ordination must be a Priest or Elder in good standing, preferably the Candidate's father. If the Candidate's father is not available, then it should be conducted by the Candidate's Godfather, or another man of similar significance. Throughout the Ordination, the Officiant and Bishop should refer to the Candidate to be Ordained by name whenever the text refers to "Candidate" in parentheses.

To start, the Officiant approaches the Bishop and the Vice-Bishops and, addressing them and the Ward, says the following:

I present unto you (Candidate) to be Ordained a Junior Deacon.

The Bishop (or a Vice-Bishop acting in his place) says:

Has (Candidate) been found qualified, in his knowledge, actions, and commitment to exercise this sacred role, to the honor of God and the Triple Path, and the edifying of this Church?

The Officiant replies:

He has.

The Bishop addresses the Candidate:

I charge and admonish you most solemnly that you must respond truthfully and sincerely, only responding with the Candidate's words for this Rite if they most surely and accurately represent your mind as well.

Have you been Baptized and Confirmed?

The Candidate answers:

I have.

The Bishop asks:

Do you, of your own free will, seek this Ordination, to serve, without any remuneration, God and this Church, to help your fellow-travelers in their journey on the Triple Path?

The Candidate answers:

Yes.

The Bishop says to the Officiant:

He has committed. Let him be Ordained.

The Officiant raises his arms and prays:

O God, we seek mercy in our infirmities that we may serve Thee and this Church, to help our fellow-travelers in their journey on the Triple Path. Let this, Thy servant to be Ordained, and all of us, act in holiness and pureness of living, with wisdom, virtue, and hope. Amen.

The Candidate is then seated before the Ward. The Officiant places a small amount of consecrated oil on his finger and says:

(Candidate), I anoint you a Junior Deacon of the Congregation of the Faithful of the Triple Path, in the name of God, and of wisdom, virtue, and hope.

Amen.

As he speaks, the Officiant uses his finger to anoint the Candidate with Consecrated Oil on the forehead, making the form of the Tricrux with the oil, forming one of each of the three prongs as he says each of the words "wisdom", "virtue", and "hope".

The Officiant says:

Now, all those previously invited, come forward to join in Ordaining (Candidate).

The Officiant moves behind the Candidate and places his hands on the Candidate's head. Others who have been previously invited join in and lay their hands on the Candidate's head as well. The Officiant Ordains the Candidate by saying:

O God,

By the authority of the Congregation of the Faithful of the Triple Path and in my office as a(n) Priest (or Elder), I Ordain this person, (Candidate), as a Junior Deacon of the Congregation of the Faithful of the Triple Path.

The Officiant then pronounces words of blessing, counsel, and comfort to the Candidate as he feels inspired to speak, taking care not to overstep the bounds of prudence or propriety. He then closes by saying:

Amen.

The Bishop then invites the Junior Deacon to sit with the other Junior Deacons to help distribute the Bread and Water of the Sacrament. The Officiant and those assisting him return to their seats. The Communal Sacrament proceeds as normal.

Ordination of Senior Deacons

All males 16 years of age or greater who have been Baptized and Confirmed and are in good standing may be Ordained as Senior Deacons.

All Candidates for Ordination as Senior Deacons must currently fulfill the same requirements as those for Baptism and Confirmation. They must believe in God, affirm their support for all aspects of this book and the Creed, and also demonstrate through their actions their commitment to the Creed and the principles of the Triple Path. In particular, they must have demonstrated their commitment by regularly attending Church for at least one year prior to Ordination, actively participating in their Ward, and diligently following the Rites, Feasts, observances, and practices of Creeds 10 through 13 to the extent possible for their membership status. They must also affirm that they are willing to fulfill faithfully the duties of a Senior Deacon as set forth in this book.

The Bishop and the Vice-Bishops should encourage all young men approaching the age of 16 and all men who are Baptized and Confirmed after the age of 16 to ensure they qualify to be Ordained. The decision to seek Ordination, however, is the Candidate's alone. No one else should make the decision to seek Ordination on a potential Candidate's behalf. Potential Candidates for Ordination should request of the Bishop and the Vice-Bishops that they be considered for Ordination. Before a Candidate is accepted for Ordination, the Bishop and the Vice-Bishops should verify that the Candidate understands and fulfills these requirements and also the commitments the Candidate is assuming by being Ordained. This may usually be accomplished through an interview with either the Bishop or one of the Vice-Bishops.

Any person accepted by the Bishop and the Vice-Bishops as qualifying for Ordination must also be approved by the Ward. His name must be published and announced in his Ward three *consecutive Sundays during Communal Sacrament. During the announcements before the start of the meeting the Officiant for that meeting shall say the following:*

(Candidate) desires to be Ordained as a Senior Deacon and has been found qualified by the Bishop and the Vice-Bishops, but the Qualified Voters of the Ward must also approve. All Qualified Voters who are in favor, please make it known by raising your right hand.

The Officiant pauses to allow the Qualified Voters in the Ward to vote, then continues:

If any of you know cause, or just impediment, why he should not be Ordained, you are to declare it privately to the Bishop and the Vice-Bishops after this meeting. This is the first (second, or third) time of asking.

If anyone dissents, the Bishop and Vice-Bishops deal with the objections appropriately and with discretion, in conformity with this book, the Creed, the Doctrines of the Church, and Church traditions, standards, and principles.

Once the proposed Ordination has been presented to the Ward three times, and any concerns resolved, then the Candidate should be Ordained during the next appropriate Communal Sacrament. The Ordination is conducted during Communal Sacrament, just following the announcements and before the singing of the hymn and the opening prayer.

The Officiant for the Ordination must be a Priest or Elder in good standing, preferably the Candidate's father. If the Candidate's father is not available, then it should be conducted by the Candidate's Godfather, or another man of similar significance. Throughout the Ordination, the Officiant and Bishop should refer to the Candidate to be Ordained by name whenever the text refers to "Candidate" in parentheses.

To start, the Officiant approaches the Bishop and the Vice-Bishops and, addressing them and the Ward, says the following:

I present unto you (Candidate) to be Ordained a Senior Deacon.

The Bishop (or a Vice-Bishop acting in his place) says:
Has (Candidate) been found qualified, in his knowledge, actions, and commitment to exercise this sacred role, to the honor of God and the Triple Path, and the edifying of this Church?
The Officiant replies:
He has.

The Bishop addresses the Candidate:
I charge and admonish you most solemnly that you must respond truthfully and sincerely, only responding with the Candidate's words for this Rite if they most surely and accurately represent your mind as well.

Have you been Baptized and Confirmed?
The Candidate answers:
I have.

The Bishop asks:
Do you, of your own free will, seek this Ordination, to serve, without any remuneration, God and this Church, to help your fellow-travelers in their journey on the Triple Path?
The Candidate answers:
Yes.

The Bishop says to the Officiant:
He has committed. Let him be Ordained.

The Officiant raises his arms and prays:
O God, we seek mercy in our infirmities that we may serve Thee and this Church, to help our fellow-travelers in their journey on the Triple Path. Let this, Thy servant to be Ordained, and all of us, act in holiness and pureness of living, with wisdom, virtue, and hope. Amen.

The Candidate is then seated before the Ward. The Officiant places a small amount of consecrated oil on his finger and says:
(Candidate), I anoint you a Senior Deacon of the Congregation of the Faithful of the Triple Path, in the name of God, and of wisdom, virtue, and hope.
Amen.

As he speaks, the Officiant uses his finger to anoint the Candidate with Consecrated Oil on the forehead, making the form of the Tricrux with the oil, forming one of each of the three prongs as he says each of the words "wisdom", "virtue", and "hope".

The Officiant says:

Now, all those previously invited, come forward to join in Ordaining (Candidate).

The Officiant moves behind the Candidate and places his hands on the Candidate's head. Others who have been previously invited join in and lay their hands on the Candidate's head as well. The Officiant Ordains the Candidate by saying:

O God,

By the authority of the Congregation of the Faithful of the Triple Path and in my office as a(n) Priest (or Elder), I Ordain this person, (Candidate), as a Senior Deacon of the Congregation of the Faithful of the Triple Path.

The Officiant then pronounces words of blessing, counsel, and comfort to the Candidate as he feels inspired to speak, taking care not to overstep the bounds of prudence or propriety. He then closes by saying:

Amen.

The Bishop then invites the Senior Deacon to sit with the other Senior Deacons to help prepare and bless the Bread and Water of the Sacrament. The Officiant and those assisting him return to their seats. The Communal Sacrament proceeds as normal.

Ordination of Priests

*All males 18 years of age or greater who have been Bap-
tized and Confirmed, and are in good standing, may be Ordained
as Priests. Candidates are Ordained as Priests in connection with
their Initiation.*

*All Candidates for Ordination as Priests must currently
fulfill the same requirements as those for Baptism, Confirmation,
and Initiation. They must believe in God, affirm their support for
all aspects of this book and the Creed, and also demonstrate
through their actions their commitment to the Creed and the principles of the Triple Path. In particular, they must have demonstrated their commitment by regularly attending and actively participating in their Ward for at least one year prior to Ordination,
and diligently following the Rites, Feasts, observances, and practices of Creeds 10 through 13 to the extent possible for their membership status. They must also affirm that they are willing to fulfill
faithfully the duties of a Priest as set forth in this book. Candidates
may not be Ordained as a Priest unless at least one year has passed
since their Confirmation. Candidates should also be contributing
financially to their Ward in full compliance with the Ward's assessment of members' annual financial contributions. Most importantly, the Candidate should demonstrate a sufficiently mature and
spiritual disposition commensurate with the solemn and sacred nature of this Rite.*

*The Bishop and the Vice-Bishops should encourage all
young men approaching the age of 18 and all men who are Baptized and Confirmed after the age of 18 to ensure they qualify to
be Ordained. The decision to seek Ordination, however, is the
Candidate's alone. No one else should make the decision to seek
Ordination on a potential Candidate's behalf. Potential Candidates
for Ordination should request of the Bishop and the Vice-Bishops that they be considered for Ordination. Before a Candidate is*

accepted for Ordination, the Bishop and the Vice-Bishops, and
then the Archbishop and Vice-Archbishops, should verify that the
Candidate understands and fulfills these requirements and also the
commitments the Candidate is assuming by being Ordained. This
may usually be done through an interview with either the Bishop
or one of the Vice-Bishops and then an interview with the Archbishop or one of the Vice-Archbishops.

Any person accepted by the Bishop, Vice-Bishops, Archbishop, and Vice-Archbishops as qualifying for Ordination must
also be approved by the Qualified Voters of the Diocese. His
name must be published and announced in all the Wards of the
Diocese for three consecutive Sundays during Communal Sacrament. During the announcements before the start of the meeting
the Officiant for that meeting shall say the following:

(Candidate) of (state the name of the Candidate's Ward)
desires to be Ordained as a Priest and Initiated and has been found
qualified by the Bishop, Vice-Bishops, Archbishop, and Vice-Archbishops, but the Qualified Voters of the Diocese must also approve.
All Qualified Voters who are in favor, please make it known by
raising your right hand.

The Officiant pauses to allow the Qualified Voters in the
Ward to vote.

If any of you know cause, or just impediment, why he
should not be Ordained and Initiated, you are to declare it privately to the Bishop and the Vice-Bishops after this meeting. This
is the first (second, or third) time of asking.

If anyone dissents, the Bishop and Vice-Bishops (or Diocesan Council), deal with the objections appropriately and with discretion, in conformity with this book, the Creed, the Doctrines of
the Church, and Church traditions, standards, and principles.

Once the proposed Ordination and Initiation has been
presented to the Wards three times, and any concerns resolved,
then the Ordination may proceed.

The Candidate should be Ordained following the third
time of asking on the next appropriate Communal Sacrament, usu-

ally in a Fast and Testimony Sunday. The Ordination takes place just after the Creed (or Reading, if not done on a Fast and Testimony Sunday). The Officiant for the Ordination must be a Priest or Elder in good standing, preferably the Candidate's father. If the Candidate's father is not available, then it should be conducted by the Candidate's Godfather, or another man of similar significance.

The Ordination is conducted on the Sunday before the Candidate is to be Initiated. The Ordination is performed by the Officiant and the Bishop (or a Vice-Bishop). Throughout the Ordination, the Officiant and Bishop should refer to the Candidate to be Ordained by name whenever the text refers to "Candidate" in parentheses.

To start, the Officiant approaches the Bishop and the Vice-Bishops and, addressing them and the Ward, says the following:

I present unto you (Candidate) to be Ordained a Priest.

The Bishop says:

Has (Candidate) been found qualified, in his knowledge, actions, and commitment to exercise this sacred role, to the honor of God and the Triple Path, and the edifying of this Church?

The Officiant replies:

He has.

The Bishop addresses the Candidate:

That this present group may also witness your qualification, and understand your mind and will in these things, and that this your public promise here may more move you to do your duties, I would examine you here as well, and you shall answer plainly to these things, which we, in the name of God and of this Church, shall ask of you.

And I charge and admonish you most solemnly that you must respond truthfully and sincerely, only responding with the Candidate's words for this Rite if they most surely and accurately represent your mind as well.

Have you accepted, and will you continue to accept. the teachings in the book of the Triple Path and our Creed?

The Candidate answers

Thus have I endeavored and will continue to so endeavor.

The Bishop asks:

Have you been Baptized and Confirmed?

The Candidate answers:

I have.

The Bishop asks:

Have you observed, and will you continue to observe, the practices of repentance; daily spiritual study, meditation, and prayer; celibacy before marriage and fidelity within it; maintaining Sunday as a day of rest, spiritual focus, and family, free from work and spending of money; completely abstaining from tobacco; not eating gluten; drinking alcohol, if ever, only in moderation; eating in a healthy and moderate manner and exercising to keep your body fit and strong; and avoiding excessive consumption of caffeine and refined sugar?

The Candidate answers:

Thus have I endeavored and will continue to so endeavor.

The Bishop asks:

Have you faithfully celebrated, and will you endeavor faithfully to celebrate, and now to minister, our communal and private Rites and Feasts: Communal Sacrament; the Consecration of Chapels, Churches, Basilicas, and Cathedrals; the Feast Days of New Year, Lent, Easter, May Day, Mid-Summer, Tricrux, Allhallowtide, Thanksgiving, and Yule; Repentance; the Consecration of Oil; the Consecration of Stoles; Private Sacrament; the Anointing and Blessing of the Sick; Father's Blessing; Blessings of Counsel and Comfort; and the Dedication of Homes?

The Candidate answers:

Thus have I done in celebration and will I continue to do in celebration and ministration.

The Bishop asks:

Have you recognized, and will you continue to ever recognize and honor, that your highest moral duty is first to spouse and children, then to parents and family, then to friends and community, then to nation, and finally toward all humankind?

The Candidate answers:
Thus have I endeavored and will continue to so endeavor.

If the Candidate is unmarried and childless, the Bishop asks:

Will you seek out a wife and be fruitful and multiply, and replenish the Earth?

If the Candidate is childless and married to a wife of child-bearing age, the Bishop asks:

Will you seek to be fruitful and multiply, and replenish the Earth?

The Candidate answers:

I will.

The Bishop asks:

Have you been seeking the truth and striving for it, that you may discover where you are in error? (Wisdom 3:1, 4)

The Candidate answers:

Thus have I endeavored and will continue to so endeavor.

The Bishop asks:

Have you banished and driven away, and will you continue with all faithful diligence to banish and drive away, from the Church all erroneous and strange doctrines contrary to the book of the Triple Path?

The Candidate answers:

Thus have I endeavored and will continue to so endeavor.

The Bishop asks:

Have you accepted, and will you continue to accept, the importance of traditional values and in honoring and following the traditions, morals, and practices of our ancestors?

The Candidate answers:

Thus have I endeavored and will continue to so endeavor.

The Bishop asks:

Have you been, and will you continue to be, fearless and fierce in defense of the Church and the Triple Path, and our traditions, and those to whom you owe your greatest duties?

The Candidate answers:

Thus have I endeavored and will continue to so endeavor.

The Bishop asks:

Have you been, and will you continue for the rest of your life to be, as self-sufficient as possible and to hold yourself accountable, never shrinking from your own actions and the consequences that flow therefrom?

The Candidate answers:

Thus have I endeavored and will continue to so endeavor.

The Bishop says:

We commend you for your dedication. And so finally, I ask, do you, of your own free will, seek this Ordination, to serve, without any remuneration, God and this Church, to help your fellow-travelers in their journey on the Triple Path?

The Candidate answers:

Yes.

The Bishop addresses the Candidate:

In this most solemn and important office, I charge you to act with great care, to apply yourself to this office and to show yourself dutiful and thankful unto God and the Congregation of the Faithful of the Triple Path, which have placed you in so high a dignity, and also to beware that neither you yourself offend, nor give occasion that others offend. Remember how studious you should be in reading and learning the book of the Triple Path, the Codex, and the best books of our civilization, and also that you should forsake, as much as practicable, worldly and frivolous cares and pursuits.

Let the Officiant proceed with the Ordination.

The Officiant raises his arms and prays:

O God, we seek mercy in our infirmities that we may serve Thee and this Church, to help our fellow-travelers in their journey on the Triple Path. Let this, Thy servant to be Ordained, and all of us, act in holiness and pureness of living, with wisdom, virtue, and hope. Amen.

The Candidate is then seated before the Ward. The Officiant places a small amount of consecrated oil on his finger and says:

(Candidate), I anoint you a Priest of the Congregation of the Faithful of the Triple Path, in the name of God, and of wisdom, virtue, and hope.

Amen.

As he speaks, the Officiant uses his finger to anoint the Candidate with Consecrated Oil on the forehead, making the form of the Tricrux with the oil, forming one of each of the three prongs as he says each of the words "wisdom", "virtue", and "hope".

The Officiant says:

Now, all those previously invited, come forward to join in Ordaining (Candidate).

The Officiant moves behind the Candidate and places his hands on the Candidate's head. Others who have been previously invited join in and lay their hands on the Candidate's head as well. The Officiant Ordains the Candidate by saying:

O God,

By the authority of the Congregation of the Faithful of the Triple Path and in my office as a(n) Priest (or Elder), I Ordain this person, (Candidate), as a Priest of the Congregation of the Faithful of the Triple Path.

The Officiant then pronounces words of blessing, counsel, and comfort to the Candidate as he feels inspired to speak, taking care not to overstep the bounds of prudence or propriety. He then closes by saying:

Amen.

Those assisting the Officiant return to their seats.

The Officiant says:

As a symbol of your office of Priest, we present you with this Stole.

The Officiant presents to the candidate the Stole of a Priest, which is made of dark red fabric with two embroidered gold or yellow Tricruxes, placed so that when the Stole is worn, one Tricrux is on each side at about chest level. At the bottom on each side is a gold or yellow Trimonvia. The Stole of a Priest has no border. The Stole may include other additional appropriate decorative or symbolic elements as defined by local custom and practice. The Officiant dresses the Candidate in the Stole.

The Officiant continues:

You must wear a Stole whenever you act as an Officiant in any required Rite, private or public. As a symbol of your office in the Church, treat this Stole with solemnity and reverence. And of even greater importance, live your life so that you treat this office of Priest with the solemnity and reverence to which it is due.

The Officiant presents to the Candidate a vial of unconsecrated oil and says:

I also present to you this vial of oil for blessing and anointing. This Stole and oil are not yet consecrated. Upon your return home from this Ordination, you must consecrate them yourself, for now you are a Priest of the Congregation of the Faithful of the Triple Path.

The Communal Sacrament proceeds as normal.

Ordination of Elders

Elders must be men of enduring maturity and sober mind, who have been consistent in seeking wisdom, practicing virtue, and laboring with hope. They must have been Baptized, Confirmed, Initiated, and Married, and be in good standing in the Church. They must have shown, and continue to show, their abiding commitment to God and the Triple Path.

All chosen for Ordination as Elders must currently fulfill the same requirements as those for Baptism, Confirmation, and Initiation. They must believe in God, affirm their support for all aspects of this book and the Creed, and also demonstrate through their actions their commitment to the Creed and the principles of the Triple Path. In particular, they must have demonstrated their commitment for the ten years prior to Ordination by regularly attending Church, participating and contributing actively to the success of their Ward (if they have changed Wards, their active participation in their prior Wards should be confirmed), and diligently following the Rites, Feasts, observances, and practices of Creeds 10 through 13. They must also affirm that they are willing to fulfill faithfully the duties of an Elder as set forth in this book. Candidates may not be Ordained as an Elder unless they have at least three children of good moral character who actively participate in their Wards (with allowance to be made for those with deceased children and for converts to the Church whose children were not born within the faith). To be Ordained an Elder, he must be married to one wife. After Ordination, an Elder must be married to remain in good standing as an Elder, and thus authorized to act in that capacity. For any person baptized before the age of 18, the marriage requirement can only be fulfilled by being married to another member of the Church of the West.

Candidates should also be contributing financially to their Ward in full compliance with the Ward's assessment of members' *annual financial contributions. Most importantly, the Candidate should demonstrate a sufficiently mature and spiritual disposition commensurate with the solemn and sacred nature of this office. No one may seek Ordination to the office of Elder. Only those who have been selected by the Ward's Qualified Voters for listing on a sortition list for a position as a Bishop or Vice-Bishop may be Ordained an Elder. Each Qualified Voter should vote according to his or her own best judgment, except that male voters cannot vote for themselves, and female voters cannot vote for their husbands. A man eligible for Ordination to the office of Elder may refuse the offered Ordination. He may later accept the Ordination if the sortition list on which he was listed has not been replaced with a new list, or whenever he appears on a subsequent list.*

Any person accepted as qualifying for Ordination must also be approved by the Qualified Voters of the Diocese. His name must be published and announced to all the Wards of the Diocese for three consecutive Sundays during Communal Sacrament. During the announcements before the start of the meeting the Officiant for that meeting shall say the following:

(Candidate) has been found by the Qualified Voters of his Ward as being qualified to be Ordained as an Elder.

I would remind you that all Elders in this Church must be in good standing in the Church and be men of enduring maturity and sober mind, who have been consistent in seeking wisdom, practicing virtue, and laboring with hope. They must have shown, and continue to show, their abiding commitment to God and the Triple Path. They must believe in God, affirm their support for all aspects of the book of The Triple Path and the Creed, and also demonstrate through their actions their commitment to the Creed and the principles of the Triple Path by the following: regularly attending Church; participating and contributing actively to the success of their Ward; diligently following the Rites, Feasts, observances, and practices of Creeds 10 through 13; being married to one wife; and having at least three children of good moral character who actively participate in their Wards (with allowance to be made for those with deceased children and for converts to the Church whose children were not born within the faith). More than this, Elders must also be vigilant, sober, of good behavior, given to hospitality, apt to teach; not given to wine and not greedy; patient and not a brawler, not covetous; one who rules well his own house; not a novice, lest being lifted up with pride he fall into condemnation. Moreover, he must have a good report of them which are without; lest he fall into reproach and bring the Church into the same.

He has accepted the Ordination and affirmed that he is willing to fulfill faithfully these duties of an Elder, but his selection must be ratified. All Qualified Voters who are in favor, affirming that, to the best of their knowledge, he fulfills the qualifications of an Elder, please make it known by raising your right hand.

The Officiant pauses to allow the Qualified Voters in the Ward to vote.

If any of you know cause, or just impediment, why he should not be Ordained, you are to declare it privately to the Bishop and the Vice-Bishops, or the Archbishop and Vice-Archbishops, after this meeting. This is the first (second, or third) time of asking.

If anyone dissents, the Bishop and Vice-Bishops, or Archbishop and Vice-Archbishops, deal with the objections appropriately and with discretion, in conformity with this book, the Creed, the Doctrines of the Church, and Church traditions, standards, and principles.

Once the proposed Ordination has been presented to the Ward three times, and any concerns resolved, then the Ordination may proceed.

The Candidate should be Ordained in the first Communal Sacrament after the third time of asking has been completed in the Diocese. The Officiant for the Ordination must be an Elder in good standing, preferably the Candidate's father. If the Candidate's father is not available or able to perform the Ordination, then it should be conducted by the Candidate's Godfather, or another man of similar significance. If the Candidate is also to be Ordained a *Bishop or Vice-Bishop, then he should be Ordained an Elder during the Rite of Ordination of Bishop or Vice-Bishop. The Candidate's father (or Godfather or other similar man) would Ordain him an Elder, then the relevant Steward would Ordain the Candidate to his Stewardship.*

The Ordination is performed by the Officiant and the Bishop (or by a Vice Bishop if the Bishop is not available). Throughout the Ordination, the Officiant and Bishop should refer to the Candidate to be Ordained by name whenever the text refers to "Candidate" in parentheses.

To start, the Officiant approaches the Bishop and the Vice-Bishops and, addressing them and the Ward, says the following:

I present unto you (Candidate) to be Ordained an Elder.

The Bishop says:

Has (Candidate) been found qualified, in his knowledge, actions, and commitment to exercise this sacred role, to the honor of God and the Triple Path, and the edifying of this Church?

The Officiant replies:

He has.

The Bishop addresses the Candidate:

That this present group may also witness your qualification, and understand your mind and will in these things, and that this your public promise here may more move you to do your duties, I would examine you here as well, and you shall answer plainly to these things, which we, in the name of God and of this Church, shall ask of you.

And I charge and admonish you most solemnly that you must respond truthfully and sincerely, only responding with the Candidate's words for this Rite if they most surely and accurately represent your mind as well.

Have you accepted, and will you continue to accept. the teachings in the book of the Triple Path and our Creed?

The Candidate answers:

Thus have I endeavored and will continue to so endeavor.

The Bishop asks:

Have you been Baptized, Confirmed, Initiated, and Married?

The Candidate answers:

I have.

The Bishop asks:

Have you observed, and will you continue to observe, the practices of repentance; daily spiritual study, meditation, and prayer; celibacy before marriage and fidelity within it; maintaining Sunday as a day of rest, spiritual focus, and family, free from work and spending of money; completely abstaining from tobacco; not eating gluten; drinking alcohol, if ever, only in moderation; eating in a healthy and moderate manner and exercising to keep your body fit and strong; and avoiding excessive consumption of caffeine and refined sugar?

The Candidate answers:

Thus have I endeavored and will continue to so endeavor.

The Bishop asks:

Have you faithfully celebrated and ministered, and will you endeavor faithfully to celebrate and minister, our communal and private Rites and Feasts: Communal Sacrament; the Consecration of Chapels, Churches, Basilicas, and Cathedrals; the Feast Days of New Year, Lent, Easter, May Day, Mid-Summer, Tricrux, Allhallowtide, Thanksgiving, and Yule; Repentance; the Consecration of Oil; the Consecration of Stoles; Private Sacrament; the Anointing and Blessing of the Sick; Father's Blessing; Blessings of Counsel and Comfort; and the Dedication of Homes?

The Candidate answers:

Thus have I endeavored and will continue to so endeavor.

The Bishop asks:

Have you recognized, and will you continue to ever recognize and honor, that your highest moral duty is first to spouse and children, then to parents and family, then to friends and community, then to nation, and finally toward all humankind?

The Candidate answers:

Thus have I endeavored and will continue to so endeavor.

The Bishop asks:

Have you been seeking the truth and striving for it, that you may discover where you are in error? (Wisdom 3:1, 4)

The Candidate answers:

Thus have I endeavored and will continue to so endeavor.

The Bishop asks:

Have you banished and driven away, and will you continue with all faithful diligence to banish and drive away, from the Church all erroneous and strange doctrines contrary to the book of the Triple Path?

The Candidate answers:

Thus have I endeavored and will continue to so endeavor.

The Bishop asks:

Have you accepted, and will you continue to accept, the importance of traditional values and in honoring and following the traditions, morals, and practices of our ancestors?

The Candidate answers:

Thus have I endeavored and will continue to so endeavor.

The Bishop asks:

Do you take upon yourself the solemn and sacred responsibility as a Steward of our traditions, committing that if you ever think you have found a way along the path that appears shorter and smoother to travel, that you will scout out miles far ahead to verify its soundness, always being ware that you do not shortsightedly fool yourself into following what ends up being a dangerous or faulty path, when the safety of the old road was there all along? (Hope 9: 11)

The Candidate answers:

I take upon myself this most solemn and sacred responsibility. I will endeavor with my greatest effort to be present and vigilant, and wise, that I not choose wrongly. I will watch carefully that I not fool myself by rationalizing away the wisdom of the past and of tradition. I will endeavor always to remember that a break from tradition is more likely to bring decline, ruin, or collapse, than improvement. (Virtue 1:11; Hope 9:13)

The Bishop asks:

Have you been, and will you continue to be, fearless and fierce in defense of the Church and the Triple Path, and our traditions, and those to whom you owe your greatest duties?

The Candidate answers:

Thus have I endeavored and will continue to so endeavor.

The Bishop asks:

Have you been, and will you continue for the rest of your life to be, as self-sufficient as possible and to hold yourself accountable, never shrinking from your own actions and the consequences that flow therefrom?

The Candidate answers:

Thus have I endeavored and will continue to so endeavor.

The Bishop says:

We commend you for your dedication. And so finally, I ask, do you, of your own free will, accept this Ordination, to serve, without any remuneration, God and this Church, to help your fellow-travelers in their journey on the Triple Path?

The Candidate answers:

Yes.

The Bishop addresses the Candidate:

In this most solemn and important office, I charge you to act with great care, to apply yourself to this office and to show yourself dutiful and thankful unto God and the Congregation of the Faithful of the Triple Path, which have placed you in so high a dignity, and also to beware that neither you yourself offend, nor give occasion that others offend. Remember how studious you should be in reading and learning the book of the Triple Path, the Codex, and the best books of our civilization, and also that you should forsake, as much as practicable, worldly and frivolous cares and pursuits.

Let the Officiant proceed with the Ordination.

The Officiant raises his arms and prays:

O God, we seek mercy in our infirmities that we may serve Thee and this Church, to help our fellow-travelers in their journey on the Triple Path. Let this, Thy servant to be Ordained, and all of us, act in holiness and pureness of living, with wisdom, virtue, and hope. Amen.

The Candidate is then seated before the Ward. The Officiant places a small amount of consecrated oil on his finger and says:

(Candidate), I anoint you an Elder of the Congregation of the Faithful of the Triple Path, in the name of God, and of wisdom, virtue, and hope.

Amen.

As he speaks, the Officiant uses his finger to anoint the Candidate with Consecrated Oil on the forehead, making the form of the Tricrux with the oil, forming one of each of the three prongs as he says each of the words "wisdom", "virtue", and "hope".

The Officiant says:

Now, all those Elders previously invited, come forward to join in Ordaining (Candidate).

The Officiant moves behind the Candidate and places his hands on the Candidate's head. Any other Elders who have been previously invited join in and lay their hands on the Candidate's head as well. The Officiant Ordains the Candidate by saying:

O God,

By the authority of the Congregation of the Faithful of the Triple Path and in my office as an Elder, I Ordain this person, (Candidate), as an Elder of the Congregation of the Faithful of the Triple Path.

The Officiant then pronounces words of blessing, counsel, and comfort to the Candidate as he feels inspired to speak, taking care not to overstep the bounds of prudence or propriety. He then closes by saying:

Amen.

Those assisting the Officiant return to their seats.

The Officiant says:

As a symbol of your office of Elder, we present you with this Stole.

The Officiant presents to the candidate the Stole of an Elder, which is made of dark red fabric with two embroidered gold or yellow Tricruxes, placed so that when the Stole is worn, one Tricrux is on each side at about chest level. At the bottom on each side is a gold or yellow Trimonvia. The Stole of an Elder has a yellow or gold border. The Stole may include other additional appropriate decorative or symbolic elements as defined by local custom and practice. The Officiant dresses the Candidate in the Stole.

The Officiant continues:

You must wear a Stole whenever you act as an Officiant in any required Rite, private or public. As a symbol of your office in the Church, you must treat this Stole with solemnity and reverence. And of even greater importance, live your life so that you treat this office of Elder with the solemnity and reverence to which it is due.

This Stole is not yet consecrated. Upon your return home from this Ordination, you must consecrate it yourself, for now you are an Elder of the Congregation of the Faithful of the Triple Path.

The Officiant returns to his seat. The Communal Sacrament proceeds as normal.

Thanksgiving of a Mother After Childbirth

The Rite of Thanksgiving of a Mother After Childbirth is performed during Communal Sacrament. It is only performed for Baptized, Confirmed, and Initiated Mothers who gave birth to a child in wedlock. It is usually performed on a Fast and Testimony Sunday, generally directly after the Naming and Dedication of her child (but this is not required). The Officiant for the Rite shall be a Priest or Elder in good standing selected by the Mother, usually her Husband, or her Father or Godfather if her Husband is unavailable or unable to perform the Rite.

The Mother shall approach the Officiant and kneel. The Officiant raises his arms and prays:

O God,

By the authority of the Congregation of the Faithful of the Triple Path, I anoint you as a Mother in this Church, to be honored and revered forevermore as you nurture your child in wisdom, virtue, and hope.

Amen.

As he speaks, the Officiant uses his finger to anoint the Moth with Consecrated Oil on the forehead, making the form of the Tricrux with the oil, forming one of each of the three prongs as he says each of the words "wisdom", "virtue", and "hope".

The Officiant says to the Mother:

Rise and face the congregation, that they may praise you.

The Mother stands next to the Officiant, facing the Ward. The Ward says:

Praise be to you, Mother.

The Officiant says:

Inasmuch, by the grace of God, you have safely delivered a child and have persevered and been preserved through the great pains and perils of childbirth, let us give a Prayer of Thanksgiving unto God.

561

The Officiant addresses the Ward.

Brothers and Sisters, please be upstanding, and let us pray.

All in the Ward stand, while the Officiant prays, his arms upraised:

O God, we give thanks for all the good things in our lives, which come by Thy grace. We give thanks for deliverance from afflictions and tribulations. We give thanks for kindness and affection and love, and any teaching that is sweet and plain that guides us toward wisdom, leads us to practice virtue, or inspires us to labor with hope. We rejoice in the Divine illumination that flows into us from following the Triple Path.

We have known hardship and sorrow; we are grateful for the lessons we learned from them. But we dwell not on our misfortunes, and instead marvel at all the great blessings in our lives.

We give thanks for family, food, clothing, shelter, and the simple joys of life, and we pray for all those who find these lacking.

We are grateful for thought and conscience, for the freedom to act and not be acted upon, and for the consequences that naturally flow from our actions.

We give thanks for the spark of Thy divinity we feel in our best moments and the chance to do better after we have passed through our worst.

And most of all, on this day, we give thanks for the safe deliverance of this Mother and her child, and for her courage to bear the next generation.

May she and we all be preserved on the Triple Path and protected from faltering or stumbling through life. We here resolve again to move forward with firmness on the Triple Path, always, and progress toward a brighter day.

Amen.

Brothers and Sisters, please be seated.

The Ward is seated. The Officiant and Mother remain standing. The Officiant says:

O God, may this woman, your servant, be blessed.

The Ward answers:
Who puts her trust in Thee.
The Officiant says:
Be Thou to her a strong tower.
The Ward Answers:
From the face of her enemy and all that assail her.
The Officiant says:
Our God, this is our prayer.
The Ward Answers:
And let our cry come unto Thee.
The Officiant and Ward say:
Amen.
The Officiant says:
Let us pray.

O almighty God, we give Thee humble thanks that this Mother, Your servant, has safely delivered a child and has persevered and been preserved through the great pains and perils of Childbirth.

We pray that she might continue faithfully to live and walk the Triple Path according to Thy will, through Thy grace, and that she feel Thy fortitude and strength during the many trials of motherhood, and that she also enjoy its sweet rewards.

Amen.

Now, Brothers and Sisters, please be upstanding, and let us again praise this Mother.

The Ward rises and says:
Praise be to this virtuous woman, perpetuator of our people, nurturer of our heritage, and creator of our future.

Amen.

The Mother returns to her seat among the Ward and the Sacrament continues as normal, except that the Prayer of Thanksgiving after the talks is omitted.

Burial of the Dead

The Rite of Burial of the Dead should usually be performed only for Church members in good standing.

Where something in the Rite is described as being left up to "Preference", it is to be decided either by the Departed before his or her passing or by those responsible for the Departed's affairs (usually spouse, children, and/or parents).

The Rite should normally be conducted first in a Church building and then at the graveside as indicated, but the first part may be performed at the home or a mortuary or other similar location, instead of at a Church, and then subsequently at the graveside, or the Rite may entirely be performed at the graveside, according to Preference. The Officiant for this Rite should be an Elder in good standing, chosen according to Preference. He performs the Rite dressed in his Stole. The Rite should be conducted in a way that is simple, impressive, and in keeping with the principles of the Triple Path. It should usually be held on a day other than Sunday.

Wherever possible, the departed should be consigned to the earth, with nothing done that is destructive of the body. Cremation is therefore discouraged.

Those who have been Initiated should be buried in their ceremonial Initiation clothing.

The Officiant meeting the body of the departed at the entrance of the Churchyard, and going before it, either into the sanctuary, or towards the Grave, shall say, or sing, the following passages from the book of The Triple Path.

All things perish, everything passes; even the universe, immortal and enduring as it is, changes and never remains the same. Only God stands firm, perfectly unchanging. (Wisdom 12:3)

We brought nothing into this world, and how can we carry anything out? God gave, and He has taken away. Blessed be the

Name of God. (Hope 14:19)

Stand in awe and stillness, and sin not. Let us offer right sacrifices and put our trust in God. (Hope 3:1)

Hope is an anchor to our hearts, making us sure and steadfast, always striving for improvement, abounding in virtue, and growing in wisdom. (Hope 1:7)

This is the day in which God has placed us. Let us rejoice and be glad in it. (Hope 8:2)

After they are come into the Church, the Officiant shall read the following passages from this book.

The deep flood of time rolls over all. Neither the infamy of the fool, nor the renown of the wise, will endure forever. The wise die just like fools. Eventually all will be forgotten and everyone will depart into the same realm of silence. Yet, the wise still follow God and the Triple Path; to them, the need to do so is self-evident. (Wisdom 13:11)

Death comes to everyone: to the wise and foolish, to the virtuous and evil, to the hopeful and pessimist alike. Followers of the Triple Path, though, leave the world better than they found it, just as their forebears, whether spiritual or physical, did for them. (Hope 15:2)

A hymn may next be sung, if desired. A prayer is offered by someone previously invited.

At this point, a program as determined according to Preference may be conducted, including talks, eulogies, and music, all of which should be reverent and in accord with the principles of this book, and also avoiding excessive length.

Following the program, when it comes time to lay the Departed's body in the earth, the Officiant shall say the following at the graveside:

All that are born have but a short time to live. We come up, and are cut down, like a flower; we flee as it were a shadow, and never continue in one stay. In the midst of life we are in death.

As the sorrows of death compass us and the pains of hell grasp, let us pray and call on the name of God for deliverance.

(Hope 14:18):

Almighty God, whose mercies cannot be numbered,

To whom may we turn for succor at this time of sorrow,
but to Thee?

We commend unto Thee the soul of our (Brother/Sister),
(Name of Departed), Thy servant, which is departed hence from
us with the sign of faith.

We pray that (his/her) soul be not delivered into the eternal death, but that (he/she) obtain Thy mercy and everlasting
peace and be received unto Thee in the fellowship of all Thy departed servants, in eternal rest with Thy perpetual light shining
upon (him/her). May (his/her) soul rest in peace in Thee.

We in the country of the living give Thee hearty thanks
for the good examples of all those Thy servants, who, having finished their course in faith, do now rest from their labors. And we
beseech Thee, that the soul of our dear departed (Brother/Sister),
with all those who are departed in the true faith of Thy holy
Name, may also be received unto Thee, in Thy eternal and everlasting glory.

Amen.

While some earth is cast upon the coffin by some standing by, the Officiant shall say,

Forasmuch as God has taken unto Himself the soul of our
dear (Brother/Sister) here departed, we therefore commit (his/her)
body to the ground; earth to earth, ashes to ashes, dust to dust.

See how soon everything is forgotten. Look at the chaos of
infinite time on each side of the present and then understand the
emptiness of applause, and the changeableness and lack of judgment in those who pretend to give praise. Let us thus quiet our
vanities at last and think on the serenity and peace of following God
and the Triple Path and content ourselves with this. (Wisdom 13:
13)

*Those casting earth on the coffin cease and the Officiant
prays:*

Almighty God,

We mourn the passing of our fellow traveler on the Triple Path, (Name of Departed). Into Thine hand we commit (his/her) spirit.

We meekly beseech Thee to raise us from the death of sin unto the life of righteousness, that Thy grace and love be with us all ever more, and that we stand firm in our faith in Thee, moving forward on the Triple Path until the end of our lives. Amen.

The Officiant addresses those gathered:

Dear Brothers and Sisters, you here present, live your lives well, so that when you are laid to rest it may be said of you that you sought wisdom, practiced virtue, and labored with hope until the end of your days.

The living know they will die. What do the dead know? They have no more earthly reward, and even the memory of them will eventually be forgotten. Whatever good you can do while you are alive, do it well, and with courage and enthusiasm. What more earthly works or thoughts can you accomplish in the grave to which you are headed? (Hope 15:3)

Whether you live a life of wisdom, virtue, and hope or whether you live a life of foolishness, evil, and lazy despair, you still will be buried, reduced to dust, and be quiet at last. Before that happens, how much better to work to increase the wisdom virtue, and hope in the world, rather than idly lamenting the foolishness, evil, and lazy despair already here. (Hope 2:4)

We are weak, watery beings standing in the midst of unrealities; therefore let us turn our minds to the things that are everlasting and real—God, truth, and wisdom, virtue, and hope. (Foundations 6:10)

Let us not just obey God, but train ourselves to agree with Him, obeying Him not because we must, but because our souls will it. (Foundations 6:18)

Let us take refuge in God, that we may be at peace. (Foundation 6:20)

Let us commend our souls to God, putting our trust in

Him. Let Him be our rock and fortress of shelter. Let Him guide and lead us. (Foundations 6:21)

In Him let our hope and trust rest. Let His faithfulness and truth be our defense. (Foundations 6:21)

Brothers and Sisters, let us depart this place with the memory of our dearly departed (Brother/Sister) imprinted forever in our hearts and let us also always remember:

Each who passed through this life, rich or poor,

Chose a path to walk 'til at death's door.

You who yet breathe are still choosing yours.

Church Organization and Practice

Note: This section sets forth a tentative, basic vision for the general contours of Church organization and practice through its initial phases of growth to the point of reaching a more mature, stable status.

This section is subject to change as real-world practice reveals the need for adjustment and further detail. As the Church grows, this section will be expanded and changed as needed.

In the Church's early phases, many provisions in this section (such as numbers of members per Ward and length of time as a member before Ordination) will of necessity be waived.

Name of the Church

The name of the Church shall be the Church of the West.

First Principles of Church Organization and Governance

The first principle of Church Organization and Governance that should rule all Stewards and members in Church affairs is seeking wisdom, practicing virtue, and laboring with hope.

Second, that we respect and follow the traditions and values of our ancestors.

Third, that all things shall be done by common consent of the Church members as represented by the Qualified Voters; that there should be absolute transparency at all levels of the Church and in all decisions and actions; and that all aspects of Church administration and governance should be as local as possible; and that the members, Qualified Voters, and Stewards of the Church watch themselves always, that they act with wisdom and virtue to seek that they never lead the Church astray to choose evil instead of good, for if they do fail in this, their wrong choices will sow the seeds of the Church's destruction.

Fourth, that no action shall be performed in the Church, and no action should be taken by the Church as a body, that is contrary to this book; and

Fifth, that all things be done in an orderly manner, with much prayer, meditation, and faith, with wisdom, virtue, and hope.

Each Church member and Steward has an unceasing duty to ensure there is no abuse or corruption in the Church. When abuse or corruption of any kind is discovered, each Church member, and especially Stewards, has an independent, solemn duty to speak up and do what is necessary to ensure that it is promptly and decisively stopped and that perpetrators are held to account before civil and ecclesiastical authorities.

Church Units of Organization

The most fundamental unit of organization of the Church is the family. Families organize themselves into congregations: smaller congregations as Branches (either Unrecognized and Recognized), stewarded by a Chief Elder and two Vice-Chief Elders; larger congregations as Wards stewarded by a Bishop and two Vice-Bishops, and governed a Ward Council of the Qualified Voters.

Five to ten Wards are organized into a Diocese stewarded by an Archbishop, two Vice-Archbishops, and a Diocesan Council of 12 Elders. When there are at least ten Dioceses in a designated, separate geographical or political area (such as a country or a U.S. state), then they are organized into a Province stewarded by a Cardinal, two Vice-Cardinals, and a Provincial Council of 12 Elders. All Stewardship positions are held for limited periods of time and are filled by sortition from a list of those deemed qualified to serve by the Wards involved.

At all levels of the Church, newcomers should prove themselves over time to be faithful, trustworthy, and true before being given responsibility.

Private Practice

Anyone not living within the geographical boundaries of a

duly organized congregation of the Church of the West who wishes to be counted among the Congregation of the Faithful of the Triple Path and participate in its Rites may administer the Rites at home, within the family, but still taking care to ensure that all qualifications are met before administering them. Generally, such Rites are administered by the father, or in cases where the father does not desire participation in the Triple Path, by a grandfather, uncle, or other close male relative. The person administering Rites within the family would administer them to the other family members and then self-administer them to himself. In cases of individuals wishing to join the Faithful, the Rites may also be self-administered.

The Rites of Ordination, Initiation, Marriage, and Burial may only be administered within an officially recognized congregation of the Triple Path, or by an Ordained Elder from recognized congregation.

Unrecognized Branches

When there is more than one family or household of adherents to the Triple Path who all reside within about 30 minutes' travel (or other reasonable, acceptable distance) from each other, they should organize themselves together as an Unrecognized Branch. They should follow all the same procedures as a Recognized Branch, except they may not Ordain Deacons, Priests, and Elders. Instead, males should be designated as Acting Deacons, Priests, and Elders to fulfill the required functions.

Recognized Branches

Once established, Unrecognized Branches should apply to the Province within which they reside (or other provisional, interim authority if there is not yet a Province) to be recognized as, or organized into, a Recognized Branch (hereafter referred to just as a "Branch"). Before they are recognized or organized by a Province, they shall be known as an unorganized Branch.

A Province (or other provisional, interim authority) may also directly organize members living within a geographical area into a Branch.

After a Branch is recognized, men may be Ordained. If

credibly attested, prior observance of the Church's Rites, Feasts, and practices, and regular attendance and participation while the Branch was Unrecognized, may count toward the prescribed times required for Ordination as Deacons and Priests. Once Priests have been Ordained in the Branch, then all previously administered Rites of Passage must be re-administered through the Branch as if being received for the first time. During this period, if there is no one meeting the qualifications for Ordination as Elder, a Priest may be Ordained as Chief Priest (as well as two Vice-Chief Priests) until there are men in the Branch who qualify as Elders.

Any Rites administered before the Branch was officially recognized should be re-administered, but prior observance of the Church's Rites, Feasts, and practices, and regular attendance and participation while the Branch was Unrecognized, if credibly attested, may count toward the prescribed times required for receiving the Rites.

Anyone who has received self-administered or private Rites who later joins a Branch should newly receive the Rites through the Branch if receiving them for the first time.

Wards

When a Branch has at least 100 active members and enough Qualified Voters to fill all the necessary positions for a well-functioning Ward, then it is organized into a Ward. Once a ward has 200 active members and enough Qualified Voters to fill all the necessary positions for two well-functioning Wards, then the Diocese should recommend that the Ward be divided and suggest boundaries that would lead to an even and equitable division (both in terms of geography and the number and level of experience of members). The Ward division is finalized when the Ward's Bishop and Vice-Bishops concur and three-fifths of the Ward's Qualified Voters have agreed (after any modifications to the boundaries according to their best judgment).

The defining difference between a Branch and a Ward is size. In most respects, they should otherwise function identically. Accordingly, in most parts of this book, for brevity's sake, only the term "Ward" is used to refer to either type of congregation.

A Ward is governed by its Qualified Voters. A male Qualified Voter is a Priest or Elder who still complies with the requirements for Ordination to his office; actively participates in the Ward;
demonstrates a wise and virtuous disposition; is married within the
Church (with allowance to be made for converts baptized after the
age of 18); and has at least three children of good moral character
who actively participate in their Wards (with allowance to be made
for those with deceased children and for converts to the Church
whose children were not born within the faith). A female Qualified
Voter has been Initiated and still complies with the requirements
for Initiation, actively participates in the Ward; is married within
the Church (with allowance to be made for converts baptized after
the age of 18); and has at least three children of good moral character who actively participate in their Wards (with allowance to be
made for those with deceased children and for converts to the
Church whose children were not born within the faith).

Any major decision about Ward governance must be approved by the Qualified Voters. The number of votes each voter
may cast is equal to the number of the voter's children in good
standing in the Church (even if they are adults, and even if they do
not live in the Ward), plus one. Wards, on most matters, operate
with a great degree of autonomy (so long as they follow the principles of this book). Branches are administered with more direct involvement of the Diocese.

Any person meeting the requirements may apply for status
as a Qualified Voter. The current Qualified Voters of the Ward
decide whether the person fulfills the necessary requirements, and
if so, accepts the person as a Qualified Voter; the rest of the Qualified Voters of the Diocese must vote to ratify that decision before
it takes effect. When a Qualified Voter moves to a Ward in a different Diocese, that person must re-apply for Qualified Voter status in the new Ward, and only after at least one year of residence
in the Ward.

The title of the Steward of a Branch is Chief Elder; he is assisted by two Vice-Chief Elders who act in his stead when he is absent and help him fulfill his duties. The title of the Steward of a Ward is a Bishop; he is assisted by two Vice-Bishops who act in his stead when he is absent and help him fulfill his duties. Other than a difference in title, the role of each position is virtually the same. In most parts of this book the term "Bishop" is used to refer to both Bishops and Chief Elders, and "Vice-Bishops," is used to refer to both and Vice-Bishops and Vice-Chief Elders.

All Bishops and Vice-Bishops must fulfill the same qualifications for Ordination to the office of Elder, as described in the Rite of Ordination of Elders. The Bishop and the Vice-Bishops administrate the ward in accordance with the direction they receive from the Qualified Voters; they are accountable to the Qualified Voters. The Bishop and the Vice-Bishops should delegate as much as possible to spread the burden and the blessings of experience. All Qualified Voters in the Ward make up the Ward Council. Bishops and Vice-Bishops must meet with the Ward Council at least once a month to discuss Ward business, planned future courses of action, to seek counsel, and for the Qualified Voters to vote on Ward business, and to approve persons to receive Rites before they are presented to the Ward in Sunday Sacrament.

A Bishop normally serves a term of two years. When the Stewardship of Bishop becomes vacant, if the Qualified Voters of the Ward approve, the First Vice-Bishop is Ordained Bishop, the Second Vice-Bishop becomes the First Vice-Bishop (no Ordination is necessary), and a new man is selected and Ordained as the Second Vice-Bishop. In the normal course of events, a Ward Steward serves for a total of six years, two years in each position.

Whenever the Bishop is absent or removed from his position, the First Vice-Bishop acts as Bishop; the Second Vice-Bishop acts as Bishop in the absence or removal of the Bishop and First Vice-Bishop. If the Stewardship of first Vice-Bishop becomes vacant, then the second Vice-Bishop becomes first Vice-Bishop.

When there are disputes between members of the Ward, the Bishop and Vice-Bishops may jointly adjudicate disputes between members of the Ward (or if the Bishop or one of the Vice-Bishops is an interested party in the dispute, then the dispute may be taken to the Diocese).

Ward Conferences should typically be held every six months, during Communal Sacrament, for the conducting of special ward business and the sharing of inspiring messages.

On the Saturday evening three weeks before the Ward Conference, the Qualified Voters of the Ward meet during their regular monthly meeting to counsel together about the Ward and make binding decisions for it. Generally, a Bishop's or a Vice-Bishop's term expires at Ward Conference. Thus, at this meeting the Qualified Voters select the next Ward Steward to be Ordained at Ward Conference, as well as selecting men to fill positions made vacant since the prior Ward Conference (if the man left his Stewardship early because he was removed or moved away). The selection is made through sortition. When the Qualified Voters meet, each should carefully assess the qualifications of all men who have not already served as a Ward Steward who are Priests or Elders, to determine who among them is best qualified. No man should serve more than one six-year course as a Ward Steward, unless there are no other qualified men in the Ward who have not done so.

At the meeting, if only one Stewardship is being filled, the Qualified Voters individually rank-order their top four choices from one to four, with their top choice receiving a four, and their lowest choice receiving a one. Each score is multiplied by the Voter's number of votes. The score for each ranked person is added together. The four selectees with the highest scores are then announced. (If there is a tie for fourth place, then the top five selectees are announced). Each of the four men must then affirm whether he is willing to serve as a Ward Steward. If he is not, then the next-highest scoring man is announced and given the opportunity to affirm whether he will serve. This continues until a list of four men willing to serve has been obtained. One name is then selected at random from the four, in full view of the assembled Qualified Voters (generally by writing each name on an identical piece of paper, placed into a hat or bowl, and then drawing one name out). That person will be the new Ward Steward. If two positions are to be filled, then the Qualified Voters rank their top five choices and the two selectees are chosen from five highest scorers; if three positions are to be filled, then the Qualified Voters rank their top seven choices and select from the seven highest scorers. When two or three names are drawn, the older man takes the higher position. If any of the three have not yet been Ordained as an Elder, he must be Ordained as an Elder before being Ordained as Bishop or Vice-Bishop. Both Ordinations may be performed in the same Rite. Any of the remaining five men on the list who have not been Ordained an Elder may also be Ordained an Elder if he so chooses. Men selected to serve as Ward Stewards are Ordained at the Ward Conference following the vote and sortition after their names have been presented and approved three times.

If one or both of the Stewardships of Vice-Bishop become vacant, then the Bishop may designate any Elder to be acting Vice-Bishop until the vacancy be filled at the next Ward Conference.

Every adult member of the Ward who has been baptized and confirmed and is in good standing should have a position of responsibility in the Ward allowing him or her to contribute to the Ward's smooth operation and success (for example, some such positions would be those of Sunday School teacher, music leader, and usher).

Geographical Boundaries and Ward Membership

Residence determines congregation. When a member or prospective member resides within the geographical boundaries of an established Ward, then that person should participate in and attend that Ward.

Anyone who lives within the geographical boundaries of a Ward of the Church of the West and who wishes to be counted among the Congregation of the Faithful of the Triple Path and participate in its Rites should do so by participating in his or her local Ward and receiving the Rites within it (and not through self-administered Rites), once properly approved by the Ward.

Dioceses

A Diocese is governed by its Qualified Voters. It is stewarded by an Archbishop, first Vice-Archbishop, a second Vice-Archbishop, and a Diocesan Council made up of twelve Elders, with at least one Elder from each Ward; they should delegate as much as possible to spread the burden and the blessings of experience.

An Archbishop normally serves a term of two years. When the Stewardship of Archbishop becomes vacant, if the Qualified Voters of the Diocese approve, the First Vice-Archbishop is Ordained Archbishop, the Second Vice-Archbishop becomes the First Vice-Archbishop (no Ordination is necessary), and a new man is selected and Ordained as the Second Vice-Archbishop. Typically, four members of the Diocesan Council are selected each year. They serve two years as junior Councilors, two years as Councilors, and two years as senior Councilors. In the normal course of events, a Diocesan Steward serves for a total of six years, two years in each position, whether on the Council or the Archbishopric.

The qualifications for serving as a Diocesan Steward are the same as for Ordination as an Elder, except that a man must already be an Elder to be voted onto the sortition list for a position as a Diocesan Steward.

Archbishops and Vice-Archbishops must meet with the Diocesan Council at least once a month to discuss Diocesan business, planned future courses of action, and to seek counsel. They should meet every two months with the Bishops and Vice-Bishops of all the Wards in the Diocese to do the same.

Dioceses should hold a biannual conference during which the members of all the congregations of the Diocese meet together for an extended Communal Sacrament of about two hours (no other Church worship services should be held that day). The extended time is to allow for the conduct of Diocese business and for additional talks and testimonies.

On the Saturday evening four weeks before the Diocesan Conference, the Qualified Voters of the Diocese meet to counsel together about the Diocese and make binding decisions for the Diocese. Generally, the terms of Diocesan Stewards expire at Diocesan Conference. Thus, at this meeting the Qualified Voters select as necessary the next Diocesan Stewards (whether because a Steward's term is set to expire at the upcoming conference or because a position was made vacant since the prior Diocesan Conference because the man left his Stewardship early), as well as current or anticipated vacancies at the Provincial level. The Qualified Voters of the Diocese fill any vacancies through a similar process of sortition as used at the Ward level. If three or fewer positions are vacant, then the ten highest-scoring names are placed on the sortition list. If between four and eight positions are to be filled, then the twenty highest-scoring names should be placed on the sortition list. If more than eight positions are to be filled, then thirty names should be placed on the sortition list. In all cases, if there is a tie for last place, then an extra name may be placed on the list. All names are presented for approval to the Qualified Voters in the Wards of the Diocese over the next three weeks. Men thus selected and approved to serve in Diocesan Stewardship positions are Ordained to their Stewardships at the upcoming Diocesan Conference. If more than one Steward is to be Ordained, then the preliminary question and answer parts of the Rite may be conducted jointly with all of the Candidates, with each responding in turn to the questions, and then each being individually Ordained.

If the Stewardship of first Vice-Archbishop becomes vacant, then the second Vice-Archbishop becomes first Vice-Archbishop. If the Stewardship of second, or both first and second, Vice-Archbishop becomes vacant, then the Archbishop may designate any member of the Diocesan Council to be acting Vice-Archbishop(s) until the vacancy be filled at the next Diocesan Conference. If the Stewardship of Archbishop becomes vacant, then the first Vice-Archbishop acts as Archbishop until a new Archbishop (usually the first Vice-Archbishop) is selected and Ordained. If the Stewardships of Archbishop and Vice-Archbishop all become vacant at the same time, then the longest-serving three members of the Diocesan Council become acting Archbishop and Vice-Archbishops until new men be approved.

No man should serve more than one six-year course as a Diocesan Steward, unless there are no other qualified men in the Diocese who have not done so.

A Diocesan committee of three disinterested Elders randomly selected from the Archbishops, Vice-Archbishops, and Diocesan Council may adjudicate disputes between members of different Wards in the same Diocese. They may also adjudicate disputes between members of the same Ward, if no resolution was achieved at the Ward level.

Provinces

A Province is the highest level of Church organization. Each Province is co-equal with each other Province.

A Province is governed by its Qualified Voters. It is Stewarded by a Cardinal, a First Vice-Cardinal, a Second Vice-Cardinal, and a Provincial Council of twelve Elders (if there are twelve or fewer Dioceses in the Province, each Diocese should have at least one Elder on the Council; if there are more than twelve Dioceses in the Province, each Councilor should be from a different Diocese). The Provincial Stewards should delegate as much as possible to spread the burden and the blessings of experience.

A Cardinal normally serves a term of two years. When the Stewardship of Cardinal becomes vacant, if the Qualified Voters of the Province approve, the First Vice-Cardinal is Ordained Cardinal, the Second Vice-Cardinal becomes the First Cardinal (no Ordination is necessary), and a new man is selected and Ordained as the Second Vice-Cardinal. Typically, four members of the Provincial Council are selected each year. They serve two years as junior Councilors, two years as Councilors, and two years as senior Councilors. In the normal course of events, a Provincial Steward serves for a total of six years, two years in each position, whether on the Council or the Cardinalate.

The qualifications for serving in a Provincial Stewardship position are the same as for Ordination as an Elder, except that a man must already have first served as a Ward or Diocesan Steward to be voted onto the sortition list for a position as a Provincial Steward.

Provinces should hold a Provincial Conference once a year during which the members of the Province meet together for an extended Communal Sacrament of about two hours (no other Church worship services should be held that day). The extended time is to allow for the conduct of Provincial business and for additional talks.

The Cardinal, Vice-Cardinals, and the Provincial Council conduct the conference. Each Diocese within the Province should be represented by their Archbishop, Vice-Archbishops, and Diocesan Council. Each Ward should be represented by its Bishop and Vice-Bishops. Provincial, Diocesan, and Ward Stewards should invite and encourage every member of the Church within the Province to attend. A Provincial Conference should always be recorded for retransmission to the Province members, and should be broadcast live whenever the capability is available.

Generally, the terms of Provincial Stewards expire at Provincial Conference. During the Diocesan Conferences just prior to the planned Provincial Conference, the Qualified Voters also vote to fill all anticipated or current vacancies in Provincial Stewardship positions through an identical process of voting and sortition as used at the Diocesan level, except any man considered for a Stewardship position must have already served as a Ward or Diocesan Steward. If three or fewer positions are vacant, then the ten highest-scoring names are placed on the sortition list. If between four and eight positions are to be filled, then the twenty highest-scoring names should be placed on the sortition list. If more than eight positions are to be filled, then thirty names should be placed on the sortition list. In all cases, if there is a tie for last place, then an extra name may be placed on the list.

Each Diocese transmits its vote information to the Province five weeks before the Provincial Conference is to happen. All sitting Provincial Stewards jointly meet as soon as possible after receiving the vote information. At this meeting any Diocesan Steward, Bishop, or Vice-Bishop may also attend. In full view of all, the Provincial Stewards draw out the required number of names and then immediately publicize these names to the Dioceses of the Province. All names are presented for approval to the Qualified Voters in the Wards of all the Dioceses over the next three weeks. All new, approved Provincial Stewards are Ordained at the upcoming Provincial Conference. If more than one Steward is to be Ordained, then the preliminary question and answer parts of the Rite may be conducted jointly with all of the Candidates, with each responding in turn to the questions, and then each being individually Ordained.

If the Stewardship of first Vice-Cardinal becomes vacant, then the second Vice-Cardinal becomes first Vice-Cardinal. If the Stewardship of second, or both first and second, Vice-Cardinal becomes vacant, then the Cardinal may designate any member of the Provincial Council to be acting Vice-Cardinal(s) until the vacancy be filled at the next Provincial Conference. If the Stewardship of Cardinal becomes vacant, then the first Vice-Cardinal acts as Cardinal until a new Cardinal (usually the first Vice-Cardinal) is selected and Ordained. If the Stewardships of Cardinal and Vice-Cardinal all become vacant at the same time, then the longest-serving three members of the Diocesan Council become acting Cardinal and Vice-Cardinals until new men be approved.

Provincial meetings should always be recorded for retransmission to all Church members in the Province and should be broadcast live whenever the capability is available.

No decision taken at a Provincial Conference may take effect until approved by a majority of the eligible Qualified Votes within the Province.

No man should serve more than one six-year course as a Provincial Steward.

A Provincial committee of three disinterested Elders selected from the Cardinal, Vice-Cardinal, and Provincial Council may adjudicate disputes between members of different Dioceses in the same Province. They may also adjudicate disputes between members of the same Ward or Diocese, if no resolution was achieved at the Ward and Diocese level.

Any decision by Provincial Stewards regarding interpretation of this book or Church practice made at the Provincial level must first be ratified by a majority of Qualified Votes of the Province and then ratified by a Churchwide vote in conjunction with the next Churchwide meeting. If it is not ratified, then the General Conference or Holy Synod that declined to ratify the interpretation must substitute its own approved interpretation that must then be approved by a Churchwide vote.

Churchwide Meetings

A General Conference of the whole Church shall meet every two years to discuss Churchwide business and, if necessary, changes to Church policy. The General Conference is hosted by one of the Church provinces on a rotating basis to be decided at a prior General Conference or Holy Synod.

Every ten years instead of a General Conference shall be held a Holy Synod of the Church at which changes to Church scripture and core Church practice may be made. Only Qualified Voters who are Elders and their wives who are Qualified Voters may vote on such changes.

All Provincial Stewards should be present at Churchwide meetings. Stewards should invite and encourage every other member of the Church within their Province to attend. Never Churchwide meetings (or at any other time) should any one person or small group purport to take upon themself or themselves leadership of the whole Church.

Churchwide meetings should always be recorded for retransmission to all Church members and should always be broadcast live whenever the capability is available.

Decisions at a General Conference must be approved by a three-fifths vote of the eligible Qualified Votes of those present. No decision taken at a General Conference may take effect until approved by three-fifths of the eligible Qualified Votes within the entire Church and by majorities of Qualified Votes in a majority of

Wards, a majority of Dioceses, and a majority of Provinces. Decisions at a Holy Synod must be approved by a two-thirds vote of the eligible Qualified Votes of the Elders and their wives present. No decision taken at a Holy Synod may take effect until ratified first by two-thirds of the eligible Qualified Votes of Elders and their wives Churchwide, after which it is to be presented for a Churchwide vote and must be approved by two-thirds of the eligible Qualified Votes within the entire Church and by majorities of Qualified Votes in a majority of Wards, Dioceses, and Provinces, and then again approved at the next General Conference following the normal procedures for General Conference votes.

A General Conference or Holy Synod may establish judicial committees to adjudicate disputes between members of different Provinces and to offer interpretations of this book and Church practice. Any decision regarding interpretation of this book or Church practice does not become binding on the Church until it is first ratified by the same process as ratifying a change to that section of this book.

The General Conference shall establish and update (as needed) standardized financial, clerical, and administrative procedures for Wards, Dioceses, and Provinces to follow to ensure the wise and faithful collection and expenditure of funds, consistent keeping of records, and the orderly function of Wards, Dioceses, and Provinces. Each Ward, Diocese, and Province, however, shall exist as independent entities maintaining their own separate finances and ownership of property and buildings.

The first General Conference shall create interim standardized rules for evaluating a candidate's qualification for a Rite and granting permission to receive the Rite. It shall also create interim rules about when remarriage within the Church of divorced members would be permissible and also about excommunication (both to clarify procedures to be followed and what offenses are excommunicable). The first General Conference shall also consider whether the Church should recognize and venerate saints, and if so, the process by which this should be realized. These interim rules about Rites, remarriage, excommunication, and saints shall be amended and ratified as needed by subsequent General Conferences and then finalized by the first Holy Synod.

Women's Organization

There shall be a parallel auxiliary women's organization organized, created, headed, and run by the women of the Church. It shall have similar organizational principles and structure to that of the rest of the Church.

Stewardship

The guiding principle for all Stewardship positions in the Church is that leaders serve limited terms. Stewards should always consider their role as foremost being to conserve the nature, practices, and conditions of the Church, and members should only vote for Stewards who have demonstrated a disposition to do so. Anyone filling such a position is acting as a Steward to ensure the proper and smooth functioning of the organization of the Church.

During initial stages of Church organization, temporary measures and waivers will be made as necessary to allow for the organization of congregations and Ordination of Stewards even though the required familial situation, or time periods of membership or practice have not been met.

Removal of Stewards

The qualified voters may remove any Steward from his position, by a majority of the qualified votes within the Ward, Diocese, or Province.

Excommunication

Any Church member who has engaged in, or is engaging in apostasy, gross indecency or immorality, criminal behavior, other egregious unvirtuous conduct, unjustified divorce (if the divorce was not mutually agreed upon, then only for the party that sued for divorce), or other conduct that brings the Church into grave disrepute, shall be excommunicated. Any qualified voter may refer a Church member who has engaged in such conduct to the member's Diocesan Stewards for consideration for excommunication. The case shall be heard by a joint meeting of the Archbishop, Vice-Archbishops, and Diocesan Council of the Church member's Diocese. They shall follow formal procedures of a judicial nature to weigh the evidence in favor and against the person and then decide upon the excommunication, which must be ratified by the Province's Cardinal, Vice-Cardinals and Provincial Council, even if the excommunicant has not appealed the excommunication.

Once the Diocese has decided to excommunicate a member, the person shall no longer be considered to be a Baptized member of the Church. The Diocese may decide to exclude that person from attendance at Church meetings and gatherings if it determines this to be in the best interest of the Church and its members. Otherwise, the person may attend Church meetings and gatherings and should be treated as any other non-member.

If the excommunicant disputes the decision, he or she may request an appeal of the Diocese's decision to the Cardinal, Vice-Cardinals, and Provincial Council, who shall meet jointly, following formal procedures of a judicial nature, to determine whether the Diocese's decision conforms with the principles of this book, the Creed, the Doctrines of the Church, and Church traditions, standards, and principles.

The excommunicated member may appeal the decision of the Province to the Judicial Council of the next General Conference or Holy Synod, which shall follow formal procedures of a judicial nature to determine whether the Diocese's and Province's decisions conform with the principles of this book, the Creed, the Doctrines of the Church, and Church traditions, standards, and principles.

During the time of appeals, the person's status shall remain as excommunicated. If the person's appeal is granted, then the person shall be restored to full membership with all its rights and responsibilities.

An excommunicated person who does not appeal the excommunication, or who has not prevailed in his or her appeals, shall usually only be eligible for re-Baptism after five years, unless

587

the Province establishes a different time period. The person must then be newly Baptized, Confirmed, Initiated, and Ordained as if a new member.

Amendments to This Book

During the life of the author of this book, changes may be made only with the consent of the author, either on his own initiative or with input from Church members or others; once the Church is duly and fully organized, such changes only become final after accepted at a General Conference or Holy Synod, and such changes may be proposed at a General Conference or Holy Synod, as set forth above. After the death of the author of this book, changes to the Meditations and Parables, Creed, and Rites and Feasts sections of this book may only be made through a Holy Synod; changes to the other sections of this book may be made through a General Conference.

Changes to this book should be made incrementally and slowly, and only when suggested changes originate from the body of the Church (not from its Stewards), and have a super-majority of support within the membership. After the death of the writer, changes to the Meditations and Parables, Creed, and Rites and Feasts sections of this book should be avoided absent highly compelling circumstances. As new doctrine and inspiring words are needed, members of the Church should write them and propose them to the body of the members of the Church for inclusion in a new book to be titled the Book of Further Elaboration, which shall grow by accretion, addition, and editing, as changing circumstances require and as further light and knowledge are gained.

More detailed procedures for making the changes and additions described in the above two paragraphs shall be introduced as Church growth requires such procedures.

Priesthood Offices

The following offices may be held by male Church members: Junior Deacon, Senior Deacon, Priest, and Elder. Elders may also serve as Stewards of their Wards, Dioceses, and Province, as Chief Elders, Bishops, Vice-Bishops, Archbishops, Vice-

Archbishops, Cardinals, Vice-Cardinals, and Councilors. The qualifications for each office are explained in the introductory explanation for each Rite of Ordination.

Junior Deacons

Junior Deacons are usually Ordained at 14 years of age and serve until turning 16, at which time they are ordinarily Ordained as Senior Deacons.

Junior Deacons assist the Bishop (and Vice-Bishops), the Officiant of a Rite, and Senior Deacons as needed to ensure the proper and smooth functioning of Communal Sacrament services. Their primary role is to prepare the Bread and Water of the Sacrament before the start of Communal Sacrament services and to distribute them during the service. They prepare it by placing unbroken bread in Sacrament trays, filling small Sacrament cups with water, and placing them all on a table to be blessed. They distribute it by carrying trays to each row of the Ward to be passed down the row by those seated on the row.

Senior Deacons

Senior Deacons may be Ordained starting at 16 years of age and usually serve until turning 18, at which time they are ordinarily Ordained as Priests.

Senior Deacons assist the Bishop (and Vice-Bishops) and the Officiant of a Rite as needed to ensure the proper and smooth functioning of Communal Sacrament services. Their primary role is to bless the Bread and Water of the Sacrament during Communal Sacrament services and to act as ushers, when needed, at Church meetings. They also assist the Bishop and Vice-Bishops as needed in working to help ensure the welfare of Ward members in need.

Priests

Priests are usually Ordained at 18 years of age, in connection with their Initiation.

Priests should be familiar with the teachings of this book and are to teach, expound, exhort, and watch over the Church. They may plan and conduct Communal Sacrament meetings, according to the teachings of this book and the requirements of wisdom, virtue, and hope. Priests should care for the Church's physical and spiritual needs, in harmony with the requirements of this book and the norms, rules, and practice of the Church.

Two Priests or Elders (or, if the Priest or Elder has a son who is a Deacon, the father should be assigned with his Deacon son) should be assigned to each family or household in the Ward to visit the household once a month to share a spiritual message in harmony with this book, to support and assist the family as needed, and to inquire into the family's welfare (and report any urgent needs to the Bishop and Vice-Bishops).

Priests must be sober, sensible, devout, and respectable. They must hold to the mystery of the faith in a pure conscience. They must not be double-tongued, drinkers of much alcohol, or greedy. They must be lovers of wisdom, virtue, and hope. They must have proved themselves through their prior service and participation in the Church. (Timothy 3:8-10; Titus 1:8; D&C 20:38-45; 107:12).

Priests serve as needed in their Ward to ensure its smooth functioning. They act as Officiants for all Rites, except for the following: the Ordination of Elders; the Ordination of Stewards; Marriage; or the Burial of the Dead.

Whenever Officiating a Rite, private or public, a Priest should be dressed in a formal and respectful manner, also wearing his Stole (except when acting as a Baptizer).

Priests may fulfill any of the functions of the Deacons when the need arises.

Elders

An Elder is Ordained when a man has been deemed worthy of and qualified for the calling by the Qualified Voters in his Ward, as demonstrated by his placement on a sortition list for selection as a Bishop or a Vice-Bishop.

Elders should be intimately familiar with the teachings of this book and be able to independently teach, expound, exhort, and watch over the Church. They may plan and conduct Communal

590

Sacrament services, according to the teachings of this book and the requirements of wisdom, virtue, and hope. Elders should administer the Church's physical and spiritual needs, in accord with the requirements of this book and the norms, rules, and practice of the Church.

Elders must be upright, blameless, and above reproach. They must not be slanderers, double-tongued, drinkers of much alcohol, greedy, quarrelsome, or quick-tempered. They must be sober, sensible, prudent, temperate, self-controlled, respectable, hospitable, patient, disposed to teach, devout, and lovers of wisdom, virtue, and hope. They must hold to the mystery of the faith in a pure conscience. They must have a firm grasp of the words of this book to both preach sound doctrine and refute those trying to contradict it. They should manage their own household well and also be well thought of by outsiders. They must have proved themselves through their prior service and participation in the Church.

Elders serve, administer, and lead as needed in their Ward to ensure its smooth functioning. Any Elder may act as Officiant for all Rites of the Church of the West except for the Ordination of Stewards, which are to be conducted by someone holding an equivalent or higher Stewardship at the time of Ordination.

Whenever Officiating a Rite, private or public, an Elder should be dressed in a formal and respectful manner, also wearing his Stole (except when acting as a Baptizer).

Elders may fulfill any of the functions of the Priests or Deacons when the need arises.

Church Buildings

A "Chapel" is the name of 1) a building or space used by a branch for Communal Sacrament; 2) any private space set apart for worship, prayer, and sacrament services; or 3) any smaller space in a Church, Basilica, or Cathedral used primarily for worship, prayer, and or private sacrament services, separate from the larger sanctuary used for Communal Sacrament.

A "Church" is a building used by a Ward for its main meeting place and for Communal Sacrament.

A "Basilica" is a building used as the main meeting place for a Diocese and where the Diocese's Archbishop is based. A Basilica may also be used by one or more Wards within the Diocese as their main meeting place.

A "Cathedral" is a building used as the main meeting place for a Province and where the Province's Cardinal is based. A Cathedral may also be used by one or more Dioceses or Wards within the Province as their main meeting place.

That we might more easily love our Church, our churches should be made lovely (Hope 11:13). All Church buildings should be traditionally beautiful and inspiring in appearance. A Church building that is purpose-built should preferably be in the nature of one of the following architectural styles: Neo-Gothic, Neo-Classical, Beaux-Arts, American Colonial/Georgian, or American Federal.

A Church, Basilica, or Cathedral should, wherever possible, have a tower with church-bells. As permitted by local laws, regulations, and customs, the bells should be rung five minutes before the start of Communal Sacrament and also immediately following the closing prayer. The bells should also be rung as appropriate during Feasts and other Rites and observances. Wherever possible, the grounds of a Church, Basilica, or Cathedral should have a sacred tree, and also an accompanying sacred grove to be used as a quiet, sacred, beautiful place for contemplation and prayer. Wherever possible, the grounds should also have a grass field with a maypole. Between the Feasts of May Day and Tricrux, weather permitting and at the discretion of the Bishop, Vice-Bishops, and Officiant, Communal Sacrament may be held outside on the field.

The Final Charge

You have received the right principles you ought to accept. What sort of teacher, then, do you still wait for, to put off reforming yourself? You are no longer a child.

If you are negligent and slothful, procrastinating day after day the time for seeking wisdom, practicing virtue, and laboring with hope, then, without realizing it, you will sit stagnant until the end, persevering in your foolishness, evil, and lazy despair.

This instant, then—right now—stand tall and think of yourself as worthy of living as a man or woman progressing forward on the Triple Path.

Let the principles of wisdom, virtue, and hope be to you as a law which must never be violated.

What now?

If this book speaks to you and you would like to consider getting more involved, go to **TriplePath.org/Newsletter** to sign up for the email newsletter. Signing up will allow you to receive regular updates (never more than once a week) and to find out about others in your area who are also interested.

To find out if there is a Ward in your area, contact us. If there is no local Ward, you can start practicing the Rites and Feasts of the Church of the West as an individual or with your family. If you would like to start an Unrecognized Branch in your area, we can put you in contact with any others in your area also desiring to do so. Find more information at **TriplePath.org/Congregations.**

Please tell your friends about this book, or give a copy to a friend, or donate a copy to your local library. Also, please leave positive reviews of this book online. It is available for sale at all major outlets (this book's purpose is not to generate a profit; proceeds from its sale will generally be used to defray development and publishing costs, and to further spread the word about it).

If you are in the Washington, D.C. area and would like information about attending Communal Sacrament and other worship services, send an email to **DC@TriplePath.org.**

This book is the first complete draft presented to the world, but it is not the final draft. It represents more than ten years of sincere effort, but there is much room for improvement in all aspects. The intent is that this book might become a communal effort. It is open to contribution, correction, and feedback from all readers. To contact the author or send any suggested contributions or corrections, send an email to: **Inquiries@TriplePath.org**

Made in the USA
Coppell, TX
11 October 2020